THE ART OF
REMEMBERING

VISUAL ARTS OF AFRICA
AND ITS DIASPORAS

A SERIES EDITED BY

KELLIE JONES AND STEVEN NELSON

Gwendolyn DuBois Shaw

THE ART OF REMEMBERING

ESSAYS ON AFRICAN AMERICAN ART AND HISTORY

Duke University Press Durham and London 2024

Library of Congress Cataloging-in-Publication Data
Names: Shaw, Gwendolyn DuBois, [date] author.
Title: The art of remembering : essays on African American art
and history / Gwendolyn DuBois Shaw.
Other titles: Visual arts of Africa and its diasporas.
Description: Durham : Duke University Press, 2024. | Series: The
visual arts of Africa and its diasporas | Includes bibliographical
references and index.
Identifiers: LCCN 2023037624 (print)
LCCN 2023037625 (ebook)
ISBN 9781478030171 (paperback)
ISBN 9781478025924 (hardcover)
ISBN 9781478059165 (ebook)
Subjects: LCSH: African American art. | Art, American—
Historiography. | African American artists. | Black people in art. |
Race in art. | Slavery in art. | African diaspora in art. | Art and
society. | BISAC: ART / American / African American & Black |
SOCIAL SCIENCE / Ethnic Studies / American / African American
& Black Studies
Classification: LCC N6538.B53 S54 2024 (print) | LCC N6538.B53
(ebook) | DDC 700.89/96073—dc23/eng/20231129
DC record available at https://lccn.loc.gov/2023037624
LC ebook record available at https://lccn.loc.gov/2023037625

Cover art: Sheldon Scott, *Abide in Me*, 2019–21. Archival digital
print, 37 × 25 in. © Sheldon Scott. Photography by Jon-Sesrie
Goff. Courtesy CONNERSMITH.

Contents

‖‖‖

PART I. PAST AS PRELUDE 15

1 Facing Phillis Wheatley

PORTRAITURE AND PUBLISHING IN
THE ERA OF THE AMERICAN REVOLUTION

— 19 —

2 Profiling Moses Williams

SILHOUETTES AND RACE IN THE EARLY REPUBLIC

— 42 —

3 The Freedom to Marry for All

PAINTING INTERRACIAL FAMILIES DURING
THE ERA OF THE CIVIL WAR

— 62 —

4 Landscapes of Labor

RACE, RELIGION, AND RHODE ISLAND IN
THE PAINTING OF EDWARD MITCHELL BANNISTER

— 73 —

Illustrations

Acknowledgments

I would like to begin by acknowledging the long-standing support and inestimable patience of Ken Wissoker, editor in chief at Duke University Press, who has supplied me with encouragement, guidance, and honesty since 2003, when I brought him my first book on the artistic practice of Kara Walker. Thank you, Ken.

Ongoing dialogues with fellow critical race art historians Huey Copeland, Jacqueline Francis, Kellie Jones, Steven Nelson, Jordana Moore Saggese, Cherise Smith, Adrienne Childs, and Krista Thompson have shaped my scholarship in untold ways. Their collegiality and pathbreaking scholarship have consistently impacted my research methods and writing practices for the better. First as students and now as colleagues, Mia Bagneris, Brittany Green, Rebecca Keegan Vandiver, Charlotte Ickes, Jill Vaum Rothschild, Luiza Repsold França, Ross Karlan, and Juliet Sperling have all pushed me to think more deeply about the art at the center of these essays. In the art history department at the University of Pennsylvania, I am grateful to successive department chairs David Brownlee, Holly Pittman, Karen Redrobe, Michael Leja, and Julie Nelson Davis, who encouraged my interests and helped support my research and teaching goals. Finally, I have nothing but respect and admiration for David Young Kim and Andre Dombrowski. Year after year these two have always been ready with tea, empathy, and advice on making it through to the end of the manuscript with a clean conscience and clear skin.

Some of the chapters in this book first saw publication in magazines, journals, and exhibition catalogs. I thank the various editors, curators, and museum publications staff who offered me those opportunities and provided me with invaluable feedback, especially Carlos Basualdo, Barbara Haskell, Asma Naeem, Rhys Conlon, Kathleen Krattenmaker, and Seph Rodney. Accordingly, I must acknowledge Thom Collins at the Barnes Foundation and Kim Sajet at the National Portrait Gallery for providing me with numerous writing and curatorial opportunities and for consistently inspirational models of excellence in museum leadership and visionary exhibition practice. Over the past two years, while I was preparing this book for submission, independent editor Donna Sanzone provided me with invaluable attention and wisdom. And I give special thanks to Fábio D'Almeida Lima Maciel for his help during the final stretch in late 2022 and early 2023. Finally, the publication was supported by subvention funds from the University of Pennsylvania's Williams Fund, for which I am grateful.

THE ART OF REMEMBERING

INTRODUCTION

As we maneuver the third decade of the twenty-first century, Black artists are experiencing an extraordinary level of visibility within the museum and gallery world. Their work fills the walls of blue-chip galleries and art fair convention halls and breaks records for contemporary and living artists at auction. Colleges and universities are scrambling to hire both emerging and senior specialists in African American and African diaspora art, just as art museums and exhibition spaces are recruiting highly trained curators tasked with building collections, conceptualizing relevant thematic shows, and organizing retrospective exhibitions of established Black artists whose contributions may previously have been overlooked or actively ignored by those same spaces. During the first week of October 2022, as I sat in my home office diligently revising this introduction, an exhibition devoted to the Black art community that Linda Goode Bryant had nurtured in the 1970s and 1980s at the legendary gallery Just Above Midtown had just opened at the Museum of Modern Art, and the Loophole of Retreat symposium, organized by curator Rashida Bumbray, visual theorist Tina Campt, and historian Saidiya Hartman on the occasion of Simone Leigh's landmark presentation at the Fifty-Ninth Venice Biennale, as the first African

American woman to exhibit in the US pavilion, was underway at that city's Giorgio Cini Foundation. The celebratory pictures of Black art world royalty celebrating at the Monday evening *Just Above Midtown* opening dominated my Instagram feed at the same time the livestream of potent Afrofemmergy appeared on YouTube.

In this moment, there is an undeniable appetite for the culturally specific visual discourses to which so much African American and diasporic Black art alludes, and it feeds a hunger in Black people's souls as much as it does in those who have no African heritage in their backgrounds. Whether it be futurist, pessimist, banal, abject, or baroque, art by Black artists that features Black people's bodies or engages with ideas of Blackness (both solid and liquid) has indeed captured the attention of the art world. But along with the rewards in this shift in visibility and plethora of platforms comes the question of what cost is being paid and how long this new Black Renaissance will last. It is a question that begs for our attention and deep consideration.[1] This book is an attempt to gather some of my early and more recent contributions and to claim a certain space within these discourses—a space that stresses the importance of history and legacy, of welcome and accessibility.

Written between 2002 and 2022, the essays assembled in this book touch on a large swath of African American art and representation, from the height of the British colonial period through to the current moment, as Black producers have worked to create primarily within the context of what is now known as the United States. These essays use various methodologies to engage and create African American art histories, both object based and biographical, but in each essay, theory is employed solely with the aim to make the work of Black artists more legible and accessible to fellow thinkers, cultural workers, and the audiences who seek to engage their production through in-person exhibitions, in books, or online. This emphasis on clarity comes in part from my own decades-long struggle with excessively complicated theoretical discourses and my desire to produce art history and criticism that can be immediately useful to people who may not have the luxury of devoting time to researching every other word that is used to describe or analyze a work of art. Accordingly, some of the essays included here first saw publication in museum exhibition catalogs or in print and online media. Also included in this collection are previously published journal articles (updated for this work), unpublished lectures, original essays, and new section introductions.

Embracing Rememory

This is a book about engaging in a process of "rememory" in the practice of critical race art history and visual culture studies. I take the terms *remember* and *disremember* from Toni Morrison's novel *Beloved,* in which the protagonist Sethe uses them as descriptive mechanisms to elucidate the tactics and strategies that must be engaged for psychological survival to be possible following the unspeakable traumas of enslavement. Those who have survived to the period of post–Civil War Reconstruction in which *Beloved* is set must tell their stories to remember what they have purposefully disremembered. Similarly, Black people continue to navigate what Christina Sharpe identifies in *In the Wake: On Blackness and Being* as the enduring sway of "the wake" borne from the Middle Passage and slavery and must also remember that past by gathering up its pieces, like parts of a dismembered body communal, in ways that honor the sacrifices and journeys of the ancestors. As artists, critics, historians, and engaged viewers, we must acknowledge the reality of the epigenetic, that which moves with our DNA through time, as we seek dynamic strategies for remembering that will contribute to the making of new and more equitable worlds.

The concepts of remembering and disremembering that I cull from Morrison also inform the ways that I see some of the differences between art history and art criticism. The historian of African American art writes about what was, effectively remembering the disremembered from the materials that have been purposefully undervalued and disregarded by white supremacist historians of American art, whereas the critic of African American art has the latitude to focus on what is and what might have been, proposing new memories of Black artistic practices. In the essays that complete the final section of the book, I engage with contemporary art from both a critical and a historical perspective, providing context and comparative examples for objects and practices that I find compelling and interesting, while also trying to imagine what might be. Accordingly, my writing reflects a palpable distress regarding the ways that the voracious consumption of contemporary art has discouraged challenging curatorial didactics in exhibition environments and accommodated habits of minimal research by curators and other arts writers, whose interpretations, interventions, and insights might otherwise have had the potential to mediate in an assistive and generative way between artists and their audiences. This is, of course, a delicate dance. As a historian, teacher, and curator of historical and contemporary art, as a member of a broader arts community, I would like to be supportive of artists whom I believe are doing important work, while also encouraging those whose efforts fall short to reconsider some of their strategies for culture making. But because we are in a moment of rising fascism and white supremacy, solidarity is important, and negative criticism must be given judiciously and with care.

This book also reflects my own personal desire to see things a certain way, from what theorist Mieke Bal, in her essay "Dispersing the Gaze: Focalization," terms a very singular point of focalization. It reveals my desire to subvert the way that others see things, too—not solely to bring them around to my way of seeing but rather to make them question their own way of understanding the visual world. Because of this impulse, it is a very personal project, although it is not one in which I interrogate images of myself or my family members. Instead, it is a collection of essays in which the images that are important to me and that have impacted the way I see ideas, self, and society are allowed to take center stage. In it, I examine the competing mythologies that have accrued to objects and image worlds. I want to look hard at the cultural moments that produced these objects and the allegorical impulses, if you will, that often allow them to be read as showing one thing while (perhaps) meaning another. In some ways this approach is similar to the kind of critical fabulation that has been artfully perfected by historian Saidiya Hartman, in which the critic "flatten[s] the levels of narrative discourse and confus[es] narrator and speakers . . . to illuminate the contested character of history, narrative, event, and fact, to topple the hierarchy of discourse."[2] And even though I value the ways that this approach augments and enlivens archives that have purposefully excluded Black voices, I remain primarily interested in utilizing existing voices and objects as evidence, without melding my voice into those of the ancestors. That said, there are moments when I opt for a more speculative mode of interrogation to prompt the reader's consideration of alternative interpretations and internal dialogues.

In this book I discuss works of art that have kept me up at night and that have plagued my days with hours of fretful handwringing about the veracity of the content, creation, and the relevance of my own critique. I work to center objects, some of which have been with me through the past three decades, beginning with work done in graduate school, and will probably remain vexing to me long after this book is published. Many of these works of art and the lives of the artists who made them present questions of experience and representation that cannot be easily or satisfactorily explained away, which is undoubtedly why I have taken up the challenge of their explication and why some readers will surely find even my best efforts wanting. I can offer no guarantees of satisfactory conclusions. Perhaps this is due to my own skepticism regarding the idea of truth and the possibility of a truthfulness of the stories that have been spun around objects, images, and the individuals who made them. I am not an Afro-pessimist in the vein elucidated by Frank Wilderson III in his recent book *Afro-pessimism,* where living in Blackness becomes akin to a state of a perpetual cycle of slavery; I still find solidarity with many people of color, while also having lost all faith in the possibilities of decolonizing the institutional contexts of the university and the museum, in which I have labored for the past thirty years.

I understand the importance of evidence and facts, but I am a natural nihilist, and "truth" has always eluded me as something fixed and inviolable. I often find that the evidence can be interpreted in multiple ways. Scholarly obsessions with truth that manifest in the need for established canons and Ur-stories to support their origins are a big part of what makes the academic practice of art history so terribly frustrating while also being incredibly interesting at the same time. Because of art history's traditional dependence on national and other sorts of geographic boundaries, specific chronological demarcations, and cultural traditions to subdivide an otherwise untenably broad area of study, scholars in emerging subfields have often felt compelled to actively engage in similar activity to establish an equitable footing for the locus of their intellectual interests. I believe that if disciplines like art history and the field of American art in which I was trained, as well as the various semi-agglutinated subfields like African American art history that it both contains and ignores, are to continue to expand and prosper in the twenty-first century, it will only be through the reexamination of the problematic myths that have been formed out of a necessity to assuage a misplaced sense of national, racial, or cultural inferiority. As art historians (and the cultural critics who push back on or trample our gates), we must repeatedly turn our attention to finding the disremembered fragments of history that have been ignored and remembering them.

The disremembered narratives of Black creativity and self-representation that lurk at the edges of American art history have often reminded me of the apocryphal stories that that were cited in the survey courses of my first and second year of college to explain Old Master paintings that depicted obscure episodes from the Old Testament and the life of Christ or the Virgin Mary. It strikes me that many of the stories that have become these biblical apocrypha, stories whose canonicity was doubted by Jewish rabbis and Christian church fathers, are the ones that meant the most to me as a Black woman, including the stories of Lilith, Judith, and Susanna; stories that were excluded from various versions of the Bible, including the one that Americans know best today, the King James Version. These apocrypha, or hidden writings, were often ignored by early rabbis, while competing Christian sects argued over them. Since ancient times there has been competition over which version of the Hebrew Bible is the most accurate. Whether it is the Septuagint (an Egyptian version of the Bible from the third century BCE that was commissioned by Ptolemy II Philadelphus and written in Alexandria, which is not only the longest but supposedly the most authentic version of the Hebrew Bible), the Palestinian version, or the Babylonian version, there has long been doubt as to which books are in fact the authorized word of God: that is, the truth. The books that remained in each version of the Bible were the ones that (in that moment) were viewed as religiously acceptable and did not contradict established social mores. These canonical stories were emotionally moving and compelling to readers, and they kept communities together by reinforcing moral standards and social unity. Extracanonical texts that did not meet at least one of these criteria were often relegated to the realm of apocrypha because of their disruption of the status quo and their inability to be fully integrated into the dominant narrative.

Despite the concerted exclusion of extracanonical apocrypha from the religious texts we are familiar with today, such stories persisted and continued to impact popular understandings of the narratives that they were originally created to modify. For example, it is an extracanonical text that gives us the names of the three wise men (kings or magi) who visited Jesus in the manger in Bethlehem: Melchior, Caspar, and Balthazar. Apocrypha are with us; they haunt the margins and impact the present regardless of whether we want them to take center stage. And yet embracing apocrypha is different from the contemporary practices called *revisionist history* or *alternative history*, in that those two terms imply a rewriting or rejection of an established narrative and chronology. Embracing apocrypha is also different from the strategies of critical fabulation, which imagine a "what if" scenario in the presence of an unfillable absence.

In many ways, religious apocrypha are akin to the modes of disremembering and remembering that have resulted from the trauma that has been present in the Black lives that are at the center of novels like *Beloved*, which employs the presence of a ghost as a manifestation of a purposefully suppressed past, or the paintings of Titus Kaphar that derange the historical traditions of Black marginalization in portraiture. "What if identity had to be constituted out of a strategic amnesia," asks literary critic W. J. T. Mitchell, "a selective remembering, and thus a selective *dis*(re)membering of experience?"[3] Would the shape of the self and its representation be affected by the piecemeal evidence that has been allowed to stay visible and the buried bits that have been recovered?

For me, some of the work that the historian of African American art might engage lies in the realm of remembering a past that has been profoundly impacted by white art historical coloniality. In recent years historians of American art have more explicitly engaged decolonial research methods and pedagogical approaches, aiming to dismantle what Aníbal Quijano has termed the "coloniality of power," a condition that has enabled the hegemonic structures of power governing forms of knowledge, including ideology, to endure from the era of European conquest to the present moment.[4] As a result, more diverse subjects, objects, and alternative histories have offered a counterweight to mainstream narratives, helping to elucidate the ongoing problem of Americanist art historical coloniality. This book examines the ways that the dominant culture's need for a coherent history often causes alternate stories of cultural objects and artistic practices to be assigned a place outside of the accepted canon to satisfy or maintain the status quo.

Lessons in Remembering

In 2005 Kara Walker (b. 1969) completed a portfolio of fifteen lithographs that featured her signature black, silhouetted forms superimposed over mass media illustrations selected from the 1866 publication *Harper's Pictorial History of the Civil War*. The artist titled this work of appropriation and adaptation *Harper's Pictorial History of the Civil War (Annotated)*—in reference to the series' direct engagement with a specific historical construct that had been produced by the dominant organ of a recolonizing force.

With a circulation that reached nearly 500,000 by the end of the Civil War in 1865, the illustrated magazine *Harper's Weekly* was one of the most popular sources of news among Northern, pro-Union audiences. The magazine supplied readers on the home front with stories and wood engravings that reproduced images of battle and daily life among the troops by illustrators such as Winslow Homer and Thomas Nast. Following the end of the conflict, the magazine's editors, Alfred H. Guernsey and Henry M. Alden, carefully selected articles and images from back issues to create a two-volume history that both expanded on and reframed what had come before. In a conciliatory move to shed the pro-Union, antislavery position that had characterized the magazine during the war, Guernsey and Alden chose two titles for the new publication: *Harper's Pictorial History of the Civil War* and *Harper's*

Pictorial History of the Great Rebellion. However, in both volumes Guernsey and Alden purposefully minimized the Black presence and participation in the war as their reporters and illustrators had recorded it. They chose not to republish most of the hundreds of illustrations of the enslaved, the freed, and the freeborn African-descended people who had originally been included in the magazine. In so doing, the editors recast the conflict as a disagreement over states' rights and a struggle for economic dominance between white men, some protecting the livelihoods of planters in an agrarian South, and others representing the interests of an industrial North that was struggling to absorb waves of European immigration.

In its recognition of the recolonizing action that was at the heart of the source material, *Harper's Pictorial History of the Civil War (Annotated)* reflects Walker's ongoing artistic practice of remembering the disremembered parts of nineteenth-century American visual culture. As her black figures (who may also be read as racially Black figures) engage in provocative and oblique dramas, they make visible to us the continuing impact of racism and perceptions of racial difference on the way that factual events are recorded in both words and images.

Walker's work also helps viewers to draw a direct line between the historical demonization and degradation of Black people that flourished during the period following the era of Civil War and Reconstruction to the civil rights and Black Power movements and the contemporary era of Black Lives Matter and calls to defund the police. "I'm interested in . . . the fact of slavery's influence on the American system," Walker related in a 2002 interview, "and the power of its influence over the American imagination."[5]

If the writing of history is about certitude in facts; if it is about assembling a chronology, recording things that happened, and delineating the things that were; if it is about providing information and facts to a reader in a way that fixes an event or series of events in time, so that they may be known and understood, then *Harper's Pictorial History of the Civil War (Annotated)* serves as a profound remediation of the act of factual exclusion performed by the original volume's purposeful elision of the Black presence in the Civil War. It is also representative of Walker's provocative insertion of Black figures, both real and imagined, into the historical image worlds that were created in the immediate aftermath of the devastating national reckoning over slavery and political union that was the American Civil War. The kind of remembering that Walker achieves here operates from the margins of history. It is unfixed and uncertain. It seeks to elucidate history, but it does not determine its course or alter its interpretation; it elucidates it instead.

The remembering of history, as practiced by artists like Walker, is about the expansion and explanation of narrative by bringing to light facts that have been purposefully set aside or actively ignored, that which has been disremembered. Like critical fabulation, it finds the given boundaries of "what was" to be insufficient, and by offering more, it asks us to imagine "What if?" In this way, the intellectual embracing of the purposefully disremembered and consciously neglected expands the possibilities of history by acknowledging the existence of multiple forms of knowledge and multiple ways of understanding an event or interpreting an object. Embracing rememory allows for interpretation and the creation of narrative to be both speculative and open-ended; it is also about flavoring and augmenting, rather than revising or re-positioning. To embrace remembered art history is to think beyond canonical interpretations of works of art or objects of material and visual culture to ask, "What else did we once know that has now been disremembered?"

In a nod to the power of history and the structuring of rememory as an act of conscious procession, this book is divided into three parts that proceed chronologically. Each one is prefaced by an introduction that frames the chapters that follow it within a historical and methodological context as well as within a personal one. The first part focuses on the eighteenth and nineteenth centuries, the second on the twentieth century, and the third on the last thirty years.

I begin in the colonial period in New England with a discussion of a portrait frontispiece of the poet Phillis Wheatley, questioning the identity of the maker of the original portrait and examining the impact that the printed frontispiece had on the representation of subsequent generations of women writers who followed Wheatley in the Anglo-American world. An essay on the work and world of the portrait profile cutter Moses Williams follows, taking us to Philadelphia in the period of the early republic and considering the ontological position of Black artisans, their bodies, and those of Indigenous Americans. The next essay discusses the role of portraiture in the formation of enslaved and free Black families before the Civil War. The final essay in this section examines the career of the painter Edward Mitchell Bannister, both before and after the war, and the ways that legacies of slavery still permeated the landscapes that he made in Rhode Island well into the 1870s and 1880s.

The second part of this book takes up questions of race, identity, and diasporic history in relation to modernism, museums, and memory. It begins with a biographical sketch of the sculptor May Howard Jackson, whose representational sculpture often dealt with the same issues of racial ambiguity that impacted the artist's own life. The next essay focuses on modernist work made by Jackson's nephew, the sculptor Sargent Johnson, who is often associated with the New Negro movement and the Harlem Renaissance, despite his being based across the country in the Bay Area of California. At the center of the essay that follows is an early-career representational drawing of a Dan mask from Africa made by Norman Lewis, whose mature abstract painting is now seen as integral to a full understanding of abstract expressionism; the impact of Mexican muralism on other Black artists of his generation comes next. The last two essays in this section focus on work made in the last third of the twentieth century that engages other ways of knowing, both spiritual and phenomenological, by sculptor Barbara Chase-Riboud and painter Richard Yarde.

I close the book with a group of essays that examine the nexus of art and race in the current century. I begin with an exploration of what it meant for artists in New Orleans and elsewhere to create art after the remarkable material, social, and spiritual destruction wrought by Hurricane Katrina. It is followed by an exploration of photographer and installation artist Carrie Mae Weems's use of focalizing perspective to engage complicated interracial histories; a discussion of the impact of *30 Americans*, the landmark exhibition of contemporary African American art drawn from the Rubell Family Collection; and a look at the work of two performance artists, Sheldon Scott and Wanda Raimundi-Ortiz, who engage in independent reparative practices that deal with histories and contemporary realities of dispossession and disenfranchisement in the African diaspora in the American South. The final essay in the book began as an opinion piece about the highly problematic photographic practice of Deana Lawson; it has been revised and expanded for this volume. In many ways, this final essay is a manifesto for the kind of work that I hope to produce from here on out, a challenge to myself to always come correct and never forget why I am doing this work.

Remembering the Self

In the past decade, a trend has emerged in the work of African American art historians and cultural critics who concern themselves with Black art and visual culture to remember their own selves in the pages of their scholarly texts. Whether it is Darby English's interweaving of his personal and professional struggle to come to terms with police violence against Black people through a limited curatorial practice at the Museum of Modern Art in *To Describe a Life: Notes from the Intersection of Art and Race Terror*, or the "Confessions of an Unintended Reader: African American Art, American Art, and the Crucible of Naming" provided by Kirsten Pai Buick, which describes her own coming into visibility as a Black art historian, we have become increasingly comfortable with placing our own experiences in dialogue with our discipline. This stems, I would argue, from an increasing realization that our stories matter and have always informed what we write about and why we persist despite the antagonism that often greets our efforts.

My own interest in researching and writing about African American art, artists, and representations of Black people began in the early 1990s when I realized that the stakes of doing art history extended beyond the academy or the museum and into the streets. In 1991, fresh out of a college experience that had included two years of art school and three at a large research university, I began working on a master's degree in art history at the University of California, Los Angeles (UCLA). My first year of coursework was irrevocably marred by the urban rebellion that occurred after the acquittal of the LA Police Department officers who were on trial for the spectacularly brutal beating of motorist Rodney King. On April 29, 1992, I watched the announcement of the verdict on the television at Jimmy's Coffee House on campus. Later that day, looking down from the university's perch between the elite neighborhoods of Bel Air and Westwood, I could see the fires burning down in South Central Los Angeles, a world that I had never entered and knew little about beyond its representation in the media. When the mandatory curfew was lifted the following week, a friend and I drove down to South Central to volunteer at a church that was accepting donations and serving as a hub for relief work. The streets were a war zone. After a week of violence and destruction, army tanks filled the parking lots of burned-out strip malls, and members of the National Guard surveilled a physically, emotionally, and spiritually devastated community.

Up until then, I had been studying nineteenth-century European sculpture, but now I worried that it might be a pointless endeavor. How could I spend my time and energy researching and writing about a cultural tradition that seemed to have little to offer the very real people who were in desperate struggle in the communities around me? At the end of the school year, I returned home to San Francisco, and then, with the encouragement of art historian Janet Berlo, who had been a visiting professor at UCLA while I was there, I applied for a museum internship at the Saint Louis Art Museum (SLAM). Berlo had convinced me that spending time in a museum, being with the objects, might help me to discover what I wanted from art history and what I might do with a graduate degree.

My application to SLAM was successful, and in 1993–94 I spent a year in St. Louis as the third Romare Bearden Graduate Museum Fellow (this important program continues almost thirty years later) before going on to a similar diversity-focused fellowship at the San Francisco Museum of Modern Art. In both positions (because of my own Blackness), I was expected to know something about African American art, and at SLAM I was tasked with directly engaging the local African American community. However, I had never received any formal training in African American, American, or African art. As a Northern Californian from Santa Cruz, a mostly white university town by the beach, I was also an outsider to the Black community of St. Louis (just as I had been to the Black community in South Central). I sensed in some way that I was entering the suffocating racism of another world to understand the thinly veiled oppressive alienation of my own. As a result, I took it on myself to begin to acquire proficiency in aspects of Black life, culture, and art that were separate from my own unique experience as the product of a mixed marriage between a middle-class, Black, Pan-Africanist photographer and jazz producer and a white, Jewish (later, out lesbian) sociology professor, AIDS activist, and prison researcher who met as fellow members of the Student Nonviolent Coordinating Committee during the civil rights movement of the 1960s. My parents named me Gwendolyn after the Pulitzer Prize–winning poet Gwendolyn Brooks and DuBois in honor of W. E. B. Du Bois. At both SLAM and SFMOMA, I found that racism, sexism, class hierarchies, and my unfinished graduate degree repeatedly hindered my progress. While I could not change who I was or where I had come from, I began to understand that not having my MA or a PhD would always limit my opportunities and that it was something that I could change.

During my year at SFMOMA, I applied to the art history PhD program at Stanford University, where I would ultimately specialize in American art. Because Stanford's art history department did not offer any courses on African American art, and the faculty teaching American art included almost no Black artists, objects that engaged Black culture, images of Black people, or writings by Black scholars in their lectures or on their syllabi, I chose to write most of my seminar papers on works that contained images of Black people, portraits of Black sitters, or art that was by African American artists. I also questioned my professors about these omissions. In response to my query about why there was no section on African American art on the list of readings required for PhD students in American art, my adviser, Wanda Corn, immediately suggested that we add one—and then asked me what I would like to include. I requested that articles by Richard J. Powell and Judith Wilson be included. To that Corn added selections from James A. Porter's 1943 book *Modern Negro Art*. In a lecture class on American art since 1940, Alexander Nemerov focused a single week on a Black artist: Jean-Michel Basquiat. When I asked him about this choice, he said that Basquiat was the only African American artist for whom he had found art historical writing or criticism that he felt was of sufficient quality (he had assigned essays by bell hooks and Robert Farris Thompson), and, he explained, there was the problem of "the indignity of speaking for others," which he ascribed to Michel Foucault. When I finally located this phrase, I learned that it had been uttered by Gilles Deleuze in 1972, at a conference where he congratulated Foucault on elucidating the power relationships that cause "difference" to be co-opted by the dominant culture and minoritarian voices to be overlaid by neoliberal advocacy.[6] While I understood this position, I knew there was much that I still had to learn about African American art and art history, and I needed someone to help me locate this knowledge—I did not care if that mentor was Black or not, I just cared about the artwork and the contexts in which it was created. A quarter century later, I was flabbergasted to see that Nemerov was teaching a course titled Black Aliveness—based on Kevin Quashie's book *Black Aliveness, or A Poetics of Being*—which promised students in its online course description "intense discussion and emphasis on developing powers of black aliveness in one's own writing."[7] It would appear that the possible indignity of speaking for the other has been supplanted by the irresistible allure of self-manifesting Blackness.

By the time I advanced to PhD candidacy, I had carved out a niche for myself working on portraiture and the representation of Black identity in American art as well as the challenges that negative imagery and stereotypes had presented to those interested in creating sympathetic and humanistic images of Black people in the United States since the British colonial period. I was interested in the ways that Black self-identity and imposed identity could be made visible through portraiture of all kinds, paintings, silhouettes, prints, photographs, and contemporary performance art, theater, and film. Before I received my PhD, I was hired as an assistant professor of African American art at Harvard University, where I spent the first five years of my professional teaching career. Not only was I the first tenure-track faculty member to specialize in African American art at Harvard, but for my first two years I was also the first full-time appointment in American art, period. All along the way, I kept telling myself that Black art mattered, that Black representation mattered, and that Black art history could do important things in a country that was constantly eating its young and tearing itself apart over issues of difference and inequality.

Thirty years after I first began graduate study in the history of art, I still believe that Black representation of all kinds matters. I have invoked this mantra almost every day over the past two decades as a professor of art history, first at Harvard University and now at the University of Pennsylvania, and throughout as a curator working with various collecting museums and non-profit art galleries. In many ways, these exhibitions and my other public-facing writing have been the work that has been the most rewarding and meant the most to me on a personal level. I have long believed that it was my mission to help bring Black art to broader audiences outside of the academy and that curatorial practice was the best way to make that happen. However, I am saddened that despite these efforts, not much has truly changed regarding the art world's understanding of Black artistic representation in the time I have been working in the field of art history. We are constantly (re)introducing audiences to the Black artistic experience. The 2022 iteration of the *Afro-Atlantic Histories* exhibition at the National Gallery of Art in Washington, DC, reminded me of a less focused version of the *Two Centuries of Black American Art* exhibition organized in 1976 by David Driskell for the Los Angeles County Museum of Art.[8]

Throughout this book issues of Black representation are centered and re-membered. Each essay explores instances of the self-construction of identity that African-descended artists and patrons have actively engaged to establish a sense of humanity in the face of the dehumanizing structures imposed by the colonialist and imperialist societies that have dominated North America since the late eighteenth century. By remembering the connective tissue between an artist's lived experiences and the external constraints placed on them, these essays explicate and place in context the lives and art of Black artists from the nineteenth century to the present. They consider the ways that the epigenetic traces of trauma carried by the descendants of the formerly enslaved "living in the wake" may be witnessed in portraits, representations of the landscape, and elsewhere. I have worked to place artists and the objects they make at the center of each essay, and some of the essays are indeed more information driven than thesis driven. This is due to the foundational and truly groundbreaking research that is presented on artists such as Richard Yarde and May Howard Jackson, for which there are no monographs, no major exhibition catalogs, and very little extant scholarship to be found. The project of this book is not to present a general critique of the field or to try to define its parameters per se. Rather, these writings are an argument for the continued viability of the subfield of African American art history as vitally integral to a history of both diasporic African art and especially American art—whose practitioners had long tried to underplay African American art's kinship and importance to a dynamic remembering of the discipline of the history of art itself.

PAST AS PRELUDE

During the eighteenth and nineteenth centuries—throughout the period of British colonization in North America, the era of the early republic, the Civil War, and the decade of Reconstruction that followed—issues of race and representation were always at the heart of American culture as "these United States" became the United States, and as ideas of liberty and freedom continued to conflict with the lived realities of slavery and racial oppression. Questions of how a Black American identity might be represented and formed by African-descended artists, and how Black patrons might also participate in this process, were often determined by an individual and their immediate community's experience of enslavement, whether they were freeborn, enslaved, emancipated, or self-freed. And while freedom did not always delimit who was represented, the social strictures connected to the concept of liberty often held sway. The art objects that I engage in the first part of this book present different instances of what it meant to be a person of African descent living and working in a nation that tethered so much of Black identity to various states of enslavement and freedom.

When I conceived the exhibition *Portraits of People: Picturing African Americans in the Nineteenth Century*, which originated at the Addison Gallery of American Art before traveling to the Delaware Art Museum and the Long Beach Museum of Art in 2006, the engraved frontispiece portrait of Phillis Wheatley provided an excellent way into the question of where to locate the origins of Black portraiture. It presents the first moment in the history of art in the United States that a Black sitter became the primary subject of a portrait, separate from an image of an unidentified Black figure, that was distributed widely in printed form. This portrait is the subject of the first essay in part I; it has been updated to include new work on the frontispiece by subsequent scholars.

The next chapter focuses on the life and career of silhouette artist Moses Williams, who worked in Philadelphia during the first decade of the nineteenth century. As the early republic emerged from colonial status and began a journey to concretize its own forms of colonization through westward expansion and redoubled oppression and dispossession of Indigenous peoples, Williams forged a career in the museum owned by his onetime enslaver, the painter, naturalist, and statesman Charles Willson Peale. While examining the ways that Williams may have worked to create a self-conceived identity for himself within his own artistic production, I also consider the contemporary interest in racial difference that included the representation of Indigenous people, and the limits and potential of cut paper silhouettes. My work on Williams began in a graduate seminar led by the late Roger B. Stein, and I continue to be fascinated by cut paper silhouettes made before the advent of photography. Revisiting the life and work of Moses Williams once more in 2021, I looked at James Rush's collection of silhouettes (bequeathed to the Library Company of Philadelphia in 1869 and recently digitized), which included the paper profile known as *Moses Williams, Cutter of Profiles*, and found that there were at least five other enigmatically raced silhouettes in the collection that could be interpreted as being of African-descended people, attesting to the ongoing ambiguity of the racial information contained within cut paper profiles made during the first decades of the nineteenth century. Accordingly, the chapter is a much expanded, edited, and revised piece that combines portions of my article "'Moses Williams, Cutter of Profiles': Silhouettes and African American Identity in the Early Republic," first published in the *Proceedings of the American Philosophical Society* in 2005 with ideas developed in "'Interesting Characters by the Lines of Their Faces': Moses Williams's Profile Portrait Silhouettes of Native Americans," from the National Portrait Gallery catalog *Black Out: Silhouettes Then and Now* (2018).

Moses Williams was a mixed-race man who was descended from at least one interracial union (his parents are believed to have been mixed race), and he himself married a white woman, factors that impacted the way that he presented in self-portraiture and images made by others. This crossing of the color line for love animates the family portraits of the two families of mixed descent from 1840s Philadelphia and 1850s Boston placed at the center of the third chapter in this book. The portraits made for the Montier and the Copeland families provide a window onto the ways that middle-class Black families chose to commemorate their unions and provide visual touchstones for their descendants in the decades leading up to the Civil War. *Three Sisters of the Copeland Family* is one of the few nineteenth-century American paintings that focuses exclusively on African American girls. As such, it is indicative of the profoundly anti-racist practice of the artist, William Matthew Prior, a white man whose family studio produced numerous paintings of free Black New Englanders between 1840 and the start of the Civil War. Prior's openness to painting all sitters regardless of race with the same frank "plainness," to borrow a descriptive phrase from historian John Michael Vlach, speaks to certain American ideals of equality that were rarely realized in the artistic production of the period. In this chapter Prior's portraits and those of Franklin R. Street, a Philadelphia-based portrait painter about whom far less is known, are considered for the ways that they helped to forge Black familial identity and manifest legacies of love and freedom in the middle of the nineteenth century.

Like Prior, the landscape painter Edward Mitchell Bannister, the subject of the final chapter in this section of the book, began his career as a portraitist in the Boston area. Not only did Bannister paint members of the free Black middle-class community of which he was himself a part, but he was also politically engaged, working for the abolition of slavery and supporting the Union cause during the Civil War. Bannister then spent the 1870s and 1880s, the period of Reconstruction and the beginnings of the Jim Crow era, making images of rural Rhode Island that were subliminally suffused with that state's history with the slave trade and plantation labor. Bannister's landscape paintings demonstrate the enduring impact of African enslavement in the Americas as something both corporeal and terrestrial. In this essay I consider Bannister's practice in the context of other professional artists of African descent who also worked in the period between the Civil War and World War I, including Mary Edmonia Lewis, Robert S. Duncanson, and Henry Ossawa Tanner.

In each of these studies, it is the act of self-creation and remembering through the visual, either as maker or as subject, that is centered. How did these Black artists, poets, and patrons use fine art and visual culture to make a space for themselves within a nation that wanted to define them solely in relation to the dehumanizing construct of slavery?

1

FACING
PHILLIS WHEATLEY

PORTRAITURE AND PUBLISHING
IN THE ERA OF THE
AMERICAN REVOLUTION

On deathless glories fix thine ardent view.
—**PHILLIS WHEATLEY, "To S. M., a Young African Painter,
on Seeing His Works" (1773)**

Myths about the origins of the arts are abundant in Western history; they have created the Ur-stories that have helped to structure the formation of a canon. In the history of ancient Greek art, for example, there is the story of the Corinthian maid who is credited, in chapter 35 of Pliny the Elder's *Natural History*, with the invention of painting. The story is so enduring that Joseph Wright (1734–97) painted this scene (figure 1.1) during the eighteenth century when the tale was receiving renewed attention. Wright's painting shows a young woman kneeling beside a sleeping youth as she uses a piece of charcoal and light from an unseen hearth to trace his outline and make what was imagined to be the first drawing of a human body. In this way, Pliny tells us, she was able to create a visible mimetic memento of her lover before his departure for war the next morning. This is one such origination myth that has persisted through time, engaging scholars at different moments in different ways, some of them clinging to it as fact, others dismissing it as

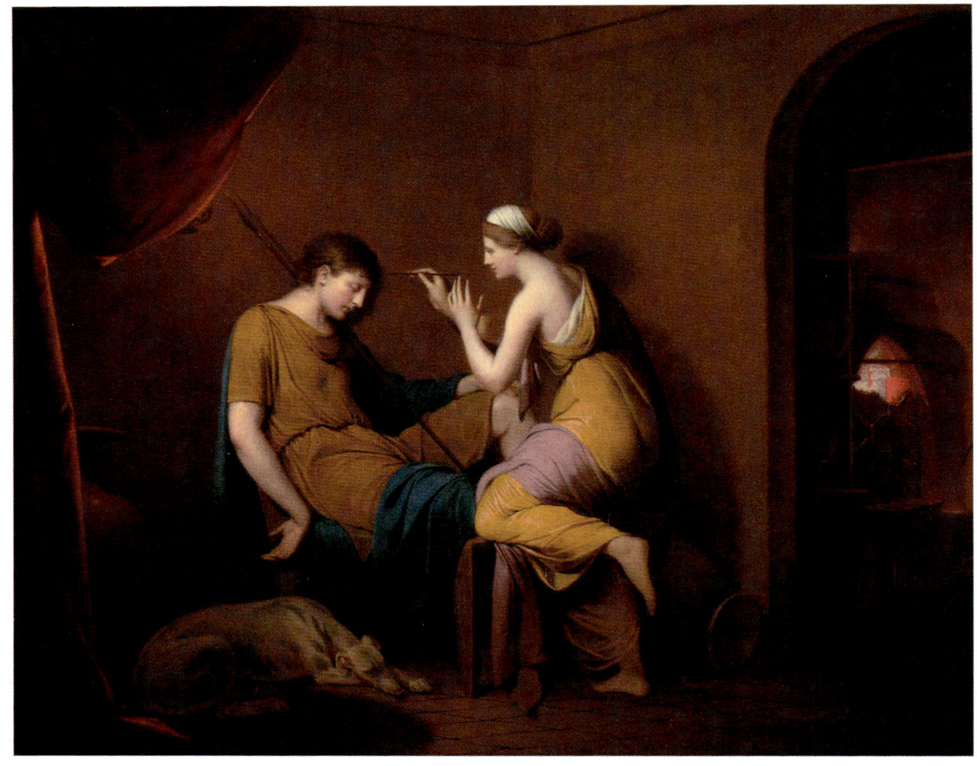

1.1 Joseph Wright, *The Corinthian Maid*, 1782–84.
National Gallery of Art, Washington, DC

conjecture. Similar explanations for the origins of other histories and subhistories of artistic traditions also exist, most of them much younger than that of the Corinthian maid, but no less romantic or problematic.

One important example of such a mythic story in the comparatively youthful history of American art is that of the origins of the African American entry into the European-based portrait tradition. It has traditionally been understood as having come with the creation of the engraved portrait frontispiece (figure 1.2) of the African-born poet Phillis Wheatley (ca. 1754–84) that was first published in her 1773 book, *Poems on Various Subjects, Religious and Moral*, when she was enslaved in the Boston household of John and Susanna Wheatley.[1] This unsigned image has frequently been attributed, using speculation and conjecture, by both literary historians and historians of African American art and culture to another enslaved African in Boston, a young man named Scipio Moorhead (ca. 1750–at least 1775).[2] Over the years, the once speculative ideas about this image's creation have been repeated so many times that they have ceased to be questioned and have become an American Ur-story.

The image and its myth have become so embedded in the canonical history of American and African American art that the portrait itself is threatened with becoming a mere trace of an important sitting for which there was no precedent. Not only was Wheatley the first person of African descent from New England to have her poetry published in English in the British public sphere, but she was also the first colonial American woman of any race to have her portrait printed alongside her writings. No other woman from the Anglo-American world prior to Wheatley can claim such a distinction. Along with her writings, this is an achievement that has been much touted by scholars of African American arts and letters, and yet it has not been clearly understood.

Literary historian and critic Henry Louis Gates cites the importance of Wheatley's volume of poems for marking the beginning of a canon, which "unlike almost any other literary tradition . . . was generated as a response to eighteenth- and nineteenth-century allegations that persons of African descent, did not, and could not create literature."[3] Social critic Paul Gilroy concurs, stating that the publication of "Wheatley's volume represented the beginning of a process in which the attributes of universal humanity for which the production of imaginative literature was emblematic [were] seen to be within the grasp of Negroes."[4] Other critics have similarly argued that the physical existence of the book and its portrait frontispiece were revolutionary: "Within the discourse of racial inequality in the eighteenth century," states Betsy Erkkila, "the fact of a black woman reading, writing, and publishing was in itself enough to splinter the categories of white and black, and explode a social order grounded in notions of racial difference."[5]

It is significant that despite literary scholars' continued interest in Wheatley's writing, art historians have become complacent about the Ur-story of the creation of the frontispiece, and since the 1940s very little has been done to investigate the compositional strategies at work in the artistic construction of her portrait. Despite the inherent power of the image, it has become so obscured by its role in canon formation that its original transatlantic sources, context, and impact as an innovative image of an Anglo-African woman writer were never studied. Instead, the image was mentioned only in passing by authors of studies of American and African American art as an early example of portraiture of a named African in America. Important questions about what models it was based on and what impact it may have had on subsequent portraits of other authors went unanswered.[6] James A. Porter, the pioneering historian of African American art, wrote in his germinal 1943

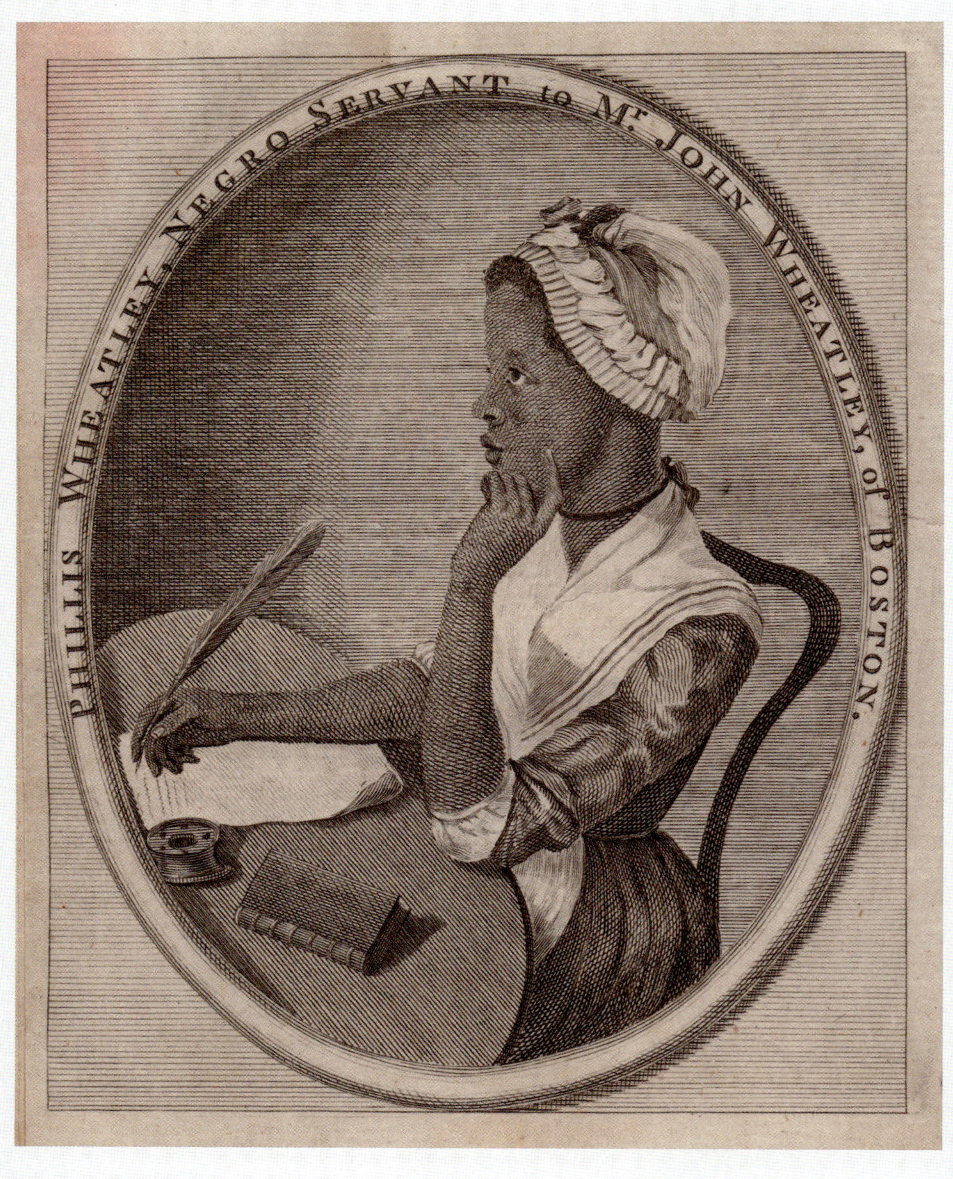

1.2 Scipio Moorhead (attr.), *Phillis Wheatley*, frontispiece from *Poems on Various Subjects, Religious and Moral*, 1773. National Portrait Gallery, Smithsonian Institution, Washington, DC

survey *Modern Negro Art*, "We may conjecture that [Moorhead] may have tried his hand at portraiture and even surmise that he is the author of the unsigned portrait of Phillis Wheatley that adorns several of her published work. The work is of provincial character and exhibits several naïve traits of design . . . [and] these traits are the strongest reasons for attributing the work to an amateur, which Scipio undoubtedly was. The conjecture is strengthened by the fact that this portrait and the poem to Scipio first appeared in the 1773 London edition of the poems."[7] Beyond Wheatley's poem, "To S. M., a Young African Painter, on Seeing His Works," almost nothing is known about Scipio Moorhead's personal life.[8] There is no informative archive of personal letters, and no signed works of art by him have ever been located.[9]

Despite the lack of evidence, and out of what may be a misplaced need to have a Black artist present within canon formation, many art historians have unquestioningly repeated Porter's narrative. Subsequently, the image long remained underdiscussed in surveys of American art and African American art published at the end of the twentieth century by Romare Bearden and Harry Henderson, Samella Lewis, Frances Pohl, Wayne Craven, and others.[10] Like the story of the Corinthian maid and her epiphanic wall tracing, its importance is as an event rather than as an object to be formally and visually analyzed; its importance to American art history is reduced to a novel commission between an artist and a sitter. Sharon Patton's discussion of the portrait in her survey text *African-American Art* is the most imaginative recitation of this event. Patton writes, "Wheatley was required to have her portrait engraved on the frontispiece, ostensibly to verify the author's race. She remembered that the Reverend John Moorhead of Boston, where she had spent her youth, owned a slave named Scipio Moorhead, who was a poet and an artist. Scipio Moorhead had learned the craft from the Reverend's wife, Sarah, who was a drawing instructor and painter. Wheatley requested that Scipio Moorhead render her portrait. The ink drawing that Moorhead did of Ms. Wheatley (untraced) was engraved in London."[11]

Patton, like most other art historians who have taken notice of this image, clings to the narrative that casts the desired artist, Scipio Moorhead, and the designated sitter, Phillis Wheatley, as the Adam and Eve of African American portraiture: he brilliantly painted a portrait of his good friend before her imminent departure for London on a tour to promote the impending publication of her book. Patton creates an apocryphal narrative by speculating about the commission, creating memories for Wheatley, and presuming an untraceable ink drawing. In this way, a creation moment for, and a canon of, African American art history is both launched and reinforced. By focusing primarily on establishing a mythic moment of creation and ignoring the lack of evidence, simply taking for granted the actual construction of the image, the possible sources for its composition, and its subsequent impact on the practice of portraiture in late eighteenth-century Britain and in what would soon become the United States, Patton and previous art historians lost sight of the importance of the actual work of art. In so doing, the possibility of Wheatley's agency in the creation of her portrait is undermined, the image becomes a mere trace of a sitting, and our conception of the sitter becomes a mere shadow of the real self.

By examining the understudied historical evidence that surrounds the portrait frontispiece of Phillis Wheatley, this essay argues for the manumission of this image from its traditional, arrested place at the beginning of the African American art historical canon. It shows that the portrait is valuable visual evidence of a heterocultural Atlantic world. This image is a remarkable and highly influential depiction of an early transatlantic woman's body, a depiction that was conceived and created using a revolutionary and defiant visual rhetoric. It is a portrait not of an objectified and subordinated woman but of an empowered wielder of agency. It is a portrait of a subject.[12]

In the confines of the engraved oval frame, Wheatley sits alone. She is a slim, dark-skinned girl with a long face. Shown in profile, her head is cylindrically shaped, with a high, pronounced forehead, a heavily lidded eye, a slightly flared nostril, and full, pursed lips. Her elbows rest on a small oval writing table on which a pewter inkwell, a book, and a sheet of paper await her poetic impressions. She wears an elaborately beribboned lace bonnet, full of pleats and accented with a colored ribbon at its top. A black band encircles her neck, ending in a bow at the back, while a white shawl covers her shoulders. The extended index finger of her left hand rests against her cheek, and the other fingers curl inward in support of her chin. She directs her gaze upward, toward heaven, as if searching for inspiration to direct the long quill pen that she holds in her right hand. In turn, the top of the feather points back up at her head.

Considerable effort has been taken to balance the composition. For example, the shape of the bonnet that Wheatley wears rhymes with the curving back of the wooden chair on which she sits, which in turn follows the line of her shoulder down to her waist before merging with her skirt. Despite this balance, many of the elements within the image seem at odds with one another. The oval of the table echoes the oval of the frame. But it slants upward, hard against the picture plane. In so doing, the space of writing seems to actively compete with the space of drawing, as if to equate the power of both types of creative presentation.

Similarly, the poet's quill pen hovers a bit above where it last marked the paper and seems to gesture toward the edge of the frame. Like the rebellious table, it too seems to challenge the confines of a frame that would contain it, a frame that has inscribed on its perimeter "Phillis Wheatley, Negro Servant to Mr. John Wheatley, of Boston."

To fully understand the tremendous importance of what Wheatley's portrait achieves, it is necessary to consider the intellectual formation of the sitter and her considerable interest in visual art, the life of the mind, and the world of British visual culture that surrounded her in eighteenth-century colonial Boston. At the time of the publication of Wheatley's writings and the creation of the accompanying frontispiece, the nineteen-year-old author was, as the inscription implies, enslaved. She was seven or eight years old when she experienced the Middle Passage. As a child she had been abducted from the Senegambian coast and brought to Boston in 1761. And when Susanna Wheatley, the wife of a well-to-do Boston tailor, John Wheatley, bought the child either off the boat that had transported her or from a nearby slave market, she was just "shedding her front teeth."[13] In a memoir that was included in an 1834 printing of Wheatley's poems, Margaretta Matilda Odell, a much younger relation of the white Wheatley family, recalled that Susanna Wheatley's choice of the child was influenced by "the humble and modest demeanor and the interesting features of the little stranger."[14] Odell chose to recall Phillis as a child prodigy and recorded that the young enslaved girl soon "gave indications of uncommon intelligence, and was frequently seen endeavoring to make letters upon the wall with a piece of chalk or charcoal."[15] John and Susanna Wheatley, who could have dealt with a property-defacing enslaved person in any manner they saw fit, chose instead to teach her to read and write, allowing their daughter, Mary, to serve as head tutor. They ensured that Phillis had a wide-ranging yet classical education, one that was far beyond what most white women received, and she flourished. By the time Phillis was a teenager, she was steeped in Ovid and Alexander Pope, and she was writing her own poetry.

Susanna Wheatley worked hard to publish her young protégé's work and was successful in having a number of poems, including several funeral elegies, printed in Boston-area newspapers, including the *Boston News Letter*, during the late 1760s and early 1770s. In 1772 the Wheatleys advertised for subscribers for a volume of poems by Phillis, but they were ultimately unsuccessful in raising the minimum amount needed to finance the book's publication. This failure has been attributed to a mix of racism on the part of many colonials, who did not believe that a person of African origins could compose poetry, and the unwise placement of the initial advertisement in the

Boston Censor, a short-lived newspaper that was overtly Loyalist and locally unpopular.[16] Despite these setbacks the Wheatleys persisted, and after having assembled a group of prominent white male Bostonians (including the future revolutionary John Hancock and the royal governor Thomas Hutchinson, who were a Patriot and a Loyalist, respectively) to "examine" Phillis and sign an attestation that she was indeed capable of writing the poems that she claimed to have authored, they were able to secure a printer in London, Archibald Bell, who specialized in religious tracts, to advertise for subscriptions and undertake the publication of the book.[17]

Poems on Various Subjects, Religious and Moral was dedicated to Selina Hastings, the Countess of Huntingdon, an English noblewoman from Bath who, despite having inherited land and slaves in Georgia, in later life had become an active promoter of the abolition of slavery and the repatriation of enslaved Africans to the continent. The countess was also well known at the time as one of the leading supporters of the Reverend George Whitefield, the force behind what we now call the First Great Awakening. Like many of her contemporaries who were swept up in the tide of Anglo-American evangelical religious fervor of the period, Wheatley admired the countess and was a dedicated follower of Whitefield, who preached frequently in Boston. When the minister died, the young believer elegized him in a poem that was widely distributed. Because Whitefield had at one time been Hastings's personal minister, Wheatley was able to use the publication of her poem to establish correspondence with the countess in 1770. "The Occasion of my addressing your Ladiship will I hope, apologize for this my boldness in doing it," Wheatley wrote to Hastings. "It is to enclose a few lines on the decease of your worthy chaplain, the Rev'd Mr. Whitefield, in the loss of whom I sincerely sympathize with your Ladiship: but your great loss which is his Greater gain, will, I hope, meet with infinite reparation, in the presence of God, the Divine Benefactor whose image you bear by filial imitation."[18]

In a letter dated January 5, 1773, Susanna Wheatley was informed that the countess was honored by their request to dedicate the forthcoming book to her; however, "the one thing she desir'd which she said she hardly thot would be denied her, that was to have Phillis' picture in the frontispiece. So that if you would get it done it can be Engrav'd here. I do imagine it can be Easily done, and think would contribute greatly to the Sale of the Book."[19]

Evidently, the Wheatleys heeded the countess's request, and Phillis sat for her portrait shortly thereafter. In the image she appears to have chosen to follow the countess in issues of fashion: from the shawl around her shoulders to the bonnet with its elaborate ribbons, Phillis's costume directly imitates that of her benefactress, as seen in several portraits from the period. It is unclear whether Wheatley would have owned such clothes. As Margaretta M. Lovell has shown, it was fairly typical during the period for colonial American sitters to wear a costume that was borrowed from the artist who was painting their portrait or copied from the clothing worn by a sitter in a mezzotint engraving that was being used as a model.[20] In a letter written by Susanna Wheatley to the countess in advance of Phillis's arrival in England, she requests that the countess help Phillis to dress appropriately but states that she would prefer Phillis's clothing to be simple and plain. However, looking at the clothes that Wheatley wears in the portrait, it is hard to see her costume as being exactly plain. And it is certainly not the costume of a house servant, let alone that of an enslaved person. The mere fact that she is dressed sets her apart from the typical images of enslaved women that were circulating at the time.

Wheatley is pictured as totally self-possessed, fully clothed, unlike other European and colonially produced representations of other African-born or -descended women made during the late eighteenth century, which show Black women primarily as objects of sexual desire or painful humiliation. *The Voyage of the Sable Venus, from Angola to the West Indies*, a 1794 illustration from a painting by Thomas Strothard (1755–1834) for a poem by the pro-slavery British historian Bryan Edwards, is a play on age-old images of Venus's birth from the sea, by imagining the arrival of a voluptuous, nearly nude African temptress on the shores of the New World (figure 1.3). She holds the reins to two magical sea creatures and is surrounded by a young Triton, amorini, and a Neptune/Oceanus figure (who waves a Union Jack).[21] She is a shapely black pearl ensconced in giant scallop shell. As she prepares for landfall, she is ready to embrace enslavement in an unknown land.

The absurd fantasy of the Sable Venus demonstrates the sexualized nature of images of enslaved African women that were common in the printed materials that circulated in the British public sphere during the period when Wheatley's *Poems* were published. Similarly, the *Flagellation of a Female Samboe Slave*, engraved by William Blake (1757–1827) from a drawing by John Gabriel Stedman, explicates the way that sadistic violence was frequently mixed into such objectifying and dehumanizing images (figure 1.4). Here a Black woman hangs from the limb of a tree; her bound wrists and the tattered rag that both covers and draws attention to her pudenda heighten the pornographic nature of the image, while the presence in the far background of white men with whips reinforces the violence of the scene and at the same time highlights its voyeuristic nature. Their remoteness and her expression of terror hint at the presence of another flagellator, one who is perhaps closer to her

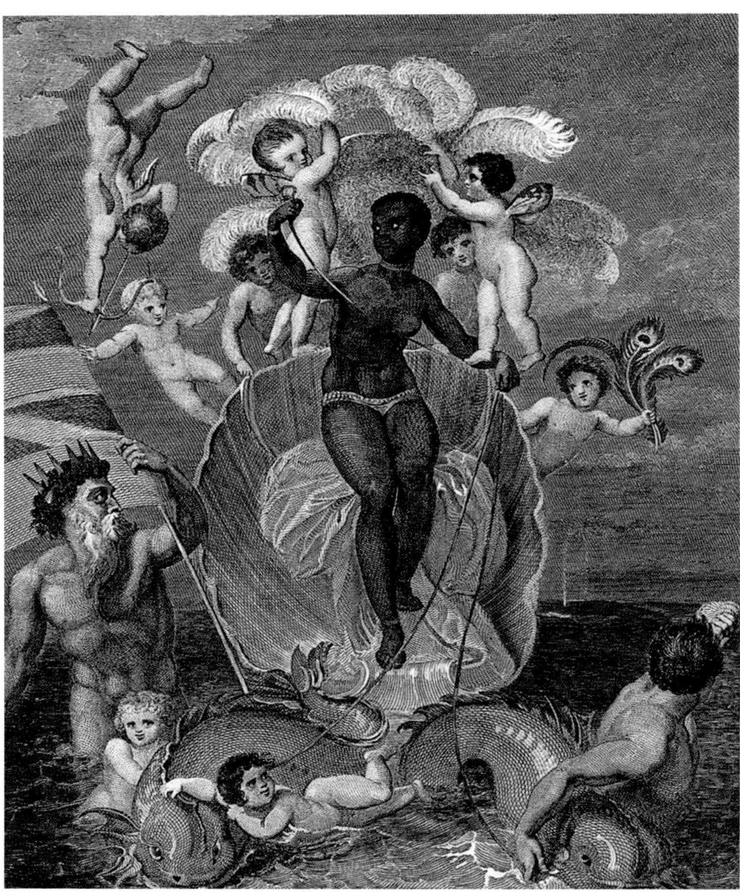

bared and bloodied body, perhaps occupying the space of the viewer. Like in the *Sable Venus*, her body twists on its axis as though writhing in sexual ecstasy.

Given the other images of women of African descent that were circulating in print during the era in which Wheatley's frontispiece was first published, her portrait must be appreciated for the revolutionary visual rhetoric of agency in representation that it both employs and attempts to propagate. Unlike the others, Wheatley's portrait shows a woman whose body is fully clothed and conservatively styled. Wheatley has been intellectualized, her form cropped within the composition so that the viewer is given visual access only to her head and her hand, the parts of her body that are active in the creative process. The portrait presents her to the viewer as a part of the literary world of her time, not as a commodified object to be taken or traded.

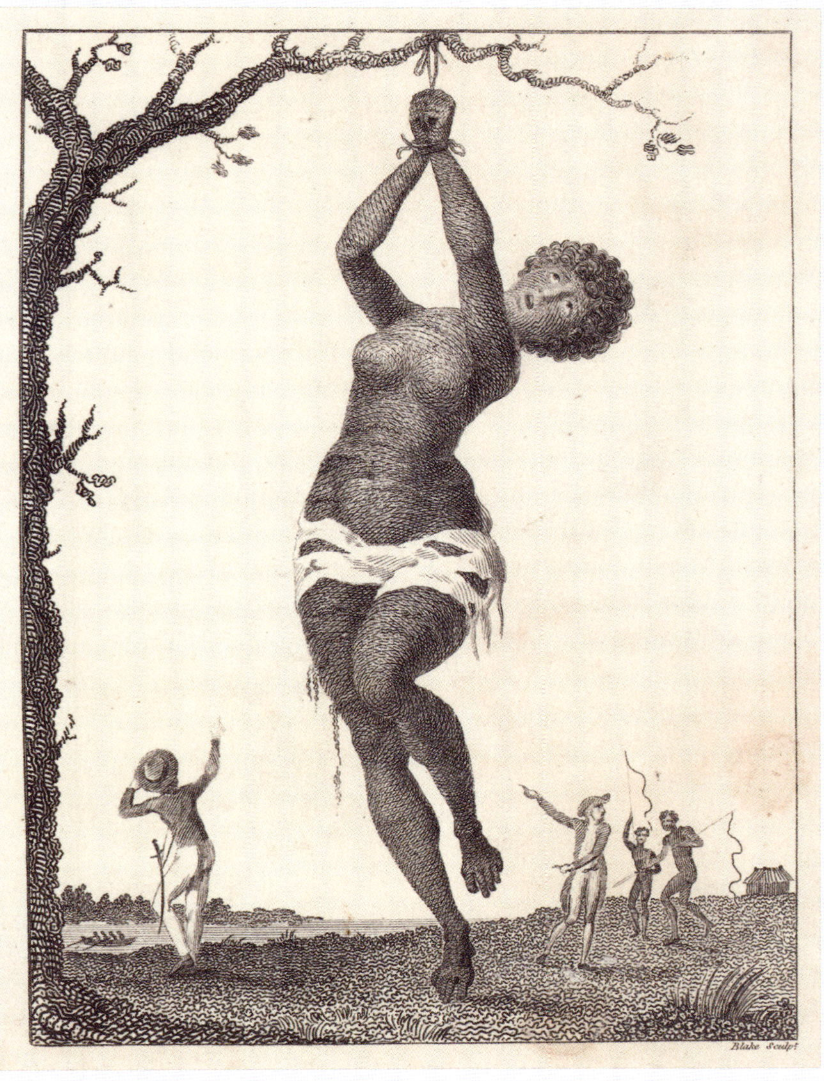

1.4 Engraving by William Blake, after a drawing by John Gabriel
Stedman, *Flagellation of a Female Samboe Slave*, 1790.
National Gallery of Art, Washington, DC

The frontispiece of Wheatley, and the poems that it accompanied, serves to visually emancipate Wheatley's middle-class, Black, female body from a dehumanized social identity. The frontispiece portrait introduced viewers/readers to the author as a respectable young woman who, despite her enslaved condition, is the epitome of learning and refinement.

During the late eighteenth century, only a few other Anglo-Africans would make similar visual impacts, and they were all men. One example is Ignatius Sancho (ca. 1729–80), who was born on a slave ship and then later brought to England; he was an accomplished composer who became well known within the diverse public sphere of late eighteenth-century England.[22] In 1768 the painter Thomas Gainsborough (1727–88) made an elegant portrait of Sancho as a gentleman, wearing a jacket with gold buttons and matching the trim along the edge of his red vest (figure 1.5).

In 1782, when Sancho's collected letters were published posthumously, the image was engraved so that it could be printed as a frontispiece (figure 1.6). Similar portrait strategies can also be found in the frontispiece portrait (figure 1.7) in the 1789 autobiography of Olaudah Equiano (ca. 1745–97). Equiano was born in the Kingdom of Benin and then enslaved to a British Royal Navy officer while still a child. By his late twenties, he had saved enough money to purchase his own freedom. After becoming active in Black abolitionist circles, he wrote and published a hugely popular memoir, which went through nine editions in less than a decade. The frontispiece engraving that accompanies *The Life of Olaudah Equiano, or Gustavus Vassa, the African*, presents the author elegantly dressed in gentlemen's clothing and holding a Bible on his lap. As Paul Gilroy argues, since significant parts of the lives of Wheatley and Equiano "were lived on British soil . . . it is tempting to speculate here about how an acknowledgement of their political and cultural contributions to England, or perhaps to London's heterocultural life, might complicate the nation's portraits of itself."[23] Like in Sancho's and Equiano's images, Wheatley's proper attire, her reflective pose, and the literary props that surround her all advertise the potential of her assimilation into British society—in both the colony and the metropole—and show her as decidedly Anglo-African, inhabiting a newly conceived identity, a "hybrid third term meant to mediate between the opposites signified by 'African' and 'Anglo-Saxon.'"[24]

The actual sitting for the portrait of Phillis Wheatley may have occurred sometime during the nine months that elapsed before the book was printed in late August 1773, but it could have occurred either before or after John and Susanna Wheatley decided to send her to London to promote the book.[25] The original image (whether it was a painting or a drawing is now impossible

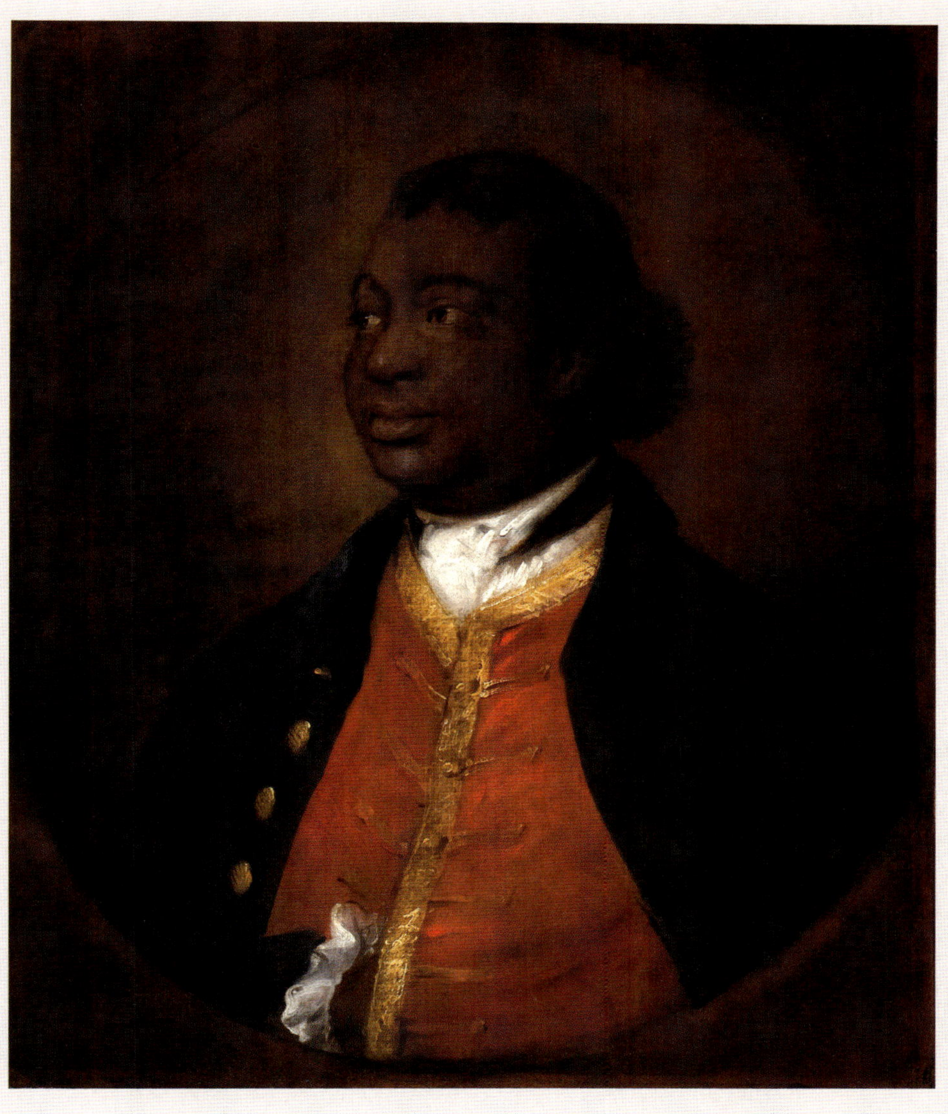

1.5 Thomas Gainsborough, *Ignatius Sancho*, 1768.
National Gallery of Canada, Ottawa

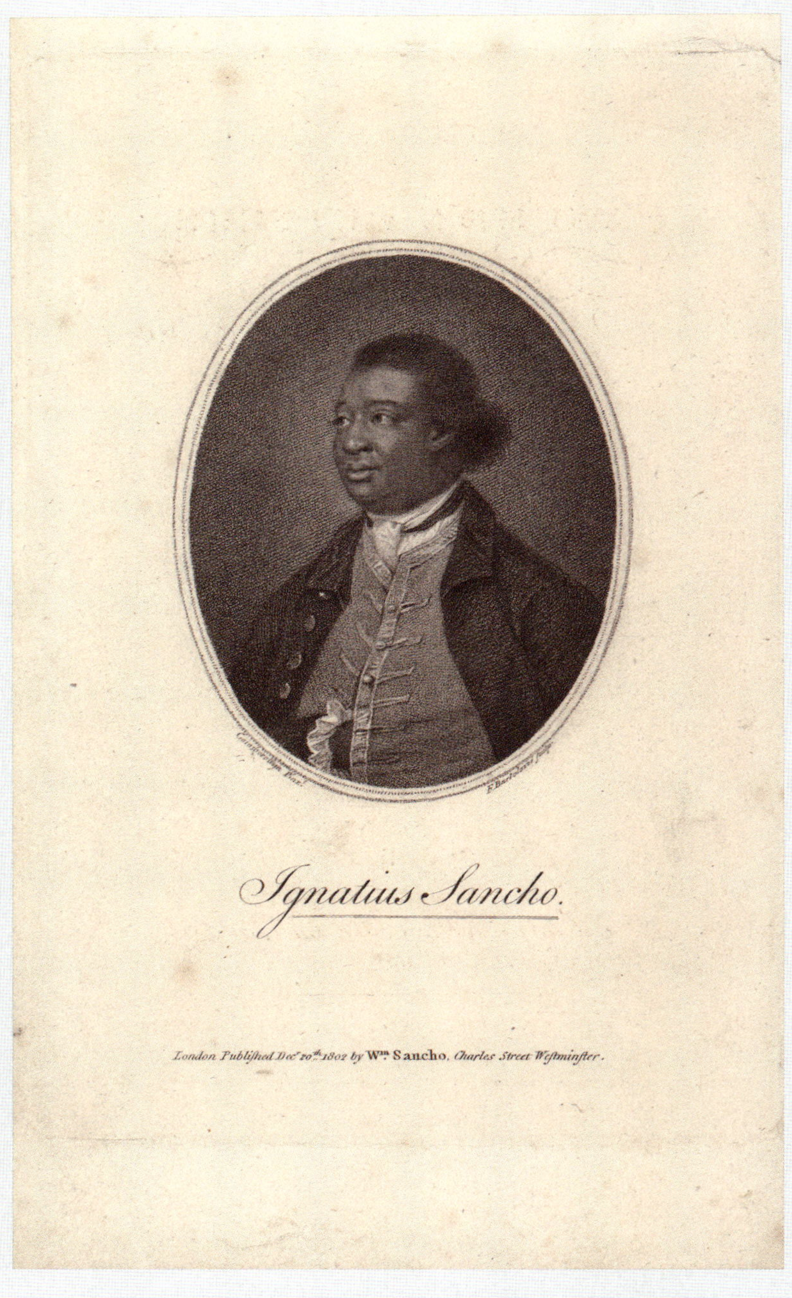

1.6 *Portrait of Ignatius Sancho*, engraved by Francesco Bartolozzi, after Thomas Gainsborough, 1781–1802. Metropolitan Museum of Art, New York

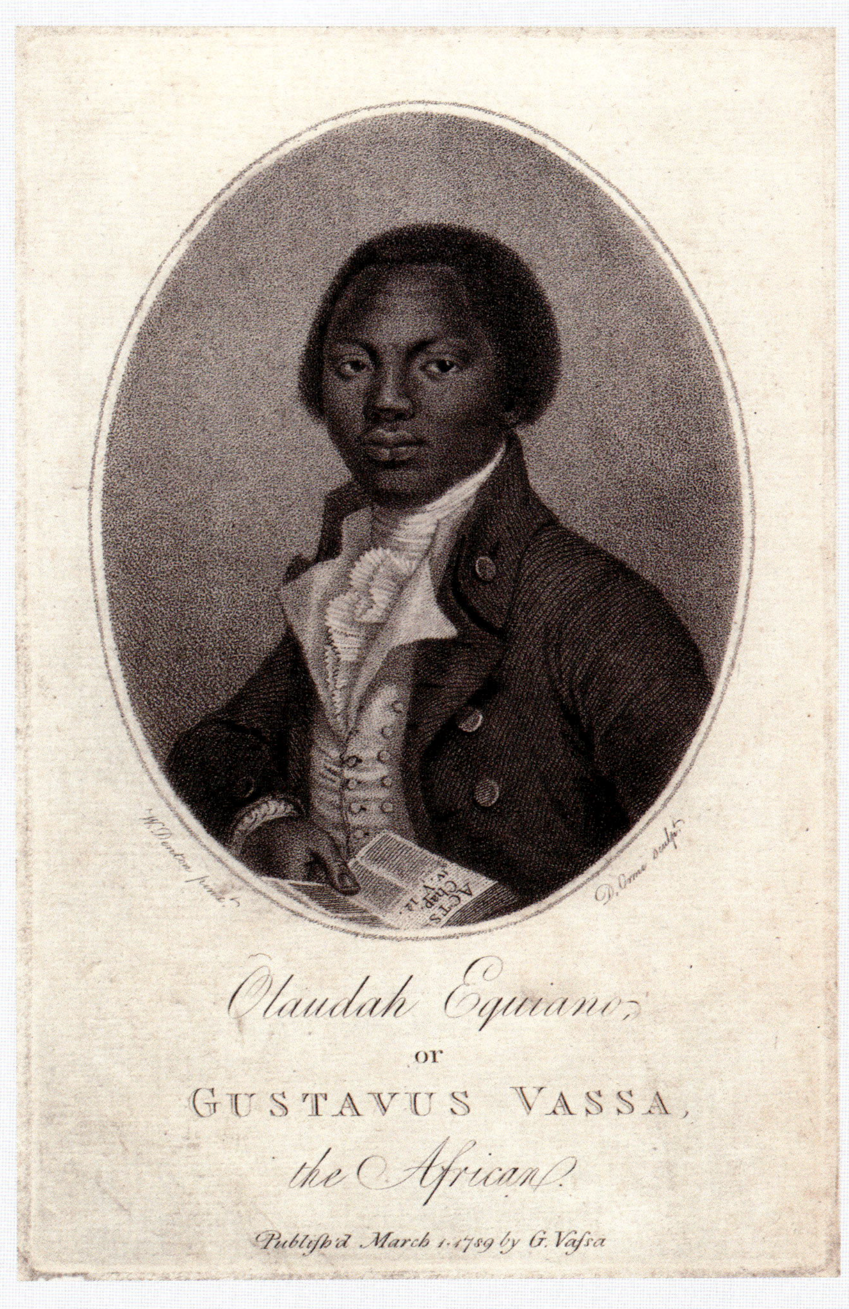

1.7 Frontispiece to *The Life of Olaudah Equiano, or Gustavus Vassa, the African*, 1789. National Portrait Gallery, London

to know), and the subsequent engraving that would furnish the published prints, could have been made in London rather than in Boston.

The choice to depict Wheatley in the act of composition may have followed the contemporaneous British practice of depicting famous male writers, such as Alexander Pope (1688–1744), one of Wheatley's other chief influences, who were commonly imaged with pen in hand (figure 1.8). Numerous reproductions of portraits of Pope circulated widely in the eighteenth century, and it is likely that Wheatley, whose own writing often echoed the earlier poet's, had access to these in the form of book frontispieces or mezzotints, and she may have asked her portraitist to pose her accordingly. In a portrait from 1727 that shows him with his pen lifted from the paper as though he has just been interrupted by the arrival of someone in his chamber. Pope's pose is like Wheatley's, and yet hers differs considerably in that neither Wheatley's body nor her attention turns from the task at hand. Unlike Pope, Wheatley is fully focused on her work, with pen to paper and eyes raised, poised to receive divine inspiration. In many ways Wheatley's pose is a pious one; it signals an intense focus on divine inspiration and closely resonates with Italian Renaissance images of studious church fathers, for example, the fresco of St. Augustine at the Chiesa di Ognissanti in Florence, Italy, by Sandro Botticelli (ca. 1455–1510), which depicts the saint with an inkwell in hand and surrounded by numerous books and other objects of scholarly inquiry, his gaze tilting heavenward (figure 1.9).

The divine inspiration that Wheatley worked so hard to receive and then channel into her writing is in evidence in her ekphrastic poetry. Through ekphrasis, by not only describing what she was seeing in a painting or print but also addressing the image directly, reflecting on its context and content, Wheatley was able to enter a multilevel relationship with a work of art.[26] The poem "To S. M., a Young African Painter, on Seeing His Works" is an enthusiastic and evocative ekphrasis on a no longer extant image. A brief examination of this poem emphasizes just how deeply the young writer was interested in the denotative and connotative discursive field that can be generated by a rhetorical engagement with an image. It begins:

> To show the lab'ring bosom's deep intent,
> And thought in living characters to paint,
> When first thy pencil did those beauties give,
> And breathing figures learnt from thee to live,
> How did those prospects give my soul delight,
> A new creation rushing on my sight?
> Still, wond'rous youth! each noble path pursue,

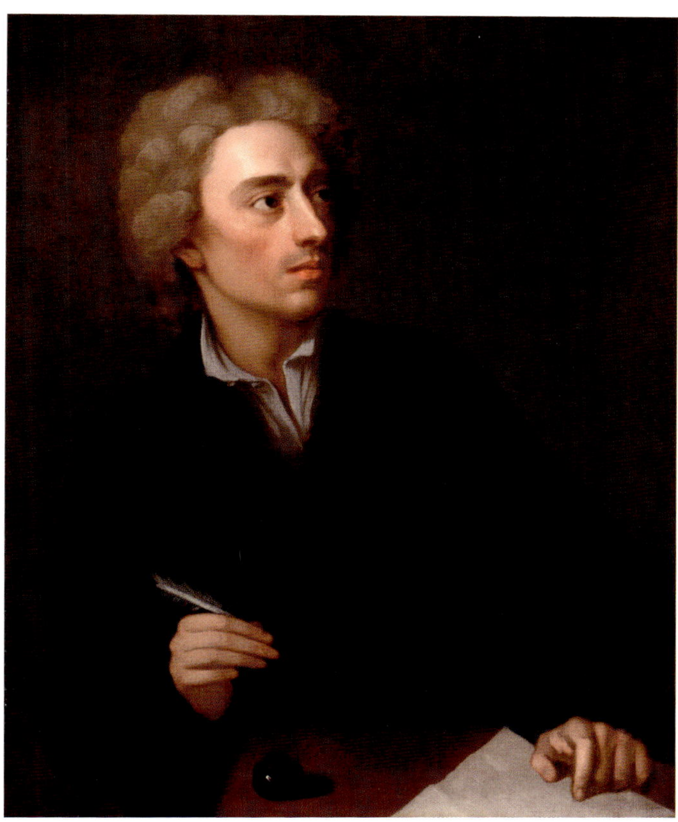

On deathless glories fix thine ardent view:
Still may the painter's and the poet's fire
To aid thy pencil, and thy verse conspire![27]

Wheatley's interest in ekphrasis indicates that she did not only wish to see with words but may herself have wanted to be seen beyond words. And because the world in which she was raised, the world within which her sight-filled words operated, was one that had a set of objectifying tropes associated with the bodies of women of African descent, Wheatley and her portraitist had to employ a strategy to manipulate and defy the visual rhetoric associated with these conventions, in order to assert control over them and to present the poet as a creative, intellectual Black woman whose body was in sync with her text.

The importance of mezzotints and other engravings within the visual culture of the Boston middle-class society of which the Wheatleys were a part

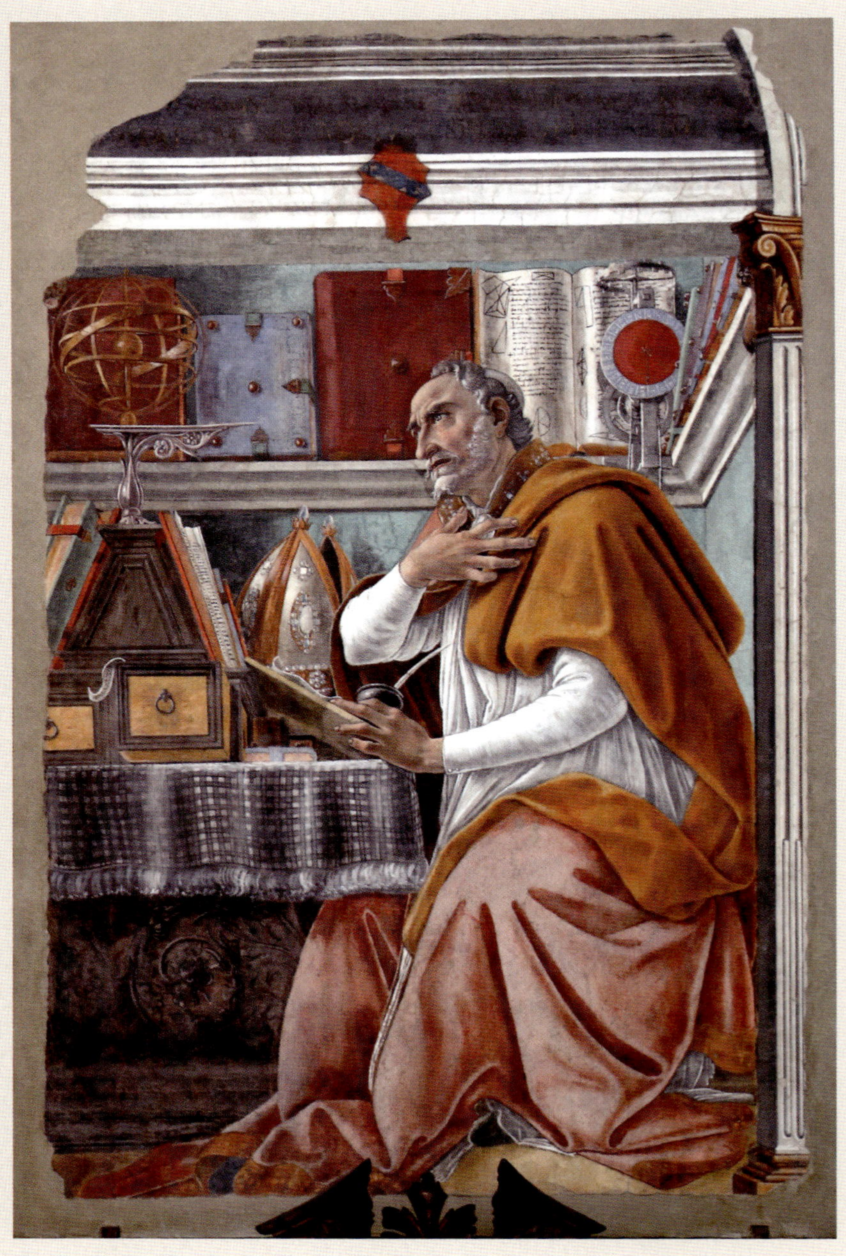

1.9 Sandro Botticelli, *St. Augustine*, 1480. Fresco.
Chiesa di Ognissanti, Florence, Italy

cannot be overstated. There is little doubt that Phillis Wheatley's interest in this sophisticated, yet popular art form may have been furthered during her three months in England in 1773.

Wheatley's experiences with the visual and the print culture of the public sphere of the late eighteenth-century British world are an important component to understanding the construction of her image. In colonial Boston of the period, there was a long-established and surprisingly rich portrait tradition within the Anglo-American community that included the Wheatley family. As a provincial portrait tradition, it drew heavily on the use of engraved or mezzotint reproductions of popular contemporary British and French portraits. Paul Staiti and Aileen Ribeiro have argued that the Boston-born portraitist John Singleton Copley trained himself to paint highly desirable portraits by adapting the work of English and continental artists that he saw in local collections and using mezzotints as templates.[28] This practice of adaptation was common for most British and continental artists of the day and especially typical for colonial artists, who had little opportunity to study high-quality portraits.[29] Mezzotint prints were used with great frequency by Copley as the templates from which to construct fashionable portraits until he left the American colonies for Europe the first time in 1774.

Although James Porter claimed that "the work [Wheatley's frontispiece] is of provincial character and exhibits several naïve traits of design," as far as the formal design of the frontispiece of Wheatley is concerned, the image is quite sophisticated for the visual rhetoric that it demonstrates and may be compared favorably to mature works by Copley and others that feature subjects seated at tables with occupied hands.[30]

The portrait of Wheatley employs a specific visual rhetoric that was often used in the presentation of educated, cultured, middle-class and elite women of the period, such as Copley's 1772 portrait of Dorothy Wendell Skinner (figure 1.10). In this enigmatic image done just a year before Wheatley's book was published, Mrs. Skinner sits at a highly polished table. The fingers of her right hand touch her chin, just as Wheatley's do, and her gaze is directed beyond the picture frame. Her left hand, rather than holding a pen, toys absently with a sprig of blue Canterbury bells.

While many seated portraits of upper-class women from this period share a reflective pose like the one Wheatley adopts, none shows them in the act of writing. Further, there are few, if any, paintings, engravings, or mezzotints of British women writers made prior to 1773, the year that saw the publication of Wheatley's *Poems on Various Subjects, Religious and Moral,* that feature them at their craft. For example, Peter Cross's 1690 portrait miniature of Ann Finch,

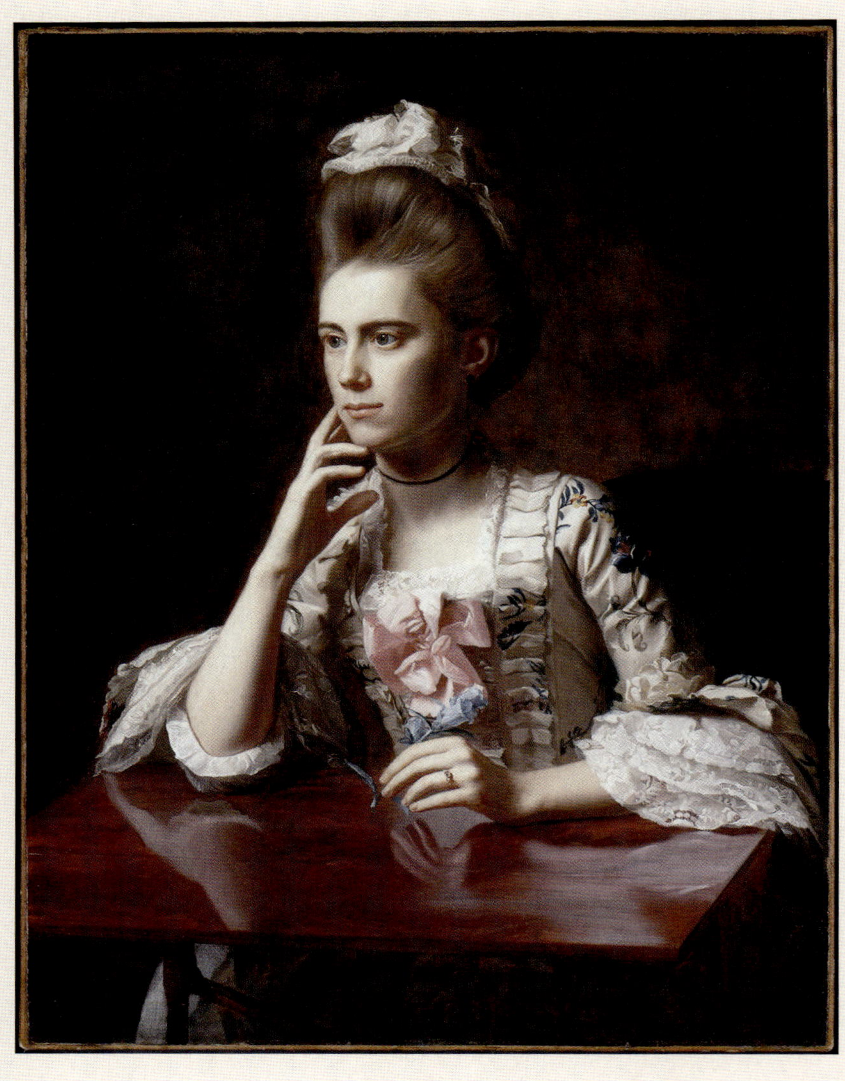

1.10 John Singleton Copley, *Mrs. Richard Skinner (Dorothy Wendell)*, 1772.
Museum of Fine Arts, Boston

Countess of Winchilsea, presents the poet and Stuart loyalist like any other lady of her era but gives not a hint of her literacy or her political activism. Only portraits of women painters such as Angelica Kauffman reveal an interest in being portrayed with the tools of one's trade. Given that Wheatley's portrait was the first frontispiece reproduction of an American woman writer, it is interesting that it was so visually innovative as to feature its subject in the act of writing.

When *Poems on Various Subjects, Religious and Moral* was published in London in August 1773, Archibald Bell could not print copies fast enough to keep up with the demand. And although he had promised to begin to send them over to Boston within a few weeks, it was several months before he was able to do so. The book entered the critical discourse of the British public sphere rapidly, where its intellectual merits and its political importance were hotly debated. Abolitionists trumpeted it as evidence of African and African-descended people's inherent intelligence and humanity, proof that their commodification and exploitation were morally reprehensible and ought to be outlawed. British politicians used the book as a counterpoint to what they saw as the ironic cries for independence and political freedom that were increasingly coming from the colonies; after all, what moral right did "the drivers of slaves" have that they might make a plea for independence? As a result of the public discourse that followed the publication of the book in England, pressure soon came to bear on the white Wheatley family for continuing to hold Phillis in a state of bondage. Rather than be viewed as hypocrites, they chose to legally free her, and as a means of support, she was granted a 50 percent royalty from the sale of her books. The receipt of this stipend became the primary source of support for her and her family until her early death, just ten years later around the age of twenty-nine.

It is remarkable that following the publication of Wheatley's book, with its maverick portrait frontispiece, there occurred a sea change in the way that women writers and poets began to present themselves in British portraiture. For example, Robert Edge Pine's portrait of Catherine Macauley from around 1774 shows the historian in the costume of a classical muse, and her right arm rests on five of the eight volumes of her monumental *History of England*.[31] Her right hand holds a quill pen while her left hand toys absentmindedly with a piece of paper.

Despite the impact that Wheatley's frontispiece seems to have had in England on the portrayal of women writers, it would be a full fifty years before an example of an African American author's emulation of the portrait would appear. But we do eventually find one in the 1836 autobiography *The Life and Religious Experience of Mrs. Jarena Lee*, the first woman to make a

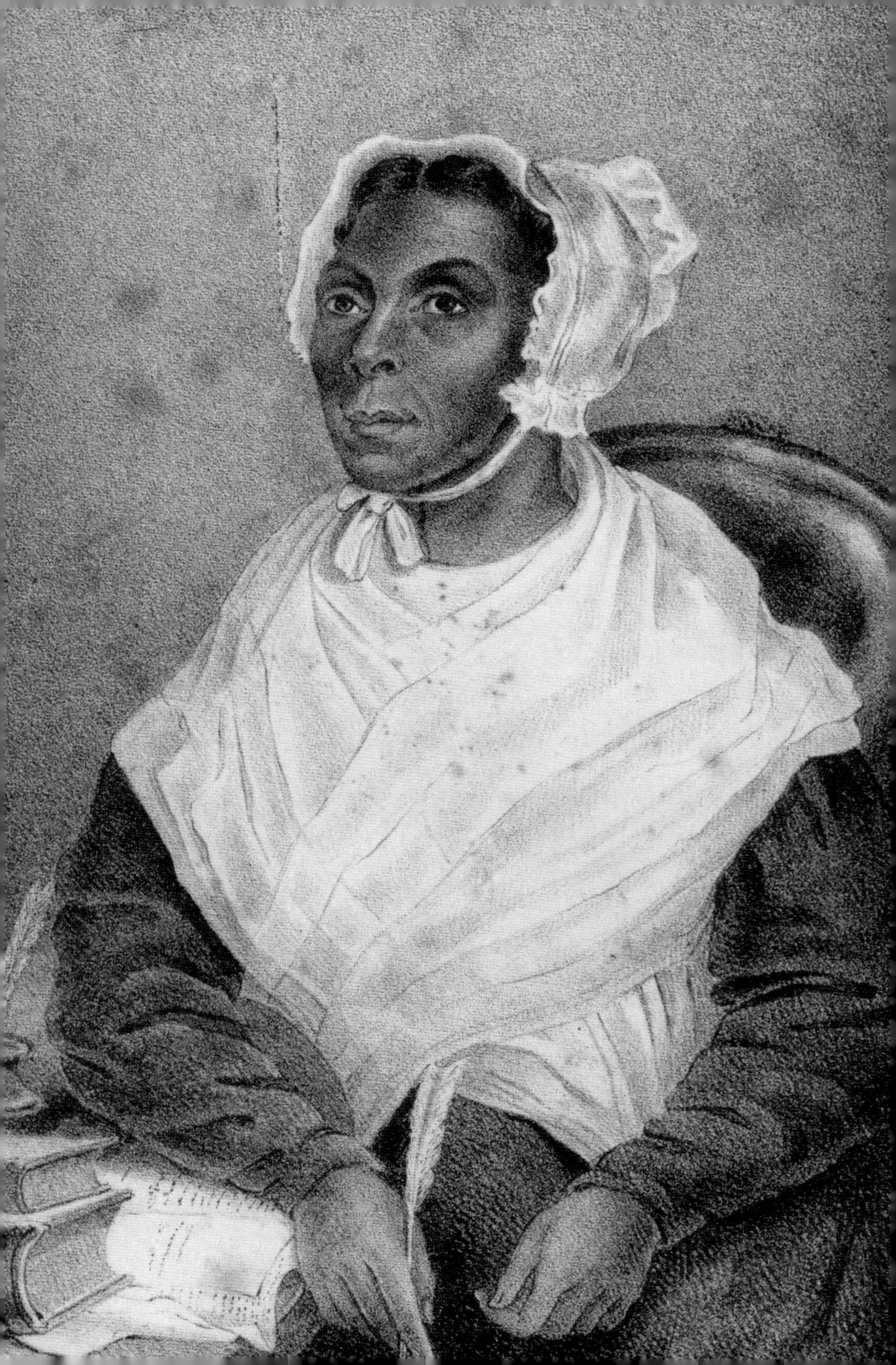

career as a licensed preacher in the African Methodist Episcopal Church (figure 1.11).[32] Like Wheatley, Lee is shown plainly dressed in a white shawl and bonnet with a quill in her hand and papers and books on the table beside her. The Bible that is placed beside Lee indicates that she is a religious woman and a literate one. Just as Wheatley had turned to specific sources for the construction of her frontispiece portrait to fashion an identity that would assert defiance from ideologically controlled visual codes in which Black women were subjected to structures of social dominance, so too did Lee. But in this case, she only had to look to Wheatley's model. One might say that she was "doing Phillis" when she sat for this portrait. And although Lee's situation as an African American in the nineteenth century might have been vastly different from that of the eighteenth-century Anglo-British writer and abolitionist Hannah More, her position as an anglophone woman writer remains a point of difference on which all these women may be connected.

It is imperative for historians of African American art to move beyond the mythic moment of the creation of this important image and others like it. It is necessary to range widely within the study of American and British art to uncover the myriad histories of the broader Atlantic world. The clothing Wheatley wears, the pose she has been placed in, the world of British visual and print culture that often inspired her writing, all tell us a great deal about the portrait of her. The possible visual sources and the probable visual descendants that bracket Wheatley's portrait are of critical importance and show how this image of an Anglo-African woman departed from earlier portrayals of Anglo-British women writers and defied the conventions of portraying enslaved African and African-descended women.

When we remember purposefully disremembered pieces of evidence, this seemingly unassuming portrait of a nineteen-year-old Anglo-African woman yields its secrets. Wheatley's portrait is a pivotal image that subverts a hegemonic visual culture that would otherwise have depicted her as less than human and incapable of the creativity that defined her life. It is an image that revolutionized the way in which numerous writers, including Anglo-Africans, African Americans, and Anglo-British women in Britain, asserted their right to exist as authors in the public sphere.

1.11 Unknown artist, *Jarena Lee*, 1836.
New York Public Library Digital Collections

2

PROFILING MOSES WILLIAMS

SILHOUETTES AND RACE IN THE EARLY REPUBLIC

In 1996 the curators of the Library Company of Philadelphia attributed a hollow-cut paper silhouette of a young man—from a collection amassed by the American psychologist James Rush (1786–1869)—to the multitalented artist Raphaelle Peale.[1] In it, a man's face, neck, and shoulders are formed by the course of a complex linear cut that has been made in white laid paper (figure 2.1). The black album stock revealed within creates the subject's forehead, the rounded tip of his nose, the full lips pressed tightly together, and an undulating hairline, with a long queue at the back that extends past the collar of the subject's coat. From between the lapels, the form line becomes a neckerchief, the end of a bow jutting out into empty space while also mirroring the thong that secures the end of the queue. And while the carved white paper deftly creates physiological characteristics and costume details, the black stock on which it rests seems to create a veil of darkness rather than reveal a "truth" about the "identity" of the sitter.

Handwritten across the lower edge of the white paper are the words "Moses Williams, Cutter of Profiles," information that seems to lift a part of this veil. But at the same time the text adds to the mystery of the portrait itself. Who was Moses Williams, and why was it necessary to inscribe his occupation next to his name? How might we interpret the denotative and connotative meanings found within this image/text combination today? What do they tell us about the silhouette's ability to contain and communicate a specific sitter's identity? Specifically, how did such a minimalist medium impact the ability of artists to communicate a sitter's race, gender, and class position in a remarkably diverse city, that of Philadelphia, during the era of the early republic? Further still, how might the silhouette's conventions be harnessed by an artist to assert a self-fashioned identity, one that might stand in opposition to hegemonic ideals and social prescriptions?

2.1 *Moses Williams, Cutter of Profiles*, ca. 1803.
Library Company of Philadelphia

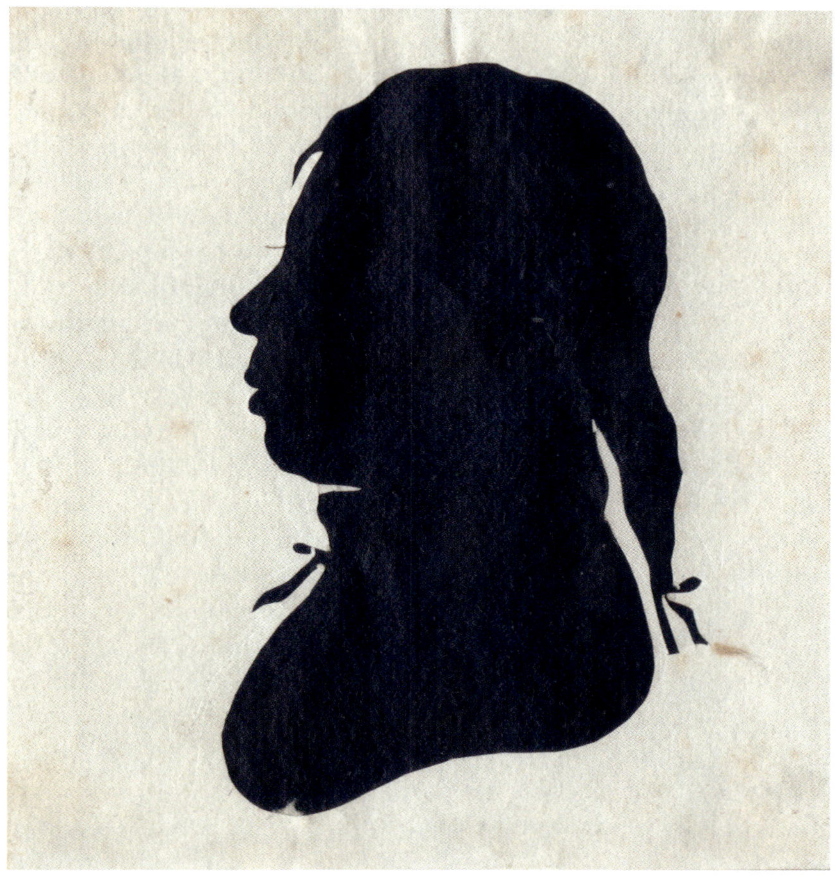

By considering the life and work of Moses Williams (1777–ca. 1825) within the historical context of the early republic, and by discussing the profile-making process itself, I attempt to remember the identity of this Black artist. In so doing, I argue that the silhouette *Moses Williams, Cutter of Profiles* may in fact be a self-portrait and that the Library Company's initial attribution of this image to the hand of Raphaelle Peale was an act of disremembering.

For many years Moses Williams was known to scholars only by a few references that constructed him as a onetime enslaved worker belonging to Charles Willson Peale (1741–1827), the foremost painter, naturalist, and museum proprietor of the early republican period of the postcolonial United States.[2] Peale's diary entries, letters, and assorted newspaper clippings provide evidence that Williams was born and raised within his master's Philadelphia household and that after his manumission he worked as a silhouette maker in Peale's Museum. Textually present yet physically invisible until 1996, when the silhouette of him was formally cataloged by the Library Company of Philadelphia, Williams existed as a shadowy enigma for historians, what Toni Morrison might term an "Africanist presence" within the well-documented legacy of the Peale family. Research conducted at the end of the last century, however, began to examine Williams's function within the museum and the impact of the silhouettes that he cut on the visual culture of early nineteenth-century Philadelphia. By synthesizing the foundational research and analysis presented in Ellen Sacco's dissertation, "Spectacular Masculinities: The Museums of Peale, Baker and Bowen in the Early Republic," and David Brigham's book *Public Culture in the Early Republic: Peale's Museum and Its Audience*, one can reconstruct Williams's life within the Peale household and his important relationship to the family's patriarch, Charles Willson Peale.

Beginning in the 1760s, Charles Willson Peale fashioned for himself a career in the arts and natural sciences that was unparalleled in his day. In addition to painting portraits of such notables as George Washington, Peale maintained a museum that featured hundreds of North American animals that he had preserved and ethnographic artifacts that he had collected. He was active in the politics of the time, serving in the Pennsylvania legislature, and was a friend and correspondent of Thomas Jefferson, Benjamin Rush, and many other prominent statesmen of his era. With three different wives, he fathered seventeen children, and while not all of them reached maturity, the ones who did tended to follow their father's example and his teachings by choosing work as visual artists, naturalists, and museum proprietors.

Like many other citizens of moderate means living in the mid-Atlantic states before and after the War of Independence, Peale enslaved people.

While working in Annapolis, Maryland, he acquired Williams's parents, a mixed-race couple named Scarborough and Lucy, as payment for portraits he painted for a wealthy client, sometime between 1769 and 1775, in the period leading up to the Revolutionary War. Shortly thereafter, in 1777, Moses was born to the couple, and following the condition of his mother, he became Peale's property. Had Moses's birth come just three years later, when the Act for the Gradual Abolition of Slavery passed the Pennsylvania legislature (with Peale's assistance), he would have been born free. After the act's effective date of March 1, 1780, Moses's status then fell into the category of indentured servitude, which allowed Peale to hold him until his twenty-eighth birthday, despite his parents having gained their freedom with the law. To Peale, Moses was a "Molatto," belonging on a lower stratum in the order of humankind, one that may not have deserved to be enslaved for life but that certainly could be subordinated and controlled, treated in the same manner as one would a child.

Growing up apart from his natural parents, Moses was functionally the "eighteenth child" of his master, and prevailing ideological attitudes pre-scribed that he would be treated as a child throughout his lifetime despite being freed a year early, in 1802, at the age of twenty-seven.[3] Raised alongside the numerous Peale children, who by necessity were trained to be useful members of the museum's staff, Moses was instructed in taxidermy, animal husbandry, object display, and eventually the use of a silhouette-making machine known as the *physiognotrace device*. This tool for image making was closely related to what was then called a polygraph machine (Thomas Jefferson owned one, as did Peale), which was designed to make two copies of the same document at once. While the polygraph was intended for making multiple documents, the physiognotrace was intended for making multiple images.[4] And yet both came from the desire that their co-inventors, Sir John Isaac Hawkins and Peale, had for devising a way to propagate and control the production of visual and textual meaning.

As a mechanically mediated visual presentation, the portrait profiles made by the physiognotrace promised the nineteenth-century viewer a certain indexical primacy that other forms of image making could not. Like the photographic media that would eventually eclipse it, the physiognotrace produced what was viewed by many to be a pure act of mechanical mimesis, an image practically unaltered by human hands. But because hand-cutting was a necessary part of their creation, physiognotraced profiles also retained what Walter Benjamin would term an aura of individuality.[5] The revolution in portraiture that accompanied the physiognotrace device was nearly as

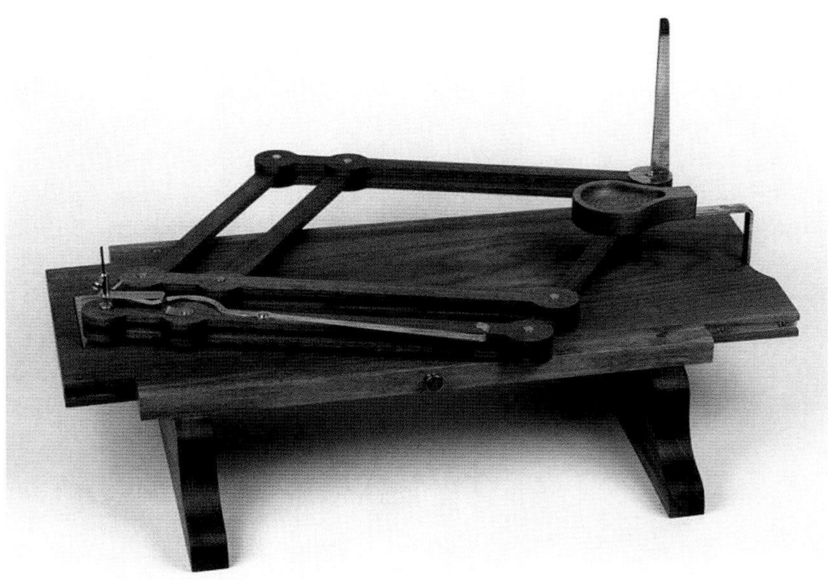

2.2 Physiognotrace, 1982, made by Terry Conable, after John Isaac Hawkins's 1802 design. National Portrait Gallery, Smithsonian Institution, Washington, DC

significant as the subsequent development of inexpensive paper photography would be during the second half of the nineteenth century. The physiognotrace silhouette retained a great deal of its "aura" because of the physical link between sitter and machine and cutter via the prosthetic arm of the wooden tracer that was attached to the device (figure 2.2).

The physiognotrace that Williams began operating at the museum in 1802 soon became one of the chief attractions for visitors. In its first years, about 80 percent of attendees, as many as eight thousand a year, had their profiles made by Williams, at a cost of eight cents each.[6] In 1805 Peale wrote to his partner Hawkins in England, "The Physiognotrace has done wonders, profiles are seen in nearly every house in the United States of America, never did any invention of making the likeness of men, meet so general approbation as this has done. . . . It would be too great a task for Mosis [*sic*] to write the Name on each. . . . However he shall give such names as he may think worthy of being known and remembered."[7]

At the time of its installation, Williams was taught to operate this portrait maker, but unlike the other junior members of the Peale household, he was not taught the "higher art" of painting. This point is significant, for virtually all of Peale's immediate descendants were painters. This was perhaps for no other reason than that they had to live up to the names he had given them: Raphaelle, Rembrandt, Angelica Kauffman, and Titian Ramsay are among the best known of Peale's artistically inclined progeny. And while these white members of the household were given a full palette of colors with which to express themselves, the enslaved was relegated to the mechanized blackness of the silhouette, effectively removing him from any significant artistic and financial competition with the others.

This situation reveals the complex nature of the elder Peale's control over artistic learning in his household and the role that slavery played within it. "It is a curious fact that until the age of 27, Moses was entirely worthless: but on the invention of the physiognotrace, he took a fancy to amuse himself in cutting out the rejected profiles made by the machine, and soon acquired such dexterity and accuracy, that the machine was confided to his custody with the privilege of retaining the fee for drawing and cutting," recalled Rembrandt Peale (1778–1860), who was well known for his vivid portraits of George Washington and others. "This soon became so profitable, that my father insisted upon giving him his freedom one-year in advance. In a few years he amassed a fund sufficient to buy a two-story brick house, and actually married my father's white cook, who during his bondage, would not permit him to eat at the same table with her."[8]

Rembrandt Peale and Moses Williams were unequal peers in a peculiar family relationship. As laboring son and enslaved worker, they were both under the control of their paterfamilias for the first half of their lives, and the role of the all-powerful head of household was one that the elder Peale relished. Further insight into the peculiar dynamics present in the Peale family, and the role that slavery played in them, may be gleaned from the way that Williams was mentioned by the elder Peale in letters to family members and close friends. For example, in an 1803 letter to Raphaelle Peale (1774–1825), who was then working in Virginia making silhouettes and painting portraits, Peale praises the work of his former chattel: "I have just spoken to a Gentleman who says he was at your Room in Norfolk which was so crouded that he could not get his profiles. Moses has made him a good one, being from Carolina he did not at first relish having it done by a *Molatta*, however I convinced him that Moses could do it much better than I could."[9]

And in an 1808 letter to Rembrandt, then studying in Paris, the patriarch records the birth of Moses's daughter in the same paragraph and sentence as the events of his natural children and grandchildren: "I have the agreable intelligence to communicate of the (safe) recovery of your sisters [*sic*] Angelica's health, and the birth of an other (Daughter) Son, after which she had a severe attack of bilious colick, Raphaelle has also another Son, and Moses a Daughter."[10] In this environment of complicated familial relations, attention to the formerly enslaved may have been seen as a slight to the son. I would speculate that Rembrandt's antipathy toward his father may have been redirected toward the easiest possible target, Moses Williams.[11]

The hegemonic language of American white supremacy has created designations for people of color that are not only derisive but problematic as well. In a diary entry of 1799, Peale refers to Moses Williams as "my Molatto Man Moses," in a manner quite like that found in the 1803 letter to Raphaelle.[12] In the term "Molatto," estimations of color, blood quantum, and subhuman, equine origins seem to confront each other. The liminal racial identity that these words constructed for Williams, his enslaved status, his racially mixed heritage, and his conditional masculinity caused him to be viewed as profoundly *other* within the public sphere of Philadelphia that defined American identity as decidedly white.

Whether living as an enslaved person with the Peale family or as a freed householder, Williams would have spent a good deal of time negotiating his visible difference from the dominant population of white Philadelphia. The 1820 census, for example, found him and his mixed-race family in the Lower Delaware Ward of Philadelphia, an area bounded by the modern Race Street, Arch Street, North Fourth Street, and the Delaware River.[13] In 1820 the ward contained 3,143 whites and 94 free Blacks, and it only contained three Black households—just two others besides that of the Williams family. Nearly all the other people of color in the neighborhood resided in white households as servants. Remarkably, ten years earlier, in the 1810 census, when Williams was listed as living in the adjacent North Mulberry Ward (covering a similar area stretching two blocks north from Arch Street to Vine Street), the entire Williams family is listed as white.[14]

Just as his ambiguously raced body made it difficult for census enumerators to record Williams's identity with consistency, so too did it enable him, with the right costuming, to inhabit multiple guises of otherness, including that of a Native American.[15] Sacco argues that despite being a vital part of the museum's workings, "Williams's presence in the museum, as silhouette cutter, or, as sent out by Peale dressed as an Indian to pass out handbills for the exhibit of the mastodon in 1802, [put] Williams up for the same scrutiny as the displays—because it featured his subordinated status within a practice of visual order."[16] This "practice of visual order" is well illustrated by *The Artist*

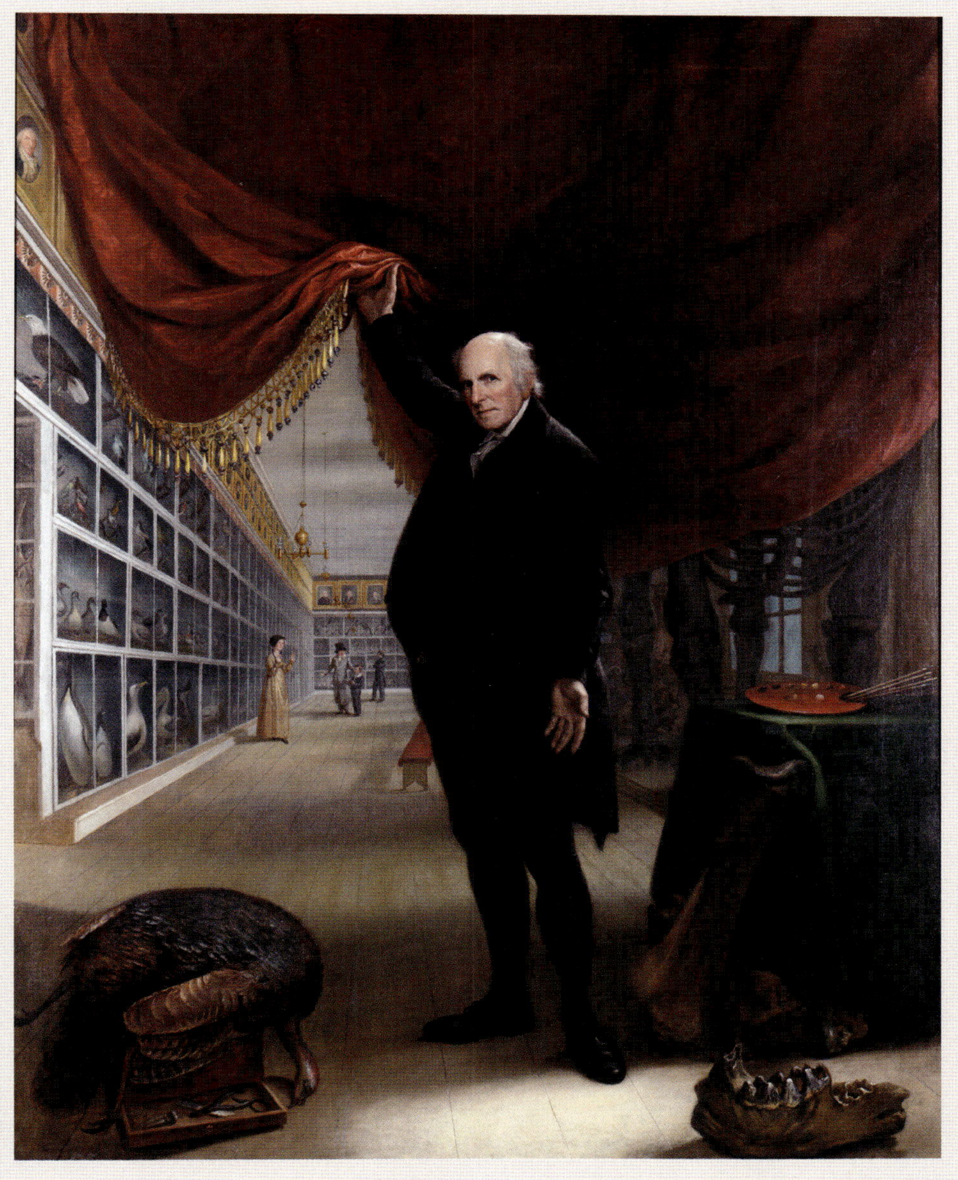

2.3 Charles Willson Peale, *The Artist in His Museum*, 1822. Courtesy of Pennsylvania Academy of the Fine Arts, Philadelphia

in His Museum, an emblematic self-portrait that Peale made toward the end of his life (figure 2.3). Here the elderly proprietor, still virile, lifts a curtain to reveal the contents of the Longroom, the main exhibition space of his museum. On the left side of the composition, near the ceiling, are arranged portraits by the proprietor of the leading white men whom he saw as being foremost among the nation's founders. Hierarchically arranged beneath them on the lower levels are various ethnographic artifacts and preserved animals collected from throughout North America. *The Artist in His Museum* is a visual biography of Peale's lifelong endeavor to create and control the production of meaning within a circumscribed space that bore his family's name.[17]

Peale was not the only person in the museum who was actively working to create meaning through the collection and creation of objects. As the resident silhouette cutter, Moses Williams was also producing information about the world that extended to the west of the original thirteen states by recording the profiles of the diverse people who visited the museum. What must he have thought, then, when Native American representatives from west of the Mississippi arrived at the museum to sit for their portraits?

In February 1806, Waconsca, a Kaw (Kansa) delegate from west of the Mississippi, sat on a chair in the Longroom. He kept his head still for the minute or so that it took Williams to use the physiognotrace (see figure 2.2) to reduce and then transfer the lines of his profile onto a piece of twice-folded paper. The surviving example from the original set of four silhouette portraits that were cut that day reveals a striking profile. The cut line denotes the facial features of a well-formed young man with a high forehead, smooth brow ridge, and strong jaw; a lock of hair is pulled back from the face and tied high, with a feather ornament thrust into its cinch; it finishes with a high-collared coat and neckerchief. The coat, in seeming competition with a lush flow of hair at the nape of his neck, juts out at the back, making him appear broad-shouldered and thickly muscled. But for the unusual arrangement of the boldly ornamented hair, Waconsca's portrait (figure 2.4) might be mistaken for that of a European-descended sitter, such as the French-Canadian interpreter Joseph Barron (figure 2.5), who traveled with the delegation of Native Americans of which Waconsca was a part.

Significantly, it is Williams's attention to what we would today call the ethnographic details and the accoutrements of cultural difference that gives the portrait profile of Waconsca its visual power, despite the limits of the mechanically aided profile silhouettes' ability to capture and codify the notions of racial difference that were essential to the era's notions of citizenship.

Having stopped first in Washington, DC, in December and January to meet with President Thomas Jefferson, the 1805–6 Indian delegation that

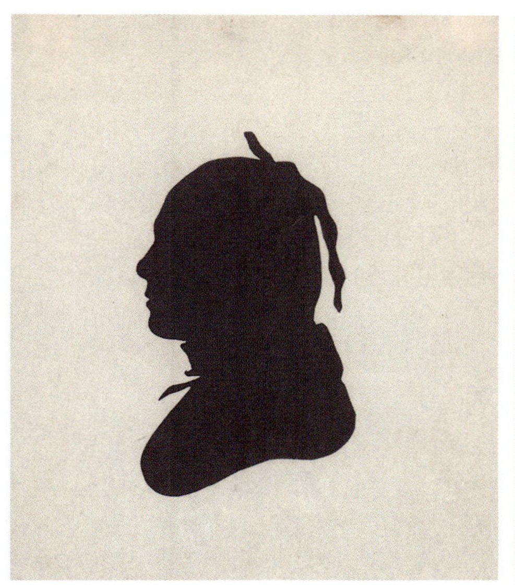 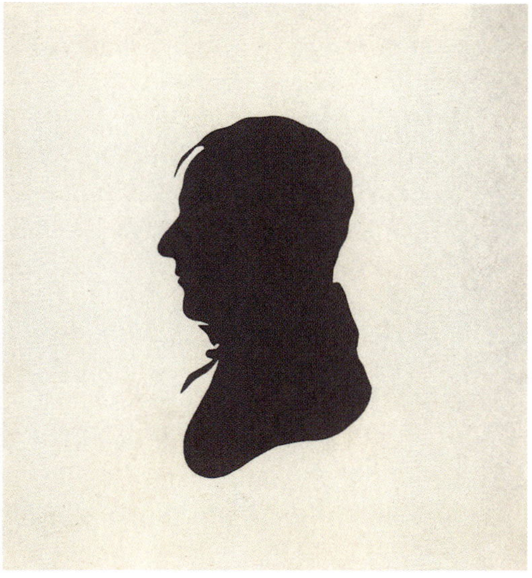

2.4 Moses Williams, *Waconsca*, 1806. Courtesy of the National Anthropological Archives, Smithsonian Institution, Washington, DC.

2.5 Moses Williams, *Joseph (Baume) Barron*, 1806. Courtesy of the National Anthropological Archives, Smithsonian Institution, Washington, DC

included Waconsca and Barron was the third group of Native peoples from west of the Mississippi to arrive in the settlers' new capital.[18] The first of these groups had received an invitation to visit Washington, DC, and meet the president in 1804 when Meriwether Lewis (1774–1809) and William Clark (1770–1838) first arrived in Saint Louis, in the new territory of Missouri, on their expedition of exploration and diplomacy that followed the Louisiana Purchase of 1803. The US federal government, under the direction of President Jefferson, exchanged $15 million with Napoleon Bonaparte (1769–1821) and the French government for sovereignty rights over the 530 million acres of land that the French had controlled intermittently since the late seventeenth century. This territory, which stretched west of the Mississippi River and up into what is now Canada, was home to vast numbers of Indigenous peoples who now found themselves compelled to negotiate with a different foreign power for their right to exist on lands that their ancestors had called home for thousands of years. In fact, France had only recently regained control of the territory from Spain in a secret treaty signed in 1801, holding it for less than two years before selling it to the United States. Over the next few years, at the behest of Lewis and Clark, dozens of Native American emissaries from as far west as Sioux territory, in what is now Wyoming and the Dakotas, would make their way east to Washington, DC, to meet with President Jefferson and his representatives.

When the first delegation of Native emissaries from west of the Mississippi arrived in Washington, DC, in July 1804, their physical and sartorial differences were one of the things that European Americans seemed most fascinated with on meeting or seeing them. Augustus John Foster, the secretary to the British legation in Washington, DC, wrote of the 1805–6 delegation, which included Waconsca:

> I had the opportunity of seeing them in their procession and accompanied them to their lodgings. . . . The interpreters and Americans who came with them went first, and the Orator went before the rest. He was in a great coat but his left eye was surrounded by a circle of green and white paint and the rest of his face was red. He carried a tomahawk which was extremely well made, serving at the same time as a pipe, otherwise in shape like a common hatchet. It came from the Northwest Company. Next followed two, naked to the waist and painted reddish yellow, their hair shaved as far as the crown where it was ornamented with feathers and formed into a tail behind inclosed in silver. They wore blankets about their middles and moccasins and pantaloons of deer's skin. . . . Their ears were pierced in two places which were much widened by the weight of the ear-rings suspended from them.[19]

Foster was interested in both the manners and the appearance of the Native American delegates but says little of their attitudes or personalities. These later attributes were not things that could be easily communicated visually without relying on exaggerated facial expressions, but there were certainly choices that could be made when one went to record a sitter's likeness. Having arrived in the nation's recently built capitol, each successive group of Native representatives attempted to negotiate and ratify treaties between themselves and the European-descended men who insisted on being called their "fathers."

"My Children: By late arrangements with France and Spain, we now take their place as your neighbours, friends and fathers; and we hope you will have no cause to regret the change," President Jefferson wrote to the chiefs of the Osage Nation several months later. "It is so long since our forefathers came from beyond the great water, that we have lost the memory of it, and seem to have grown out of this land, as you have done; never more will you have occasion to change your fathers."[20] But once the physiognomic portrait profile silhouettes of the 1805–6 Native American delegation, which were made by

Moses Williams at Peale's Museum, joined Jefferson's collection of Native American artifacts at his Monticello home, in a space he created called the "Indian Hall," they became shadowy accompaniments to the remnants of the cultures that their sitters had once personified for their interlocutors.

The hegemonic white patriarchy embedded in complex ideas of "fatherhood," as expressed by both Jefferson and Peale, overhung the lives of both African-descended people and Indigenous people as they engaged the settler colonialism that drove the political agenda of the early republic. It is not accidental that we are only now beginning to change how we refer to the dominant political class of this period from the "founding fathers" to simply the "founders," as though this gender-neutral term is more historically accurate than the one it is supplanting. Issues of practical "fatherhood" and structural, race-based patriarchy were critically important for Moses Williams's life and existence. As a person born into chattel slavery, his relationship with Peale was not dissimilar to the one Jefferson asserts in his address to the Native peoples who had traveled so far to meet with him and his representatives. Just as the controlling "fathers" of Native Americans could change from the Spanish, to the French, to the former British subjects who were now attempting to extend control, with the stroke of a quill pen and an exchange of currency, so, too, could the parents of Moses Williams change hands, from those of a Maryland plantation owner to those of Charles Willson Peale.

In 1806, when Moses Williams made hollow-cut profile silhouette portraits of Waconsca and his fellow delegates during their visit to Philadelphia, his former enslaver, Peale, took both cultural and scientific interest in detailing the physical and cultural differences of the Native American visitors that could still be ascertained. The letter from Peale to Jefferson that accompanied the group of eleven silhouettes, nine of Native American sitters and two of European Americans, reveals similar representational concerns.[21] Here Peale expressed his hope that the enclosed profiles would be "acceptable" and his concern that the names written on them (in an unidentified hand that may be that of Williams) "may not be correctly spelt." He also wrote that "some of these savages have interesting characters by the lines of their faces."[22] This observation referred to the contemporary pseudoscience of phrenology, which was based on the belief that neural anatomy was expressed in the shape of the skull—in its curves, planes, and bumps—and that the deviation of these measurements from a norm could give insight into an individual's or an entire ethnic or entire racial group's level of intelligence, or even their criminal propensity.[23] Further, phrenologists subscribed to a kind of moral philosophy that argued that such physical features as a sloping brow or a straight nose could give insight into the innate character and moral capacity of a person. Phrenological research and theorizing, which was largely centered around defining class, ethnic, and racial difference via the numeric and visual construction of implied hierarchies, had begun in the late 1790s in the work of Viennese physician Franz Joseph Gall (1758–1828). It was widely believed by many European and European American scientists and laypeople to be a valid scientific pursuit throughout the nineteenth century.

Early naturalists like Peale failed to see equality across racial lines. Even though, as an elected state legislator, Peale campaigned for the eventual abolition of slavery in Pennsylvania, in practice he remained remarkably ambivalent about its premise as an ordering structure for a heterogeneous state with a racialized hierarchy that ranked and dehumanized many of the people who lived within its power.[24] For example, in addition to being the workspace of Williams, who could be ordered to dress up in Native American garb when not operating the physiognotrace and cutting silhouettes, Peale's Museum held Native American artifacts and their bodily remains. On the day that Waconsca sat for his portrait at the Philadelphia museum, not only would he have encountered Williams's ambiguous body, he would also have seen on display the skeletons of a man and a woman who had been members of the Wabash Confederacy.[25]

Whether it was Waconsca and his compatriots or the deceased Wabash, like their African-descended counterparts, who were at the mercy of an insidious, European American–dominated patriarchal structure, Native Americans of the period had little control over the way that they were imaged or explained in the hegemonic historical record. President Jefferson may have claimed to "have lost the memory" of his ancestors ever having immigrated to America; nevertheless, like his friend Charles Willson Peale, he did not want visitors to his museum to forget that the dominance of the new nation was based on definitions of racial difference and the imposition of hierarchies that separated some people into "children" and others into "fathers."

Just as Monticello became a space in which racial difference and otherness were visually dramatized, so too was the space of Peale's Museum. Williams not only created the profile portraits of nonwhite people, as in the suite of Native delegates, but also played out his own role as the *other* in this space of didactic vision. In this performance of otherness, he not only was dressed up as an Indian for advertising purposes but may also have been transformed into an Indian in a painting attributed to Rembrandt Peale, *Man in a Feathered Helmet* (figure 2.6). Sacco suggests that in this painting the "light mulatto" may have been cast as a noble savage and masqueraded against an ethnographic black background

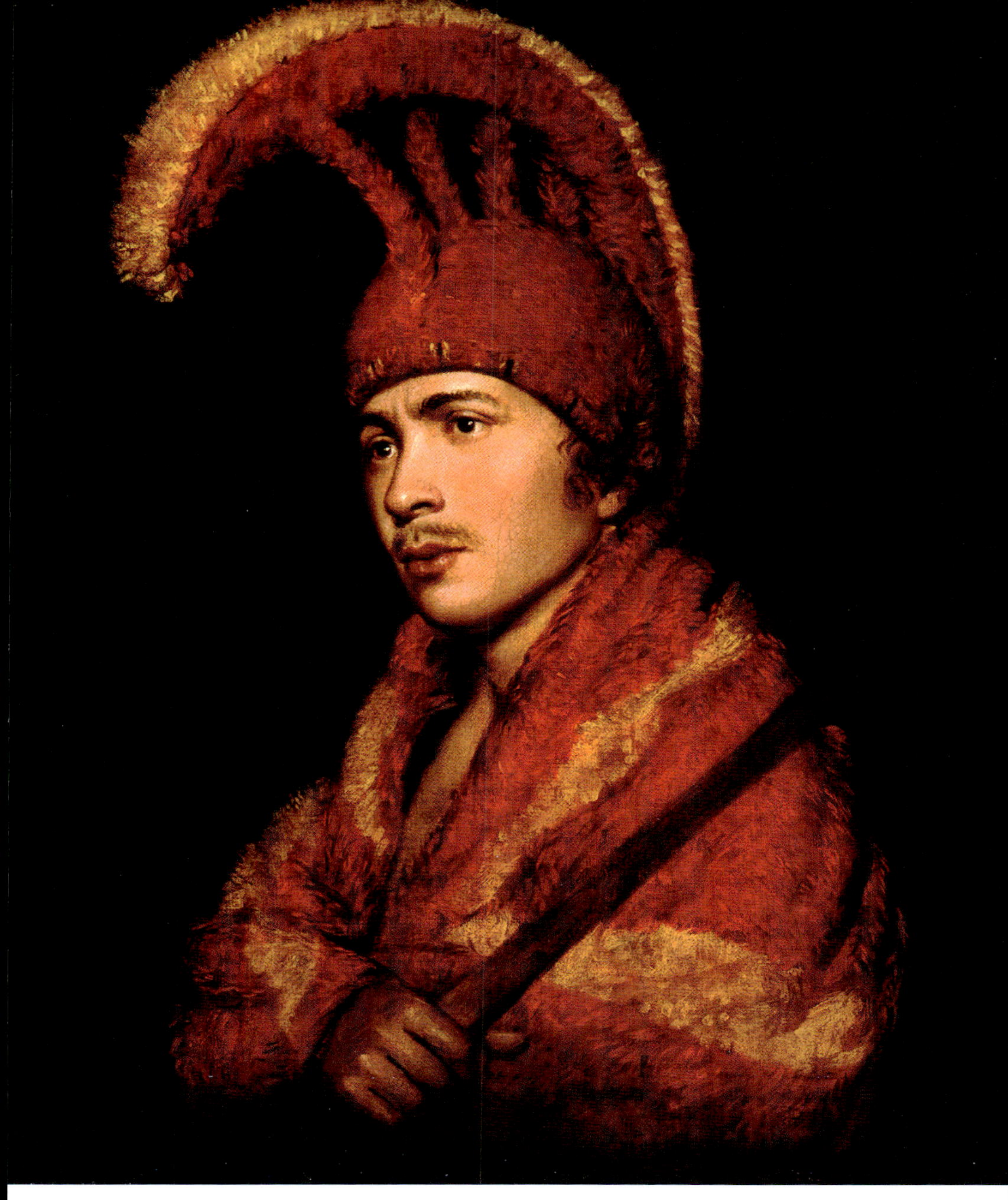

2.6 Rembrandt Peale (attr.), *Man in a Feathered Helmet*, ca. 1805–13. Courtesy of Bernice Pauahi Bishop Museum, Honolulu

as a Hawaiian chief. "A comparison of Williams's profile, with that of the young man portrayed in the painting shows the same full mouth and broader jawline." She states that through this presentation Williams has been taken out of history and environment and presented like other exhibits in the Longroom, a specimen within a hierarchical order in which nonwhites were at the bottom.[26]

Part of the problem with researching nineteenth-century silhouettes is that we often do not know who made them. There were other portrait profile artists besides Williams and the Peales who were working on the eastern seaboard in the 1810s and 1820s. Collectively they produced tens of thousands of these small images, which measure about four by five inches. The established method for attributing these images is that those made at Peale's Museum generally bear the embossment "Museum," while those made by Raphaelle in his independent practice are marked "Peale." While the designation "Museum" must be read as having subsumed the practice of Williams within it, it would also include profiles by Charles Willson Peale, or even by people who opted to save the eight-cent operator's fee by only paying for the paper and making their own. Further, there are certain stylistic details that link these profiles, such as ink-drawn curls on the head of a female sitter, or the way that a lock of hair falls over the forehead of a man, that, in the absence of an embossment, help to identify them as Peale-type profiles. But whether a silhouette has "Museum" or "Peale" embossed across its lower edge is not a concrete designation of its authorship, only of its origination within the realm of the Peale family. As a result of such ambiguities, a reasonable number of silhouettes attributed to members of the Peale family bear no embossment, and *Moses Williams, Cutter of Profiles* is one of these. These factors provide us with reasonable doubt as to the "true authorship" of this image. It is not necessarily by Raphaelle Peale; it may have been the product of collaboration on the part of the two men, or, as I suggest, it may instead be a self-portrait by Moses Williams.

Imagine for a moment, if you will, the scene of this image's creation. Moses Williams enters the Longroom of the museum; walking to the end, where the physiognotrace was located, he takes a piece of paper, folds it twice so that four copies will be made, and inserts it into the top of the machine. He sits beneath the device, adjusting his posture to fit his head within the arch at the bottom. Then, using one hand, he begins to guide the dowel over the features of his face. Chin, nose, eyes, and forehead all glide easily beneath it. The hinges of the machine, which articulate its drawing arm, act to reduce his features onto the small square of paper tacked to the top of the board. The front half of his head now drawn, he attempts to extend the reach of his arm so that it may guide the dowel over his hair and down his back. It is a difficult thing to accomplish, and the line that he achieves in this second half of the image is much choppier and rougher than in the first. The tracing of the profile now complete, Williams removes the paper and begins cutting it out. He doesn't like some of what he sees, so he corrects it to his preference. Then, using a quill and ink, he adds the finishing touch of an arching eyelash and, perhaps, writes his name and occupation at the bottom.

In *Moses Williams, Cutter of Profiles*, certain discrepancies reveal both what was ignored and what was embellished during this artistic process. On the white laid paper, embossed pentimenti from the machine's trace line appear prominently in the areas of the queue and the necktie, making a record of what was mechanically "seen" by the device. There is a significant deviation of the cut line from this path that indicates what was changed by the artist during the cutting process. Here the remaining trace lines reveal that the "cutter" altered the length of the hair by extending it nearly one-half inch beyond the original trace line, causing it to lie closer to the head. In concert with a stylized lock curling over the forehead, the altered hair follows a smoother, more flowing line.

The identifying information for Williams's silhouette is repeated on the back, but here it reads "Moses Williams, *the* Cutter of Profiles" (emphasis mine), asserting the paramount importance of the sitter's professional identity as a singular specialist. The reinscription doubles the importance of the subject's vocation in the assessment of his identity, for it constitutes a social status democratically on par with those of other artisans, defining him as a skilled worker within his community.

This profound act of naming staged beneath the profile of the artist and on the back of the mount may also be read in terms of the practice of naming Africans in America during the antebellum period. Africans newly arrived on slave ships and at domestic markets were were given new names as they were sold into slavery. It was not until an enslaved person was freed that they were able to name themselves. This practice of self-naming may be found in the case of Moses's father, Scarborough Peale, who became John Williams when he and his wife, Lucy, were freed in 1786.[27] Why John Williams chose his new name is unknown, but his son also took that last name when he was freed some sixteen years later. The first name of the son is important to consider as well. In the Bible, Moses is the one who is separated from his actual family and raised in the house of Pharaoh. Eventually, when he is confronted with his difference, his otherness, he is forced to make a critical choice not to ignore this shift in identity. At this point he is reborn when he assumes the life of an enslaved Hebrew in a newly racialized body. But it was his role as the one

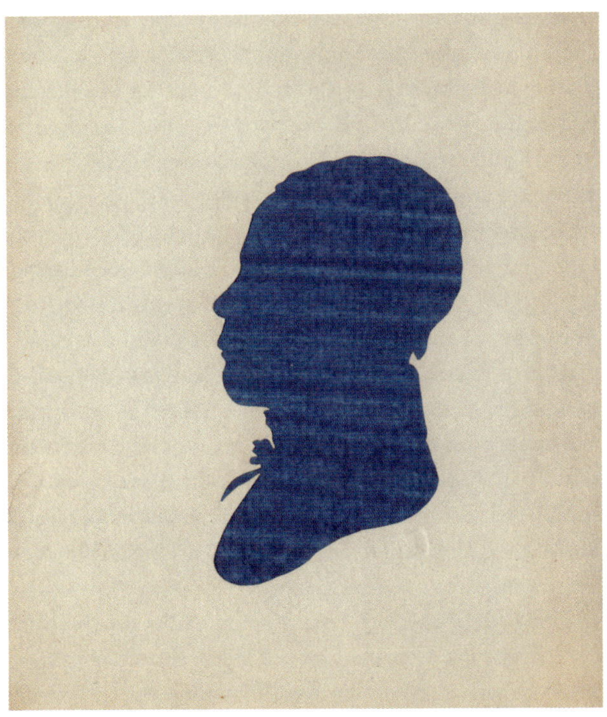

chosen by God to lead his people out of Egypt, from bondage to the promised land, that made Moses a popular one for many enslaved African Americans to give their own children. During the early nineteenth century, enslaved people went more often to another owner than they did into self-possession, and their names changed to suit the new owner's preferences.

The only other silhouette made at Peale's Museum (and attributed to Moses Williams) that is known to be of an African American is inscribed "Mr. Shaw's Blackman," thus attesting to the lack of personal and independent identity that most enslaved people endured while in bondage (figure 2.7). As historian David Brigham has recognized, it is a name that identifies the subject in relation to his enslaver and his racial category; it creates his existence solely within the institution of slavery and his skin color.[28] Without this identifying title, the viewer might not otherwise know that the sitter was enslaved or that he was dark-skinned. There is little in the image to indicate his race other than the slight fullness of his upper lip or the short wavy hair. Like the silhouette of Williams, the simple rendering of his clothes, an animated bit of necktie peeking out from a high-collared jacket, seems to give little indication of

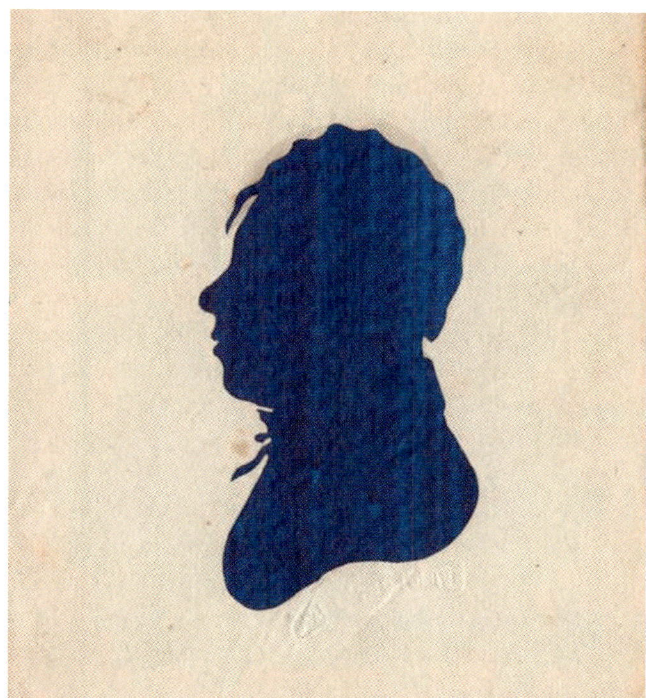

his identity, but in this case, his costume must be read as livery rather than merely contemporary clothing. The silhouette of "Mr. Shaw's blackman" is interesting to juxtapose with Charles Willson Peale's textual mode of racializing Williams's identity as "my Molatto Man Moses," described above.

The inscribed silhouettes of Moses Williams and "Mr. Shaw's blackman" are not the only ones of African-descended people that were made at Peale's Museum. The collection that holds them, and about a thousand other silhouettes, came to the Library Company of Philadelphia as part of the bequest of Dr. James Rush, a psychologist whose father, Dr. Benjamin Rush, had been a signer of the Declaration of Independence as well as one of Peale's closest associates.[29] Among these silhouettes are those of at least four other men and one woman who appear to be African descended (figure 2.8).

Moses Williams's status as a formerly enslaved and indentured person, working within the literal shadow of his former owner at Peale's Museum at a moment when racial identity and otherness were actively being constructed in the new nation, is key to understanding the complex construction of an active artist's identity that *Moses Williams, Cutter of Profiles* presents. Although the rounded nose and full lips of Williams's African ancestry remain to dominate his facial features, the European part of his "Molatto" identity crowns him in the form of long, straight hair. In comparison to the staccato waves of *Mr. Shaw's Blackman*, or the feathered accessories of Waconsca, it is decidedly anglicized. By deviating from the original form line, I believe that Williams purposely created an image in which his own features would connote tropes of whiteness rather than Blackness. But was it an attempt to deny the African part of his racial heritage? I would argue that it records the anxiety and confusion that he had about his position as a person of mixed race within a white society that despised that heritage. As a newly freed man, he needed to create an identity for himself, and he had to do it with the tools that he had been given. In this way, *Moses Williams, Cutter of Profiles* both creates and obscures its subject's identity by signifying and subsuming him beneath the appellation "Moses Williams, Cutter of Profiles."

Recall the kindred relationship between the physiognotrace and the polygraph devices. In the same manner that Peale or Jefferson might have produced multiple copies of their writings using a polygraph, so, too, did Williams inscribe a visual record of his identity using the physiognotrace. It was a related act of writing. Henry Louis Gates Jr. argues in *The Signifying Monkey: A Theory of African American Literary Criticism* that within the African American literary tradition, "to rename is to revise, and to revise is to signify."[30] In this act of redrawing, an act that I read as akin to renaming or revising, we can see Williams signifying on his own profile. Rather than letting the traced image remain as the machine had recorded it—a machine that was invented by one of his owner's cronies—he went back into it and revised it with his scissors. As they cut into the paper, Williams wrote his own story onto the one produced by the mechanical conception of his enslavers. Through this act he achieved agency over a small part of his representation within the public sphere. That this act comes around 1803, at the beginning of his career, shows both his interest in fitting into the artisanal society of Philadelphia and his ability to manipulate and defy its tenets. His marriage to the Peales' white cook, Maria, further indicates this ability, and the fact that their daughter disappeared from history, most probably by passing for white, shows the legacy of the father's own search for identity within a racialized selfhood.

And yet, despite the agency that I have attempted to remember by this account of Moses Williams's life, it was a waning silhouette business, the basic economic problem of an oversaturated market, that may have ended his career. A half century after Williams began his artistic practice as a cutter of profiles, *Philadelphia Daily News* columnist Frank Colliger wrote in his column Recollections of the Past that "Moses Williams, a light mulatto man, was brought up in the family of the elder Mr. Peale. He was, as many old folks may recollect, a pleasant, witty, as well as an expert fellow in his vocation; but as his employment gradually declined, even so did Moses, and his finale hastened by too liberal use of the 'social glass.'"[31] Peale correspondence from the summer of 1823 confirms that Williams was forced to sell the property that his initial professional success had enabled him to buy.[32] Unlike Rembrandt and Raphaelle, who could paint all manner of portraits, still lifes, or whatever else the market demanded, Williams's artistic flexibility was as limited as the black and white of the paper media with which he worked. At the time of his manumission, Williams had assumed the professional identity that was provided for him by his owner. But when this career failed, he lost the primary thing that had represented his freedom and independence: his ability to signify. Without his professional identity as "the cutter of profiles," Williams's taking of the social glass, his drinking, increased, and he descended into insolvency. Divested of property and without means to support himself, he was simply Mr. Peale's "Mulatto Man Moses," a thing that he clearly did not want to be.

The nineteenth-century artistic practice of Moses Williams demonstrates the tradition of signifying as it may have been applied by an African American artist who chose to trope the conventions of the silhouette mode. It becomes clear that Williams had a certain amount of agency and control over his artistic practice and that his signifying on the line of his self-portrait was one of the ways that he showed this ability. Regardless of whether his alterations were "good" or "bad," they were his.

While works of art by other Peale family members have been studied in detail over the past two centuries, this silhouette of Williams was discovered just a few decades ago by the Library Company of Philadelphia, although it had been in their collection since the death of James Rush in 1869. When the curators attributed this image to Raphaelle Peale, although it does not bear his signature or embossment, they participated in the two hundred years of disremembering Williams's artistic contribution to American art history by denying the possibility that it might be a self-portrait.

Over twenty years have passed since I first encountered this silhouette, and I still believe that Williams's voice may be found within what at first might seem to be the impenetrable blackness of the profile portrait silhouette. It is a voice that signified on a specific visual form and, through an active remembering, made that form its own. It demonstrates the artist's own agency in the visualization of his selfhood and subverts the negation of voice that racial Blackness connoted during the period of the early republic.

3

THE FREEDOM
TO MARRY FOR ALL

PAINTING INTERRACIAL FAMILIES
DURING THE ERA OF THE CIVIL WAR

When the United States Supreme Court struck down the Defense of Marriage Act in the spring of 2013, it had been 145 years since the ratification of the Fourteenth Amendment ensured equal protection under the law to all who were born in the United States, and 45 years since the court in 1968, in *Loving v. Virginia*, declared unconstitutional all laws prohibiting Americans from marrying across the color line.[1] As Mildred Jeter Loving, one of the two plaintiffs in that case, said on its fortieth anniversary in 2007, "I am proud that [my husband] Richard's and my name is on a court case that can help reinforce the love, the commitment, the fairness, and the family that so many people, Black or white, young or old, gay or straight seek in life. I support the freedom to marry for all. That's what *Loving*, and loving, are all about."[2]

The visual and social importance of a legal right that has long been in flux but saw one of its major milestones erected at the end of the Civil War, when large numbers of newly freed, formerly enslaved people were granted the right to marry each other, deserves closer consideration. Whether formerly enslaved people could marry across the color line, however, depended on where and when they chose to do so. "If slavery was a kind of social death for Black people in the United States, then Reconstruction held out the promise of social rebirth—rebirth as enfranchised citizens and rights holders," writes legal historian Katherine M. Franke. "During the period after the Civil War, Black people in the United States celebrated the right to alienate their labor, own property, and participate in the institutions of civil and public society that were considered fundamental to a good and free life. The right to marry figured prominently among the bundle of rights African Americans held dear in the postbellum years."[3]

Considering the distinct legal privilege that marriage represented in the nineteenth century, what did it mean for African American families to celebrate and preserve their loving unions through portraits? Several paintings of the members of two mixed-race families, the Montiers of Philadelphia and the Copelands of Boston—made in the years leading up to the Civil War—have much to tell us about the complicated history of the institution of marriage in the United States. Marriage is one of the most central and perpetually contested of the various institutions—including church and school—that help form us as fully socialized subjects. The stories of these families and the images through which they remembered themselves communicate across time and space, personal experiences of the legal transformations that marriage continues to undergo in American life and culture. Consideration of these experiences clarifies what marriage meant for interracial couples and their descendants. The visual records the families left behind reveal much about loving across the color line, both before and after the war.

The Montiers

In 1841, when the portraits of the newly married boot maker Hiram Charles Montier and his bride, Elizabeth Brown, were completed in Philadelphia, slavery was still partially legal in the state of Pennsylvania.[4] It would not be completely abolished until six years later, in 1847, when the approximately one hundred remaining enslaved people, those who had been born before 1780, when the Act for the Gradual Abolition of Slavery was adopted, were finally released from bondage. But in 1841 the Montiers had been free and freeborn for several generations. Hiram Montier could trace his origins back to the French colony of Saint-Domingue, which his father, one of the French-allied *gens de couleur*, had left as a refugee during the Haitian Revolution in the first years of the nineteenth century.[5] He was also descended from the first mayor of Philadelphia, Humphrey Morrey, an appointee of William Penn. Morrey freed his enslaved Africans on his death in 1715. His son Richard formed a common-law marriage with one of these women. Richard's wife, Cremona, or Mooney, was born in 1710 to parents who had been kidnapped in Guinea and sold into slavery.[6] According to their descendants, Richard and Mooney developed a committed, if not legally recognized, relationship that ultimately produced five children, including Hiram's grandmother, also named Cremona.[7] Richard Morrey worked hard to ensure that his family would inherit his land in Pennsylvania, going so far as to have a deed drafted in 1746 that stipulated, "Know ye, that the said Richard Morrey, as well for and in consideration of the good faithful service unto him done and performed by his now freed Negro Woman Mooney otherwise known as Cremona Morrey ... do bargain and sell for consideration of one peppercorn" a total of 198 acres "on his land in Cheltenham."[8] The deed to the land, which today includes the campus of Arcadia University in Cheltenham Township, was witnessed by a number of white neighbors. But the extralegal status of their union and the exclusion of women from the right to hold property alone made it difficult to enforce when, following the death of Richard Morrey, Cremona legally married John Fry, a man of African descent. When Cremona predeceased her second husband, Fry sued unsuccessfully for control of the property; it was ultimately awarded to Cremona and Richard Morrey's illegitimate children.

This sort of legal quandary was shared by many African American and mixed-race couples of the period, who were frequently without the legal protection that state-sanctioned marriage provided. Enslaved people in the antebellum United States, whether they lived in the North or the South, had no legal standing and no right to make contracts, including those of marriage. This was also the case for many free Blacks, whose rights were strictly curtailed and limited from state to state.

When the Montiers presented themselves to the little-known painter Franklin R. Street to have their portraits made, they were barely of age: Hiram was twenty-three, and Elizabeth was twenty-one. And yet they both look far more mature and erudite than their youth would imply.[9] Each is posed in front of a column, perhaps to suggest strength or stalwartness; a sunrise behind him and a stormy vista behind her may signify the wish for a solid relationship through sunny and stormy weather. While the artist's skills were limited, particularly when it came to painting the lower halves of his sitters' bodies, he was highly accomplished at rendering their distinct facial features, hair, and skin color: Hiram's aquiline nose, contrasting with Elizabeth's more rounded one; her long, wavy hair curled into four vines that cascade down her shoulders, and his substantial sideburns; her eyes a little darker, his skin slightly lighter. Street also suggested Hiram's literacy through the inclusion of several books, and Elizabeth's Catholic piety is on view in the form of the golden cross and looped chain at her neck. Whether it was the artist who suggested that his clients be shown against opulent drapery and classical columns is unknown, but what is readily apparent from the portraits is the couple's satisfaction with being represented as both literate and stylish. The elaborate presentation of Hiram Montier and his bride indicates the commensurate wealth and privilege from which they originated.

The 1850 federal census found the Montiers living near Market Street in what is now called Old City, Philadelphia. There they were surrounded by Black and mixed-race, or "mulatto," families whose male heads worked as seamen, cabinetmakers, waiters, barbers, laborers, and porters: unglamorous jobs that paid for modest lifestyles.[10] Hiram Montier may have been a boot maker, but he was also a landowner and literate. He was as close to a gentleman as an antebellum man of African descent could come, and as such, he had well-developed representational expectations and aspirations, seen in the form of these elegant portraits.

Within a few years of having their portraits made, the Montiers appear to have tired of living in an increasingly segregated Philadelphia and sectionally divided United States. Around 1850 they decamped to Toronto, Canada, taking with them their two young sons, Adrien and Joseph.[11] The 1861 Canadian census records them (and two more Canadian-born children) living on Agnes Street near the shore of Lake Ontario.[12] Nothing is known about why they chose Toronto, but they integrated themselves into the African-descended community that existed there in the nineteenth century. For example, in 1860 a New York–based African American newspaper recorded that a male member of the Montier family, perhaps Hiram or one of his teenage sons, was a member of the Toronto Amateur Musical Association and had participated in a concert at St. Lawrence Hall benefiting the House of Industry.[13] Regardless of their motivations for migrating to Toronto, the Montiers were determined to enjoy themselves as they waited out the sectional conflicts just to the south that then dominated most people's lives.[14]

As the Montier children grew to maturity in Toronto, they became more settled and saw themselves as a part of the new country in which they lived. In 1864 twenty-one-year-old Adrien married a young Canadian woman named Daylass Carleton.[15] A few years after Adrien Montier's first marriage, the Montier family moved back to the United States, where Hiram continued to practice boot making and shoemaking. He is listed as working in this occupation in an 1868 Baltimore city directory, and in the 1870 census, the family is recorded as living in Philadelphia.[16] In 1872 Hiram's name appears in a Philadelphia directory as the proprietor of a boot-making and shoemaking enterprise in a storefront that still stands today at the corner of South Twelfth and Christian Streets. After returning to Philadelphia, Adrien got married again, in 1871, to Emma Chase, and the couple had two children, Leanora and Joseph.[17] Years later, while he was living with his daughter and her husband, Richard S. Brown, Adrien Montier's identity was recorded as both white and Canadian, in line with census enumerator's mistaken assessment that Richard and Leanora Brown were also white.[18] This momentary passing into whiteness by Hiram Montier's son and his family is witnessed in the 1900 US census records.

The Copelands

Forever young and beautiful, Eliza, Ellen (Nellie), and Margaret, the subjects of *Three Sisters of the Copeland Family*, appear to sit patiently before us in a room with undecorated light brown walls (figure 3.1). The window behind the first sister at left, Eliza, frames the upper branches of a leafy tree, perhaps hinting at their location as the second floor of William Matthew Prior's studio at 36 Trenton Street in East Boston. Painted in 1854, the Copeland sisters are pictured in a moment of high promise. Although their youth is still visible in the form of round cheeks and petite frames, they hold in their hands the various emblems of impending womanhood. Six-year-old Eliza cradles a book, one finger inserted in its pages to hold her place. Its ownership and use indicate her precocious literacy and intelligence. Ellen, sometimes called Nellie, who stands at center, is the smallest and youngest sister. She holds a small basket of cherries in her left hand, while a cluster of three dangle from her other, alluding to her sweetness. Four-year-old Margaret, sitting at right, holds a small bouquet of mixed flowers, their stems wrapped in ribbon and nestled in her lap. The flowers not only mirror her beauty but, like the cherries held by her little sister, Nellie, indicate her eventual blossoming into a young woman as well. All three girls are modest yet elegant. They are dressed in fashionable clothes with lace-trimmed sleeves, striped stockings, and bloomers; one has ribbons on her shoulders, another a coral necklace, the third a strand of round beads, possibly pearls. Together, in their feminine promise and mid-century finery, they sit quietly, waiting for their preservation to be complete.

Their portraitist, William Matthew Prior (1806–73), was known as a racial egalitarian as well as an accomplished painter whose livelihood was quickly being eroded by the advent of cheap, reproducible photographs in the period immediately preceding the Civil War. He could work in both a "flat" style that employed a limited amount of three-dimensionality and a more naturalistic

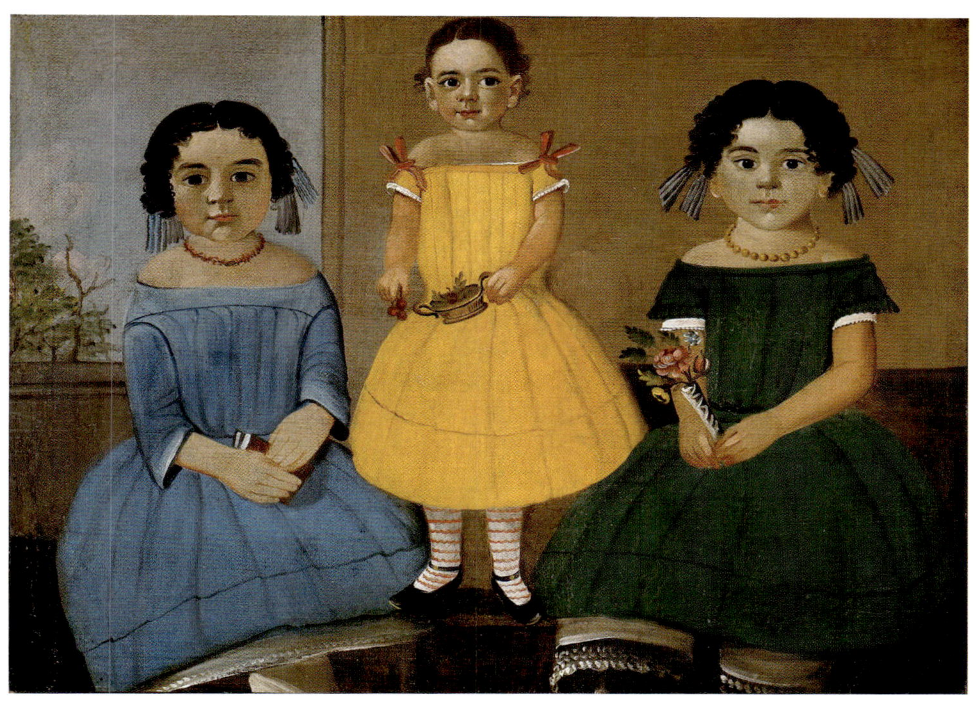

3.1 William Matthew Prior, *Three Sisters of the Copeland Family*, 1854.
Museum of Fine Arts, Boston

representational mode. His portraits of the Philadelphia abolitionist William Whipper (1804–76) and a woman identified as "Mrs. Nancy Lawson" also demonstrate his interest and ability to create detailed, emblematic images (figures 3.2 and 3.3). Whipper sits with his body turned toward the left, looking out at the viewer, his patterned waistcoat trimmed with the same gold paint that forms a delicate watch chain, the monogram on his diary, and the gold rings on his fingers. He appears both wealthy and well appointed. Like Whipper, Nancy Lawson looks both well groomed and intellectually formidable with her modest jewelry, diaphanous bonnet with brocade ribbon trim, wedding band, and well-thumbed book. As these two images demonstrate, Prior's depictions of Black sitters do not compromise or search for alternate languages with which to present their subjects; they provide us with glimpses of the ways in which the nineteenth-century color line was frequently crossed in the quest for suitable representation and artistic success.

When Prior painted the Copeland girls in 1854, his patrons, Samuel and Alice Copeland, were a rare pair in mid-nineteenth-century Boston. Like Richard and Cremona Morrey, the Copelands were a mixed-race couple,

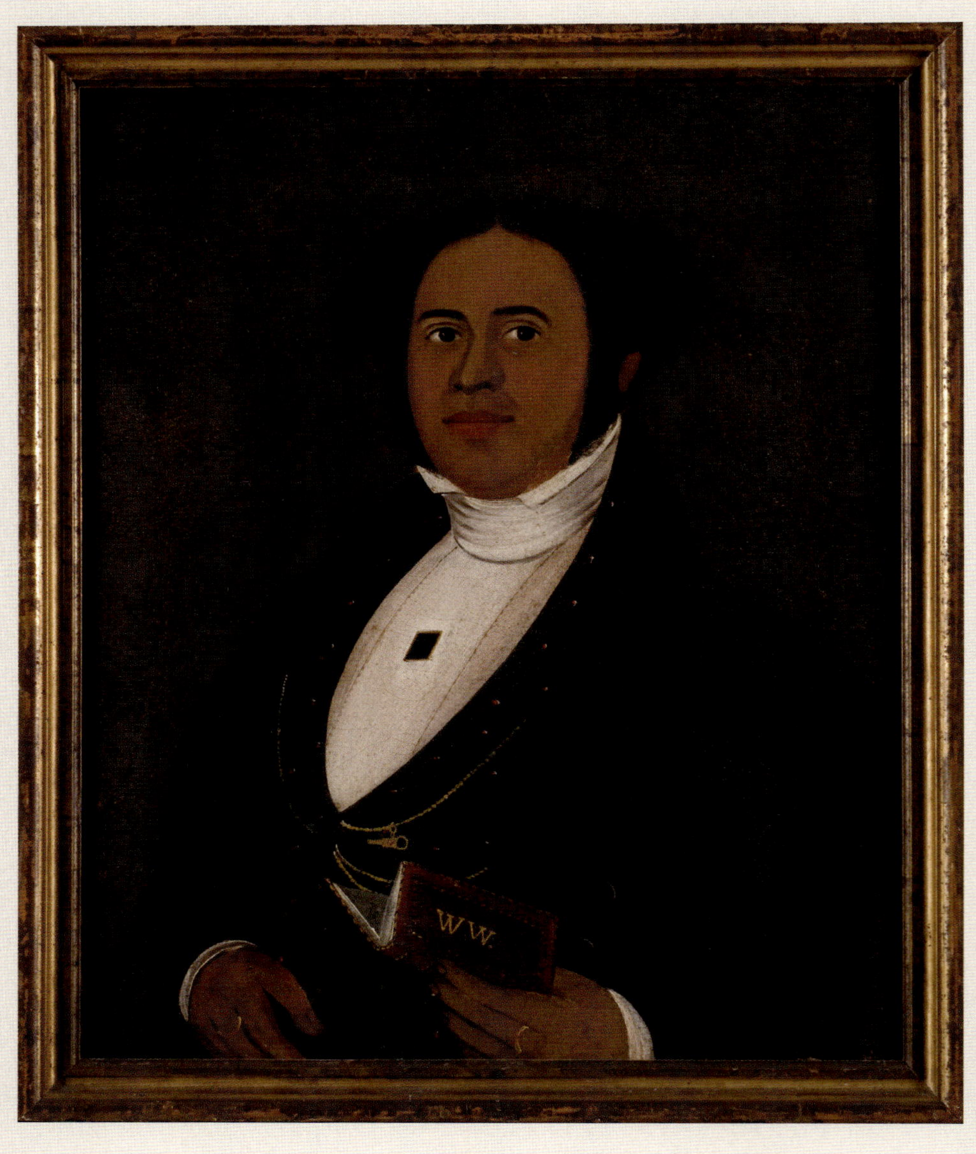

3.2 William Matthew Prior, *William Whipper*, 1845.
Fenimore Art Museum, Cooperstown, New York

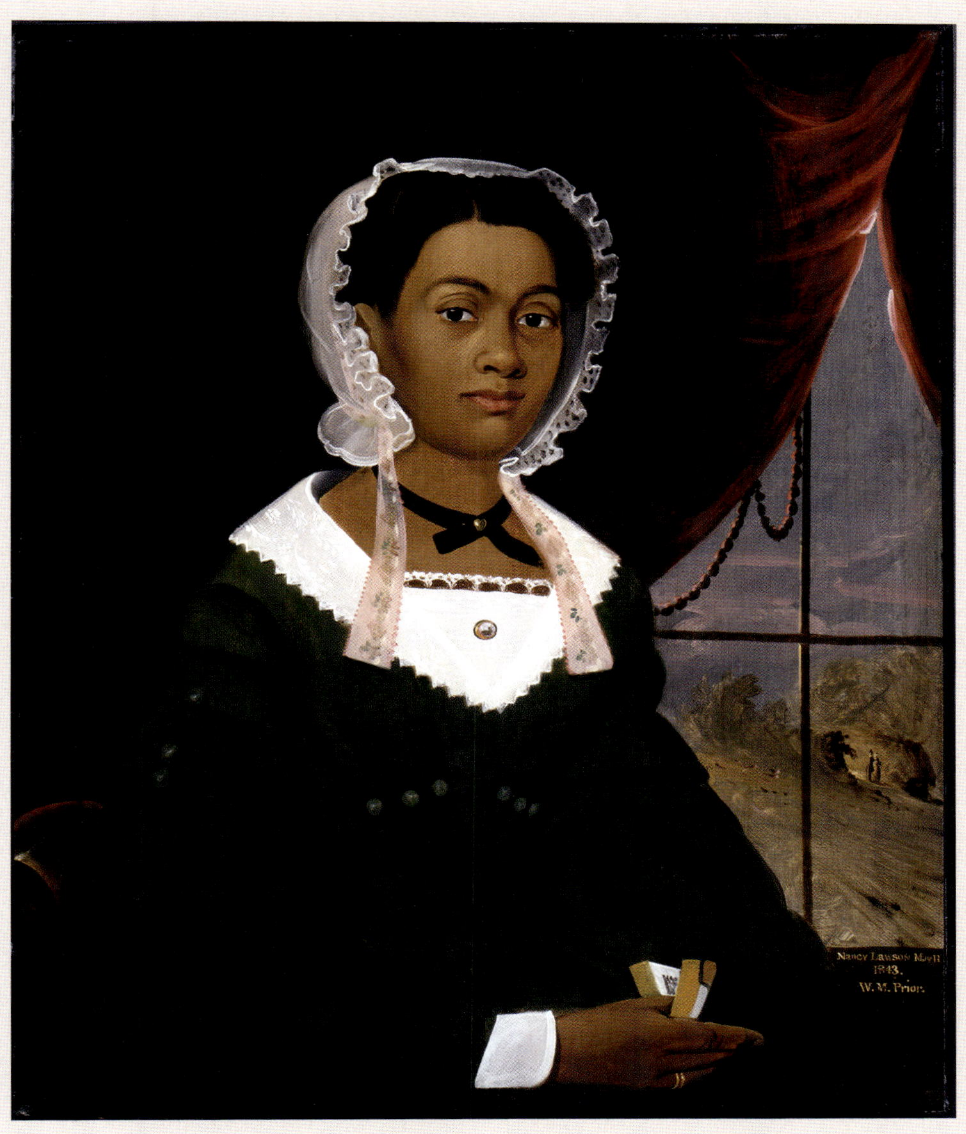

3·3 William Matthew Prior, *Mrs. Nancy Lawson*, 1843.
Shelburne Museum, Shelburne, Vermont

raising children in a community that included Quakers and members of other anti-racist sects, like the Second Advent group of Millerites, to which Prior belonged in the 1840s. The large size of the canvas, nearly twenty-seven by thirty-seven inches, on which the Copeland sisters' portrait is painted hints at the formidable cost of the object, as does the delicate rendering of the girls. Both indicate the significant expendable financial resources that were then available to the Copeland family.

The Copelands were entrepreneurs in a city with a small Black community that had largely integrated itself into the commercial fabric of Boston. It was here that Samuel Copeland began to expand his trade in used clothing to include new items, eventually establishing a thriving business that would employ several of his children and support his growing family over the next half century. But the Copelands were unique in their interracial alliance. Unlike Richard and Cremona Morrey, Hiram Montier's grandparents, a union of a white man and a freed woman of color, Samuel Copeland was of African descent while his wife, Alice, was from the British Isles. This combination was far rarer in nineteenth-century New England, and although their marriage would have been legal in Massachusetts—in 1843, just as the couple was beginning to start a family, Massachusetts repealed a century-old anti-amalgamation law—no marriage record has yet been found for them. This suggests that they may not have been legally joined, perhaps opting for a common-law arrangement, as the Morreys had done in Pennsylvania.

In 1850, when they were recorded for the first time in the US census, the Copeland family was living at 38 Blackstone Street, next to the Haymarket, in a neighborhood of recently immigrated English and Irish families headed by laborers, seamen, engravers, blacksmiths, and traders of various kinds.[19] Despite having been born in Virginia, where most people of African descent were then enslaved and kept in a legally enforced state of illiteracy, Samuel was semiliterate, in that he could read but not write. Interestingly, when assistant census marshal Elijah Pike recorded the Copelands in his ledger, he must have spoken only with Samuel or perhaps with a neighbor who described the family to him because he marked Alice as "b," or "black," the same designation given for all members of the family but the only time that she is recorded as such.[20] Earlier that year, in daughter Margaret's official birth record, the child was listed as "colored," the abbreviation "col'd" appended awkwardly, a visible stigma in a column reserved by the state to demarcate gender and color.[21] The other children registered on the same page received only an M or an F, indicating their gender, and an omission that silently signaled that their racial identity was normative, or "white." But in the row where little Margaret's name lies, the reader is witness to a newly made, newly racialized body floating in a sea of blank whiteness.

When the Civil War began, Samuel Copeland dutifully registered for the draft, but a record of his service has not yet been found. By this time, he had moved his family a few miles north to Chelsea, where he purchased a house worth $10,000 (about $370,000 in 2023). In contrast to the largely immigrant neighborhood of Haymarket, in Chelsea most of their neighbors were natives of Massachusetts or New Hampshire, while others, like Alice Copeland, hailed from England or Ireland. Over the years, the Copelands would become prosperous, amassing land and employing white servants, including the Irish-born Mary Conway, who is recorded in the 1860 census as helping care for their children. Census records show that after his wife's death, Copeland still employed white servants, including the English-born Margaret Rodman, who was working as his housekeeper in 1870.[22]

As is evident from Samuel Copeland's marriage to an English-born white woman and their mutual production of no fewer than seven children in fifteen years, he had no qualms about crossing the "color line" to satisfy his emotional or material desires.[23] So it is not surprising that when he decided to have his daughters' portrait made, he patronized William Matthew Prior, a white painter who was also unafraid of crossing the color line in the other direction to obtain work. Our understanding of the path taken by this mixed-race family is important, for it reveals both the complexity and the banality of the lived experience of race and representation in the nineteenth century.

In 1947 Ellen Brown sold the painting that included her grandmother Nellie, the smallest girl at center, to the Boston art dealer Richard C. Morrison.[24] The following year, Morrison sold it to the renowned collector Maxim Karolik, who with his wife, Martha, subsequently bequeathed it to the Museum of Fine Arts, Boston, giving that city a formidable collection of American art that makes up the backbone of that institution's impressive holdings.

Hiram and Elizabeth Montier's descendants became the modern Pickens family, who have continued to be patrons of the arts. In the 1930s, at the height of the Great Depression, Dr. William Pickens Sr. had the sculptor Augusta Savage create a portrait bust of him, which today resides in the collection of the Studio Museum in Harlem.[25] And more recently, his grandson Dr. William Pickens III generously loaned the portraits of his ancestors, which for many years were stored under the bed of an elderly relative, to the Philadelphia Museum of Art, where they hung in the American galleries from the winter of 2009 until the summer of 2011 and were reinstalled in 2021 when the museum renovated its early American galleries. The portraits of the Montiers and the Copelands, with their complex stories of love across the color line, remind us that the desire to visualize our loved ones as beautiful and perfect creations still resonates. Whether showing a young couple eager for a future together or the bright young lives formed from a committed relationship that would have been illegal in most of the country in which it occurred when it occurred, these visual records endure. It is especially important now, considering the Supreme Court's decision in 2015 to permit gay marriage, to remember that something many of us take for granted—the right to marry the person we love—has not always been a right enjoyed by all people in this country.[26]

American pendant portraits such as those of the Montiers have long stood, to borrow a phrase used by Wayne Craven to describe the iconic colonial-period paintings of John and Elizabeth Freake, as "hymns to the divinely blessed institution" of marriage.[27] In these portraits the Montiers celebrated their free and legal love in a Philadelphia where enslaved people still walked the streets. The Montiers and the Copelands did not bow to those who would have preferred they remain invisible, outside the law, and without title to their familial legacies. On the eve of the Civil War, these two families sought to create enduring representational legacies because they wanted their families, both born and yet to be born, to see the affection they had for each other and for their children, as if to say, "That's what loving is all about."

4

LANDSCAPES
OF LABOR

RACE, RELIGION, AND RHODE ISLAND
IN THE PAINTING OF
EDWARD MITCHELL BANNISTER

> The presence of Black figures [in *Workers in the Fields*], relatively
> uncommon in Bannister's work, has raised speculation that the
> painting stands as an oblique reference to the plantation system
> of Rhode Island's past and to its role in the slave trade.
> —**CORRINE JENNINGS, in Holland,**
> ***Edward Mitchell Bannister, 1828–1901 (1992)***

From his arrival in Providence, Rhode Island, in 1869 until his death there in 1901, Edward Mitchell Bannister (1828–1901) painted the landscape of southern New England in a style that has often been described as derivative of the French Barbizon school. However, unlike the Barbizon painters, who sought to create pastoral scenes of idyllic peasant life in the French countryside, Bannister frequently depicted farms and other rural locations that evoke the history of Rhode Island's chattel slavery. Bannister first emigrated from New Brunswick, Canada, to Boston, Massachusetts, in 1850, and his life is exemplary of many of the challenges and achievements that creative African Americans faced and attained during the second half of the nineteenth century. Like the paintings of Henry Ossawa Tanner (1859–1937) or the neoclassical sculpture of Mary Edmonia Lewis (1844–1907), Bannister's compositions provide a window on the intellectual and creative terrain that socially concerned artists of the period faced. *Workers in the Fields* reveals a space in which the artist could explore a legacy of racial oppression within a contemporary international artistic language of landscape and noble peasantry. In this way Bannister was able to both remember the rapidly disappearing evidence of Rhode Island's plantation history and elevate the labor of its still-disempowered Black folk.

Bannister accomplished this radical move in two ways: first, by referencing the African American religious tradition and, second, by subverting the visual vernacular of French landscape painting and its current vogue for the rural picturesque. We witness this in the rectangular canvas of *Workers in the Fields*, within whose borders a large green-and-brown hayfield set beneath a low-lying horizon opens before the spectator (figure 4.1). The field is framed from below by a bit of wild grass that sprouts wildflowers growing from the carcass of a blasted tree stump. In the middle ground and to the right, within the yellow brown of the hayfield, dark-skinned people are occupied with gathering hay to place atop the large hay wain at the back of the composition. The workers appear almost lost in the space of the hayfield,

4.1 Edward Mitchell Bannister, *Workers in the Fields*, 1890.
Museum of Fine Arts, Boston

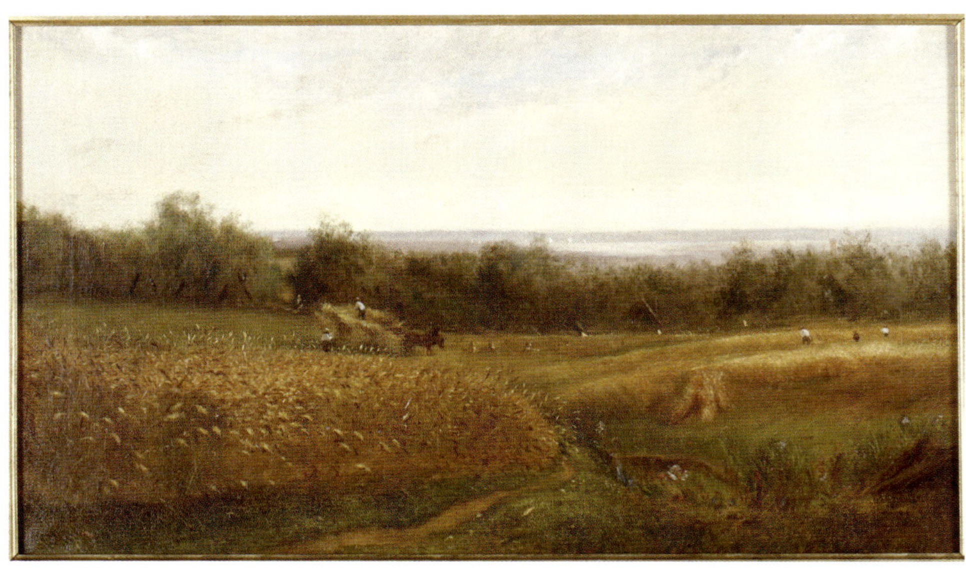

which swirls about their knees, truncating them and blocking their forward progress. There is no visible path behind them to indicate the direction from which they have come, nor is there any sign that they have cleared away the crop and are now gleaning the remains. The workers at right appear to be swimming across a great sea of grass, the trampled blades that surround them arching like waves. This swimming motion moves them apart from the other workers, as though they have strayed out from the distant harbor of the hay wain and the life of labor that it represents and are now approaching the pastoral promise that rises in the foreground.

In *Workers in the Fields*, Bannister creates for the spectator a world in which the drudgery of daily life and the curse of humble birth can be challenged, if not overcome or transcended. He renders a world in which crossing over, the action of moving from one reality to another, from labor to leisure, can be achieved by fording a river of grass as though it were the River Jordan. The juxtaposition shows these Black people as analogous to the Israelites who wandered in the wilderness for forty years waiting for the ultimate reward of the promised land, yet still within the control of the plantation system that had enslaved their ancestors, still within Pharaoh's reach. This ability to depict an unpopular reality in a popular mode makes Bannister's work in general, and *Workers in the Fields* in particular, some of the most dynamic landscape painting of the late nineteenth century.

The period between the end of the Civil War and the turn of the century when Bannister completed his mature work brought great changes to the American art world. This important half-century saw the exponential expansion of national interests, as the political wing of the fraily reunited country moved forward with the cause of domestic industrialization and newfound imperialist opportunities abroad. It also witnessed the size of the artisan class, the number of people skilled in manual arts, retract as the professional and the working classes grew. Just as those who practiced crafts felt the increasing competition of the mechanized workplace, so too did critical changes occur in the demographics of those who were able to produce so-called fine art. Painters and sculptors found new audiences as the rising bourgeoisie clamored for the various accoutrements of their position; with the rise of photography, they no longer needed painted portraits to decorate their homes, and they now longed for intimate landscapes and tasteful objects to decorate their parlors. These economic and social changes came in the aftermath of significant antebellum agitation by abolitionist and women's rights adherents who, prior to the war, had taken great interest in the creative potential of African Americans. This focus, which centered on artistic achievement to emphasize the humanity of enslaved people and their free Black counterparts, and thus their worthiness to participate in the American democracy, laid a foundation for notable, but extremely limited, African American artistic success between 1850 and 1870. During this period, several African American artists found success in abolitionist enclaves centered in Boston, Philadelphia, and Cincinnati.

Bannister was among several African American artists who received their initial support from individual abolitionists and from antislavery societies in these communities and then went on to garner prizes and acclaim from the mainstream art world following the Civil War. The landscape painter Robert S. Duncanson (1821–72) and the sculptor Mary Edmonia Lewis are two other prominent artists who received strong support from abolitionist communities.[1] Bannister was freeborn in Saint Andrews, Charlotte County, New Brunswick, Canada, and had a mixed racial heritage. His father may have been from Barbados; however, there is compelling evidence that his family immigrated to New Brunswick, fleeing the newly established United States as Loyalists following Britain's defeat in the Revolutionary War.[2] Once settled in Canada, his grandfather may have worked as a servant for the prominent Hatch family. Following the death of his parents, a youthful Bannister worked on the estate belonging to Harris Hatch before serving as a sailor on one of the many ships that plied the northeastern seaboard between Nova Scotia and New York.[3] This youthful experience on a plantation in eastern Canada must have impacted his thinking about the racial politics of field labor when he approached it as artistic subject matter much later in his life. This is perhaps why he is so sympathetic to the plight of the bodies that swim across the river of grass in *Workers in the Fields*; in many ways they repeat his experience of leaving a life of farm labor for one of self-determination.

The foundational support that Bannister received through abolitionist patronage while he struggled for artistic recognition and creative acceptance from the dominant culture and his own immediate community during the mid-nineteenth century cannot be overstated. In the late 1840s, Bannister settled in Boston with his brothers and worked as a hairdresser while pursuing a growing interest in painting on the side. As his skills developed, he began to pick up work painting portraits of the local white abolitionists and the growing Black bourgeoisie in the area. One of Bannister's earliest known portraits is of Dr. John Van Surley DeGrasse (1825–68), a noted Black physician and antislavery activist who would subsequently serve as the first Black surgeon in the Civil War.[4] The image presents the doctor as a well-dressed, middle-class professional. The tones are dark and the modeling rather flat, yet the gravitas of the sitter radiates from the eyes, and his benevolence is indicated by the slight smile that is barely readable through the great bush of beard, whose outer margins disappear into the dark background. Bannister's painting joined others in the DeGrasse family collection, including one of the doctor's father, Isaiah DeGrasse, by the African American painter and printmaker Patrick Reason. Several years later, Bannister also completed a pastel portrait of Cordelia Howard, the future Mrs. DeGrasse, which joined a painting by the European American painter William Matthew Prior of Cordelia's mother, Margaret Gardner.[5] That the DeGrasse and Howard families were able to afford multiple painted portraits of family members, and that these works remained in the family through the late twentieth century, speaks to the solidity and dynamism of the African American social system that had developed in Boston during the nineteenth century.

The portrait of Dr. DeGrasse, who was an antislavery activist and a pillar of the African American community, is a visual testament to Bannister's involvement in the abolitionist work in Boston and to his status as a midlevel but well-established artist. In the same way that many other freeborn African Americans had done before him, Bannister benefited from the attention and funding of whites who not only wanted to abolish slavery but also aimed to prove the basic humanity of Black people through educational and professional achievement and cultural contributions. He used his talent to fund the cause several times during the 1850s, and just one year into the Civil War, he made a full-length posthumous portrait of Colonel Robert Gould Shaw (location unknown) for a charity auction. His portrait of the white leader of the Massachusetts 54th, the first Black regiment to be commissioned in the Union Army, joined a number of other commemorations of the fallen hero, including a bust by Mary Edmonia Lewis.[6] Comparable to the abolitionists of Cincinnati, who applauded and supported the career of the African American painter Robert Scott Duncanson, the Boston antislavery community was vigorous in its promotion and utilization of free Black creativity to propagandize for the cause.[7]

This involvement in the Boston art world and the larger political scene enabled Bannister to make inroads into the mainstream art establishment during the late antebellum period and the Civil War. It helped him to grow and develop despite the hostile racial environment of the United States during this era. In addition, his wife, Christiana Carteaux (1819–1902), whom he met in the 1850s, was hands down his greatest patron and supporter. Carteaux, who had roots in the Native American communities around Providence, was a fellow hairdresser who owned her own salon. She was also active in the antislavery movement (during the war she served in the Colored Women's

Auxiliary), and when they married in 1858, her financial acumen enabled Bannister to devote nearly all his time to his art. During this period he received some formal art training at the Lowell Institute in Boston under the painter William Rimmer and began to expand his repertoire from portraits, to religious subjects, to genre, still life, and, later, landscape painting.

Unfortunately, much of the progress that Bannister made in the 1860s was challenged in the 1870s and 1880s as the dominant culture of the United States became increasingly hostile to Black creativity. This general hostility, which arose out of white racism's continuing need to find new ways of controlling African Americans through popular visual culture and art, retarded the spread of African American artistic culture during the Gilded Age. Following the Civil War, the climate for African Americans living in Boston changed dramatically. Many displaced formerly enslaved people began making their way north in search of work and opportunity. Within a few years the community of free Black professionals to which the Bannisters belonged, many of whom had been in the area long before the war, began to see their social status slip. As marginally skilled freed people flooded the labor markets of northern cities, working-class whites (who were themselves mostly immigrants from Ireland and other impoverished European countries) adopted racist attitudes about the right to work. Further, the members of the white community who had supported the abolitionist cause were now far less interested in the current situation of African Americans, having been more enamored of the idea of freedom than the reality of the free Blacks who now filled their city streets.[8] This tense climate led in some cases to race riots and generally made the environment of the city unbearable for many middle-class Black families, who increasingly found that their social privilege was not a protection against racially motivated violence.

In 1869 Bannister and Carteaux moved to Providence, and it was there that his style fully matured, and his landscapes started to show the influence of the Barbizon school. This anticlassical style of painting, which began in the French countryside with the work of Theodore Rousseau, focused on the spiritual and emotional properties of landscape. These serene spaces featured peasants who seemed to coexist peacefully with the beasts of the field; they were explorations of humans' harmonious interaction with God's creation. In opposition to the studio-produced "Great Pictures" in the Hudson River school style that Robert S. Duncanson had painted, Bannister's Barbizon-influenced landscapes were generally done out of doors and were intimate in scale, rarely the epic oils that characterize the elder artist's work at the height of his career in the late 1860s. That American art critics and consumers shifted their taste in landscape painting from epic to humble in the 1870s is evident not only in the rapid decline of Duncanson's reputation following his death in 1872 but also in the survival of Bannister's career, which embraced the new style.

Following his relocation to Rhode Island, Bannister developed his method of painting through the firsthand study of the regional landscape around Providence. Here he found a welcoming arts community, and in 1873, with his colleagues George Whitaker (1840–1916) and Charles Stetson (1858–1911), he helped found the Providence Art Club. Still in existence today, the club proved to be an influential organization. Its proximity to Newport and the well-heeled summer populations that the region attracted enabled members to exhibit and sell their work to an influential bourgeoisie and upper-class clientele. For more than a century, an original silhouette of Bannister has been visible behind the front door of the clubhouse, testifying to the artist's involvement in its foundation, and in 2020 the club unveiled a specially commissioned bust of the artist by sculptor Gage Prentiss.

Through his affiliation with the Providence Art Club and his work in founding the Rhode Island School of Design in 1878, Bannister saw many of his works move into private collections. Eventually he was able to devote all his time to painting, traveling up and down the New England coastline and exploring the many islands in Narragansett Bay in his small yacht. In this way he became familiar with the various locations that had factored heavily in the Rhode Island slave trade, ports where Africans were put ashore, and the like. If in *Workers in the Fields* Bannister had raised the legacy of slavery and the presence of Black folk in the landscape to a biblical level, then the paintings that he made of these historically loaded sites did something just as powerful, if slightly more covert. In these compositions he records industrial advances altering the pastoral world, and as art historian and gallerist Corrine Jennings has rightly argued, "his use of rivers and the sea reflects a lost ancestral heritage and the longing for freedom, and his ships have been identified as signifying freedom."9

This belief in the power of landscape to retain history, empowering the terrain to stand as witness to the past, is evident in the seascape *Fort Dumpling, Jamestown, Rhode Island* (ca. 1890), a rectangular composition divided up by diagonal lines and pyramidal forms. In this scene of leisure, four figural groups, made up of light-skinned men, women, and children, relax along the seashore. Three children in yellow straw hats hunch down within the shadow of the cliff at the lower right of the composition, as though examining a new-found treasure. Close by them, at the center of the space, is a group of three people, a man and two women. One woman stands with her back to the spectator, facing the sea and holding a red parasol, while another woman sits at her feet. The man faces them both. Together, the three adults, with their triangular arrangement and the arresting red of the parasol, serve to draw the spectator's gaze up and into the dark block that is Fort Dumpling. The fort, whose upper form line is clearly visible against the white clouds of the sky, rises like a forbidding piece of the living rock on which it is perched. As a military installation on Narragansett Bay, it references both the forceful conquest of Coanicut Island from the Wampanoag and Narragansett peoples (Christiana Carteaux's ancestors) and Rhode Island's establishment as a slaveholding state and a leader in the triangular transatlantic slave trade.[10] When read through the lens of history, the ship in the water to the fort's left references both the horror of the Middle Passage and Bannister's own love of sailing.

Bannister's landscapes of the 1890s, such as *Fort Dumpling*, which feature the maritime legacy of slavery in seemingly idyllic surroundings, or *Workers in the Fields*, in which Black people attempt to ford a river of endless labor, may be read as visual metaphors of the Middle Passage, attempts at passing over racial barriers as well as at passing into a heavenly reward. In this way a river painted by Bannister can be read both as a surrogate for the journey that enslaved people made as they fled from slavery to freedom in the northern states and as an allusion to the biblical River Jordan that the Israelites crossed to the Promised Land after having wandered in the wilderness for forty years following their flight from Egypt.[11] *Fort Dumpling* itself stands as though it were the Sphinx, a witness to the passage of many stolen and enslaved Black people before the cliff's side.

The identification of the plight of African Americans with biblical figures, even after the end of slavery, that we see in *Workers in the Fields* is also present in the work of Mary Edmonia Lewis and Henry Ossawa Tanner. In 1869 Lewis created a marble sculpture of Hagar, the Egyptian handmaiden of the barren Sarah, who is forced to lie with her mistress's husband, Abraham, and is then cast out into the desert once she conceives her master's heir. The subject of Hagar—a woman abused by and separated from patriarchy—was a fitting way for Lewis to comment on the social disadvantages faced by Black women in the United States both under and after slavery.[12]

In contrast to the water imagery of Bannister, or the metaphorical transposition of Lewis, Tanner approached biblical subject matter and its relationship to African American religious culture in his paintings by using the people of North Africa, whom he came to know through his travels in the region, as his models. Having expatriated to France in the 1890s, Tanner made numerous paintings of biblical scenes using Moroccans and other North Africans as models and depicting their living cities as though they were ancient scenery. His *Annunciation* (1898), for example, presents the spectator with a young Mary, looking very much like a contemporary Moroccan woman, seated alone in her room as the angel Gabriel appears to her as a great beam of white light.

Tanner's use of African models for biblical characters seems to have been a solution that he reached to deal with the vexing criticism that was heaped on him when he stopped painting African American characters following *The Banjo Lesson* (1893) and *The Thankful Poor* (1893–94).[13] Tanner was never forgiven by some critics for having abandoned the sympathetic treatment of African Americans found in these two images of Black men passing on their cultural capital, in the form of music lessons and piety, to young boys. In fact, it is for these works that he is most often recognized even though they are not representative of his mature style or of the biblical subject matter to which he was most frequently drawn. Rather, *The Banjo Lesson* and *The Thankful Poor* were explorations of ways to render the popular motif of the folk in American terms. Tanner sought to represent African Americans as an authentic folk, the rustic peasants that peopled so many French paintings of the 1880s and 1890s. In fact, during the period between 1893 and 1895 in which he painted these authentic Black folk, he also executed *The Bagpipe Lesson* (1893) and *The Young Sabot Maker* (1895), two images of Brittany peasants teaching their offspring the joys of music and the skill of shoemaking.[14]

It is notable that just as his younger colleague Tanner was searching for a way to paint African Americans in a compelling manner, so, too, was Bannister investigating modes for depicting Black people as the folk inhabitants of the countryside. And it is remarkable that, in the same vein as Tanner, he chose to render them not only as though they were the French peasants that the Barbizon painters had so adored but also in the role of biblical heroes. And yet, despite the emphasis on the contemplative and transcendent power of landscape that we find in Bannister's work, *Fort Dumpling* and *Workers in the Fields* must become more than idyllic retreats for the spectator, for they speak to the struggle with racial representation that the artist grappled with throughout his career.

Although he began his artistic practice painting many Black Bostonians, a body of work that featured commissioned portraits, including those for the DeGrasse-Howard family as well as a personal portrait of his wife that is now at the Newport Museum, he rarely included any African American figures in his landscape paintings. This absence of Black people in his images may be read as a survival mode by which he submerged his Blackness beneath a generic landscape aesthetic that called for a benign white presence in the composition, an assumed white producer of the object, and an ideal white spectator standing before it.

This sublimation into whiteness that we see in much of Bannister's painting, with obvious notable exceptions, was also apparent in the covert ways in which he submitted his work to exhibitions, often keeping his racial identity a secret. For example, in 1876 he entered an already much-lauded work, *Under the Oaks* (ca. 1876, location unknown), in the competition at the Philadelphia Centennial Exposition. There it won first prize for painting and gave rise to one of the most frequently recounted stories of nineteenth-century African American art history, one that reflects the racism and difficulties with which Black artists of this generation had to contend:

> I learned from the newspapers that "54" had received a first prize medal, so I hurried to the Committee Rooms to make sure the report was true. There was a great crowd there ahead of me. As I jostled among them many resented my presence, some actually commenting within my hearing in a most petulant manner what is that colored person in here for? Finally when I succeeded in reaching the desk where inquiries were made, I endeavored to gain the attention of the official in charge. He was very insolent. Without raising his eyes, he demanded in the most exasperating tone of voice, "Well what do you want here any way? Speak lively." "I want to enquire concerning 54. Is it a prize winner"' "What's that to you," said he? In an instant my blood was up: the looks that passed between him and others in the room were unmistakable. I was not an artist to them, simply an inquisitive colored man; controlling myself, I said deliberately, "I am interested in the report that *Under the Oaks* has received a prize; I painted the picture." An explosion could not have made a more marked impression. Without hesitation he apologized, and soon everyone in the room was bowing and scraping to me.[15]

This type of national success must have been bittersweet for Bannister because, while it garnered him recognition from the Black and white communities outside of New England, it also exposed him to the tide of racism that had continued to rise in the United States. And it was just this type of reception that probably caused him to shy away from Black characters and from overtly racialized subject matter. To the white officials and attendees of the Philadelphia Centennial Exposition, he would never be distinguishable from the Black people who labored in the hayfields he painted. Nevertheless, he continued to exhibit nationally, in 1879 at the National Academy of Design and in 1880 at the New Orleans Cotton Centennial Exposition.

The artistic production of Bannister, and that of his colleagues Duncanson, Lewis, and Tanner, speaks to the changing modes of visualizing the global African experience that occurred in the second half of the nineteenth century, and it retells the obstacles they encountered due to their socially prescribed identities as they negotiated spaces of race and representation. Because of the post-Reconstruction reactionary oppression of Black creativity, today we are familiar with the work and careers of only a handful of the African American artists who were active between 1865 and 1920. This is due in part to the limited critical reception that they received during their lifetimes and to the institutional racism that kept their work out of most large museum collections until the late twentieth century. Further, after finding the dominant art world at best unresponsive and more typically openly hostile to their efforts, many of these artists, except for Duncanson, who died in 1872 at the height of his career, chose alternate avenues for their careers. Bannister, of course, left Boston and opted for the relative isolation of Providence, where he was able to develop a strong reputation amid a growing colony of regionally motivated landscape artists. Lewis expatriated permanently to Rome after the mid-1870s, where she became a part of a community of American sculptors, many of them women. And Tanner sought the unique status and relative racial freedom of France, where he lived permanently from 1895 until his death in 1923.

Following their deaths at the turn of the century, the reputations of both Lewis and Bannister suffered a rapid descent into obscurity as the styles in which they had painted and sculpted had fallen out of fashion. Their work, and that of Tanner as well, was further marginalized by Alain Locke, the New Negro cultural critic of the subsequent Harlem Renaissance, who found it to be derivative and imitative of white aesthetics rather than authentically African American.[16] Up until the last decades of the twentieth century, there was little appreciation for Bannister's landscapes; his paintings were largely unknown to historians of American art and virtually unseen outside of Rhode Island collections. There was little reason to investigate the sea of grass, to search for the struggle of racial remembering that Bannister engaged in his landscapes of Rhode Island's plantation past.

Part II

MODERN BLACKNESS

For many years the era of the Harlem Renaissance, which spanned both the Roaring Twenties and the Great Depression, dominated the art historical work that was being produced on African American visual and material culture. It was a period when African and African diaspora culture and aesthetics were both celebrated and derided as valuable folk culture and as harbingers of radical modernism. Regrettably, as we sit within the centenary of that era, its primacy within the field has been displaced. In 2018–19 the Columbus Museum of Art mounted the nontraveling exhibition *I, Too, Sing America: The Harlem Renaissance at 100*, but as of 2022, no other shows or books about the visual art of the period had been published for the occasion.[1]

Although it is rapidly being eclipsed by the broader art world's rising interest in focusing on representational art by Black artists that is being produced in the contemporary moment, the past century still looms large in the project of African American art history. This section of the book is anchored by two essays that have their center in that moment when the New Negro movement that drove the Harlem Renaissance hoped to change the landscape for Black artists of all kinds, and it concludes with explorations of art made by artists who were born in the period itself and whose careers were propelled by its momentum.

At the dawn of the twentieth century, Black visual artists, who had long been marginalized by the white-dominated art world, were begrudgingly being allowed limited admission to the nation's art schools. However, they were still being shut out of most exhibition opportunities by the racist policies and practices that were a part of widespread segregation. The first essay in this section considers the art and career of May Howard Jackson, one of only a handful of African American women artists, most of whom were sculptors, whose careers were in full swing before the impact of the Harlem Renaissance and the Federal Art Project helped to stimulate and support visual artists in Black communities across the United States. In the 1890s she became the first Black woman to gain admission to the Pennsylvania Academy of the Fine Arts. By approaching Howard Jackson's career through her work as well as from both a biographical and a social perspective, my engagement aims to form a better understanding of the ways that the artist's liminal racial status as a white-passing Black woman and her social identity as a middle-class lady helped to influence her subject matter and circumscribe her opportunities to exhibit and sell her art. It is the most extensive research and writing that has been done on Howard Jackson to date; hopefully it will stimulate more research into her oeuvre and help unearth lost works.

Just as May Howard Jackson struggled during the first three decades of the twentieth century to make a career for herself as a classically trained sculptor in the nation's capital, so too did her nephew by marriage, the sculptor and printmaker Sargent Johnson. By 1915 Johnson had established himself in California, where he lived and worked in the San Francisco Bay Area for the next fifty years. A proficiency in the New Negro aesthetics that championed African art–influenced modernism, combined with steady commissions from the Federal Art Project during the Great Depression, enabled Johnson to achieve a much higher degree of commercial success than his uncle's wife. By charting Johnson's unique geographic mobility and by considering the likelihood that his aunt significantly aided his career by sharing her own connections within the art world, this chapter brings the networks that were established by striving Black artists during the first half of the century into greater visibility while it also focuses on the place of Blackness within the transatlantic modernism of Gertrude Stein.

Johnson's interest in Stein's modernist opera *Four Saints in Three Acts* first became apparent to me in the late 1990s when I was working at the San Francisco Museum of Modern Art as a research assistant on an exhibition of the artist's work. This occurred after I attended a stirring lecture at Stanford by cultural historian Steven Watson, a specialist on the creative and personal relationships within American avant-garde artistic circles during the early twentieth century; Watson was promoting his book *Prepare for Saints: Gertrude Stein, Virgil Thomson, and the Mainstreaming of American Modernism*. That night I was introduced to Stein and Thomson's 1934 opera, *Four Saints in Three Acts*, the first opera to not only have a successful run on Broadway but also feature an all–African American cast. Watson's discussion of *Four Saints* helped me to begin to make sense of Johnson's 1940 lithograph *Singing Saints*. In Watson's slides I saw immediate visual resonances between Johnson's dark-skinned, guitar-strumming figures and the costumed African American performers who floated through the cellophane and taffeta set decorations that were designed for the modernist opera by the artist Florine Stettheimer. Following the lecture, I was convinced that I had found a way into Johnson's enigmatic print, but I did not pursue it at the time. It was not until 2009, when I participated in a symposium at Stanford in honor of my mentor, Americanist art historian Wanda M. Corn, that I initiated my own research into the potential relationship between *Singing Saints* and *Four Saints in Three Acts*.

These themes of Black artistic community and diasporic connection are furthered by other essays in this section: an examination of the influence and confluences among African American artists; the muralism movement that originated in postrevolutionary Mexico and spread north; and the painter Norman Lewis's early engagement with African art in the 1930s. In 2015–16 the Pennsylvania Academy of the Fine Arts organized the exhibition *Procession: The Art of Norman Lewis*, the first comprehensive traveling museum retrospective of the artist's work ever mounted. The exhibition spanned the artist's career from his origins as a social realist in the 1930s through his work with the first generation of abstract expressionist artists based in New York City. This remarkable undertaking inspired several satellite publications on Lewis's work, including the special issue of the *International Review of African American Art* where this essay originally appeared. Here I focus on Lewis's early interest in African art objects and his grappling with their "thingness" in the context of modern museum exhibition practice that engaged them as aesthetic objects disengaged from a cultural context of lived practice that has been purposefully disremembered to colonize the original function of the objects.

The chapter that follows centers on the impact that Mexican muralism and radical proletarian politics had on African American artists working in the 1930s and 1940s, including Aaron Douglas and Elizabeth Catlett. Commissioned for the Whitney Museum of American Art's 2020 exhibition *Vida*

Americana: Mexican Muralists Remake American Art, this essay also seeks to connect the anti-capitalist and anti-racist sentiments that were championed in the work of midcentury Black artists, some of whom went into self-imposed exile in Mexico after being persecuted by the Federal Bureau of Investigation, with the museum's own challenges in the contemporary moment around questions of "artwashing" the reputations of controversial donors. The political positions taken by these artists helped establish expectations for how subsequent generations might create art to help forge social change and aid working-class Black communities. And yet this was not a path that all African American artists would choose to take.

Toward the end of the century, artists who were born in the 1930s began to explore new methods of making art that foregrounded aspects of process and phenomenological response within African American history and culture, probing deeply into the transhistorical and the spiritual at a time when the expectations for what Black art should look like and how it should function were profoundly politicized.

One of the most important artists of the twentieth century, sculptor and writer Barbara Chase-Riboud, expatriated to France as a young artist, following her graduate study at Yale. Despite her physical distance from the United States, she remained engaged with Black American communities, remembering our histories, making monumental sculpture, and writing historical novels such as *Sally Hemings*, which fictionalizes the disremembered life story of the African-descended and enslaved concubine of President Thomas Jefferson. The essay included here was first published in the catalog *Barbara Chase-Riboud: The Malcolm X Steles*.[2] It works to center the artist's ongoing engagement with commemorating the impact of the life of the assassinated civil rights activist Malcolm X within a larger effort to elucidate the lives of the disremembered, including those of the Black New Yorkers whose final resting place was in the eighteenth-century African Burial Ground in Lower Manhattan, where the artist's massive sculpture *Africa Rising* (1998) now stands.

The final chapter in this section focuses on the life and work of painter Richard Yarde, who is most well known for his watercolor drawings of Black historical subjects and for the interest in African diaspora spirituality that he developed toward the end of his life as he battled terminal kidney disease. I first wrote about Yarde's work for the exhibition *Pulse: Art, Healing, and Transformation* at the Institute of Contemporary Art in Boston in 2003. In the significantly revised and greatly expanded essay that I present here, I have chosen to go deeply into the artist's biography, drawing on eight hours of interviews that I conducted with him in 2011, during what would be the final year of his life.

My decision to foreground biography in both the first and last chapters in this section reflects my scholarly conviction that the lives of African American artists are important to our understanding of the work that they produce. It is a conviction that is supported by the relative invisibility of Black individual experience within the history of art. By focusing on the specificity of individual Black experience, the singular nature of an artistic life lived, I hope to remember artistic practices and creative lives that would otherwise remain disremembered.

5

"THIS GIFTED SCULPTRESS OF THE RACE"

THE INTERSECTIONAL ART OF MAY HOWARD JACKSON

In a photograph of May Howard Jackson's (1877–1931) now-lost clay sculpture *Mother and Child* (ca. 1916), we see a young woman holding a smiling baby in her arms (figure 5.1). The woman bends her head downward, touching the child's forehead to her chin, her eyes shut against the viewer's gaze. Her long hair is left unbound, parted on the right, curling tendrils pouring like waves down her shoulders and about her arms, covering both her own body and that of her child. The expressionistic surface treatment of the plaster recalls the ruddy surface of Donatello's *Maddelena Penitente* (1453–55) at the Museo dell'Opera del Duomo, Florence, and the artistic tradition that it continues from the late-medieval period forward of representing the body of Mary Magdalene with long, unbound hair that falls past her shoulders, covering her body.[1] Like the blue mantle or veil that is so often depicted covering the head and shoulders of the Virgin Mary, providing her with an appropriate level of modesty, the attribute of unbound hair frequently served to identify the Magdalene as emblematic of fallen yet redeemable womanhood. Not only does the hair of *Mother and Child* serve to situate her within a Christian visual tradition of the Magdalene, it also references nineteenth-century American and British traditions of visually depicting a sexualized, mixed-race, African-

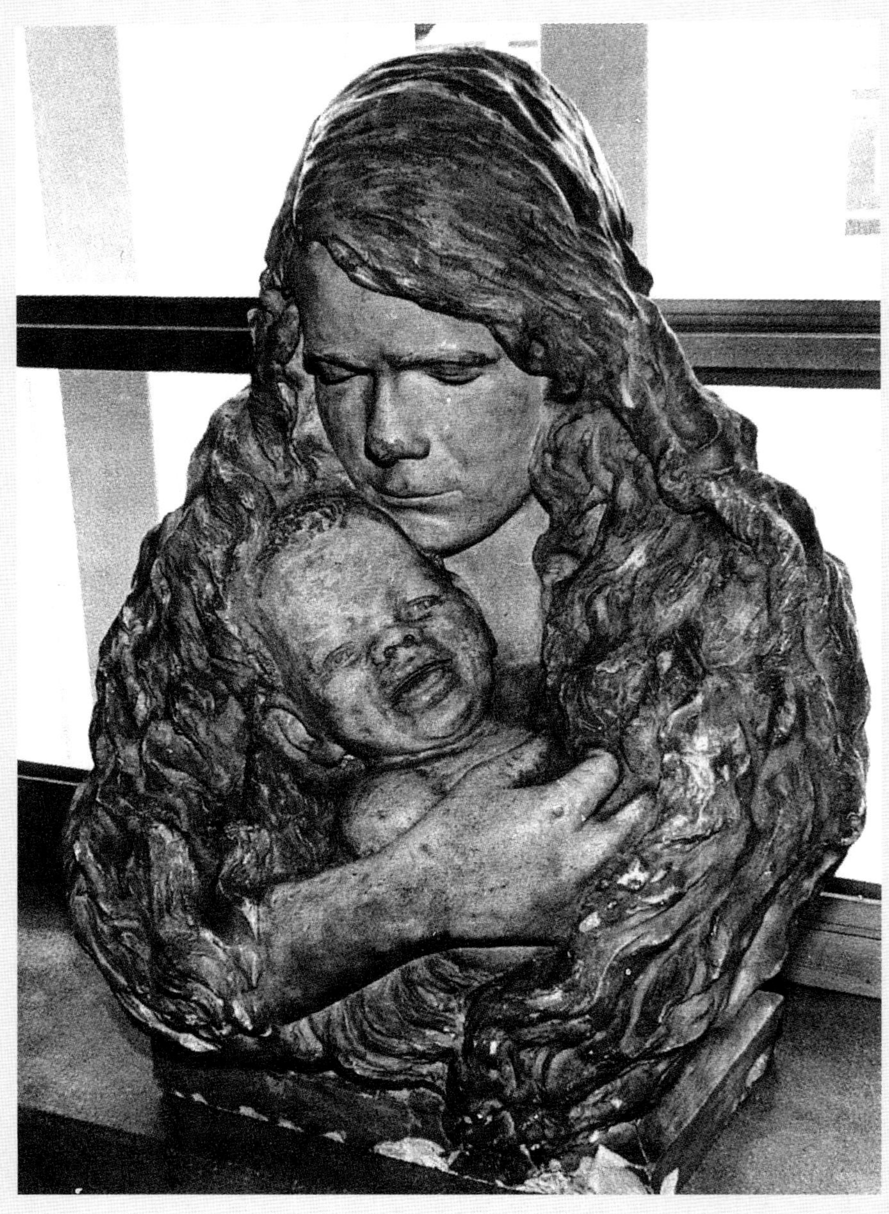

5.1 May Howard Jackson, *Mother and Child (Mulatto Mother and Child)*, ca. 1916. Published in *Crisis* 12, no. 6 (October 1916): 279

descended woman by using wavy or curly, but not kinky, hair as the most important physical mark of the illicit sexuality created by the interracial union that produced her body. This use of long, wavy, loose hair as an artistic method of representing this kind of illicit sexuality is seen in a number of nineteenth-century sculptures, most notably John Bell's *The Octoroon* (1868), which shows a nude woman who partially covers her body with her hair.[2] But unlike Bell's *Octoroon*, whose cascading hair also draws attention to her naked breasts as it falls between them, the hair of Howard Jackson's *Mother and Child* fully covers her body, forming a barrier between her nakedness and the viewer's eyes, protecting her (and also her child) from visual violation.

Shortly after its completion, *Mother and Child* was discussed at length in the *Crisis*, the publication of the National Association for the Advancement of Colored People (NAACP), the leading Black-interest magazine of the period. The article, titled "A Story in Clay," found within the "Men of the Month" section (the magazine had no feature to specifically highlight the accomplishments of women), began by stating that *Mother and Child* portrayed "a curious tale of inner tragedy" that occurs when light-skinned Black women "marry into the other race, as they have a perfect right to do being more white than black." The *Crisis* identified the two main problems of these unions as being children who viewed "the race problem from the standpoint of white folk" and the internal anxiety of light-skinned women who had felt "the call of the blood and marr[ied] within the race, often to men of darker and stronger Negro blood" and found they were unable to protect their dark-skinned children from racism. It was the progeny of this second union that the *Crisis* identified within the sculpture *Mother and Child*, describing the sculpture as communicating the pain of the light-skinned mother who "sees her child proscribed in a hundred ways where she was not, since the public did not easily sense her race identity, and she holds the little one to her in fierce protection."[3]

Mother and Child is a work about race, gender, and sexual propriety. Its subject matter was clearly set within contemporary racial issues, and its artistic sources were set deep within the history of Western art. In many ways it is exemplary of May Howard Jackson's intersectional identity as an African American woman affected by racism and sexism. It also reveals the social and class-based aspects of her larger artistic practice, which was formed in an era when a "New Negro" and the "Talented Tenth" politics of racial uplift were ascendant.[4] It is evidence that the impact of the conservative sculptural traditions of the Pennsylvania Academy of the Fine Arts (PAFA), where the artist studied in the late 1890s, had not yet been supplanted in her mind by the radical modernist aesthetics seen at the 1913 International Exhibition of

Modern Art organized by the Association of American Painters and Sculptors (known as the Armory Show), the first large-scale exhibition of avant-garde art in the United States. And yet the very existence of Howard Jackson's sculpture points to the radical aspects of the artist's practice, which defied the contemporary, conservative New Negro social norms that encouraged middle-class Black women to live their lives in service to their families. After all, here she was, a woman whose artistic accomplishment was so unusual that it was being featured in an aggressively ideological magazine in a section devoted to the activities of notable men. It is evidence of how out of place Howard Jackson's career as a Black woman sculptor was in the early twentieth century. And like the light-skinned mother in her sculpture, as a working woman who did not have children and whose father was of mixed heritage and whose mother was white, Howard Jackson was constantly in conflict with the racial and gender codes of the Black community in which she moved and with the larger dominant culture of white supremacy that sought to control her life and that of her progeny, in this case the artworks she created. A deeper understanding of Howard Jackson's life and sculptural production, which this essay seeks to provide, may elucidate the extent to which issues of identity served to shape not only the subjects that the artist chose to engage but also the reception of her work, and even her ability to have work exhibited in mainstream institutions.

The young May Howard grew up in a row house at South Twelfth and Christian Streets in a predominantly African American neighborhood in Philadelphia. From 1894 through 1898, while in her late teens, she attended PAFA, where she completed a standard course of study that included nude figure drawing, painting courses with William Merritt Chase (1849–1916), and sculpture courses with Charles Grafly (1862–1929). During the 1890s Grafly's work focused on the expressionistic treatment of mythical figures, such as his bronze bust of an emotionally tortured *Daedalus* (1892), which was acquired by the academy in the same year it was made. The impact of Grafly's interest in the expressive possibilities of the human body, particularly the face, may be seen in his pupil's work.

Despite PAFA's notable history of regularly admitting white women to study since its founding in 1805, May Howard was the first Black woman to enroll. Whether there were others before her who tried unsuccessfully is not known. Her tuition at PAFA was paid by a scholarship sponsored by the Philadelphia Public Schools.[5] Her attendance there came just a decade following that of the African American painter Henry Ossawa Tanner (1859–1937), who experienced intense racism as a student at PAFA in the early 1880s. One often repeated anecdote of his time there was relayed by a classmate who later described what happened when his peers began to see his presence as a threat to their white supremacy: "Then he [Tanner] began to assert himself and, to cut a long story short, one night his easel was carried out into the middle of Broad Street and, though not painfully crucified, he was firmly tied to it and left there. And this is my only experience of my colored brothers in a white school; but it was enough."[6]

The study of art at PAFA in the 1880s and 1890s was a decidedly white male affair. A photograph of a sculpture class from around 1888 in the Thomas Anshutz collection at the Archives of American Art reveals a room full of young white men, most sporting handlebar mustaches and bowler hats, only a few of them wearing protective smocks over their street clothes (figure 5.2). They are gathered around wooden stands on which they are building clay representations of a nude male model who poses at the center of the room. A mannequin displaying the subdermal musculature of the human body stands at the back of the room, an unacknowledged specter of the inherent biological sameness of humans. In another photograph of students that was taken at the academy in the 1880s, we see a group of young white men, again in street clothes, dissecting a cadaver, which appears to be much darker skinned than they (figure 5.3). The cadaver may be discolored due to its state of decay, or it may be the unclaimed body of an African American pauper, which was frequently the case during an era when people did not generally donate their bodies for research purposes and Black corpses without families were often commandeered into the service of medicine or art. What, one wonders, must it have been like for a young woman of mixed-race descent like May Howard to enter such a world?

Despite the feelings of unwelcome that young May Howard may have experienced at PAFA, she emerged resolute in her determination to be an artist. Following the premature death of her mother, Sarah (or Sallie), a white woman whom she would later describe as "Quaker of good old abolitionist stock," May Howard grew up in a household that was headed by her widowed father, Floarda Howard Sr.[7] They lived in a neighborhood of two- and three-story row houses, occupied primarily by African American strivers, including the retired abolitionist William Still (1847–1902), who lived just a few blocks away.[8] The neighborhood was also home to the Institute for Colored Youth, the nation's oldest African American private school for higher education.[9]

On the first day of June 1900, May Howard and her three siblings, Harriet, Floarda Jr., and Elizabeth, were visited by federal census enumerator George W. Anderson. As a part of the family's census enumeration, Anderson noted that the head of the household, Floarda Sr., was a "caterer," while

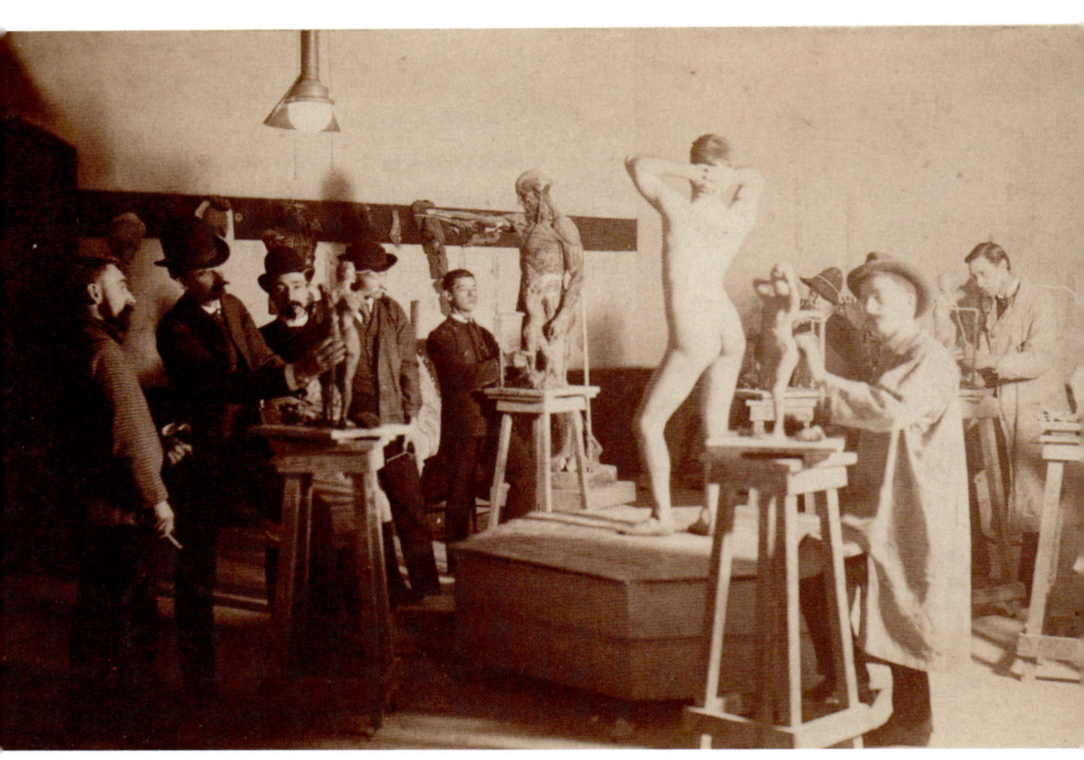

5.2 Sculpture class at the Pennsylvania Academy of the Fine Arts, ca. 1888. Unidentified photographer. Thomas Anschutz papers, ca. 1870–1942, Archives of American Art, Smithsonian Institution, Washington, DC

twenty-two-year-old May was an "artist," sixteen-year-old Floarda Jr. was a "student," and fourteen-year-old Elizabeth was "at school." He did not record the eldest Howard sister, Harriet, who was in Virginia at the time, serving on a mission with the Episcopal Church. The occupation designations that Anderson recorded on the census form are remarkable for several reasons. First, an examination of the adjacent census record pages finds that May Howard is the only woman in her immediate neighborhood whose occupation was not recorded as "house servant" or left blank by the enumerator, probably indicating that they were homemakers. May Howard is recorded as an artist: a professional identity that sets her solidly apart from the other Black women in the community of her youth.[10] Second, her father, Floarda Howard Sr., is listed as a caterer, implying that he, too, was a professional, a man who ran a business and commanded an array of high-level business and social skills. Interestingly, Floarda Howard Sr. is also listed in a second federal census

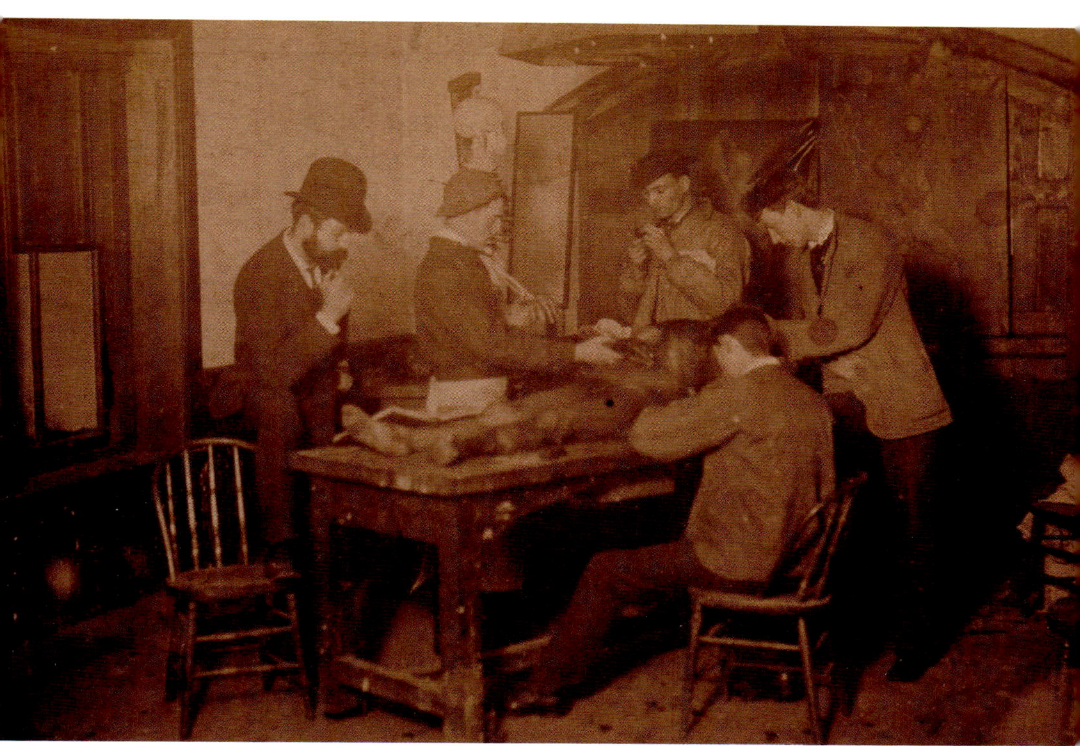

5.3 Students dissecting a cadaver at the Pennsylvania Academy of Fine Arts, ca. 1882. Unidentified photographer. Thomas Anschutz papers, ca. 1870–1942, Archives of American Art, Smithsonian Institution, Washington, DC

record taken on the very same day, a little over sixty miles away in Atlantic City, New Jersey. Here he is recorded as serving as a waiter in a small seaside hotel at South Michigan and Pacific Avenues, less than a block from that city's famed Boardwalk on a lot that is presently occupied by Bally's Casino.[11]

Sometimes called the "Plantation by the Sea" for the way that the resort community exploited Black labor at the turn of the nineteenth to the twentieth century, Atlantic City in 1900 was home to a large Black population that worked in the service industry. When the population of the seaside resort swelled during the summer months as the middle- and upper-class white communities of Philadelphia sought refuge from the unhealthy weather of the city, so too did the Black population. Because of its seasonal job market, Atlantic City was a beacon for many African Americans, especially those migrating from southern states in search of better economic opportunities. For example, it was in Atlantic City that the artist Jacob Lawrence's parents met and married and the artist was born. In a 1968 interview in the collection of the Archives of American Art, Lawrence states, "I know that my parents were part of this Negro migration which took place right after World War I, so many of the Negroes coming North to seek work. They were domestics. I think my parents met in Atlantic City. They were part of that movement from the South."[12] This topic would later become the subject of Lawrence's most well-known artistic project, *The Migration Series* (1940–41), a group of sixty tempera paintings on panels with narrative titles.

A native of Maryland, Floarda Howard Sr. had not traveled as far as many of his Black coworkers to reach the employment opportunities of Atlantic City. Although it is physically possible that Floarda Howard Sr. could have hopped on and off the Atlantic City Railroad on Friday, June 1, 1900, to be present in both places when George Anderson visited his family in Philadelphia and William A. Stefany visited his place of employment (where he also resided) in Atlantic City, it seems unlikely. Joseph Boston, the proprietor of the hotel in which the elder Howard worked, was the highest-ranking white male on the premises on the day that the census was taken. As such, he was probably the person who answered the enumerator's questions. He knew enough about Howard to say that he was "married" but did not know that Howard was by this time a widower. In contrast, the individual who answered the enumerator's questions back in Philadelphia knew that Sarah Howard was deceased. He or she also chose to answer the enumerator's question about Floarda Sr.'s occupation as "caterer" rather than "waiter," indicating a perceptual slippage about his actual work that served to elevate Howard's profession to one that sounded more elite. Despite this discrepancy, Floarda Howard Sr. may also have worked as a caterer during the winter off-season, when empty resorts down the shore sent most of their staff to find work elsewhere.

Considering Floarda Howard Sr.'s probable absence from the Twelfth Street residence, it was likely his eldest child, twenty-two-year-old May, who would have answered the enumerator's questions. If this was indeed the case, then May Howard would have had to make certain choices when asked about her family's business, such as calling her father a "caterer" and herself an "artist." However, there were some things that she may not have had a choice about. For example, one wonders if she was asked to confirm her family's African American heritage, which might have been in doubt in the mind of the enumerator given the young woman's light skin and wavy hair, which are readily witnessed in photographs of her taken later in life. Like most of the other people of African heritage in the South Philadelphia neighborhood in which they lived, the Howards were enumerated simply as "black" on that day in June 1900.

As an artist and the daughter of a caterer, May Howard embraced her African American identity fully and, like her siblings, determined to progressively improve her social and economic situation.[13] May Howard's marriage in 1902 to William Tecumseh Sherman Jackson (1868–1943), called Sherman, a protégé of the lawyer John Mercer Langston (1829–97), would serve to firmly ensconce her in the New Negro elite of the progressive era, but it did nothing to protect her from racism.

The couple probably met through the bride's older sister, Harriet, whose husband, the Rev. John Wesley Johnson, had attended the all-Black Virginia Seminary in Petersburg (now Virginia State University), where Sherman Jackson taught mathematics in the 1890s. May and Sherman's engagement was announced in the *Colored American*, a Black-interest newspaper, on April 19, 1902.[14] It was an elite union between a woman who was often mistaken for white and who had attended predominantly white schools in Philadelphia and a much darker man who was born at the end of the Civil War to formerly enslaved parents in rural Virginia. She was twenty-four while he was thirty-seven. Like the educator Booker T. Washington (1856–1915), Sherman Jackson had literally pulled himself "up from slavery" by studying diligently in an overcrowded school for freed children in the Alexandria, Virginia, community to which his family had migrated in the 1880s. After attending college at Amherst, where his tuition was paid for by Massachusetts senator George Frisbie Hoar (1826–1904), Sherman Jackson completed a master's degree at Catholic University (before that institution stopped admitting Black students in the 1910s).[15] He then began a teaching career.

As newlyweds, they settled in Washington, DC, in a large townhouse on Sixteenth Street NW near Sherman Jackson's subsequent employer, the M Street School, the city's only preparatory high school for Black students.[16] After acclimating to married life, Howard Jackson attempted to continue her studies by applying to attend classes at the recently founded school of the Corcoran Art Gallery. Unfortunately, the school rejected her application on the grounds of her race.[17] Having been refused admission to the Corcoran, she resigned herself to working on her own in a studio she fashioned at home. Soon, however, she found encouragement from the sociologist and political activist W. E. B. Du Bois (1868–1963), who moved in the same bourgeois social circles as the Jacksons. Du Bois, who frequently opined publicly on the importance of visual art to the development and uplift of the African American community, urged Howard Jackson to continue with her work.

In 1907, while teaching at Atlanta University, Du Bois commissioned Howard Jackson to create a bust of himself. He sat for her several times while in Washington, DC, and provided several photographs for the purpose of completing the bust accurately.[18] Several years later, in 1913, Du Bois lent the bust back to Howard Jackson for an exhibition at the Veerhof Art Gallery in Washington, DC. Not surprisingly, the *Crisis* magazine, which was under Du Bois's editorial direction from 1910 until 1934, helped promote the work by reprinting part of a review of the show originally written by critic Leila Machlin for the *Washington Star* newspaper. "It has been pronounced an excellent likeness and is undoubtedly well modeled," wrote Machlin. "The head is well placed on the shoulders, the expression is vital and good, and the play of muscle, the turn of surface, the intimation of mobility are well rendered."[19] Similar sentiments were expressed several years later by the editors of *La Follette's Magazine*, who praised the work for its "sensitiveness of expression" and the way that the artist's work consistently "reproduced both faithfully and with sympathetic touch" her subjects.[20]

During the 1910s Howard Jackson continued to receive commissions for busts of prominent African American men, including one of William Henry Lewis (made in 1912), an assistant attorney general in the administration of William Howard Taft who was also her husband's close friend from undergraduate studies at Amherst College; Kelly Miller (made in 1914), then dean of Howard University; and a posthumous bust (figure 5.4, made in 1919) of the poet Paul Laurence Dunbar, whose famous poem "Sympathy" declares, "I know why the caged bird sings."[21] While no installation views of any of Howard Jackson's work have yet been located, the bust of Du Bois may be seen in a photograph of Howard Jackson manipulating the clay model for the work with a set of calipers (figure 5.5). A comparison of several of Howard Jackson's portrait busts reveals a consistent goal on the part of the artist to create representations of her sitters as contemplative, intelligent men, in possession of upright and cultured outward appearances and rich internal lives. For example, the bust of Du Bois shows him wearing his academic robes, which he received on completion of his PhD in sociology at Harvard University. The bust of Dunbar shows the poet in a tidy high-buttoned suit, stiff collar, and tie. Probably working from photographs of Dunbar, as she had done with Du Bois, Howard Jackson emphasizes the physical characteristics of the sitter, taking care to include the distinctive part that Dunbar always wore in his hair. Similarly, the bust of Miller (figure 5.6), which was reproduced in the November 1917 issue of the *Crisis* magazine in lieu of a photographic portrait, is distinguished not only by the sitter's suit jacket, vest, collar, and tie but also by his bushy mustache and furrowed brow, emphasizing his dedication to the life of the mind.[22]

In 1915, at the Washington Art Club, Howard Jackson exhibited the busts of Lewis and Du Bois, along with one of the Rev. Francis Grimké. A reporter for the Black-interest newspaper *Washington Bee* noted, "This is the first time the Washington public has had the opportunity to view Mrs. Jackson's work in a collection."[23] In 1917, when Howard Jackson exhibited a portrait bust of a young boy named Clark Bailey (figure 5.7), titled *Head of a Child* (ca. 1916), at the Corcoran Gallery, which had by that time relaxed its exclusionary policies to a certain degree, it was praised by another *Washington Bee* reporter as an "admirable piece of work, well-constructed, nicely modeled and expressive and it takes its place well among the works in the gallery by sculptors of more experience and greater reputation."[24] In 1920, when the Dunbar bust was first exhibited publicly, a reporter for the *Washington Bee* described it as "a most excellent likeness," adding that "the eyes look straight toward the observer, but one feels that the vision is inward, that the man was one who searched his own soul. The expression is peculiarly sad, almost tragic, as though the writer himself realized the sadness of his own to [*sic*] short career."[25] Perhaps because of its celebrated subject, Howard Jackson's bust of Dunbar received a great deal of notice in the African American press with an additional appreciation appearing in the *Negro Star* newspaper.[26] The positive reception of the Dunbar bust proved to be one of the few high points in May Howard Jackson's career; she was nearly forty years old and had only just begun to make a place for herself in the Washington, DC, art world.

During this period, the philosopher and cultural tastemaker Alain Locke praised Howard Jackson for using "frank and deliberate racialism" in the representation of her Black subjects to "convey more than the individual personality of the subject" in order to create work that "penetrates the depths of the collective soul."[27] Art historian Lizzetta LeFalle-Collins points to the anxiety that is manifest in Locke's comments with her astute observation that Howard Jackson chose to visually racialize her figures along specific gender lines, giving the female bodies more European features, such as narrow noses and straight or wavy hair, and giving the male subjects the more African characteristics of full lips and curly hair.[28] Interestingly, this practice has also been previously recognized in the work of at least one other mixed-race sculptor: the nineteenth-century Native and African American woman sculptor Edmonia Lewis. Art historian Kirsten Pai Buick has famously argued that Lewis sought to feminize her female subjects by giving them features

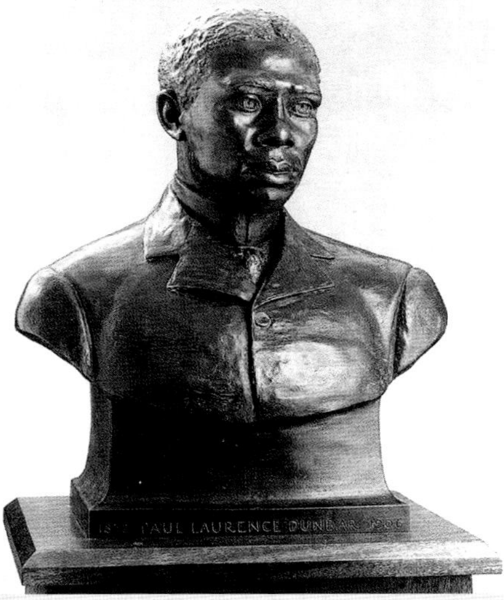

5.4 May Howard Jackson, *Paul Laurence Dunbar*, 1919. Uncredited photograph published in *Crisis* 20, no. 2 (June 1920): 75

5.5 May Howard Jackson with bust of W. E. B. Du Bois. Uncredited photograph from Belle Case La Follette and Caroline L. Hunt, "Woman of the Hour: May Howard Jackson," *La Follette's* magazine 4 (June 22, 1912): 10

HOME AND EDUCATION

The home is the real seat of government, and the Wise Men of all nations bring their gifts to the cradle.

Conducted by BELLE CASE LA FOLLETTE and CAROLINE L. HUNT

Women of the Hour
May Howard Jackson

THERE HAVE recently been exhibited in one of the art stores of Washington two portrait statues by May Howard Jackson—one of the Reverend F. J. Grimke, for over forty years pastor of one of the colored churches of the city, the other of Professor W. E. Burkhardt Du Bois. The latter has attracted special attention because of the fact that Dr. Du Bois is being talked of as a possible successor to Dr. Thirkield, who has just resigned the presidency of Howard University to become a bishop in the Methodist Church. Many people hope that at this time, when the rapidly increasing power and independence of the colored people are creating a need for wise leaders among them, Howard University will make an exception to its rule, elect a colored man as president and give to the great body of students the inspiration of Dr. Du Bois's deep scholarship and high ideals. But this was to have been a sketch of Mrs. Jackson, not of Dr. Du Bois.

Mrs. Jackson is herself colored, or is classed as such, though she has much more white than colored blood. She was born in Philadelphia. Her mother was a Quaker of good old abolitionist stock. The small amount of colored blood she has came through her father. She was brought up among white people and attended the public schools. At a very early age she showed talent for modeling and became a pupil in Professor J. Liberty Tadd's art school, which is part of the public school system. Here she won a scholarship in the Pennsylvania Academy of Fine Arts, where she studied several years.

About ten years ago she married Mr. Sherman Jackson, who is at the head of the mathematics department of the High School for colored people in Washington. She had expected to continue her studies at the art school connected with the Corcoran Art Gallery but was refused admission because of her color. Somewhat discouraged, she decided to keep her talents to herself, to model only for the pure delight of it and not to seek public recognition. It was chiefly through Dr. Du Bois's influence and urging that she again took up her work with the determination to make the most of her gifts for the sake of the encouragement it would be to her people, as well as for her own satisfaction. She is now making a bust of Mr. W. H. Lewis, assistant Attorney-General.

It is not at all customary for Washington art stores to exhibit the work of colored artists, particularly if the subjects too are colored, and the fact that Mrs. Jackson's work has been displayed is evidence that her talent is being recognized. Her statues have in fact been very favorably noticed by critics, and pronounced "well constructed and skillfully modeled." She could hardly have found a greater contrast than that presented by Mr. Grimke's strong, rugged features and the delicacy of Dr. Du Bois's face and the sensitiveness of its expression. But she has reproduced both faithfully and with sympathetic touch and has made studies which have not only artistic merit but also a distinct scientific and sociological value.

Those who, like myself, are not art critics will be likely to be even more interested in this woman than in her work. Though she has beauty and great personal charm one feels after talking with her that he has been in communication not with an individual but with that great, new, brave spirit of the colored people which is turning the bitterness of the wrongs they have suffered and are still suffering into the joy of independence and mutual helpfulness.

* * *

¶ TO HAVE what we want is riches; to be able to do without is power.—GEORGE MACDONALD.

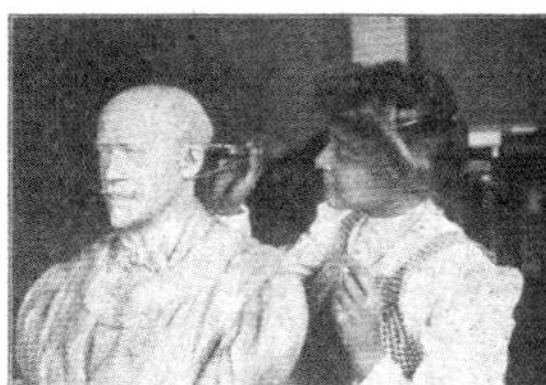

MAY HOWARD JACKSON

Working on a bust of Dr. Du Bois in his office in New York City.

Simplified Dietary Standards

THOSE WHO HAVE more than an intellectual interest in dietetics, those, for example who teach or who have charge of the food of children, or of those who have been placed on a diet, will welcome the simplified form in which dietaries are being stated in Government publications and elsewhere. These dietaries used to be stated in terms of three food principles, proteids, fats, and carbohydrates,—and those who tried to plan meals approximating even roughly to a given standard, found themselves in a maze of arithmetical difficulties. Now the dietary is usually stated in terms of fuel value and proteids, which reduces the factors to be taken into consideration from three to two, and simplifies correspondingly these mathematical difficulties involved.

* * *

What Shall We Do With Our New Magazines?

TIMES CHANGE and with them our pressing problems. We used to ask "What shall be done with our old magazines?" But now when social affairs are in a state of peculiarly unstable equilibrium, and when a few people seem to have the power to turn the tide toward or away from social justice and when every great movement publishes its own organ, the greater problem is what to do with our new magazines. How shall we make them reach the greatest number of people? Where shall we place the magazines like the *Woman's Journal*, which gives the latest news of the suffrage movement and provides an answer for every argument that can possibly be raised against the enfranchisement of women? How shall we spread abroad the record of women's trade union history as given in *Life and Labor?*

There are some magazines, of course, which one feels he can make more useful by keeping than by giving away. The *Public*, edited by Louis F. Post, is one of these. In the very beginning this magazine adopted a system of references from the current issue to previous issues which makes it possible for the reader to follow a topic back to the time when it was first mentioned in the publication. This, combined with the fact that *The Public* is one of the best edited magazines in the country makes it desirable to keep the volumes intact.

But, suppose one is willing to break a volume for the good of a cause, how can he bring the magazines to the attention of

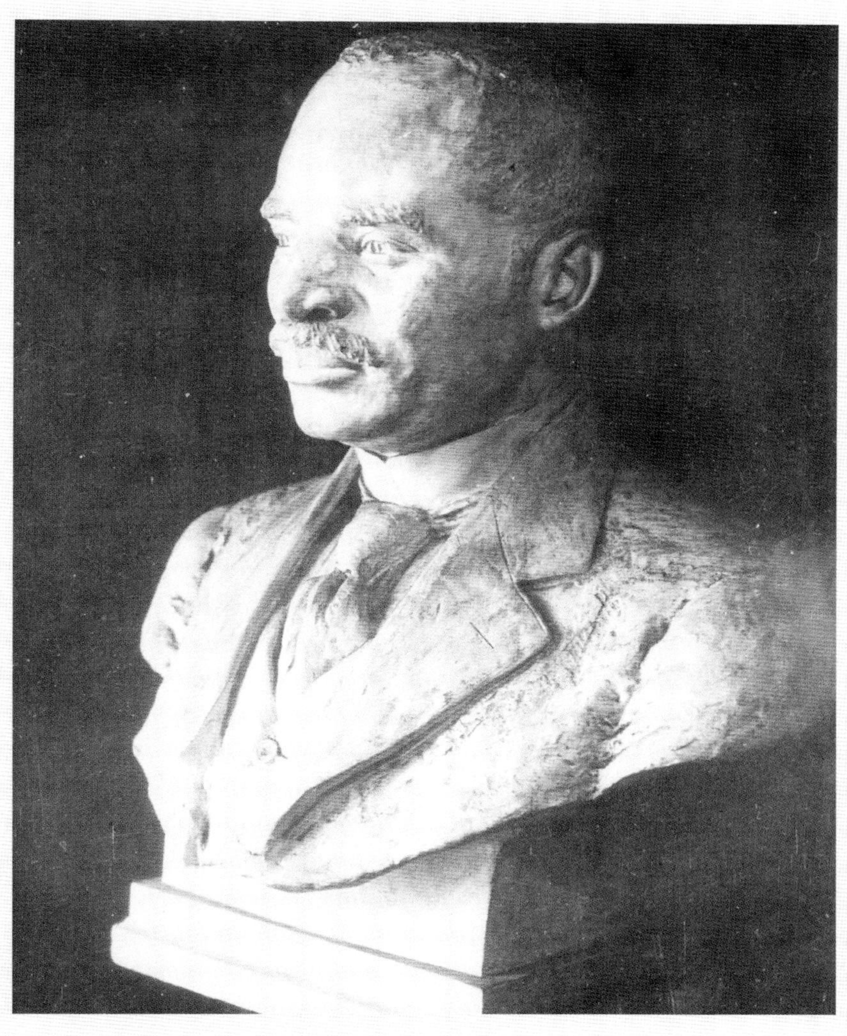

5.6 May Howard Jackson, *Kelly Miller*, 1914. Uncredited photograph
published in *Crisis* 15, no. 1 (November 1917): 23

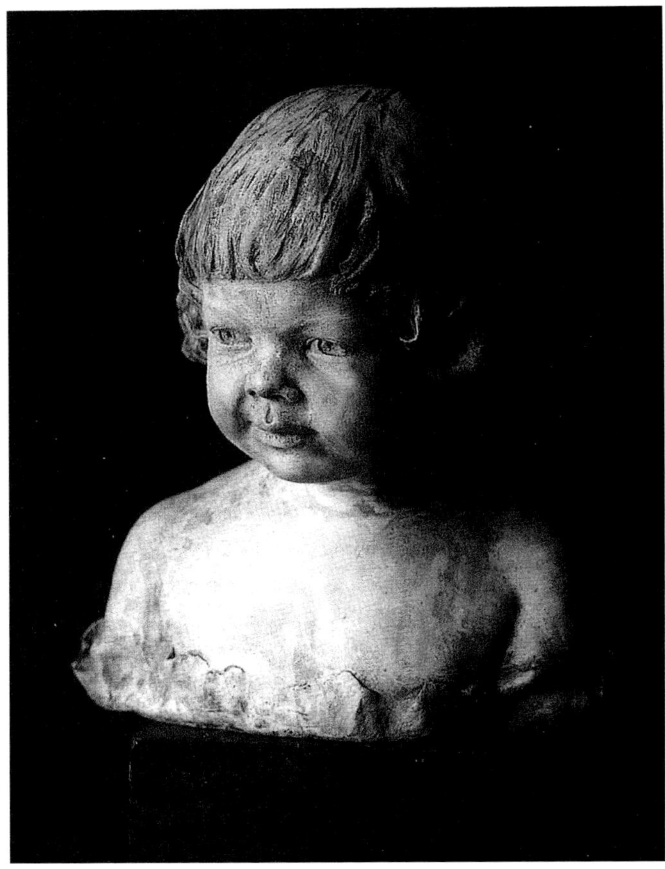

that were closer to European ideals than those of African beauty as a way to counteract the prevailing reality that Black womanhood did not exist as a protected and valued gender identity during the nineteenth century.[29] In this way, Lewis's sculptures of Black women might be considered deserving of male protection under the ideological "Cult of True Womanhood" that was embraced by the dominant white supremacist culture of mid-nineteenth-century America.[30]

This practice of gendered racial representation in Howard Jackson's work is especially evident in a comparison of her undated *Bust of a Woman* and the portrait bust of Paul Laurence Dunbar. *Woman* (figure 5.8) is an idealized image of femininity in full bloom: the smooth shoulders are bare; the neck, long and gracefully curving to the left, supports a well-shaped head with even features. The eyes are obscured by nearly closed lids and set beneath a strong brow, while the lips turn up at the corners in a bemused smile. *Woman's* luxurious, wavy hair is pulled atop her head in a Gibson Girl knot, creating an hourglass form. With his neat suit and tie, Dunbar is set in the present moment; his curly cropped hair is parted down the middle and combed to the sides (figure 5.4). The head is tilted to the right, and the face carries an expression of deep concentration. His nose is larger and wider than that of *Woman*, as are his lips. Compared to the grounded portrait bust of Dunbar, Howard Jackson's *Bust of a Woman* is all fantasy.

In addition to making portrait busts that she modeled both from life and from photographic sources, Howard Jackson's artistic production was characterized by works that engaged with biblical topics and Christian religious imagery. One of the most notable examples for which we have an image is the clay sculpture *Brotherhood* (figure 5.9), which was featured on the cover of May 1919 issue of the *Crisis*, celebrating Easter week.[31] A small advertisement placed by Howard Jackson in the back matter of the issue tells us much about the circumstances of the artist's production. The advertisement begins, "Have you studied the cover of this issue of the CRISIS? Do you grasp its deeper

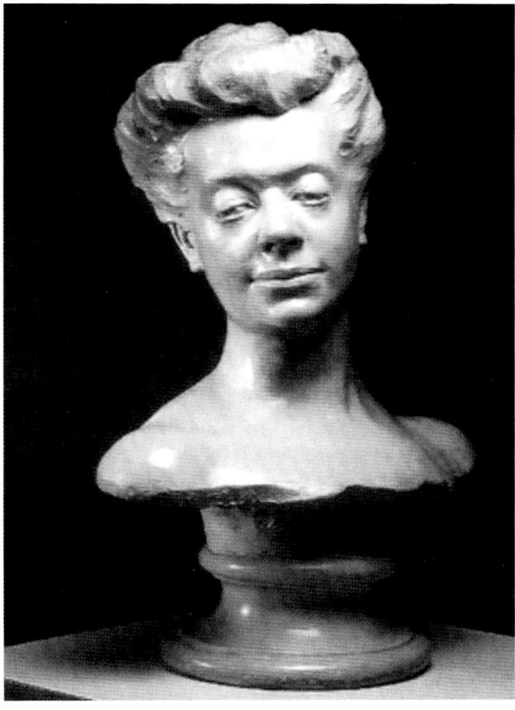

5.8 May Howard Jackson, *Bust of a Woman (Miss Alice Jackson)*, 1899. Location unknown

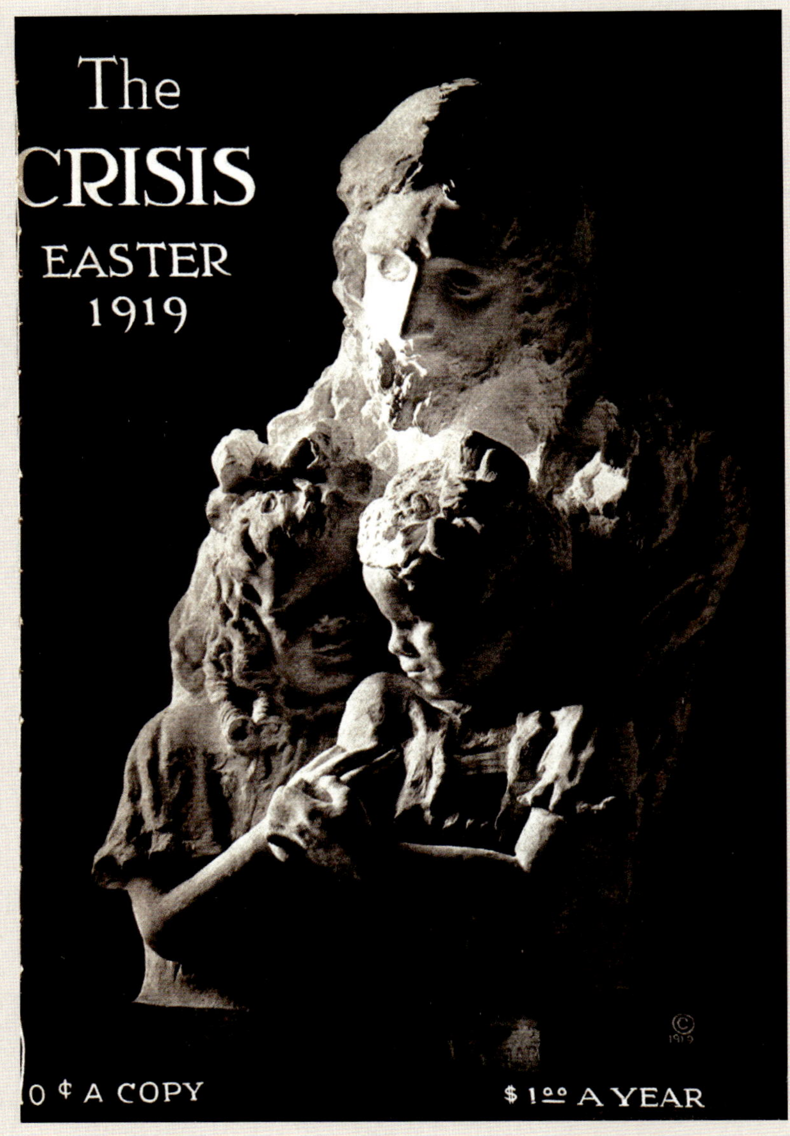

5.9 May Howard Jackson, *Brotherhood*, n.d. Uncredited photograph on the cover of *Crisis* 17, no. 6 (April 1919)

meaning? It is May Howard Jackson's way of expressing 'Brotherhood'—
the great message of the risen Christ. This sculpture is on exhibition at the
independent Art Society Exhibit now being held at the Waldorf Astoria in
New York City." It continues by entreating the reader to consider adding images of Howard's work to the walls of their home and community: "Would
you like to adorn the walls of your home, your library or your school with
photographs of these and other works of this gifted sculptress of the race?"[32]
The advertisement concludes by listing an address on West 138th Street in
Harlem at which the artist may be reached.

Interestingly, Howard Jackson's advertisement offers photographs of
sculptures for sale, rather than originals or copies of the works themselves.
This provides important insight into her working practice in the 1910s as well
as into her expectations for sales within a Black community that had scant
tradition or experience in buying fine art. In the late nineteenth and early
twentieth centuries, many working- and middle-class African American
homes were decorated with photographic reproductions and popular prints,
while poorer homes in rural areas often used catalog pages and other advertising papers for insulating wall covering.[33]

Further, Howard Jackson does not appear to have cast many of her works
in bronze, which would have been hugely expensive, more frequently opting to fire the original terracotta works. It was not until the late 1920s that a
record exists of her attempting to market bronze casts of her work. On the
reverse side of an application to the Harmon Foundation Fine Art Exhibitions of 1929, the artist lists several works she is sending, including *Bronze
Shell Figure, Negro Baby* (figure 5.10).[34] A follow-up letter to the secretary of
the Harmon Foundation notes that the "little bronze [*Shell Baby*] is being sent
without the required registration card. . . . price at $40.00."[35] In a subsequent
letter, the artist notes that "the price on the 'Shell Baby' . . . will be $15.00 a
piece. I would sell them for $25.00."[36]

There is no evidence confirming that Howard Jackson sold any of the
copies of *Shell Baby* through the Harmon Foundation or that her advertisement in the *Crisis* generated many requests for photographs of her sculpture.
However, in 1929 she received the bronze medal award of $100 at the Harmon
Foundation exhibition for her bust of Kelly Miller, which she also submitted
along with *Shell Baby* and four other works that remained in her possession,
including *Head of a Child*, *Mother and Child*, and *Brotherhood*.[37] Several
months later she wrote to Alain Locke that her work, which had previously
been exhibited at the National Academy of Design in Washington, DC, was
now being rejected. In fact, the academy had sent someone around to her

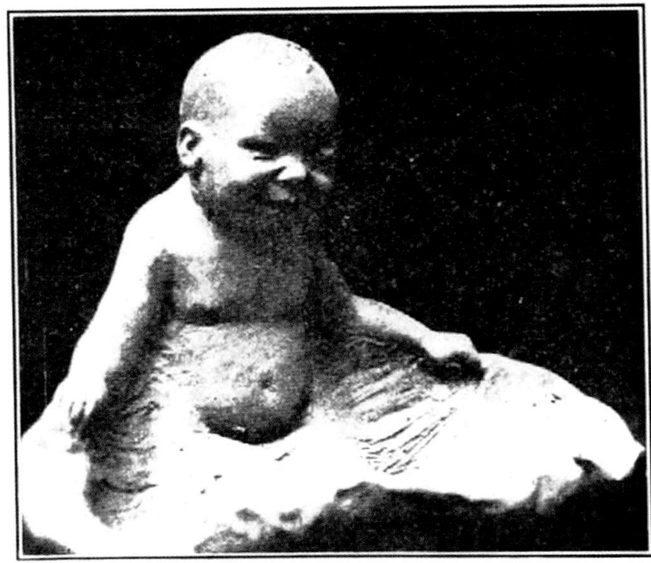

home to inquire if she was of "Negro blood" and, on hearing that she was indeed African American, told her that her work would no longer be welcome in their exhibitions. "I have no satisfaction," she wrote Locke, "only a deep sense of injustice. Something that has followed me and my efforts all my life."[38] May Howard Jackson never came close to achieving the fame or recognition she (and others) believed she deserved. In large part this was due to the limitations that racism put on African American artists working in the United States during this period.

In 1910, when May Howard and Sherman Jackson were visited by a census taker for the first time since their marriage in 1902, they had long been settled into a large townhouse on Sixteenth Street NW in Washington, DC, which was located not far from Howard University and Dunbar High School.[39] The artist's father, Floarda Howard Sr., was living with them, working as a waiter in a hotel, just as he had been doing in Atlantic City ten years prior. (Perhaps he had never been a caterer.) Sherman was listed as a teacher, while May was now described as a "sculptress" and a "housekeeper," attesting to her attempt to balance both work and domestic life, and her sense of identity as a player within the world of the New Negro. The years that followed were ones of great excitement and optimism for the Jacksons as they sat firmly ensconced among this Talented Tenth bourgeoisie. During the height of the Harlem

Renaissance, the two shuttled back and forth between Washington, DC, and the New York City area. They attended Christmas parties at the home of Madame C. J. Walker (1867–1919), the hair-care entrepreneur who became the first African American woman millionaire, and spent late nights at the salon hosted by Howard Jackson's close friend, poet Georgia Douglass Johnson, where they rubbed shoulders with the likes of Jean Toomer, Alain Locke, Jessie Fauset, and Richard Bruce Nugent.[40] But by the time the 1930 census was taken, Howard Jackson had begun to see herself as without a notable occupation.[41] This is evidence not just of her advancing middle age but also of the toll that her frequent brushes with art world racism, like that described in her letter to Locke, had finally taken on her self-conception as an artist, let alone as a sculptress.

While the often-racist art world served to dampen Howard Jackson's spirits and impede her career, she had found a life partner in Sherman Jackson, whose work and inheritance provided a very comfortable middle-class existence for the couple. In 1919 the couple divested themselves of four properties in Alexandria that were Sherman Jackson's inheritance from his parents, both of whom, despite beginning their lives under enslavement, had risen to become well-off property and business owners.[42] In addition to the townhouse at 1816 Sixteenth Street NW in Washington, DC (which in 2023 was worth well over $1.6 million), at different moments the Jacksons also owned summer homes in the Hudson River Valley and on Long Island.[43] All of this real estate capital helped to make the Jacksons a very comfortable couple by 1930 when they told the census enumerator that their personal property was worth in excess of $20,000.[44] These resources allowed Howard Jackson to pursue her artistic ambitions without the burdens of a day job, and the fact that the couple remained childless allowed Howard Jackson to focus on her work.[45] Even though she lived most of her adult life in Washington, DC, when she died in 1931, it was at a family home in Long Beach, New York. Over the years she kept in close touch with her three siblings, all of whom lived in New York City, where she maintained the residence on West 138th Street, frequently attended social events, and often exhibited her work.[46] When funeral services were held for her, they were conducted at St. Martin's Episcopal Church in Harlem, where her older sister Harriet's son, the Rev. John Howard Johnson, was vicar.[47]

After May Howard Jackson's death, W. E. B. Du Bois, long a close friend of the artist and still the head of the NAACP and editor of the *Crisis*, reflected on the challenges that the artist had faced as a light-skinned African American woman who was interested in portraying racially mixed people in her work:

The death of May Howard Jackson is a loss to art. She was a sculptor with peculiar natural gifts. With her sensitive soul she needed encouragement and contacts and delicate appreciation. Instead of this she ran into the shadows of the Color Line. Problems of race, class, of poverty and family may affect different persons quite differently. It may inspire some and discourage others. It may give new determination or set a soul wandering. In the case of May Howard Jackson the contradictions and idiotic ramifications of the Color Line tore her soul asunder. It made her at once bitter and fierce with energy, cynical of praise and above all at odds with life and people. She met rebuffs in her attempts to study, and in her attempts at exhibition, in her chosen ideal of portraying the American mulatto type; with her own friends and people she faced continual doubts as to whether it was worthwhile and what it was for. Thus the questing, unhappy soul of the Artist beat battered wings at the gates of day and wept alone. She accomplished enough to make her fame firm in our annals and yet one must with infinite sorrow, think how much more she might have done had her spirit been free![48]

Despite the significant amount of class privilege that Howard Jackson enjoyed as the wife of a successful and well-connected Black man, ultimately she found that her liminal racial identity—her light-yet-not-whiteness—and the confusion that it often provoked in her social relations with art-world whites, served to undercut her artistic ambitions. Despite having studied at PAFA, she was turned away from the Corcoran. Later that institution chose to exhibit her work, while the National Academy of Design, which had once been welcoming, decided to reject her submissions. Her career was a series of small successes and little satisfaction. Her identity as a light-skinned woman of African descent often limited her access to art exhibitions and widespread recognition. Like *Mother and Child*, created at the zenith of her career in 1916, May Howard Jackson was forever at the mercy of a racist society's perception of her as a racialized and gendered body, one that bore the marks of its troubling origins on its surface. As a woman who never bore her own children, her work became her sole legacy, and like that of the *Mother and Child* she had created from clay, the figures that she sculpted could never be freed from the materials with which they were made.

6

SINGING SAINTS

SARGENT JOHNSON'S
MODERN BLACKNESS

On Monday, March 18, 1940, the *San Francisco Chronicle* featured a large reproduction of a lithograph called *Singing Saints* (figure 6.1) by Sargent Johnson (1888–1967). The linear composition showed two dark-skinned people, their eyes cast downward and their mouths rounded in song. The person in the foreground strums a guitar, while the one to the left wears a wide-brimmed hat. Set against a blank white background, the two musicians appear to be seated on a low bench, and yet their bodies, formed by a series of arcing lines, make them both rounded and buoyant, as though lifted along with the lilting melody of their silent chorus. While the shading of their skin marks them as dark skinned or African descended, their genders are much harder to determine: an undulating line on the chest of the person on the left echoes the elbow of the one on the right, making a breast-like line. Although this line may indeed indicate a female body beneath the voluminous gown, there is nothing more to argue for this person's (or their partner's) femininity or masculinity. These ambiguously gendered "saints" exist above and apart from carnality and the specificity of the socialized body, having already been beatified.

According to the news article that accompanied the image (figure 6.2), *Singing Saints* was offered to the public for sale as a part of an ongoing

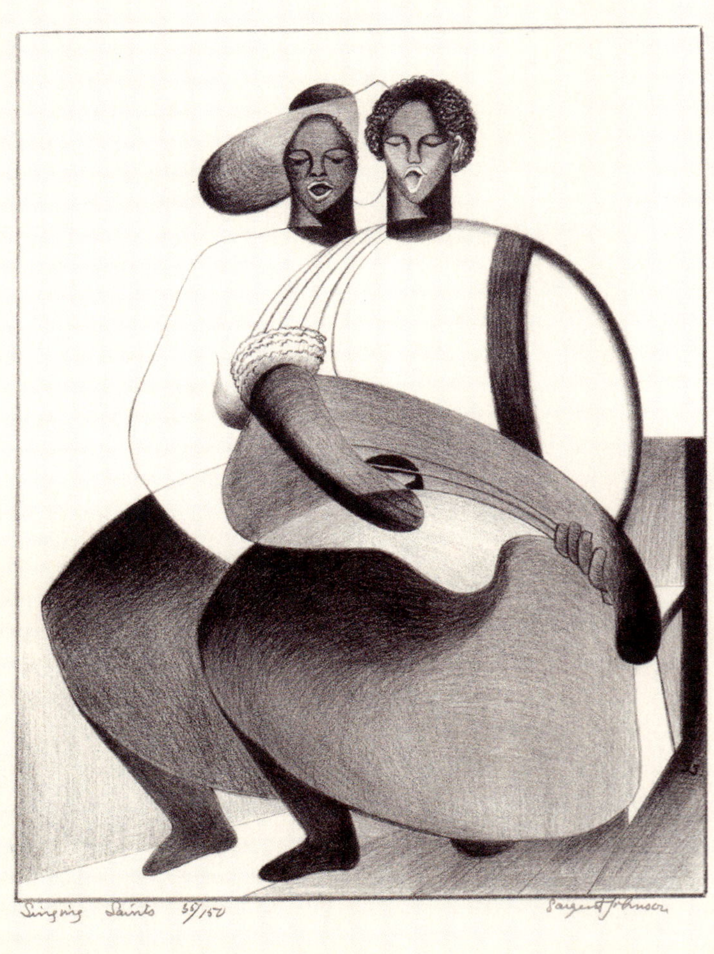

6.1 Sargent Johnson, *Singing Saints*, 1940. Metropolitan Museum of Art, New York. © Metropolitan Museum of Art. Image source: Art Resource, New York

"contemporary" graphics series. Each print was available for $2—the price of a good-quality men's shirt at the time—at the newspaper's business offices as well as at several merchants around the city, including the stationer Schwabacher-Frey, the department store City of Paris, and the luxury retailer Gumps. Works from the series were inexpensive and easy to purchase to stimulate sales and artistic support among readers; as the editors of the paper put it, "Artists like to eat. Their work must bring them some profits, so their patrons used to be kings and princes and nobles and the church. Today their patrons are the modern counterparts of these—the government and its agencies and of course a few wealthy collectors."[1]

The previous day, Sunday, March 17, 1940, the *Chronicle* featured a full-page story that outlined the biographies of the artists featured in the series, including that of Johnson. Under the headline "Sargent Johnson's *Singing Saints*," the article provided his life story in brief: "Sargent Johnson was born in Boston. He studied at the Worcester Art School, five years at the California School of Fine Arts and three years (of sculpture) with Beniamino Bufano. Among his awards have been the Otto H. Kahn prize in 1927, the bronze award in 1929, and the Robert C. Ogden prize in 1933 from the Harmon Foundation, and from the San Francisco Art Association, the medal for sculpture in 1925, 1931 and 1935, with the Graphic prize in the 1938 exhibition."

As the *Chronicle*'s writer implies, Johnson was a special artist. He was the most highly lauded and successful African American artist of a generation that came to prominence during the period known as the Harlem Renaissance. During that era he participated in more exhibitions and received more prizes, awards, and commissions than did Aaron Douglas, Archibald Motley Jr., or any number of artists who are today better known and more widely exhibited. He belonged to the elite San Francisco Art Association (SFAA) and served on its council board for several years. He received numerous awards from the SFAA, the National Association for the Advancement of Colored People (NAACP), and New York's Harmon Foundation. His works of art were featured in international expositions and reproduced in national magazines and foundational art historical texts, and they inspired numerous artists in their own work. His large-scale public works, made under the auspices of the Federal Art Project in the late 1930s, remain focal points in many public buildings in the San Francisco Bay Area, where he lived and worked between 1915 and 1967. His art and his life story are especially compelling, for they reveal the complexity of being an artist of African and European descent working with racial subject matter in the United States of the twentieth century.

The Arts

he de Young useum Given x Doré Books

books containing works by e Doré, nineteenth century famed for his grotesque ures and moody illustra- of such classics as Dante's Comedy," have been pre- to the M. H. de Young co bibliography.

n, a vice president of the rancisco Club, auxiliary of useum, donated the volumes h the club to the newly- d museum art library. The i- collection bears on exhibits museum and are available for se and research.

n's donation is expected to ate further contributions.

Doré items, it was an- ed yesterday, are "Histoire Sainte Russie," with 500 vings, one of Doré's earliest , published in 1854; "Two red Sketches," 1869; "The ry of Croquemitaine," with esigns on woods, 1871; "Ad- res of Baron Munchausen," 30 full page drawings, 1871, a volume of 100 Doré illus- s for "The Bible" and an of "Colla's Whispers," pub- in 1869, with illustrations by nd George Cruikshank, famed strator of many of Dickens' are included.

books were placed on the shelves, after ceremonies museum Colonial room, by Cecile Sorbier, president of lub, and Mrs. Vincent S. club treasurer.

ted to the books is the n's noted Doré bronze vase, a metal masterpiece.

eption to Mark den Anniversary

years of married life will be sted by Mr. and Mrs. John T. next Sunday at a reception r home, 1479 Twenty-seventh , from 2 to 5 p. m., with a dinner at the Hotel Can- to follow later.

s, who is 75, has been super- ent of buildings for the Board rks for 38 years. Mrs. Burns e were married in Denver and to San Francisco 47 years

The Bohemian Club's Art Shop Opens

The Bohemian Club's annual spring exhibition of paintings and sculpture by artist members opened in the club gallery yesterday and will continue until the end of the month.

Haig Patigan, the only sculptor with work in this year's show is rep- resented with four classically con- ceived and executed pieces, "The Earth Dormant," "Harvest," "Sun- shine" and "Rain," and with a larger group called "Creation."

Gleb A. Ilyin and Peter A. Ilyin, whose styles are remarkably simi- lar, have contributed a number of portraits notable for their almost photographic technical perfection. Arthur Cahill is showing his por- traits of Frank Van Sloun and Farnham Griffiths.

Two San Francisco architects, W. B. Faville and Harald Wagner, have water colors of Sierra and Monterey peninsula landscapes hung side by side, exhibiting the entirely different approach to the same subject achieved by different artists. Faville's style is in the con- ventional tradition, while Wagner's technique is faintly reminiscent of Japanese prints.

Some of the other Bohemians represented in the show with oils and water colors, mostly of Califor- nia scenes, include Dr. W. H. Streitmann, Lee Randoph, Francis Todhunter, Maurice Logan, Spencer Macky, G. Liljestrom, Douglass Fraser, William A. Gaw, Arthur Hill Gilbert, Percy Gray, Ferdinand Bergdorff, L. P. Latimer, Paul Daugherty and R. Jerome Jones.

ant Plays With Symphony Sunday

r Levant, wit and musical of radio's "Information will pound the ivory keys e San Francisco Symphony tra at a special "pop" con- the Memorial Opera House y evening at 8:30.

nt has chosen as his selec- George Gershwin's Concerto to be played with the orches- d "Rhapsody in Blue." The al master mind is a composer

of both light and serious music and the author of a best seller.

Other orchestral numbers listed by the orchestra under the direc- tion of Pierre Monteux are "Pre- lude to Die Meistersinger," Wagner; "Clouds" and Festivals," Debussy; "Pomp and Circumstance," Elgar; "Overture to Die Fledermaus," Strauss; "Waltzes from Rosenkava- lier," Richard Strauss; "Valse Triste," Sibelius, and "La Valse," Ravel.

Rossi Proclaims A 'Hobby Week'

"Hobby and Leisure Time Week," April 29 to May 5, inclusive, was an- nounced yesterday by Mayor Angelo J. Rossi and it will feature the sec- ond annual National Hobby Show, sponsored by the San Francisco Junior Chamber of Commerce, to be held at the Civic Auditorium, May 2 to 5 inclusive.

The four-day show will be open both afternoons and evenings.

Drama

C. Little Theater Stages ays by Saroyan, O'Neill

JOHN HOBART

iam Saroyan's play, "My s in the Highlands," the one so baffled and disturbed the York critics last spring, had t production hereabouts last end when the University of rnia Little Theater staged it eeler Auditorium.

n it was billed another play amous Bay Region resident— God's Chillun Got Wings," by e O'Neill of Contra Costa . The two plays, both un- ational in technique, provided usual and stimulating double ll the more interesting be- both, after their fashion, are s against the injustice of the as it is regulated today.

NTLE PROTEST

the Saroyan work protests with a kind of rueful smile. Ben Alexander, the best un- poet alive, and his small ohnny are dispossessed and th uncertainly on the high- the boy says "I'm not men- g any names, Pa, but some- wrong somewhere." That is as Saroyan cares to go in sing a concrete opinion.

God's Chillun," on the hand, was written in such se of anger that its mean- es straight to the spectator's

s a stinging rebuke, over- ing in its emotional impact. system that allows racial tice to warp human lives. is no room in O'Neill's smar- rid, as there is in Saroyan's r one, for the solace of or for the song that stirs

of character and its quiet mood of melancholy, like a musical ob- ligato in a minor key.

Edwin Duerr, in directing it at U. C., kept the unreal quality, bor- rowing a few ideas from "Our Town" (the knock on the non- existent door, the trumpet that was obviously being tooted offstage) and one or two scenic suggestions from the Russian expressionists. Some of the whimsy of the staging struck me as a little forced.

MIXTURE OF REALISM

Among the actors there were Wil- liam Fisher and 14-year-old Fred- erick Moreton, who made the re- lation between the poet and his son an ideally pleasant one (although Mr. Fisher should control that booming voice of his); John Bren- neis, wonderfully magisterial as the aged duffer; Seth Ulman, whose Mr. Kosak was too highbrow for a Fresno grocer, and Hugh Koford as Mr. Wiley, the genial mailman.

Mr. Duerr's approach to "All God's Chillun" was non-realistic in the first half, realistic in the second, and the shift in styles was not altogether satisfying.

But the play itself, one of O'Neill's mightiest, survived the eccentricities of staging and the mechanical mis- haps of the Friday night perform- ance.

POWERFUL PORTRAYAL

Thanks to Robert Nielsen's amaz- ingly powerful portrayal of the Negro, Jim Harris, and Jeanne Tay- lor's equally fine one as the white woman he married, "All God's Chillun" had the effect of a fire lit by indignation. Particularly in its final scenes, the play burned and blazed.

When white actors don blackface the danger is a minstrel-show look, but that danger was happily avoided at U. C. by Mr. Nielsen, who looked his part, and by the two actresses who played his sister and mother, Elizabeth Berryhill and Amelia Standke.

Today's 'Contemporary' Graphic

Graphic Artist Sargent Johnson's lithograph "Singing Saints," one of a series of contemporary graphic prints being presented to Western readers by The Chronicle, contains a true lyrical feeling for the tones of Negro voices. It is but one of many fine signed originals now made available to local collectors at moderate prices. The limited number of contemporary graphic originals which are available to the public at $2 each may be obtained at The Chronicle's first floor office, or from the City of Paris, O'Connor-Moffatt, Paul Elder, Schwabacher-Frey, or Gump stores. When ordering by mail, check or money order (not stamps or currency) should be enclosed.

'Pax Americana'

Lectures to End Tonight

Brothe Leo, famed writer and lec- turer, will conclude his series of Lenten lectures when he discusses "Pax Americana" at 8:15 o'clock tonight in Veterans' Auditorium.

The series has been sponsored by the St. Mary's College Guild in the interests of international, na- tional and personal peace. Proceeds are turned over to the Guild schol- arship fund.

The musical program will fea- ture the lyric-coloratura, Mrs. Norma Andreotti. Mrs. Andreotti attended Girls' High School and Dominican Convent. She recently returned from Europe, where she studied at the Salzburg Mozarteum, and at Milan, with the celebrated Maestro Vittorino Moratti.

Her program will include "My Lovely Celia," by Munro; "La Violette," by Scarlatti; "Una Voce Poca Fa," by Rossini. She will be accompanied in her rendition of "Ave Maria" by Eleanor Costello Schroth, harpist. Other accompani- ment will be by William Tyroler, of the San Francisco Opera Associ- ation.

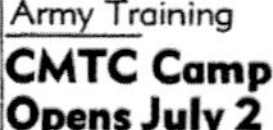

MRS. NORMA ANDREOTTI

Featured on peace program. (See story, Column 3.)

Angna Enters Will Give but One Performance in S. F.

A painter, author and playwright billed as "The One-Woman The- ater" will arrive here Thursday in the person of Angna Enters to en- tertain San Francisco theater-goers in a single matinee performance at the Curran Theater Sunday after- noon.

Hailed by the artistic world as one of the most striking figures on the American stage today, Miss Enters will present a new repertoire inspired by her paintings featured in exhibitions in New York. She is on the last leg of her annual trans- continental tour.

A $500,000 Fire

NEWARK, N. Y., March 17 (P)— destroyed the Jackson - Perkins Nursery Company plant tonight with loss estimated at $500,000.

Civic Club

Exposition Will Honor District Leaders at Di

By BILL SIMONS

THE DISTRICT ANGLE—Last year we had a great Exposition on Treasure Island. It deserved all the superlatives in Webster's. But speaking strictly from the district angle there was one phase that might have been improved—district participation. True, the districts went wild during Exposition open- ing week. And there were many civic club days on the island. But somehow the clubs seemed to feel they were a little left out of the picture.

The World's Fair this year, how- ever, is starting with the district angle very much in mind. The man- agement wants every district civic and merchant group in San Fran- cisco to feel the Exposition is theirs. To further this feeling of co- operation, Marshall Dill and the Exposition directors are arranging for a big dinner party, guests at which will be some 1000 civic lead- ers. The date: Next Monday, March 25.

Here are some of the details as announced by Major Oscar J. Keat- inge, in charge of special events:

The dinner will be in the Admin- istration building. Free parking space will be provided for guests coming by automobile. For those without cars, bus transportation has been arranged, also without cost.

One of the night's high spots will be reached when a citizens' com- mittee turns on the lights of Treas- ure Island for the first time this year. And there will be many other features for the Exposition's guests of the evening.

It will be, in short, a night ded- icated solely to the civic workers of San Francisco—a brilliant ges- ture of recognition and friend- ship by the Exposition to those people who work so consistently for this city's welfare.

CHINATOWN HOUSING—A note from Gordon Berendsen, president of Twenty-seventh District Munici- pal Council: "Our civic club joins the San Francisco Board of Super- visors and the San Francisco Junior Chamber of Commerce in unani- mously pledging ourselves to sup- port the Chinatown low-cost hous- ing project."

Well, that makes it unanimous all around. Not one single civic club has opposed this project. It is one project whose successful completion tickles us enormously. One of our most pleasant experi- ences last year was working with the Junior Chamber and the Chi- nese Senior and Junior Chambers on it.

Happy indeed about the whole thing is Mark Daniels Jr. who headed the Junior Chamber com- mittee that started the campaign for Chinatown housing. He deserves a great deal of credit for his un- selfish work, as do all the other men and women who gave so generously of their time and energy.

NEIGHBORHOOD—Drop around to North Beach Annex at 555 Chest- nut any time this week between noon and 6 o'clock and see boccie ball played as only North Beach knows how . . . That reminds us: We have a game coming up with you, Sieve Bertone; be- tween Dick Gorman, too . . . Wonder how Joe Arata is at rolling the ball. Joe (full name: Joseph V. Arata, assist- ant manager of Columbus branch Bank of America) is president of the Salesian Oldtimers . . . He's a good-natured fellow, one of the best liked in North Beach . . . Say, we are sorry about a slipup in this column last Friday. Credit for last year's membership drive of Ingle- side Terraces Homes Association was given to George Bevan, chair- man of the committee this year. . . Well, it should have gone to Lionel Moriarty, who worked hard and successfully as chairman of the 1939 committee. To him: We're very sorry for the error.

Ah, here's the list of new direct- ors of North Beach Merchants As- sociation: J. B. Accampo, A. Bero- nio, Ray Bianchi, E. A. Bonzani, Pete Leveroni, Felix Nebbia, William J. Paganini, S. Portos, ill Raffetto, T. Ravazzini, Louis Rocca, Vic Sbra- gia, Dismo Scatena, L. Segale, Har- old Tosetti . . . Tosetti is the one with all the sons . . . Lots of luck to Frank and Reno who last week opened the Silver Bowl and are at Hunters Point. They come from Joe DiMaggio's . . . And welcome, John

Army Training

CMTC Camp Opens July 2

Special to The Chronicle

PRESIDIO OF MONTEREY, March 18—Colonel Homer M. Gron- inger, camp commander of the Eleventh Cavalry, today announced that the Citizens' Military Training Camp will be held here from July 2 to July 31.

Stressing the importance of early enrollment, Groninger said, "the tentative quota for the Presidio has been set at 1145 men, not including regular and reserve officers.

"The Presidio here is the largest Citizens' Military Training Camp west of the Mississippi river."

Young men between the ages of 17 and 24, who are accepted by their local M.T.C.A. commissioners, as well as former candidates, may join the camp. Transportation, food and clothing expenses will be paid by the Government.

Sport Pageant Luncheon The

"A Pageant of Spor theme of the Down tion luncheon, with commentator, Thursd in the Hotel St. Fran

Sports of the San Area will be symbol ness, and what it Francisco in financia be discussed.

And yet the article did not make any mention of Johnson himself being of African descent and raised the issue of race only at the point where the content of the print is reviewed, referring to "Negro voices."[2] The voices may well have belonged to Negroes, but what were they singing? And why were they dressed so outlandishly, in flowing robes, ruffles, a rakish hat, and such? Despite its serviceable overview of Johnson's professional career, the *Chronicle* offered no consideration of the source material for the print or of Johnson's motives for imaging such a scene. The editors simply offered the stereotyped musicality of African Americans as explanation enough and presented the work as the product of an artist who had become known for his sympathetic images of African Americans and his positivist racial ideology. In so doing, they failed to mention the most likely inspiration or source for Johnson's composition: the 1934 opera *Four Saints in Three Acts*.[3]

A landmark of modernism, *Four Saints in Three Acts* featured a libretto by Gertrude Stein (1874–1946) and a score by Virgil Thomson (1896–1989). It is "both an opera and a choreographic spectacle," explained Maurice Grosser in the official scenario for the piece that was published in 1949.[4]

It is an elaborate fantasy of saintly life centering on the sixteenth-century Spanish Saint Teresa.[5] In the first act she enacts imaginary scenes from her own life: each scene is told through the mechanism of a tableau in which a second Saint Teresa performs. The second act revolves around saintly activities at a garden party in Barcelona at which the saints dance, play games, make toasts, and take turns regarding the "Heavenly Mansion" through a telescope. The third act is set in the garden of a monastery where Saint Ignatius discusses monastic life, describes his own vision of the Holy Ghost, and predicts the Last Judgment. Act 4 concludes with all the saints in heaven, singing happily of their previous lives on earth. The opera ends with the singing of "When this you see remember me." "One should not try to interpret too literally the words of this opera, nor should one fall into the opposite error of thinking that they mean nothing at all," warned Grosser. "On the contrary, they mean many things at once."[6]

Four Saints in Three Acts had its first public performance, an "audition rehearsal," at Saint Philip's Protestant Episcopal Church in Harlem on February 1, and its premiere at the Wadsworth Atheneum in Hartford, Connecticut, on February 7, 1934.[7] It opened on Broadway several weeks later, where it

6.2 "Today's Contemporary Graphic," *San Francisco Chronicle,* March 18, 1940

was performed at the Forty-Fourth Street Theatre, from February 20 through March 17, and at the Empire Theatre, from April 2 through 14, for a total of forty-eight performances.[8] The production was much lauded, and theater aficionados and the culturally aware public—even those who had not seen the production in person—soon knew of the opera for the stunning freshness of its evocative, abstruse lyrics by Stein. Those who could already quote "Rose is a rose is a rose" could now add to their repertoire such Steinian phrases as "To know to know to love her so" and "Pigeons on the grass alas," two lines from the opera's libretto. *Four Saints* was also celebrated for what was seen as the unique "Americanness" of Thomson's score. [9]

Another fact made *Four Saints* a pivotal and uniquely American modernist project: its cast was entirely Black, made up of both professional opera singers—including tenor Edward Matthews in the role of Saint Ignatius and soprano Beatrice Robinson-Wayne in the role of Saint Teresa of Avila I—and church choir members. While the cast was Black and Eva Jessye coached the choir, making her the first African American to serve as a choral director for a Broadway show, the original production company was mostly staffed by white professionals: it was directed by John Houseman; the sets, which included swags and curtains of cellophane, and the costumes, made from gauzy lace, satin, and taffeta, were designed by the painter Florine Stettheimer; and Frederick Ashton created the choreography.

Four Saints in Three Acts arrived during a period of American cultural history when opportunities for African Americans in the visual and performing arts were limited and circumscribed by race prejudice. As such, the success of the opera was an important beacon of hope for creative Black folks throughout the country, and the Black periodicals of the day took notice. News of *Four Saints* was first reported before the production opened by an African American newspaper, the *New York Amsterdam News*, and subsequently traveled swiftly through the African American community of New York and beyond, continuing long after its closing performance.[10] Between its casting in December 1933 and its New York closing in April 1934, *Four Saints* received more than a dozen mentions in the *New York Amsterdam News*, the *Pittsburgh Courier*, the *Afro-American*, and the *Chicago Defender*, all popular, race-focused papers that reached most of literate Black America during this period.[11]

The popular magazine *Crisis*, founded in 1910 by W. E. B. Du Bois as the official organ of the NAACP, carried several articles by managing editor George W. Streator that focused on the success of *Four Saints*. In his commentary Streator expressed mixed emotions about composer Virgil Thomson's public explanations for choosing an "all-colored" cast:

Thomson has concocted a strange mixture of sacred and vulgar sequences. At times one feels "churchy," and at times one wants to guffaw. But at no time is one quite certain what it is all about. The composer has said again and again that this is why he wanted a colored cast. "They would not worry about the sense of words." Some critics declare that this is no great reason, citing that many an opera star from the hinterland has sung in Italian, German, and French without troubling with the words. The same might be said for the audience.... But most people who attend "4 Saints in 3 Acts" leave the theatre looking quite serious. There must be something in it.[12]

White-owned newspapers also took note, seeing *Four Saints* as a cause célèbre, especially insofar as the notorious librettist Stein was concerned. In November 1934 Stein and her partner, Alice B. Toklas (1877–1967), arrived in New York City from Paris to promote the opera. Over the next few weeks, Stein proceeded to give several lectures on the opera at different venues, including a musicale and luncheon at the Ritz Tower Hotel for "the benefit of the New York American Christian and Relief Fund." At this event the *New York Times* reported that "Miss Stein said St. Therese and St. Ignatius were her 'favorite saints, almost my only favorites.' As a part of the event at the Ritz Tower Hotel, [Virgil] Thomson himself accompanied the two starring 'saints' of the show, Edward Matthews, the Fisk-trained baritone who had portrayed St. Ignatius, and Beatrice Robinson-Wayne, who had portrayed St. Theresa, as they sang selections from *Four Saints* for the assembled guests."[13]

We do not know whether Johnson saw the original production of *Four Saints*, though it is possible: the New York run coincided with a period when he was participating in juried traveling exhibitions of African American art mounted by the Harmon Foundation. In fact, on May 1, 1934—just two weeks following the close of *Four Saints*' initial run—Johnson's work appeared in a group show at the New School in Manhattan that was co-organized by the Harmon Foundation and the College Art Association.[14] Even if he did not see the opera performed, it would have been hard for a person as culturally attuned as Johnson to ignore the swirl of excitement that accompanied *Four Saints* in both the Black and white press in 1934—or in April 1935, when Stein herself made front-page news by visiting San Francisco for a round of lectures over a two-week period. While there is little chance Johnson would have seen Stein speak at the all-white Women's City Club on April 11 and 12, he would have known of her arrival in the city through the extensive coverage it received in the region's newspapers.[15]

Regardless of how he learned about Stein's opera, *Four Saints in Three Acts* inspired Johnson's print *Singing Saints*. The artist would certainly have been attracted by an opera that foregrounded Black performance in a positive and uplifting—if not unproblematic—way. What's more, the involvement of Gertrude Stein—an orphan, a child of the Bay Area, an arch-modernist sympathetic to the Black experience, and an artist born outside the faith who was fascinated by Catholicism—may have given the work special resonance for Johnson.

It was in San Francisco that the German-Jewish-American Stein, who attended the First Hebrew Congregation of Oakland's Sabbath School throughout her childhood, first became fascinated with Catholicism. In an article about her promotional tour for *Four Saints*, Stein told the *New York Times* that she read Saint Ignatius after many hours in contemplation at the Roman Catholic Church of Saint Ignatius in San Francisco.[16] What she did not say was that she spent time at Saint Ignatius following the deaths of her mother in 1888 and her father in 1891, when the teenaged Stein left her former home in Oakland and went to live in the care of her older brother Michael in San Francisco.[17] Originally built in 1880, Saint Ignatius Church was a massive structure that stood at the corner of Hayes and Van Ness Streets.[18] It was a most impressive church built by the Jesuits, second only in historic importance within the city to the Spanish Franciscan Mission Dolores. Its elaborate interior must have held an allure for the young woman living only a few blocks away at 1118 O'Farrell Street. Perhaps the orphaned Stein found comfort in the towering columns of the church's nave or in Saint Ignatius's never-ending mission to bring the unsaved to Christ. Saint Ignatius was destroyed in the 1906 earthquake and fire, but it was later rebuilt a few miles from the original site. In 1915, when Sargent Johnson arrived in San Francisco, the new Church of Saint Ignatius had only just reopened its doors. As it was for Stein, it may have been for him too—a welcoming space in which to reflect and find solace.

Stein's effort to reconcile the profound differences between the faith of her birth and Catholicism began in San Francisco and was furthered during her undergraduate studies at Radcliffe College from 1893 to 1897, where she first formally learned about the history and beliefs of Catholicism.[19] After moving to France in 1903, she quickly became enamored of what she saw as that country's uniquely intellectual practice of Catholicism and came to see the expressive relationship between liturgy and poetry. In his definitive book on the opera *Four Saints in Three Acts*, cultural historian Steven Watson attributes the Spanish-Catholic theme of the opera to a memorable 1912 tour of Spain during which Stein and Toklas were enraptured by a chapel in the Church of Saint Teresa in Avila that was "covered in beaten gold and ornamented in coral."[20] Watson argues that the ecstatic Saint Teresa, whose own father had converted from

Judaism to Christianity, became for Stein and Toklas "the mystic bride of Jesus transformed into the bride of art."[21] Stein saw Catholicism, with its elaborately decorated cathedrals, ceremonial processions, rich costumes, and liturgy, as an art form all its own.[22] Similarly, she saw the artist as a kind of saint—a pure and devout person who was dedicated to art rather than to the church.[23] In an interview with the *New York Times*, Stein recommended "the meditations of St. Therese whose mysticism was 'real and practical.'"[24] Stein regarded creative genius as a secular way of being pure and devout to one's own project and having faith in the importance of one's creativity and artistic ability.

Although she generally told people who asked that she was not interested in religion itself, the linguistic possibilities that liturgy afforded her are apparent.[25] She exploited these parallels by playing off binary oppositions within language—using, for example, *this* and *that* over and over in the libretto for *Four Saints* and revealing the arbitrariness of distinctions between binaries.[26] By having Saint Teresa in the opera sing "Can women have wishes?" she was alluding to her own questions: Can women write? Can women aspire to public recognition?[27] In this way, using Saint Teresa as a surrogate for both herself and Toklas, Stein came to align spiritual energy and creative power as comparable acts of faith.[28] Theater critic Bonnie Marranca observes:

> A saint's life is quite like a writer's life, based as it is on the Word, revelation. . . . [A] writer-saint's life, St. Teresa's is naturally a performance because it is given to self-dramatization. . . . For Stein, the life of a convent is the life of a landscape, nuns busily moving about but the scene remaining placid as a landscape, simply there. Still life. The walled-in cloister is a natural frame. . . . Stein was able to experience the world as miraculous through the writing of her opera. . . . [F]or a time she became St. Gertrude in ecstasy.[29]

Stein's proposal, through the opera, that sainthood and artistry were comparable acts of faith—that theater was the creation of experience through word constructions that were repeated and then broken down into component parts, just as cubist painters had broken down vision—may have been highly appealing to Johnson.[30] But the question of the unusual Catholic theme, which served to secularize the spiritual by aligning spiritual energy and creative power as mutually constitutive acts of faith—a truly modern notion—might have especially appealed to Johnson, as it had to Stein, for both of them were orphans who, in the absence of their own mothers, found special comfort in the bosom of the Catholic church.[31]

In addition to being active in the visual arts community, Johnson was also interested in poetry. The poet in Johnson may have been drawn to Stein's modern verse and her innovative libretto, while the racially conscious part of his psyche was surely intrigued by the presence of the Black performers in *Four Saints*. Perhaps he knew or intuited that the two strands were tightly wound together in Stein's artistry. In his discussion of the story "Melanctha," one of three pieces that made up Stein's first published work, *Three Lives* (1909), literary historian Werner Sollors argues that Stein saw her brand of modernism as linked with her exploration of the Black experience in her writing. This first revolutionary work of Stein's came when she addressed the experiences of Black life that she encountered while assisting with births in Baltimore's Black community during her years as a medical student at Johns Hopkins. "Stein's merging of modernist style and ethnic subject matter was what made her writing particularly relevant to American ethnic authors who had specific reasons to go beyond realism and who felt that Stein's dismantling of the 'old' was a freeing experience."[32] For many contemporary readers, Stein's modernism lay in her articulation of Black experience in "Melanctha" and her use of repetition to create meaning. Throughout the story Stein repeats the phrases "warm broad glow" of "negro sunshine," instilling in the reader a numb acceptance of the ubiquitous trope of the mask historically adopted by African Americans to preserve the amicable tenor of their unequal interactions with whites as well as an abraded realization of the power fantasy that the white myth of "negro sunshine" enacts. Virgil Thomson may have seen Black folks as so simple that they would not be worried about the associative meanings of the words coming out of their own mouths, but Stein purported to have a more nuanced view of what it was to be Black in America.

At first glance the composition of Johnson's *Singing Saints* (figure 6.5) appears to radiate all that Stein found in the "warm broad glow" of "negro sunshine." In so doing, it would appear to fall in line with standard, stereotypical visual tropes of African American musical creativity. "Sargent Johnson has lithographed a true lyrical feeling of the full tones of Negro voices and accomplished it with a simple sincerity of line and tone," observed the editors of the *San Francisco Chronicle*. "Even the shape of the guitar has been developed to create the feeling of stringed music."[33] This stereotype may have been reinforced by Johnson's presentation of the two saints in choir robes, the saint with the guitar being most easily associated with Saint Ignatius, who plays one in the first act of the opera. "In the original production by Florine Stettheimer, the Compère and Commère, who represent the laity, were dressed in modern style," explains Grosser. "The two Saint Teresas were costumed in as cardinals. Saint Chavez, Saint Ignatius, Saint Settlement, and the members of the small chorus wore robes recalling those of saints in Baroque Art. The large chorus was dressed in monastic robes and surplices."[34] In Johnson's print these very specific costumes have been abstracted to a level where it is hard to tell which individual saints might be represented.

For the white editors of the *Chronicle*, Johnson's *Singing Saints* would have joined the vast visual archive of images of Black people making music for imaginary white audiences that had become commonplace from the nineteenth century forward. This type of image is perhaps best exemplified by William Sidney Mount's 1856 painting *The Banjo Player* (figure 6.3). The painting shows a handsome young African American man, nattily dressed, his lips parted, teeth gleaming, as he plays his instrument. Background imagery has been kept to a minimum: the musician sits in a nondescript space that might be a tavern or some other public gathering place. If his physical location is unclear, his temporal location is decidedly specific, as he is dressed in 1850s clothing. Unlike this antebellum entertainer, the saints of Sargent Johnson are placed in their own floating world—like those of Thomson and Stein, frolicking in Stettheimer's taffeta choir gowns amid cellophane sets—and are somehow free from the temporal specificity and social restrictions of the culture of American minstrelsy that echoes in the company of Mount's images. Mount's banjo player exists to entertain an unseen audience, which he acknowledges in his sidelong glance to the left as he picks out his tune. Johnson's saints sing for other ears—those of God, the Madonna, and Christ—and their closed eyes deny us the pleasure of easy access to their inner, sacred world. The evanescent blankness of the background reveals Johnson's saints to be sharing a transcendental space: a heaven in which their beatified souls converse freely, rather than singing for the coin that will surely compensate Mount's subject.

Unlike Mount's painting, Henry Ossawa Tanner's 1893 painting *The Banjo Lesson* (figure 6.4) has traditionally been interpreted as an image about African American familial relationships and efforts at cultural continuity. Within a specific space of humble domesticity, an older man instructs a young boy on the banjo, imparting knowledge from one generation to the next. In this interpretation Black musicianship is presented as a learned skill rather than something that is innate within Black people, as the *Chronicle*'s comment on the "full tones of Negro voices" would imply. Johnson's *Saints* are different from Tanner's musicians in that they do not enact a transfer of what Pierre Bourdieu called "cultural capital," in which the accumulation of certain valued aspects of social knowledge serves to advance an individual's progress within society.[35] Although they sing together—a musical activity that has frequently been associated with ideas of Blackness through the work-song tradition of the fields and that of the Negro spiritual or gospel tradition—they

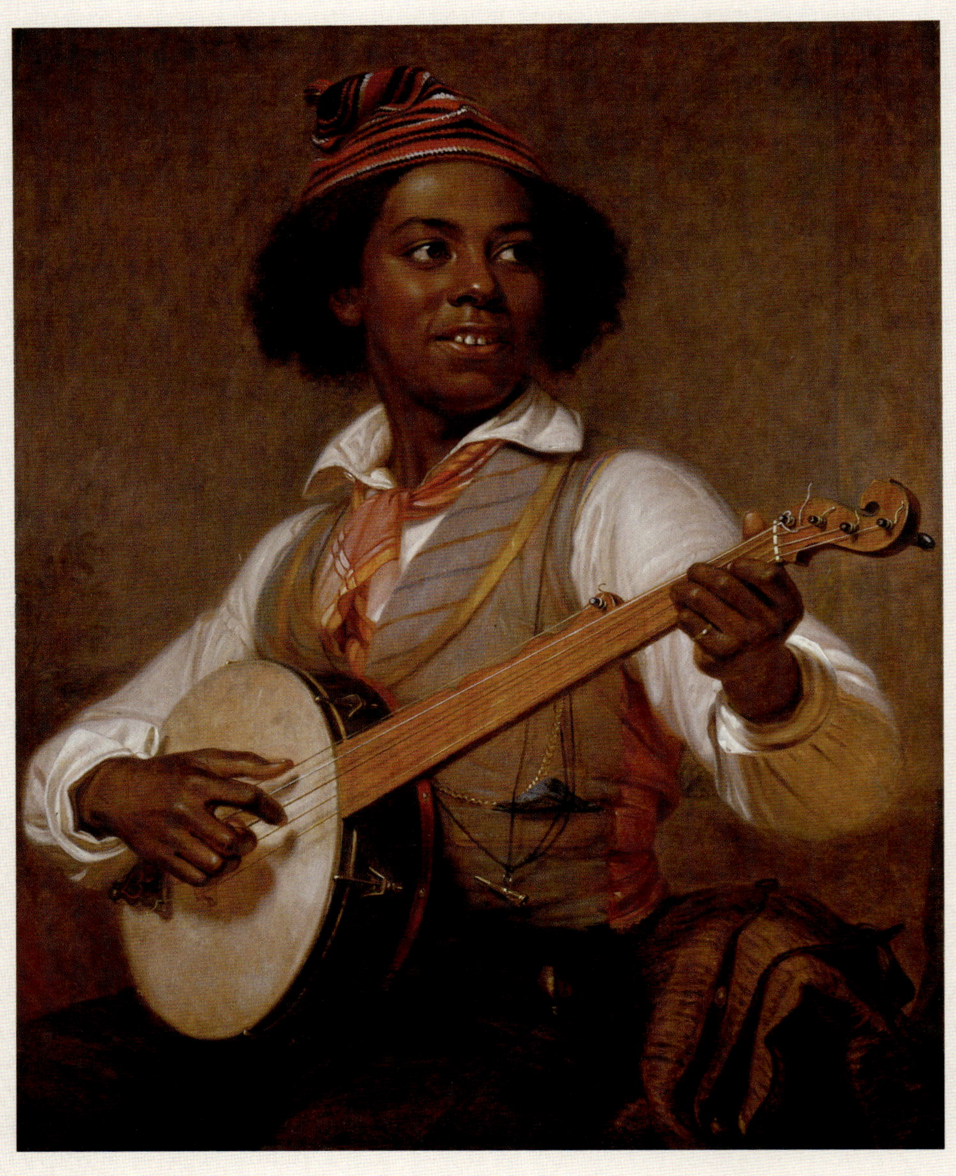

6.3 William Sidney Mount, *The Banjo Player*, 1856.
Long Island Museum of American Art, History,
and Carriages, Stony Brook, New York

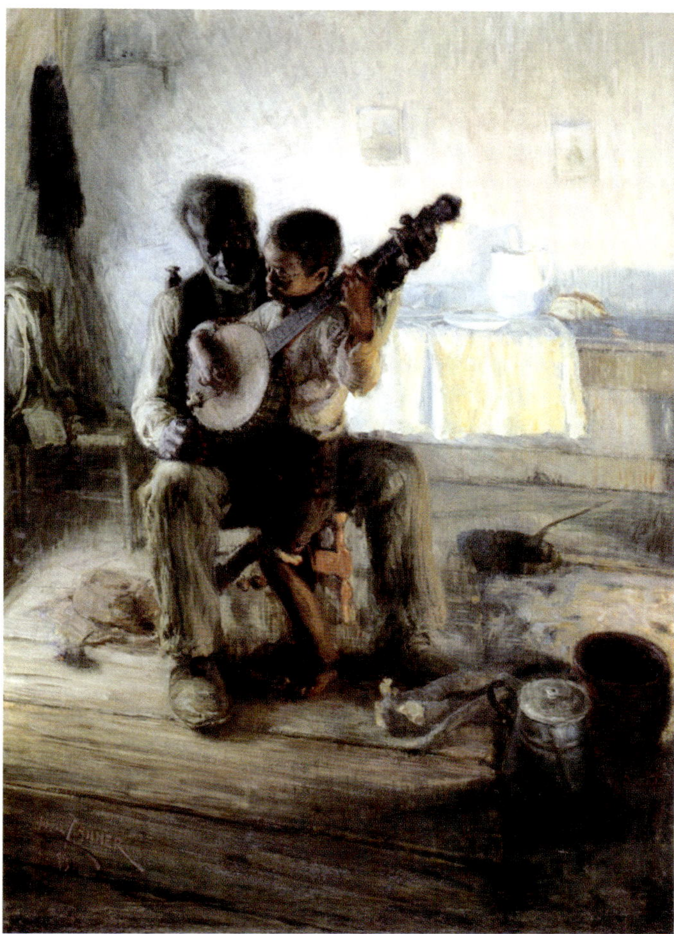

perform to the accompaniment of an instrument that holds little association with common ideas of Black people's musicality: the guitar.

Like the banjo, the guitar has roots in West African stringed instruments, but unlike the banjo, which developed under enslavement in the New World, the guitar was not generally associated with African American performance in the late 1930s when Johnson was beginning to compose *Singing Saints*. Thomas Jefferson wrote in his *Notes on the State of Virginia*, "The instrument proper to [enslaved people] is the Banjar, which they brought hither from Africa, and which is the original of the guitar, its chords being precisely the four lower chords of the guitar."[36] Throughout the nineteenth century, racist representations of Black men with banjos, based on the appearance of white performers in blackface, proliferated throughout American visual culture. Similarly, in Thomas Dixon's 1905 novel *The Clansman*, the source for D. W. Griffith's racist film *Birth of a Nation* a decade later, the banjo is also tied to Southern enslavement and sinister Blackness.[37] For Jefferson, the guitar was a more evolved form of the banjo—which it may in fact be, as the classical guitar has roots in the Moorish ouds that were brought to Spain in the twelfth century. Despite the probable African roots of the guitar, it is not an instrument that is commonly associated with Black subjects.

While the banjo has a prominent place in American visual, historical, and literary culture, the guitar has rarely appeared in painting beyond cowboy campfire scenes and the occasional gypsy-wanderer images. In the history of European art, the guitar was similarly rare, appearing infrequently in the work of Nicolas Poussin, Jean-Baptiste Greuze, and Johannes Vermeer.[38] In the late nineteenth century, it began to make its way into the work of Edgar Degas, Pierre-Auguste Renoir, and Édouard Manet.[39] The next generation of modernists continued to be enamored of guitars, and many appear in the work of Pablo Picasso, Joan Miró, and Juan Gris, perhaps because these men were of Spanish origin or perhaps because it was seen as an instrument of the folk rather than the elite.[40] In the American popular culture of the 1930s, the guitar was associated with both the folk and the avant-garde. This was the period when Delta blues artists such as Robert Johnson and Son House peaked in popularity. It was also the moment when Sargent Johnson began to learn the guitar himself, building on musical training he had received as a youth at the Brightside Orphanage in western Massachusetts, where his uncle sent him to live after the death of his parents.[41] That Johnson himself was a guitar player is significant, for it may have drawn him to the figure of Saint Ignatius, the guitar-playing character in *Four Saints in Three Acts*. Its inclusion in *Singing Saints* may have been partly autobiographical.[42]

How Sargent Johnson first became aware of *Four Saints* is unknown, but it is plausible that in this modernist performance spectacle he found a topic that spoke to him on many levels—social, political, artistic, and spiritual. He and Gertrude Stein were motherless moderns, each having been orphaned during adolescence, each seeking comfort in reimagining the decidedly anti-modern source material of Catholic saints, each recognizing African American people and culture as potentially modern vehicles for their creative projects. The beatified Black characters of Stein's opera offered a kind of spiritual and perhaps even maternal comfort to Johnson.

Late in his life Johnson returned to the subject matter of *Singing Saints*, making a brightly colored enamel plaque of the subject. The shapes visible in

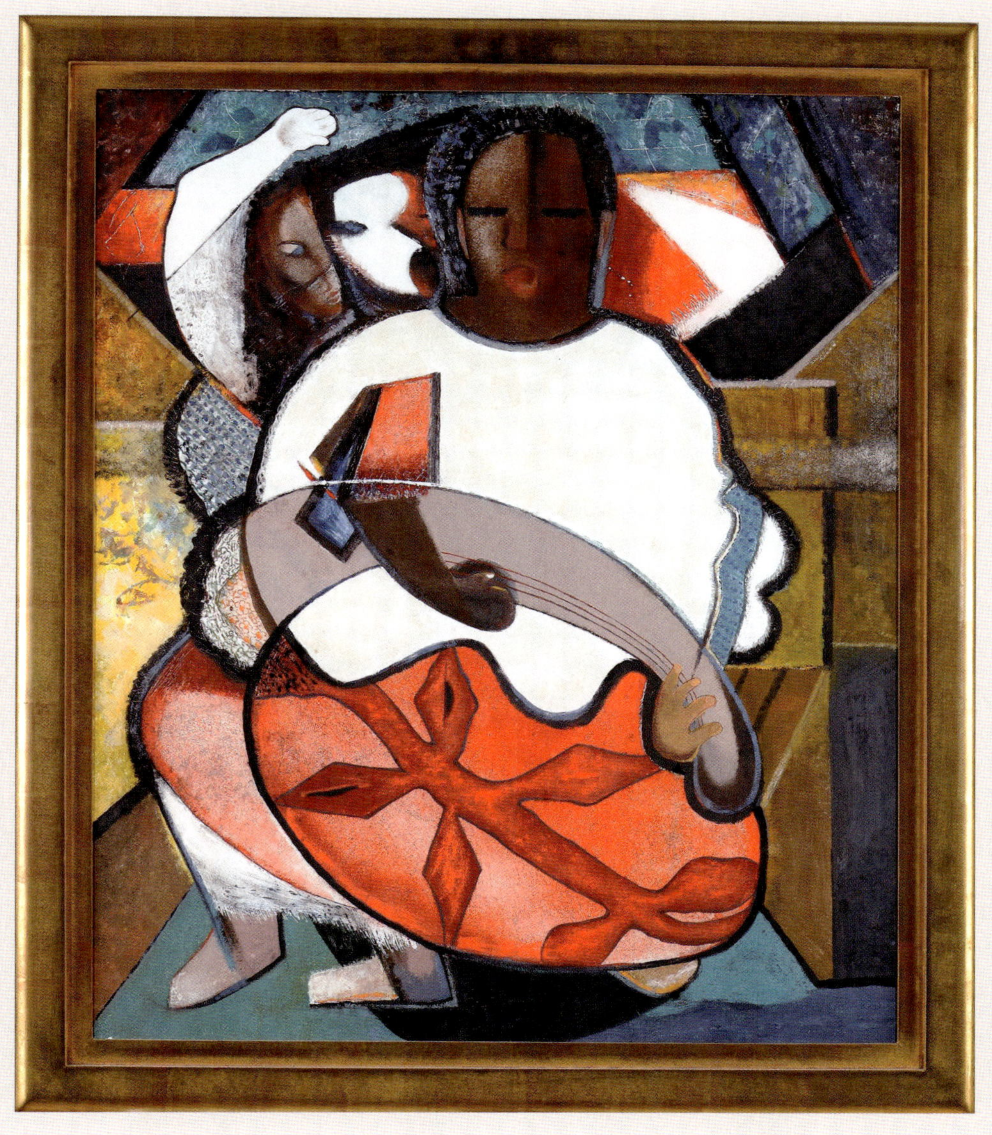

6.5 Sargent Johnson, *Singing Saints*, 1966–67. Private collection

the plaque recall the saints of the 1940 print, but they have been transformed into color and fractured into an even more prismatic composition. The saints of Johnson's old age have become further abstracted. Rather than the two distinct figures visible in the 1940 print, there appears to be only one coherent form in the 1966–67 work—a form ghosted by the bits and pieces of other bodies that float in its orbit across the recesses of the enamel's picture plane. In the later work, only the figure of the guitar-playing saint remains clear, the neck of the instrument drooping downward as it did in the 1940 lithograph, while the figure's skirt has become distinctly ovoid, shot through with a vein of red pigment that branches out organically across its surface. To the left of the figure's head, in the space where the face of the second saint had once been, we now find masklike forms—one white and red, the other brown— surrounding the figure, perched behind it, silently waiting. The figure of the remaining saint has been fragmented into discordant parts, its feet now a light pink, one hand brown, the other yellow.

The modern saints of Stein and Thomson's opera had significant resonance for Sargent Johnson, and the images that it prompted in his creative mind were lasting and important. Yet the visual world of *Singing Saints* was not inspired solely by *Four Saints*. Johnson's mature visual language is the product of an African American artist at the height of his powers during the era of the Harlem Renaissance and the Federal Art Project, yet it is also connected to his upbringing by Catholic nuns after the deaths of his parents in the 1890s. In this way, *Singing Saints* and other spiritually directed works of art that Johnson created may be interpreted as emblematic of a strongly rooted aesthetic that explored the possibilities of Black beatification in different and often surprisingly direct ways.

It was Sargent Johnson's desire to fuse his creative interest in the avant-garde world of both visual and performing arts with a culturally relevant African American past that undoubtedly drew him to Stein and Thomson's opera. In *Four Saints* he found a stunningly modern spectacle that depended on a new way of viewing African American spirituality and musicality. It would have resonated with his own Catholic upbringing, his musicianship, and his growing self-conception as an artist. In this way Johnson sought to remember spiritual belief and aesthetic aspiration into an artistic practice, a new kind of ethnic modernism that he recognized in Stein's opera.

7

NORMAN LEWIS'S
DAN MASK

THE CHALLENGE OF THE
AFRICAN "THING" IN THE 1930S

In the spring of 1935, Norman Lewis (1909–79) made *Dan Mask* (figure 7.1), an arresting pastel drawing inspired directly by a carving from the Ivory Coast that he had seen in the exhibition *African Negro Art* at the Museum of Modern Art (MoMA).[1] Set against the creamy white background of the sandpaper support, the strong, sculptural features of a carved wood mask stand out in brown, violet, and reddish tones set off by carefully placed white highlights, emphasizing the hand-polished surface of the original object. By choosing a three-quarter view from the lower right, Lewis has captured much of the phenomenological power of the original: its bold, abstract replication of human features and mysterious blankness. Lewis has noted all of the mask's key formal elements: from the high-contrast of the bulbous forehead, thinly cut eyeholes, sharp cheekbones, down-turned mouth, and firm chin, to the evenly placed holes that dot the mask's perimeter, indexes of the now-vanished raffia that would have streamed about the wearer as the piece was once danced in its original Ivory Coast context, before it became a thing hung on the wall of a museum in New York City.

The exhibition in which Lewis saw the original mask, *African Negro Art*, was organized by the MOMA's director, Alfred Barr, and its newest curator,

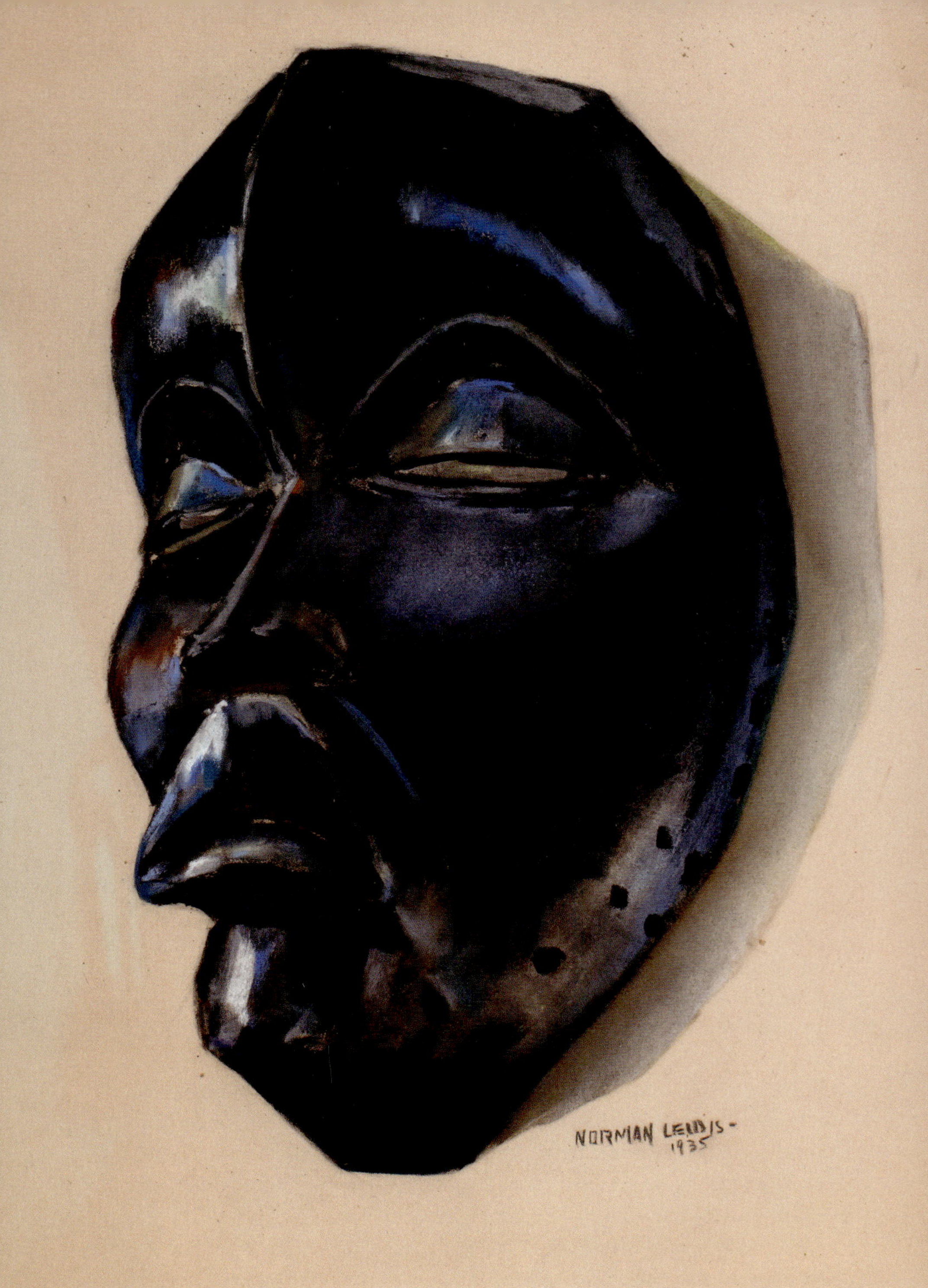

NORMAN LEWIS -
1935

James Johnson Sweeney. It was assembled from works in private European and American collections, including those of Walter Arensberg, Daniel Kahnweiler, and Arthur B. Springarn; state collections in Germany, France, Switzerland, and England; and the holdings of the museum of the University of Pennsylvania in Philadelphia. "The art of the primitive negro in its mastery of aesthetic forms, sensitiveness to materials, freedom from naturalistic imitation and boldness of imagination parallels many of the ideals of modern art," stated Sweeney in the museum's press release.[2] With 603 objects on display, the exhibition was the largest show of its kind since the landmark 1923 exhibition *Primitive Negro Art, Chiefly from the Belgian Congo*, which was held across the East River at the Brooklyn Museum. A handful of much smaller gallery shows had also been organized in New York City during the 1910s and 1920s by Marius de Zayas, Alfred Stieglitz, and others.[3] As art historian Virginia-Lee Webb has noted, "The purpose of the exhibition was to present the [African] sculptures for their formal, artistic, and abstract qualities, not as ethnographic specimens, as was the typical presentation of the time."[4] The photographs taken of the original MoMA installation (the exhibition traveled the country) reveal a now-typical modernist arrangement of works set within an ornament-free, white-walled set of galleries. One photograph shows a grouping of four masks and four pieces of Bakuba raffia cloth hung on the wall like abstract paintings, each one given its own space (figure 7.2). It is a far remove from contemporaneous natural history museum installations of African materials, and an even further one from the original context on the African continent.

At Sweeney's request, 477 of the objects in the *African Negro Art* exhibition were captured in photographs by Walker Evans. Composed as individual close-ups, like headshots for would-be movie stars, the prints were bound together in seventeen elegant portfolios. *Mask, Ivory Coast*, the photograph that Evans made of the same object that Lewis rendered in his *Dan Mask* drawing, shows the object in question from the front, evenly lit, and closely cropped against a plain background. As a part of a larger photographic project, one plate in a portfolio of hundreds, Evans's image of the Dan mask from Ivory Coast is placed within a disparate constellation of other objects that are linked not by the specific identity of their creators, or even the purpose of their creation, but by their shared continent of origin, highly refined aesthetics, and the imprimatur of their collectors.

7.1 Norman Lewis, *Dan Mask*, 1935. Courtesy of Michael Rosenfeld Gallery, New York. © Estate of Norman Lewis

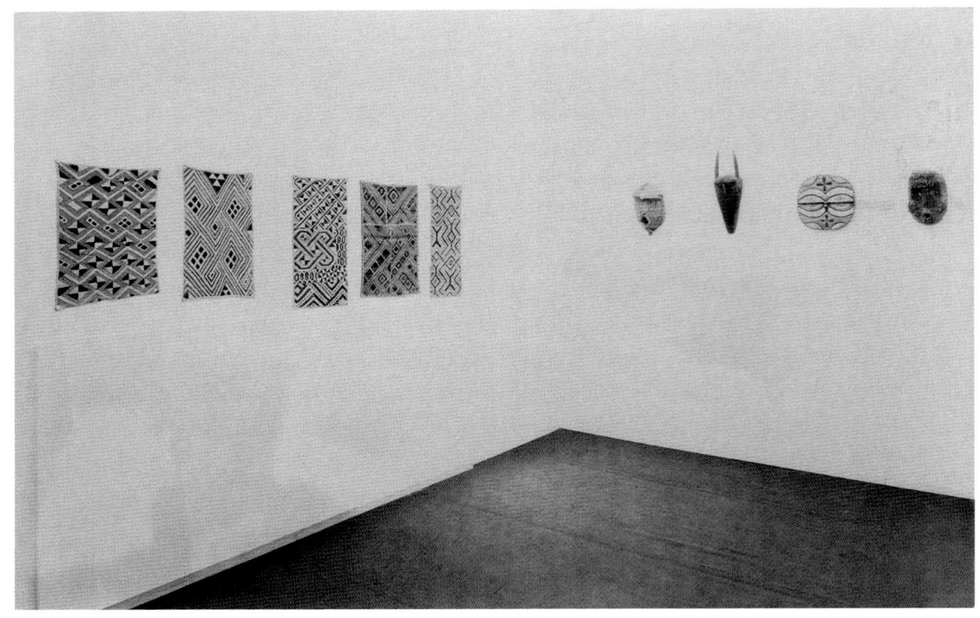

7.2 Installation view of the exhibition *African Negro Art*, Museum of
Modern Art, New York, March 18–May 19, 1935. Photograph by Soichi
Sunami. Museum of Modern Art Archives. © Museum of Modern Art /
Licensed by SCALA / Art Resource, New York

The strong sculptural qualities of the Dan mask that are evident in Lewis's drawing, the sharp undulations of the abstracted facial features, are deemphasized in Evans's photographic representation. Rather than presenting the mask in a way that focuses on its three-dimensional, sculptural qualities, as Lewis had done by rendering it in three-quarter view from below, Evans presents it to the viewer head-on and from above, highlighting the symmetrical formalism of the object. Evans's composition flattens the mask so that the elegant formal patterning and overall linear motif become the focus of the photograph.

For Evans, Sweeney, and Barr, the project of mounting and documenting the *African Negro Art* exhibition helped to announce the white American institutionalization of the international avant-garde's fascination with and aesthetic investment in what was then called "primitive" art (a term that included Native or Indigenous art forms from around the world, including objects from sub-Saharan Africa, Oceania, and Native North America). Evidence of this newly institutionalized interest in the use of "primitive" artistic aesthetics within the European and European American fine art and design world is found in the rapid consumption of the portfolios by numerous mainstream institutions in the United States and abroad, including the Victoria and Albert Museum in London, which purchased (for $50) and accessioned into their collection one of the seventeen portfolios in 1936, less than a year after it was produced.[5]

The potential role of "primitive" art, and African art and aesthetics, within contemporary artistic practice was also of concern to American artists of African descent working at the time. During the interwar period of the 1920s and 1930s, the question of what might constitute "New Negro" art in a modern context was at the forefront of the movement that is often referred to as the Harlem Renaissance. The philosopher Alain Locke, the poet Langston Hughes, and numerous visual artists in these intellectual circles, including Loïs Mailou Jones, Palmer Hayden, and Aaron Douglas, explored the potential of incorporating African art and African American folk traditions into their thinking and their work.[6] For example, between 1926 and 1936, the West Coast sculptor Sargent Johnson made a series of African-inspired copper masks (see figure 7.3), which were based on pieces in the collection of the Barnes Foundation that he may have seen in reproductions featured in Locke's 1925 anthology *The New Negro*.[7]

In Johnson's response to the challenge of adapting African aesthetics and formal qualities to modernist artistic projects, the artist retained many formal elements and motifs of the works that he encountered, such as the highly polished wood of African carvings, while also reimagining them through different media like copper.

In his direct engagement with the objects in the MoMA exhibition, Norman Lewis, barely in his mid-twenties, met his older colleague Johnson at the center of the artistic challenge that African art presented to socially and racially conscious African American artists of the period. In *Dan Mask* we see both an illustrator's and a documentarian's engagement with his subject. We might conjecture that as he positioned himself in the galleries of the museum and prepared to sketch the mask, he was careful to choose a vantage point that would provide the best view of the object as a three-dimensional object. Lewis's clarity of vision is remarkable: within the sculptural strokes and smudges of light and dark pastel, the represented mask seems to push its way up from the paper's rough, sand-covered surface.

In 1935, when *Dan Mask* was made, Lewis's career was just beginning to take off: he was coming to the end of two years of art classes at Columbia University and study with the painter Raphael Soyer at the John Reed Club School of Art, which had awarded him a scholarship and had shown his work

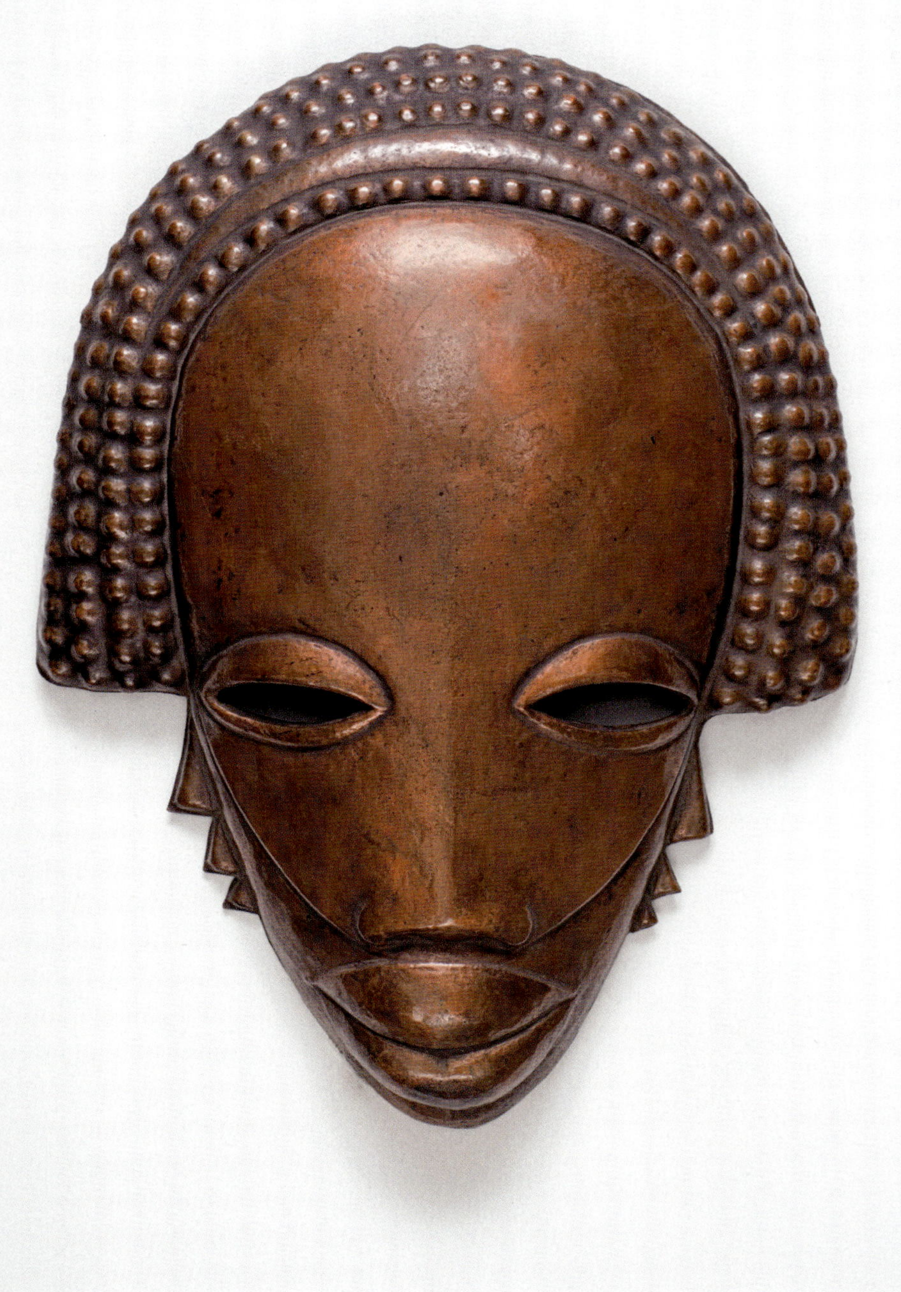

7.3 Sargent Johnson, *Mask*, 1933. San Francisco Museum of Modern Art

as part of the 1934 group exhibition *Hunger, Fascism, and War*. Like other so-cially conscious artists working during the Great Depression, he was deeply involved in progressive labor politics, including being active in the Unem-ployed Artist Group (later renamed the Artists Union). He also began to teach his own classes at the Harlem Community Arts Center, working under the auspices of the New Deal's Public Works of Art Project as it was transi-tioning into the Federal Art Project. And he became a member of the "306 Group" of artists and writers, including Romare Bearden, Ralph Ellison, and Jacob Lawrence, who met at the 306 West 141st studio that painter Charles Alston shared with several other artists.

The mid-1930s, therefore, was a moment when Lewis was fully enmeshed in the question of what it meant to be an artist, a member of the Harlem community, and an heir to what Alain Locke had famously termed "the ancestral legacy" that African art had bequeathed to the diaspora.[8] In this context of radical, modernist New Negro artistic foment, Lewis's engagement with the bold physicality of the Dan mask at first seems predictable: a part of the larger zeitgeist for both primitivism and for what Van Wyck Brooks termed the "usable past" within American culture itself.[9] But the realism and attention to detail that Lewis's drawing reveals, the effort that the artist put into representing the object that hung on the wall in the white-box space of the MoMA, brings to the fore its very present "thingness" and reveals the impossibility of its representation as an actual "Dan mask." By identifying the mask as a thing, I am referencing Bill Brown's concept of thing theory, which posits that our subject relationship to objects changes when they are no longer able or allowed to function in their original ways. "We begin to confront the thingness of objects when they stop working for us: when the drill breaks, when the car stalls, when the windows get filthy, when their flow within the circuits of production and distribution, consumption and exhibi-tion, has been arrested, however momentarily. The story of objects asserting themselves as things, then, is the story of a changed relation to the human subject and thus the story of how the thing really names less an object than a particular subject-object relation."[10]

In the context of the MoMA exhibition, the Dan mask was no longer the cultural object that it was when it had come into being when, at an unknown moment in time in an unknown workshop somewhere in the Ivory Coast, it had been carved from wood and decorated with raffia by a person with a name. There it had been danced by a person with a name, and there it had been viewed by people who knew its meanings, its contexts, its use, and its name. Hung on the white wall of the MoMA gallery, the once meaningful object had become a thing whose artistic, aesthetic, and physical excesses complicated and made ambiguous its original use.

I would argue that the state of decontextualization and thingness in which the Dan mask was now mired presented Norman Lewis with a profound challenge that helped throw into question the very possibility of representation for the young artist. What, after all, was he seeking to represent in his drawing of the mask? Its contemporary thingness as an art object? Perhaps. But certainly not its original meaning or its use, which were wholly absent from comprehension in its perch on the white wall of the MoMA. In many ways the aesthetic conundrum that the mask presented to Lewis was wrapped up in the way its materiality had been colonized, first by its European collectors and then by its American exhibitors. As the Martinican surrealist poet and politician Aimé Césaire would assert two decades later, colonization = "thingification."[11]

With *Dan Mask*, Lewis nodded momentarily to both the modernist and the New Negro fascination with African art, but he was not able to embrace it for long. In the late 1930s, Lewis's paintings turned first toward abstracted figuration before moving into nonobjective abstraction over the following decade. The figurative and abstract expressionist works that followed in these later years and that attended primarily to existential concerns of the postwar era, such as the nuclear destruction of *Every Atom Glows: Electrons in Luminous Vibration* (1951) and the ongoing racial terrorism perpetrated by the Ku Klux Klan, hinted at in *Evening Rendezvous* (1962), reveal little evidence of the impact of African art objects, from the 1935 *African Negro Art* exhibition or elsewhere.[12] Perhaps, being unable to reconcile the things that these objects had become in the modern context, Lewis chose to engage other aspects of African culture that were more real, purposeful, alive, and meaningful in his world, such as contemporary African dance, which had become a visible part of the New York art scene by the early 1950s and whose rhythmic qualities may be seen in many of the works that Lewis created later in his career.[13]

8

"BOLSHEVIZED BY CONDITIONS"

AFRICAN AMERICAN ARTISTS AND MEXICAN MURALISM

The revisionist historical imagery and radical socialist politics visible in many of the works made by Mexican muralists on their visits to the United States between 1920 and 1950 made a significant and lasting impact on the art produced by African Americans associated with the New Negro movement of the interwar period. Like their Mexican counterparts, African-descended artists in the United States were seeking to create a class-conscious artistic vision that foregrounded the fight for racial justice in the face of inequality and systematic repression. Hale Woodruff (1900–1980) in his 1938 *Amistad* murals at Talladega College in central Alabama, illustrating the true story of a violent revolt at sea by kidnapped Africans against their oppressors, took his cue from close study of Diego Rivera's murals and José Clemente Orozco's *The Epic of American Civilization* (1934) at Dartmouth College, which depicted Indigenous resistance to invading Spanish conquistadors (figure 8.1).[1]

In solidarity with their Mexican counterparts, socially conscious African American artists like Woodruff often found it difficult to reconcile their ambitions with the desires of their patrons as they sought to use art to raise political, class, and racial consciousness within their own communities. These African American artists were acutely aware of the difficulties encountered by their Mexican counterparts, whose status as international celebrities did not always insulate them from censorious backlash against their more controversial work, especially when that work challenged the racial mores of the day. One of the primary challenges shared by these politicized artists was how to create work that revealed and honored the struggles of one's proletarian ancestors or contemporary comrades while simultaneously depending financially on elitist individuals or government programs invested in maintaining a status quo based on social stratification and racial inequality.

During the 1930s, as labor unrest in the United States intensified, work made by prominent Mexican muralists was increasingly under attack by repressive institutions and individuals. In 1931 Orozco's mural *Table of Universal Brotherhood* at the New School for Social Research in New York, which featured a conference of "people of all races being presided over by a black," caused the school to lose a number of donors who were uncomfortable with a scene that depicted interracial cooperation and equality.[2] The following year, David Siqueiros's highly charged public mural in Los Angeles, *América Tropical*, showing an Indigenous man crucified beneath a US eagle, was deemed undesirable and was whitewashed shortly after its unveiling. And two years later, in New York, Rivera's mural *Man at the Crossroads* was demolished on

8.1 Hale Woodruff, *The Mutiny on the Amistad*, 1938. Talladega College, Talladega, Alabama. © 2022 Estate of Hale Woodruff / Licensed by VAGA at Artists Rights Society (ARS), New York

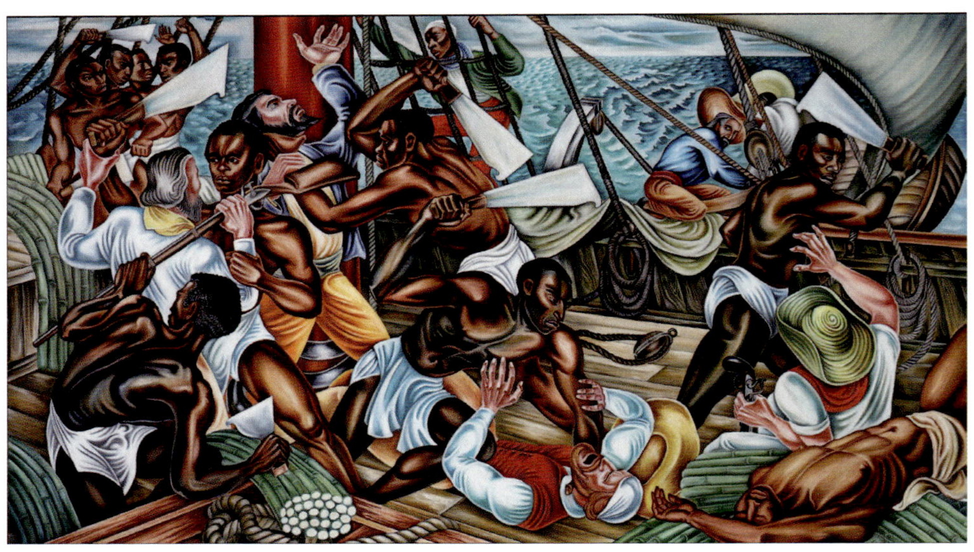

the orders of its commissioners, the wealthy Rockefeller family, after the artist refused to paint over the unwelcome face of Bolshevik leader Vladimir Lenin, which he had included in one of its crowd scenes.

The chilling effect of the censorship of work by celebrated Mexican muralists in the United States by white American elites is evident in the work of contemporaneous African American artists who held similar anti-capitalist political beliefs. In November 1934, when painter and illustrator Aaron Douglas (1899–1979) completed his ambitious *Aspects of Negro Life* mural cycle at the 135th Street Library in Harlem, it quickly became apparent that the artist had engaged in self-censorship to realize most of his artistic vision. At the time, Douglas was one of the premier artists associated with New Negro culture and the racial uplift politics of the day. His art had been championed by philosopher Alain Locke, whose 1925 edited volume *The New Negro* helped define the intellectual and aesthetic aspirations of a generation of young writers and visual artists. Sociologist and civil rights activist W. E. B. Du Bois had also featured Douglas's drawings on numerous covers of the *Crisis* magazine, the organ of the National Association for the Advancement of Colored People (NAACP), which Du Bois had helped found and which he directed during the 1920s and 1930s. But by the mid-1930s, Douglas, like many American artists, was largely dependent on New Deal government programs for his income. Working for the government came with different expectations and restrictions than a practice of creating art solely based on one's own political convictions.

Today Douglas's mural *Aspects of Negro Life* features a set of four panels: *The Negro in an African Setting, Slavery through Reconstruction, The Idyll of the Deep South,* and *Song of the Towers* (figure 8.2). Originally, Douglas had planned a fifth panel in which he had intended to depict the plight of the Black worker under an anti-union state. When interviewed by the *New York Amsterdam News,* the most important African American–owned newspaper of the day, about the ideological ramifications of the work, the artist trod carefully while explicating his passion for and ambivalence toward the project, lamenting the issues involved in creating the frescoes for the federal Public Works of Art Project.[3] While he struggled with the decision to omit the final section, Douglas ultimately decided that it would be career suicide to include it.

Since the onset of the Great Depression, Douglas's politics had been slowly drifting left until he had arrived at a place where he felt fully "bolshevized by conditions."[4] He had shifted from a 1920s Jazz Age practice that depicted the performance-based creativity and supposedly natural musicality of African

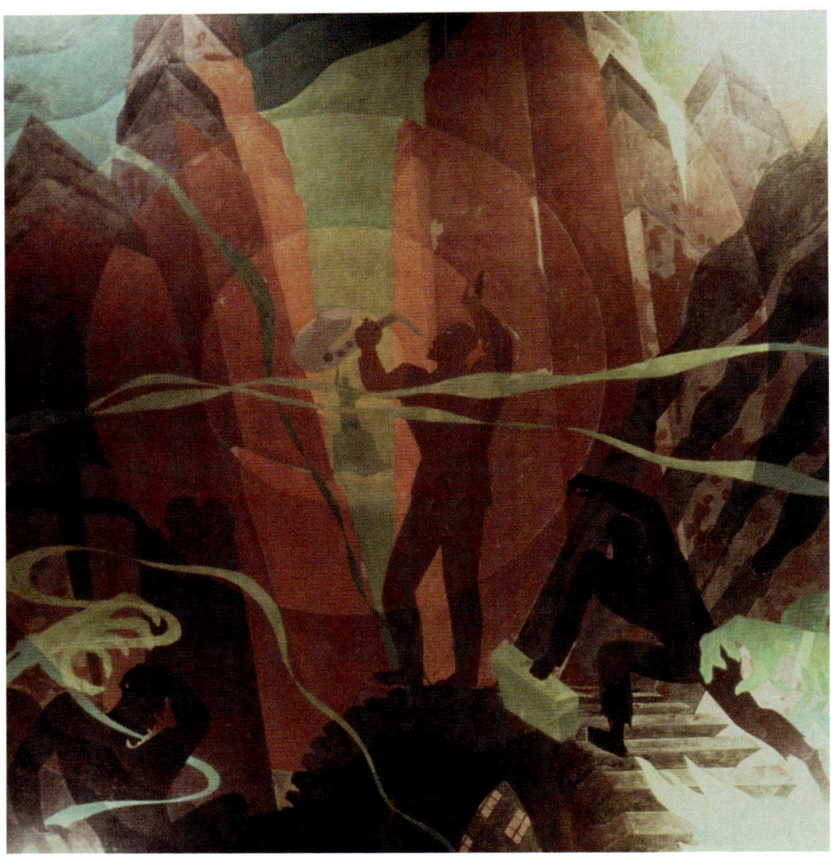

8.2 Aaron Douglas, *Aspects of Negro Life: Song of the Towers*, 1934.
Schomburg Center for Research in Black Culture, New York

Americans toward works that focused on urban workers' struggle against the
social ills, race-based discrimination, and violence that increasingly characterized Black life during the early 1930s. A significant contributor to his
artistic development, Douglas told the *Amsterdam News*, was the Marxist
social consciousness that he saw in the work of Rivera, Siqueiros, and Orozco,
who he believed painted "what they personally think the proletariat feels."[5]

Song of the Towers, the last completed panel in the chronological progres-
sion of Douglas's *Aspects of Negro Life*, depicts the economic aspirations of
the American descendants of the kidnapped and enslaved Africans shown in
the first three murals. At the center of the composition, the silhouetted form
of a man in a modern suit stands at the crest of a giant cogwheel.

He holds a saxophone in his left hand while gesturing with his right to the characteristic skyscrapers of the New York skyline, which part to reveal the iconic shape of the Statue of Liberty in the distance. His path is traced by another silhouetted man, who climbs the wheel while carrying a valise that presumably contains all his worldly belongings. Framed by industrial smokestacks and rural vegetation, the upward momentum of the second man's climb is powerfully conveyed, and he gestures forward as though exhorting a caravan of African American strivers behind him. *Song of the Towers* is a siren song of economic and social promise: the modern metropolis with its promise of liberty awaits as a sanctuary from the systematic and casual violence and the company-store serfdom of sharecropping in the South.

The 135th Street Library, the site of Douglas's murals, was an important gathering place for many recent African American migrants enticed by such a promise for themselves and their children. One young library patron was aspiring artist Jacob Lawrence (1917–2000), whose parents had left South Carolina and slowly migrated north until they eventually settled in Harlem, where they found jobs, housing, and schools for their growing family. As a youth, Lawrence attended classes at Utopia Children's House and then received studio art training at the Harlem Art Workshop, where he was taught by Charles Alston, whose Harlem Hospital murals had been strongly influenced by the work of Orozco.[6] In 1939, using resources available at the 135th Street Library, Lawrence began researching the history of African American migration with the goal of creating an epic work of art. This project resulted in a group of sixty tempera paintings, *The Migration Series* (1940–41), which chronicle the experiences of African Americans following the end of the Civil War and Reconstruction. Some of the most powerful pieces in the series address the race- and class-based violence experienced in the North by those who were fleeing similar oppression in the South, such as *Panel 42* (figure 8.3), which shows a white police officer from behind, his arms and legs spread to make an X, blocking the free movement of two Black men who are seated in a holding cell.[7]

Shortly after its completion, a portion of the series was published in *Fortune* magazine, and it was collected jointly, with the even-numbered pieces remaining in New York at the fledgling Museum of Modern Art while the odd-numbered panels traveled south to become an important part of the Phillips Collection in Washington, DC. While Aaron Douglas chose to self-censor his government-commissioned murals and Jacob Lawrence depicted his monumental interpretation of the history of Black migration in the nonpublic format of serial tempera paintings, other African American artists who were inspired by the Mexican muralists to address issues of discrimination,

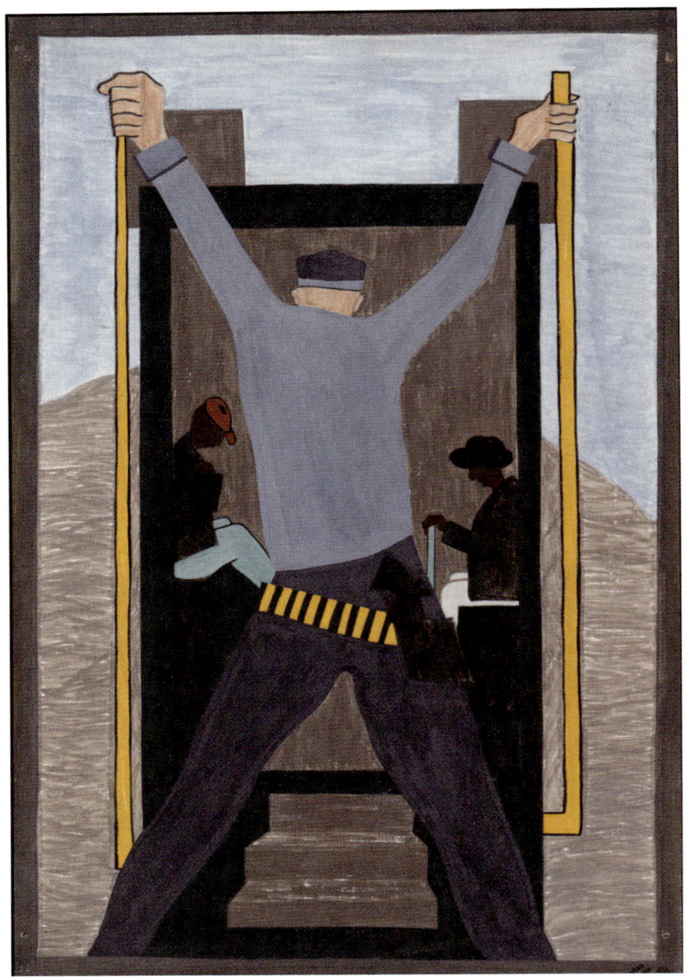

racism, and exploitation in their work often decided that they had to leave the United States to realize their artistic goals more fully.[8]

Sculptor and printmaker Elizabeth Catlett (1915–2012) and her first husband, the painter and draftsman Charles White, had spent the late 1930s creating anti-racist work inspired by the Mexican muralists' social ideals. By the 1940s the couple found themselves targeted by the Federal Bureau of Investigation for their art and their involvement with social organizations focused on interracial cooperation.[9] With funds from a Julius Rosenwald Grant, Catlett and White left the United States in 1946 to work at the Taller de Gráfica Popular (People's Print Workshop) in Mexico City. Although they

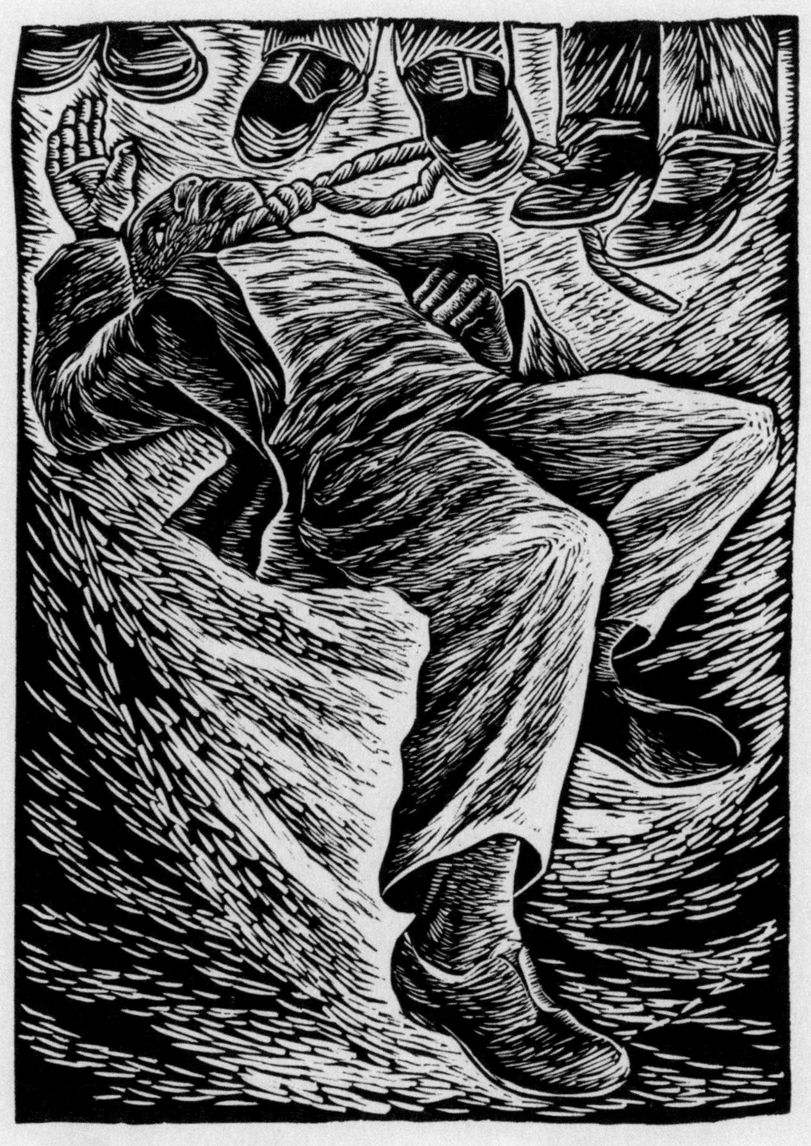

8.4 Elizabeth Catlett, *And a Special Fear for My Loved Ones*, 1947. Courtesy of the Pennsylvania Academy of the Fine Arts, Philadelphia

divorced soon after and White returned to the United States, Catlett chose to remain in Mexico, eventually adopting Mexican citizenship. During the Mc-Carthy era, she served as one of the primary liaisons for persecuted American socialists fleeing the United States for Mexico and revolution-era Cuba. The works she created at the Taller, especially *And a Special Fear for My Loved Ones* (1947), exemplify her continuing emphasis on concerted political action as a way of addressing the targeted racial violence of lynching (figure 8.4). In the print Catlett is very direct about the reality of racial violence, which permeated African American life in both Northern and Southern states.

One of the most significant attractions of Mexican muralism for African American artists was the movement's emphasis on calling out economic inequality and migration-related racial violence in both the history and the contemporary reality of both nations. Whether artists were addressing the atrocities of the Spanish conquistadors during the colonial era or the grim legacy of the Confederacy and the de facto racism of the *Plessy v. Ferguson* doctrine of "separate but equal" segregation, Mexican and New Negro artists often found common cause in the ongoing fight for racial justice.[10]

It is a sad fact that many of these issues of migration and racial violence are still a part of our world today, and as such they remain at the center of socially engaged activism by politically radical artists and cultural workers nearly a century after the Mexican muralists began working in the United States. In December 2018, while I was writing this chapter (originally for an exhibition catalog), the organizer of that exhibition, the Whitney Museum of American Art in New York, became the focus of intense protest, from within the institution as well as publicly online and on-site, demanding the ouster of Warren B. Kanders, a vice chair of the museum's board of trustees.[11] One of Kanders's companies, Safariland, had been identified as the manufacturer of tactical tear gas canisters that US border agents had used to repel Central American and other migrants and asylum seekers desperately attempting to cross the southern border of the United States near Tijuana, Mexico.[12] While shocked at the show of force displayed by US agents, protesters were specifically concerned that a significant supplier of tactical gear to the military, police, and prison-industrial complexes was using the museum to "artwash" profits that had been made from selling products used to violate the human rights of poor and Indigenous people.

To many of the concerned artists, art historians, and cultural workers who publicly objected to the museum's continued association with Kanders, the fracas at the border was part of longer histories of colonialism, racism, and the economic and military oppression of the poor and disenfranchised.

I would argue that the contemporary Central American refugees trying to breach the wastelands of concertina wire and steel slats guarding the "promised land" are not really that dissimilar from the African Americans depicted in Lawrence's *Migration Series* and Douglas's *Aspects of Negro Life*. Whether migrating north of the Mason-Dixon line in the 1920s and 1930s to escape the grinding poverty and extralegal lynching parties of Catlett's prints or crossing the southern border in the 2010s and 2020s to escape unemployment and gang violence or political oppression, desperately poor folk will always seek a better life despite the odds. Similarly, socially concerned and politically engaged artists, regardless of race or nationality, will always seek to call out injustice through their work.

After seven months of lively protests, and a growing number of artists choosing to distance themselves from the Whitney by not participating in or by pulling their works from the museum's prestigious biennial exhibition, Kanders resigned from the board. His departure in late July 2019 was hailed by many as evidence of the power of artistic activism to make meaningful change in the art world and its institutions.

In this very contemporary controversy around art and migration resound the loud echoes of the conflicts between conservative art patrons and radical artists that characterized the interwar period, when African American and Mexican artists working in the United States found that their radical messages of social justice for poor and working-class people were not always welcomed by those in power. In a twenty-first-century online meme, Kanders's visage could easily have replaced one of the predatory capitalists seated in the *Wall Street Banquet* panel of Diego Rivera's 1928 murals at the Ministry of Education in Mexico City.

9

MALCOLM X RISING

There are two ways of seeing: with the body and
with the soul. The body's sight can sometimes forget,
but the soul remembers forever.
—**ALEXANDRE DUMAS**, *The Count of Monte Cristo* (1844)

One day, may we all meet together in the light of understanding.
—**MALCOLM X**, *The Autobiography of Malcolm X* (1965)

Sunset in the ethereal waves: I cannot tell if the day is ending,
or the world, or if the secret of secrets is inside me again.
—**ANNA AKHMATOVA**, "A Land Not Mine, Still" (1922)

Malcolm X, No. 3 (1969) rises sharply against the gallery wall, a crumpled and folded cuirass of poured bronze atop a mass of undulating twisted and knotted silk cords dyed the same golden hue as the metal structure from which they issue (see figure 9.1). Towering nearly ten feet, it dominates the viewer's field of vision. This formidable sculpture, frequently referred to by the artist as a *stele*, is one in a series of "skirt sculptures" by Barbara Chase-Riboud (b. 1935) that she dedicated to the controversial African American civil rights leader who was assassinated in 1965.[1] According to the artist, the

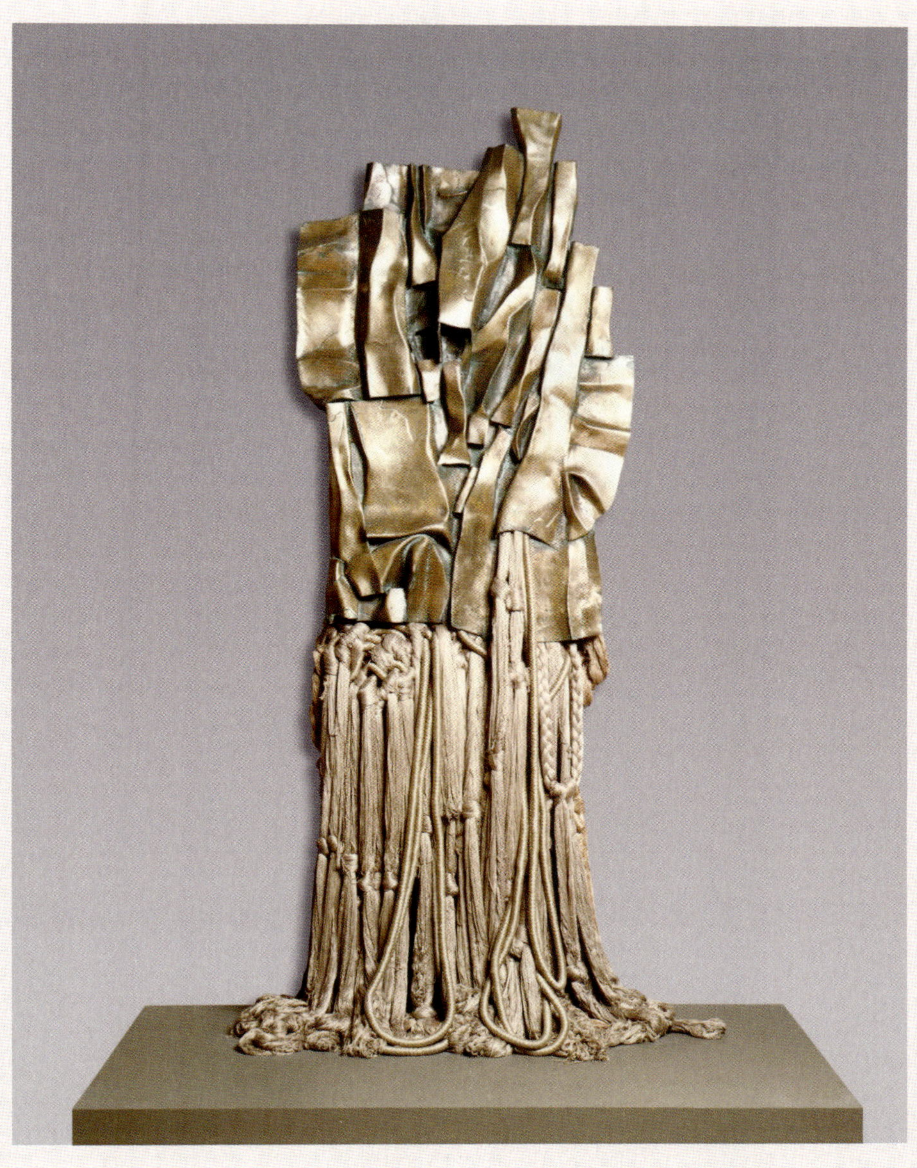

9.1 Barbara Chase-Riboud, *Malcolm X, No. 3*, 1969.
Philadelphia Museum of Art. © Barbara Chase-Riboud

bifurcated structure of these sculptures, which allows for the sudden transfer of "the characteristics of one material to another," evolved because she "wanted freedom from the tyranny of the base and legs," finding the answer in African dancing masks, in which the porters are concealed by fibers.[2] Although the work's formal connection to ancient steles (traditionally a carved or inscribed upright stone or pillar used to commemorate an important event or person) and its suggestion of human-initiated movement inspired by African masking traditions are relatively easy to see, its potential to memorialize a specific individual, Malcolm X, is far less simple to describe.

How might the abstract form of *Malcolm X, No. 3* serve as a monument to such an iconic historical figure, one whose likeness has been ingrained in popular memory through the mass reproduction and distribution of powerful photographic imagery? How does it evoke the man whose name it is given without drawing on this legacy of representation? These questions have vexed many critics and art historians who have attempted to interpret the *Malcolm X* series as well as Chase-Riboud's visual art in general. Her resistance to the formula that scholars often rely on to discuss the work of biologically similar artists (e.g., African American, or female, or both), as I outline in the following, has emphasized her exceptional place among modern abstract sculptors of the past half century.

Unlike her contemporaries, such as the Italian arte povera artists, who found an important champion in Germano Celant, or the American minimalists, who gained legitimacy in large part through their perceived opposition to the formal mandates of Michael Fried and Clement Greenberg, Chase-Riboud has rarely been examined in the context of larger artistic movements. Instead, critics and art historians have preferred to discuss the trajectory of her career; her interest in ancient Chinese, Greek and Roman, and African art forms; or her prodigious literary production, which includes best-selling novels, acclaimed books of poetry, and *I Always Knew: A Memoir*. This is not to say that these approaches are without interest or merit. Rather, my aim is to consider why the objects produced within this artistic practice have been so challenging for scholars to explicate. What I believe is missing from the literature on Chase-Riboud is some good, close looking that considers her work on its own terms and engages with the objects on the merits of their own materiality and their phenomenological impact on the viewers who stand before them. More than being about something, the art of Barbara Chase-Riboud *is* something.

Shortly after moving to Paris in 1961, Chase-Riboud started to expand the repertoire of traditional sculptural materials, including clay, plaster, and bronze, with which she had been trained to work as an undergraduate at Temple University's Tyler School of Art in Philadelphia and as a graduate student at Yale. By the end of the decade, she began to experiment with fixed viewpoints, moving away from sculpture in the round. "The last few sculptures have been in relief," she explained in 1971. "I think it is because I am combining these sculptures with another material, which is silk or wool. It seems to lend itself to a sort of flat relief surface rather than a three-dimensional one."3 She found significance in "taking a hard material and a soft material and making them work together." By 1965 she had begun using wax sheets, which she cut, stacked, and folded, melting and manipulating its surface with fire from torches. She shuttled between her home in Paris and Verona, where she worked with the Bonvicini Brothers Foundry, having them cast experimental plaster sculptures. She adopted the special wax used by the foundry in their casting process—it was a special formula that did not crack or melt excessively when the torch was applied, yet it flowed out easily from the mold when a final cast was being made. By the end of the 1960s, this special wax formula and the surfaces that Chase-Riboud was able to create with it had become part of the artist's trademark style and working method.

During the late 1960s, Chase-Riboud would sometimes incorporate bones and other found objects into her work, and by 1969 she turned to spun wool and silk. The incorporation of fiber into Chase-Riboud's work was encouraged by her Yale classmate and good friend, artist Sheila Hicks (b. 1934), who lived and worked in Paris during the mid-1960s. At the time, Hicks was becoming known for her innovative work with fiber that blurred the boundaries between what was seen as the hard, or masculine, materials of sculpture (bronze, marble, steel) and the soft, or feminine, materials of craft (beads, thread, yarn). By choosing fiber as the primary medium for her monumental abstract sculptures, Hicks challenged preconceptions about the appropriate materials for making important and formidable art. In combining fibers with bronze, Chase-Riboud threw down her gauntlet as well.

The visual sympathies between certain aspects of Hicks's and Chase-Riboud's sculptures are unmistakable. Both artists have similar ways of manipulating, of twisting and braiding, fiber materials. In Hicks's *Wow Bush / Turmoil in Full Bloom* (1977), for example, a multitude of recycled cotton fibers spills forth from an unknown source, flowing toward the viewer in a riot of red, yellow, and purple and pooling in soft eddies around the plinth on which they rest. Similarly, in Chase-Riboud's *Malcolm X, No. 3*, the combination of hard and soft materials, of the no longer malleable bronze and the inherently supple silk, is representative of the binaries and dualities that she often engages in her artistic practice, challenging oppositions that have worked to set ideas and people apart from one another. For these two artists who sought singular voices for themselves in the flux of the 1960s and 1970s, material hierarchies were too restrictive and needed to be overthrown by refutation or elevation.

The orientation of *Malcolm X, No. 3* as well as of the other works in the series controls how viewers experience the work by limiting their movements. Pressed against the gallery wall, with only a few of its silken cords resting on the plinth below, the sculpture appears to hover in midair in a space all its own. All but the front remains a mystery; viewers cannot walk behind it or see its backside. One wonders how the back of the work might look. Does it resemble its facade, a highly polished surface of folds and crimps? That the sculpture must be approached from the front, as though it were a monarch on a throne, creates a sense of formal rigidity and control that moves viewers to respond with awe and submission.

To engage with the phenomenological experience of the work, one must take time to study the bronze crevasses and cords that give it its thingness. The upper half of *Malcolm X, No. 3* is a staunched flow of once liquid metal transformed into a shiny surface of crevasses and gullies, of spaces and places for secretion. Each planar junction produces a new network of spaces where the viewer's eyes can rest, and their mind can wander. At various points between the crevasses, the planar surface is broken by thin lines that hint at superficial layers having been chipped or peeled away. In these spaces the bronze appears as if it were cast from sedimentary rock, with bits and pieces sheared from the surface to reveal the fragile layers beneath. On each side of the upper portion, a horizontally folded piece of bronze cascades downward, its borders edging up to frame the vertical mass of crimped and folded metal. Here and there a small knob of bronze breaks the surface, causing the eye to pause momentarily.

While the physical boundaries delimit the viewing orientation of *Malcolm X, No. 3*, the confluence of bronze and silk that bisects the larger form highlights the differences between the sculpture's soft and hard surfaces. A few fibers extend higher than their peers, entering the bronze form about a foot above the rest. The pliable and smoothly textured silk threads, collected and coiled into complementary groups of braids, bundles, or cords that rise and fall together—at one moment resembling a cascading braid of hair, at another a measure of rope that might bind a person's wrists or a chain that might tether a captive prisoner—create a network of veins and nerves bridging the space between the upper portion and the plinth, pushing the work just outside of the viewer's space. Each skein of silk thread makes a new relationship with space and surface, the clusters passing through complexes of knotted junctures before disappearing into the bronze and then reemerging, cascading down toward the plinth again and again and again, as though caught in an infinite loop, ends vanishing into the superstructure like snakes entering burrows or intravenous lines making subcutaneous entries. The dense layering of the fibers, knotted every few feet in some places and every few inches in others, produces a sense of infinitude and depth that appears to recede to the wall against which the sculpture rests.

The soft silk cords spilling forth from the hard bronze of the upper portion recall the innards of a gutted animal that has been hung up for slaughter, its intestines sliding out from its slit belly onto the abattoir floor, a mass of vital organs made useless, tangled and knotted. What once provided life through the extraction of nourishment for the body has been laid to waste, exposed to the consumptive gaze. Yet, beyond hinting at a kind of animistic death, the corded silk that spills from beneath the bronze references the creation of the piece by echoing the wax channels, or sprues through which the molten bronze flowed to make up the core of the sculpture. Now lost to sight by the finishing process, these channels—vestigial tentacles of bronze reaching out into space—would have been connected to the surface of the piece immediately after its casting and then removed by a professional bronze worker. The discarded spruing finds its ghost in the skeins of silk thread that jostle for space in the stele's lower half, forming a heavy skirt that hides the sculpture's support structure and inner workings.

The upper portion of the sculpture reveals concretized evidence of the artist's manipulation of her medium. What began in the studio as a smooth sheet of wax—a tabula rasa, a planar expanse of pliable material—was folded, melted, and merged, forever altered and manipulated. In the final bronze cast, a densely expressive surface on which are recorded the myriad aesthetic choices of the artist, the lost-wax process reveals itself. In the uppermost register, a horizontal splash pattern, a reminder of the liquid potential of the original wax model, breaks the vertical movement of the now-fixed bronze folds, giving the material a sense of fluidity that works against our perception of it as static. Ghosted on the surface of the bronze, the dribble and flow of wax made liquid by Chase-Riboud's torch endure, the surface of the paraffin once scumbled by her fingers standing as the indexical marker of her actions. In this way, the artist has made it seem as though the metal was crumpled and folded in on itself, gathering energy into its center before being fixed forever in time and space.

The surface of *Malcolm X, No. 3* speaks of choices made and forms manipulated, and yet it continues to change over time as patina creeps across its surface, corrupting the golden bronze with a greenish-gray tinge, making shiny parts a little duller, and rough parts a bit rougher. The delicate green film has accreted in the creases of the bronze, adding color and character to the form, helping us recognize the material's slow, organic life cycle, and its ability to morph and to endure, exemplified by ancient Greek statuary that survived a millennia or more beneath the volatile waves of the Mediterranean, as in the case of the Artemision Bronze (470–440 BCE) in the National Archaeological Museum, Athens, blackened with age and brittle to the touch yet still whole and recognizable as Zeus or Poseidon. Such temporal detritus reminds us that the only way to destroy a bronze sculpture completely is by the same mode used in its creation: by melting it down. It is this process, visible on the surface of Chase-Riboud's piece in the pentimenti of the wax sheets that formed the work's original model, that pushes the element of mortality to the fore by juxtaposing the fragility of an individual human life, such as that of Malcolm X, with the enduring nature of human civilization, in this case exemplified by the continued discovery of ancient Greek sculptures.

In places glowing with the golden tones of polished bronze, while in others darkly textured with the patina of time, *Malcolm X, No. 3* is profoundly compelling, as are the other works from this series, including *No. 2, No. 10, No. 11,* and *No. 13*, and Chase-Riboud's related sculptural series *Tantra* and *All That Rises Must Converge*, which feature bifurcated structures comprising cast forms above and silk cords below. In these works Chase-Riboud occasionally opted to combine colors; in *Malcolm X, No. 13* she added a contrasting skein of white silk cording to an otherwise homogeneous mass of dark brown threads, and in *All That Rises Must Converge, Red*, she used vibrant vermillion fibers to support the bronze cast. In the *Tantra* series, she abandoned the familiar single-skirted form in favor of a tripartite grouping of bundled and knotted silk fibers that enhance the levitational appearance of each sculpture. Such differences highlight both the similarities and the variety found in Chase-Riboud's works made since the inauguration of the *Malcolm X* series.

Like her sculptures, Chase-Riboud's drawings share a visual language that contrasts hard and soft with intransigent and malleable forms. The artist has insisted, however, that the two practices are discrete and fulfill different desires. "I don't do preliminary drawings for my sculpture. They are drawings for the sake of drawing. I draw very quietly, very meticulously. It may take me three or four or five days to do a drawing. But with the sculpture I am much more impatient. I want to see it right away. I want to see at least the basic form very quickly."[4] Despite this admonition, the upper portions of each *Malcolm X* sculpture, with their folded and scumbled wax originals, resemble the rumpled bedsheets of the artist's series of drawings from 1966 called *Le Lit*, or *The Bed*. This series reveals a transformation of form in two-dimensional space as two human figures lying side by side in a rectangular field, arranged as though yin and yang, heads against one another's thighs, evanesce into a mass of overlapping, cubist planes. It is as if the figures have become lost in the space of the bed. Swallowed up, their human identities have become materials that can be folded and reconfigured, made pliable, like the specially formulated Veronese wax that Chase-Riboud had begun using for her sculpture.

With the drawings in the *Le Lit* series, Chase-Riboud returned again and again to the sheet of paper as the image slowly emerged from the empty space; the production of each line required the artist's pencil to call it into being. Sculpting, on the other hand, allowed her to push and pull the form into existence much more quickly. In this way, the impulse to honor Malcolm X materialized in an upright, vaguely anthropomorphic form, one that seems to wear a protective bronze cuirass and twisted fiber skirt recalling the archaic uniforms of classical warriors.

Like the *Malcolm X* series, her *Monument Drawings* series—comprising large-format tributes to fictional characters, historical figures, and writers who are important to the artist, including the nineteenth-century Russian poet Alexander Pushkin and the Count of Monte Cristo, the character created by the French writer Alexander Dumas—presents distinctive phenomenological forms. Pushkin, often hailed as his homeland's greatest poet and beloved for his drama *Boris Godunov* (1825–31) and his verse novel *Eugene Onegin* (1825–37), is the father of modern Russian literature. Dumas's hugely popular adventure novels, including *The Count of Monte Cristo* and *The Three Musketeers*, both published in 1844, have made him the most widely read French author of all time. Both men were initiators of discursive practices in what literary critics and theorists would call the Foucauldian sense: Pushkin, who ushered in romantic literary form in nineteenth-century Russia, and Dumas, who formulated the genre of adventure writing, which led to the birth of pulp fiction and the late twentieth-century pocket novel, engendered new modes of popular public discourse through the creation and dissemination of their innovations. The discursive or literary paradigms set in motion by the two men's writings not only are meaningful on their own terms but also continue to have a profound impact on our contemporary understanding of what it means to be individuals in the modern world.

Chase-Riboud's ongoing engagement with (and I would say identification with) transnational histories of creative expression, exemplified by the cosmopolitans Pushkin and Dumas, both of whom were famous not only for their writings but also for their mixed African and European heritages, coupled with her interest in the possibilities for shared aesthetic experiences between artists and viewers, authors and readers, may explain many of her choices of individuals to honor through her artistic creations. By giving two-dimensional form to what I would argue is an intensely personal experience—communing intellectually and aesthetically with the creative project of another person—Chase-Riboud welcomes the viewer to engage with a uniquely transcendent, transglobal, and transhistorical discursive field where monumentalization is an ongoing aesthetic process.

Although many contemporary critics celebrated Chase-Riboud's non-objective commemorative art, and the *Malcolm X* series, they generally did not discuss in depth the phenomenological power of the works. In a 1971 essay published in *Art Journal* shortly after Chase-Riboud exhibited works from the *Malcolm X* series in the group show *Contemporary Black Artists in America* at the Whitney Museum of American Art, art historian Elsa Honig Fine highlighted the artist's sculptural practice as an elegant solution to the dilemma many American-born artists of African descent faced.[5] According to Fine, most African American artists active during the 1960s and 1970s had three choices for self-identification and marketing of their work. First, they could eschew racial content in their art and attempt to make a go of it in the mainstream. Second, they could focus on traditional social-realist subjects, such as the scenes of working-class family life depicted in the genre paintings of Jacob Lawrence (1917–2000), an approach Fine identified as "blackstream." Third, they could join the Black Arts Movement, which, according to Fine, meant working in a highly politicized manner that mandated a full commitment to a radical Black nationalist aesthetic practiced by members of Afri-COBRA, or the African Commune of Bad Relevant Artists, a Chicago-based artists' collective founded in 1968. Fine dismissed this movement as identifying wholly with the experiences and aesthetics of the urban ghetto. Despite her insistence that these three ideologically inflected modes of production predominated among contemporary African American artists, she was careful to note that there were a few exceptions, including Chase-Riboud and the sculptor Richard Hunt (b. 1935), who managed to move in the mainstream art world without entirely disavowing their Blackness or wholly excluding Black content or themes from their work. Hunt, described Fine, "separates his art and politics, claiming that his blackness is irrelevant to his art, but not to his life," and Chase-Riboud makes in her work "a purely aesthetic statement, and then dedicates the work to a Black hero [Malcolm X]."[6] As Fine implied (and as the artist asserted in a conversation with me in February 2012), it was only after Malcolm X's death that she chose "to dedicate the works to him." Malcolm X's death had a profound impact on Chase-Riboud (on more than one occasion, she discussed his death and legacy in letters to family in Philadelphia), and her thinking about the possibilities and potential for her sculpture began to turn toward the commemorative. The assassination occurred in 1965, while the artist was working closely with the Bonvicini foundry to perfect her folded-wax technique, and she maintains to this day that she did not intend to memorialize the fallen hero in the forms themselves. Rather, she wanted to share the visual and visceral experiences that the sculptures had elicited from her during their making, with the knowledge that the effort had been pledged to its namesake posthumously. In March 1968, following the birth of her second son, Chase-Riboud returned to the studio to begin preparing works for a 1969 show in New York sponsored by Air France. It was in this show that the first folded castings appeared. These sculptures were named for individuals who meant something significant to the artist, including one work named *Sheila*, in honor of Sheila Hicks, whose friendship and creative generosity had helped introduce Chase-Riboud to the powerful potential of mixed-media fiber art. By naming her works for significant singular individuals, such as Hicks or Malcolm X, Chase-Riboud was able to ground an aesthetic experience in a social reality.

Although Fine took great pains to outline the difficult paradigm of African American artistic identification that held heavy sway at the close of the civil rights era and during the height of the Black Power movement, she spent less than a sentence discussing Chase-Riboud's work. Fine's characterization of the artist's sculptures as being aesthetic first and memorials second failed to touch on her self-proclaimed radical sensibility. In an interview for the *New York Times* in 1969, Chase-Riboud proclaimed her militancy as one of the primary reasons for her expatriation to France: "I could easily go back to America now and find my place politically because Black people are fighting back. When I left in 1961 it seemed that if you were militant, you were all alone."[7] Rather than engaging Chase-Riboud's work or rhetoric, Fine demurred, mentioning only her bifurcated practice. Contemporary mainstream critics who were invested in the ideological constraints that Fine described, such as *New York Times* critic Hilton Kramer, were less convinced than Fine that the artist's approach could be viable or successful.

In a 1970 review that coupled an exhibition of sculptures by Chase-Riboud with one of collages by Romare Bearden (1911–88)—lumping together formally and materially disparate work based on the artists' affinity of racial heritage—Kramer lamented what he saw as a "Parisian sensibility" in Chase-Riboud's sculptures, namely, an "overrefinement" that was "emotionally at odds with the provocative themes announced in her titles."[8] He felt that the "discrepancy between form and motif is especially evident in the four 'Monuments to Malcolm X'—wall-hanging sculptures of considerable elegance that unfortunately suggest the ambiance of high fashion rather more than they suggest the theme of heroic suffering and social conflict." The gendered and racialized language of Kramer's assessment is glaring, especially in his assertions that Chase-Riboud's forms could speak only within the feminized language of fashion and that she had taken their "refinement" too far, as if the Black woman from Philadelphia had been corrupted by her time in France.

Similarly, the absence of an easily recognizable visual language of Black suffering in Bearden's work bothered Kramer. He derided the artist's collages as "a little too decorative . . . a little too pat, for the emotions that are not so much stated as implied in his imagery." That the white critic could not feel the Black artists' emotions seems to have been deeply troubling for him, as the visible suffering of Black people was, and I would argue remains, an ingrained part of the ideological expectations of the dominant culture in the United States, a culture within which Kramer was firmly grounded. It appears that two of the most prominent African American artists of the period simply could not win: they held back too much, or they were too sophisticated, or they were not angry enough for Kramer to make sense of them.

In response to Kramer's review, art historian Henri Ghent wrote a powerfully worded letter to the *New York Times* identifying what he saw as the author's thinly veiled racist rhetoric and assumptions:

> One strongly suspects that the real motive behind Kramer's severe criticism of Mrs. Riboud's work stems from the fact that she chose to create such tasteful and dignified sculptures in memory of Malcolm X. She, like *millions* of blacks, has come to see the civil rights activist as an eloquent and beautiful human being, one who played a towering role in helping America's black population to think better of itself. This, in the minds of many, is an unpardonable sin. . . . When black artists dare to adhere to *universal* artistic standards as in the case of Bearden and Mrs. Riboud, they are either written off as being derivative or just plain untalented.[9]

Although Ghent referred to Chase-Riboud's "dignified sculptures," he, like Fine, did not describe how this was accomplished formally.

While debate about the political categories of and aesthetic possibilities for African American art simmered in the early 1970s, the phenomenological potential of nonobjective forms to function as meaningful memorials did not become a topic of public discourse in the United States for another decade, when it was sparked by the controversy surrounding the Vietnam Veterans Memorial designed by Maya Lin (b. 1959) for the National Mall in Washington, DC. In 1981 Lin, an undergraduate architecture student at Yale, was awarded the commission for the design of the memorial to the American service members who had died or who had been classified as missing in action during the conflict. Lin's pathbreaking, minimalist design built on the recent history of abstract memorials by artists such as Robert Motherwell (1915–91), whose epic series *Elegy to the Spanish Republic* (1948–67), comprising large canvases of amorphous shapes, painted mostly black and white, laments the tragedies of the Spanish Civil War. Despite such celebrated precedents, her plan—consisting of two walls of polished black stone engraved with the names of the fallen and the missing, set below ground level and meeting at a 125-degree angle—caused an instant uproar. Critics scoffed at the possibility that a nonfigurative form could convey adequately the emotional experience of the Vietnam War to veterans and the families of those who perished or whose status was unknown. Dismayed veteran Tom Carhart, who testified in protest of Lin's plan before the United States Fine Arts Commission in October 1981, went so far as to suggest that the abstract design was a kind of aesthetic revenge perpetrated by the less-than-American artist (an Ohio-born woman of Chinese descent), who sought to deny real Americans (those of European descent) the marble monument they expected. He condemned the design as "a black gash of shame and sorrow." "Why can't we have something white and traditional and above ground?" Carhart implored.[10] Ultimately, not only did Lin's vision win over the panel of architects, critics, and sculptors (including Richard Hunt) who had been appointed to choose the memorial's design, but it convinced most dissenters when, after its dedication in 1982, they were able to experience its phenomenological power for themselves. Visitors standing before the reflective black surface traced the names of lost loved ones with their fingers and often burst into tears. The memorial's contemplative and cathartic potential quickly made it the most visited site on the National Mall.

While the memorializing potential of Chase-Riboud's *Malcolm X* sculptures had been unintelligible to Hilton Kramer in 1970, by the early 1980s the Vietnam Veterans Memorial had begun to encourage even skeptical Americans to consider how abstract forms could commemorate individuals or historical events. Like Lin's monument, the *Malcolm X* series requires viewers to submit to the experience and to embrace the act of contemplating form, texture, and presence. Through our submission to this phenomenological opportunity, we can experience the act of viewing as a significant form of commemoration.

Chase-Riboud's phenomenological, transcendent practice, which is simultaneously openly narcissistic with its focus on communicating her personal aesthetic experience and hugely selfless by way of its efforts to memorialize the creative power of others, presents a significant challenge to critics. In his review of her 1970 New York exhibition, Kramer decried Chase-Riboud's invocations of the Black militant Eldridge Cleaver and the nineteenth-century French poet Arthur Rimbaud, as though these two figures could not be contemplated in relation to each other or be equally comprehensible to the artist. Nearly thirty years later, Roberta Smith, Kramer's successor at the *New York Times*, was bewildered by Chase-Riboud's *Monument Drawings* series, complaining, "The variety of the names and the similarity of the images make everything seem formulaic and interchangeable; there is no discernible reason why a monument to Nelson Mandela shouldn't be dedicated to the Russian poet Anna Akhmatova or vice versa." Smith likened the works "to a form of academicized Post-Minimalism," claiming that the artist had fallen into a formulaic process of creation that seemed "cooked."[11] Because Chase-Riboud's drawings evoke historical events, personages, and places textually but not visually or didactically, they were indecipherable to Smith, who seemed to be carrying on the critical legacy of her predecessor. As Chase-Riboud moved into the mature phase of her career, critics continued to castigate her consistent visual rhetoric and style, and her use of titles that are independent from the formal aspects of the objects.

In recent years Chase-Riboud has become more open to incorporating increasingly recognizable abstract figural elements into her work while continuing to produce nonobjective, wall-oriented sculptures such as those of the *Malcolm X* series. Her bronze sculpture *Africa Rising* (1998), commissioned in 1996 and installed on the grounds of the Ted Weiss Federal Building of the General Services Administration (GSA), which unknowingly was built atop an eighteenth-century African burial ground in New York City, exemplifies the artist's formal journey from the 1970s to the end of the twentieth century. The burial ground, which long had been lost to history, was discovered in 1991 when construction crews working at the GSA building site unearthed the skeletal remains of the first of more than four hundred people who had been laid to rest beginning in the early seventeenth century when the location was just beyond the borders of the Dutch West India Company's settlement of New Amsterdam. Through a partnership between the GSA and Howard

University in Washington, DC, archaeologists began to excavate the site, in the process exhuming not only human remains but also pieces of coffins and grave goods with which the deceased had been interred. The scientific analysis of the materials found at the site yielded numerous unexpected insights into the lives of the people who had been buried there, creating a previously unrecorded picture of African New Amsterdam and early Anglo New York. Unfortunately, this research was disrupted irrevocably when nearly sixteen hundred boxes of artifacts from the site that were being housed in one of the World Trade Center towers were destroyed in the September 11, 2001, terrorist attacks. With the permanent loss of this material, the burial ground's memorial program at the GSA building site has taken on an added level of importance.

After the completion of the archaeological excavation, the GSA moved ahead with revised construction plans for the site that incorporated an elaborate commemorative project for the burial ground with commissioned works of art by Chase-Riboud, Houston Conwill (1947–2016), and the forensic artist Frank Bender (1941–2011), among others. These artists were tasked with visually representing the historical, experiential, and spiritual connections that influence our contemporary understanding of the African diaspora. Each artist chose a different approach. The large terrazzo-and-brass floor installation *The New Ring Shout* (1993–94), created by Conwill, with the assistance of the architect Joseph DePace and the poet and artist Estella Conwill Mojozo, draws on West African Yoruba religious practices by echoing the form of a divination board. Its title derives from the communal ritual of the ring shout, historically practiced by the close-knit communities of African-descended peoples living in the coastal communities of the Carolinas and Georgia, in which participants chant while walking rhythmically in concentric circles, men in one and women in the other. Bender created a bronze bust, *Unearthed* (2002), of three imaginary figures—two women and a man—clustered together. Chase-Riboud's contribution, *Africa Rising*, to date her most visually impressive and ambitious sculpture, dominates the lobby of the federal building.[12] The soaring, complex form features a winged female figure standing at the center of an arc supported by three vertical planes, the shape of which suggests an ancient Egyptian headrest. The arc in turn is held up by a rectangular base embedded with masses of coiled bronze that resemble the artist's signature fibers. *Africa Rising* (figure 9.2) is meant to be viewed in the round, its enormity commanding the space of its installation to a degree that Chase-Riboud's *Malcolm X* sculptures simply cannot.

In her conception for the piece, Chase-Riboud considered the experiences of the African people and their descendants who lived near the site of the

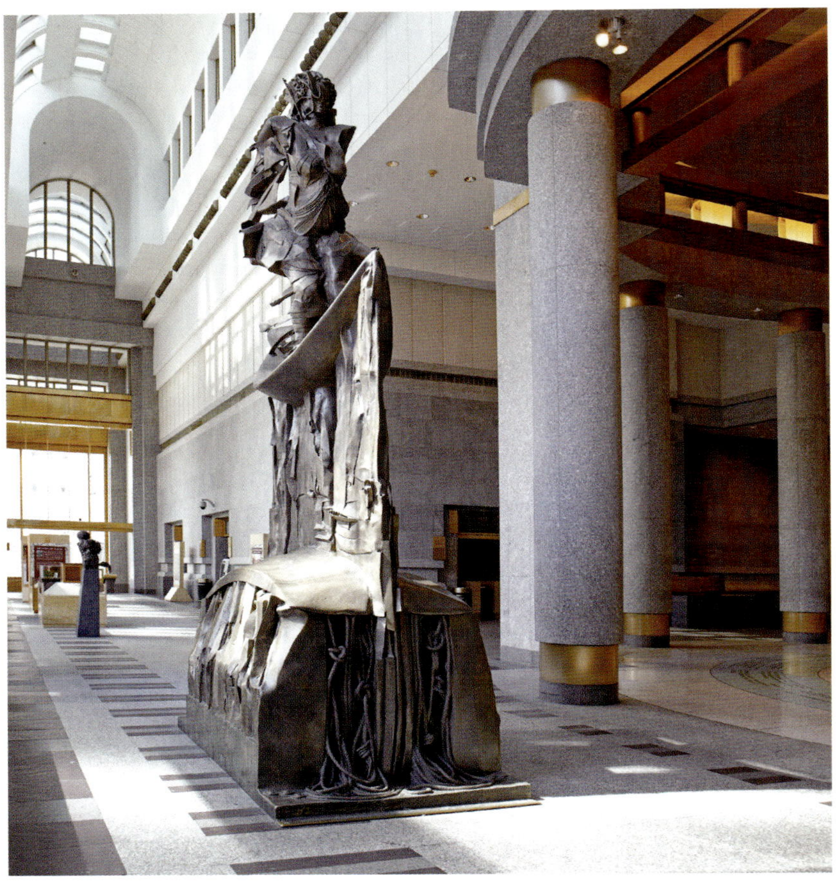

9.2 Barbara Chase-Riboud, *Africa Rising*, 1998. Ted Weiss Federal Building, New York. © Barbara Chase-Riboud

burial ground not only when it was under British colonial rule but also during its earliest history, when the area was part of the Dutch settlement of New Amsterdam. She did this by referencing the phenomenological experiences of the area's enslaved Afro-Dutch, who, in the seventeenth century, made up the second-largest population of enslaved African-descended people in North America (second to South Carolina), and of the Khoi people who came under colonial rule in 1642 when the Dutch East India Company established Cape Town, in what is the modern-day country of South Africa. For the latter, Chase-Riboud had in mind the experience of a specific Khoi woman, Sarah Baartman (1789–1815), who was abducted from her home in the Eastern Cape and enslaved by Dutch farmers before being convinced to travel to Europe, where, beginning in 1810, she was exhibited as a sideshow freak. After her death in 1815, French scientists performed an autopsy on her body, preserving her skeleton, genitalia, and brain, which were displayed in the Musée de l'Homme in Paris until 1974. In 1994 Nelson Mandela, president of South Africa, called for the repatriation of her body to her homeland, a request that was not granted for nearly a decade. In August 2002 Baartman's remains were interred in the Gamtoos Valley, near where she is believed to have been born almost two hundred years before.

In an essay on the relationship between Chase-Riboud's *Africa Rising* and her novel *Hottentot Venus* (2003), which articulates the largely unrecoverable experiences of Baartman through an existential narrative, Carlos A. Miranda and Suzette A. Spencer considered the ramifications of combining the experiences of a known African woman whose life in France is documented with those of anonymous Africans and their descendants who were interred in Lower Manhattan.[13] As interdisciplinary scholars who specialize in African American studies, Miranda and Spencer argued that the mix of abstract and representational components in *Africa Rising* contends with the "histories of those lost to slavery and white supremacy" and implied that the raw and abraded surfaces of the sculpture reference "the physical trauma evident in the excavated bodies of the African dead and in Baartman's corporealization and dissection," while "impressing the sheer impossibility of making such monumental histories of suffering intelligible much less legible."[14] This tension between that which has been seen but is now lost to sight and that which cannot be visualized is the challenge that Chase-Riboud's work presents.

One of the great strengths of Chase-Riboud's writing is her ability to convey the interior lives of Black female subjects such as Baartman, women whose perspectives and stories were elided or disavowed in their own lifetimes, but whose legacies resonate strongly in the present. Through her novels and poetry, Chase-Riboud works to reshape contemporary understandings of women whose racial designations and social positions have made them targets of cultural derision or moral condemnation, or nearly invisible to mainstream history. I would argue, however, that her work as a creator of aesthetic experience is no more about Black history or women's history or Black women's history than it is about her personal reaction to being a living, breathing part of this history and to having a responsibility to elucidate its hidden, wronged, or neglected parts. This is perhaps why the *Malcolm X* sculptures, the *Monument Drawings*, and *Africa Rising* provoke such profound phenomenological experiences in open and receptive viewers. These works operate within a space beyond simple binaries, a space of dualities and multiplicities, of potential and opportunity. To know this place, viewers must be prepared to give their attention to and to submit to the experience.

The transcendent aesthetic experience embraced by the viewer open to Chase-Riboud's work forms the commemoration of the fallen hero, the homage to the discursive initiator, the honoring of the unknowable suffering of ancestors. This profound act of submission and communion initiates a transfer of cathartic energy that enshrines and memorializes. The marks on paper, the elegantly knotted silk ropes, the gleaming bronze—these artistic mediums provide vehicles through which experiences might pass from the artist to the viewer. It is the viewer's phenomenological experience of Chase-Riboud's work that is central to its existence. Without the visceral reaction produced by the viewer's presence in the space of her work or the viewer's receptiveness to examining the form, there is nothing. No story. No emotion. No easy takeaway with which to placate the busy art critic. The art of Barbara Chase-Riboud is not about something; it is something.

10

RICHARD YARDE'S
MOJO BLUES

In 1995, as he lay ill with kidney failure, artist Richard Yarde (1939–2011) began to work on a watercolor that would prove to be a dramatic shift in his artistic vision.[1] The piece, a large, rectangular watercolor that he called *Mojo Hand* (figure 10.1), was born from the dreams that had come to him while lying in his sickbed at home in Northampton, Massachusetts.[2] After having tried unsuccessfully to visually represent these dreams in their specificity, he shifted to a more emblematic approach, gradually identifying and selecting important images that repeated from dream to dream, night after night. As the painting took shape, distinct elements emerged out of the white space of the paper, each bound within a fabric of interwoven indigo-blue squares. Six pairs of hands, shown palm up; a diagram of a DNA molecule; an enigmatic grouping of dots; an X-ray of the torso of a pregnant woman; and the Twenty-Third Psalm, written in braille. The ancestral counterpart for each element had first appeared in a dream, before being contemplated, researched, and revealed on the heavy, richly textured paper.

In many ways, *Mojo Hand* was a breakthrough piece for Yarde. It marked a significant change in the content of his paintings, which for the preceding three decades had been records of the cultural and political history of the

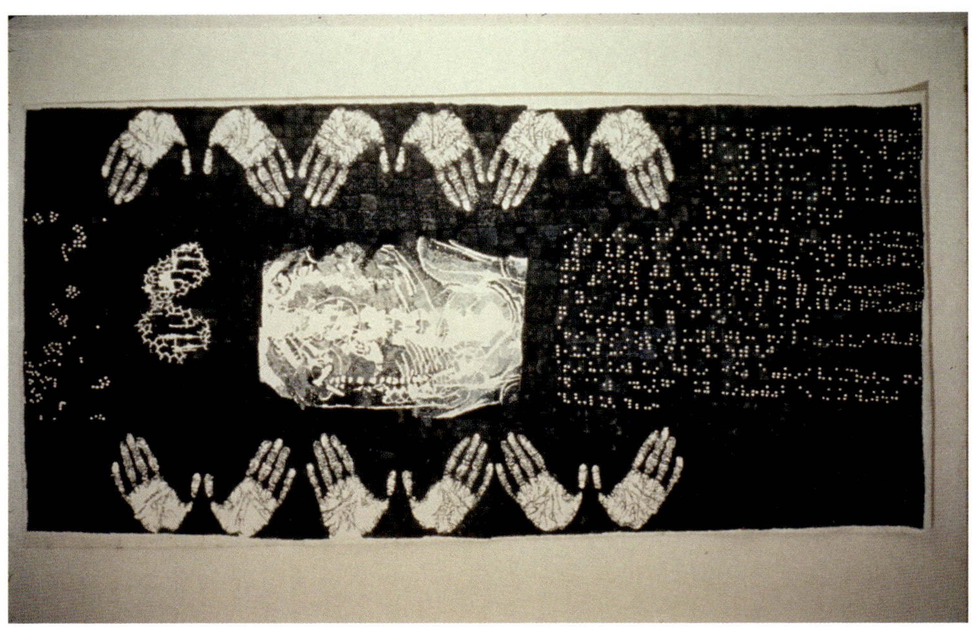

10.1 Richard Yarde, *Mojo Hand*, 1995–96.
Private collection. © Estate of Richard Yarde

twentieth-century diasporic African experience. His evocative watercolors recorded Malcolm X speaking in the Grove Hall neighborhood of Roxbury in the early 1960s or reinterpreted an iconic photograph of the controversial turn-of-the-century boxer Jack Johnson on an epic scale. He painted culturally resonant subjects as diverse as Universal Negro Improvement Association leader Marcus Garvey on parade in Harlem and made a life-size installation of dancers cavorting at the Savoy Ballroom as a part of a continuous body of work that celebrated a tangible image world that was lived and experienced, both firsthand and through popular culture. While the mystical world revealed in *Mojo Hand* was new territory for Yarde, the medium of watercolor and his use of blue pigment were as much a part of him as his signature.

Richard Yarde was born in Boston and grew up on Cunard Street in the city's South End neighborhood. "My mother and father came to the States on the same boat," he recalled. "They didn't know each other. They didn't find out until much later that they had actually come on the same boat." Born in St. Michael's Parish near Bridgeton, Barbados, Edgar St. Claire Yarde and his future wife, Enid, who hailed from Christ Church, arrived in New York City in 1923. They met several years later in Boston and were married in 1933. Their first son, Edgar Jr., was born in 1936, and their second, Richard, came three years later.

The Yarde family joined a growing anglophone West Indian community in Boston that included other Barbadians, Jamaicans, and Bahamians. Many of their friends and family were committed supporters of the radical Black nationalist Marcus Garvey, who had promoted Black enterprise and separatism as the best path forward for the African diaspora in the 1920s. "My cousins, the Bynoes, were old Garveyites, as were all these West Indians from the area. I think Garvey had been deported by that time, but they were still carrying on, having parades on Tremont Street." Sometimes they met at the Prince Hall Masonic Temple. "In the Bynoes' living room there was a shrine to Garvey . . . photographs . . . that kind of stuff." The Bynoes were deeply invested in Garvey's model for Black achievement. They were "pretty successful folks who all turned out to be lawyers and hairdressers, anything that related to making good money and having good status in the community." Yarde's father worked as a handyman and a machinist, while his mother took in laundry and worked as a seamstress.

Throughout their childhood Richard and Edgar Jr. were taken to the Garveyite parades that were held in the neighborhood. It was at one of these parades in the winter of 1942 that Edgar Jr. caught pneumonia. While confined to his sickbed, the six-year-old spent much of his time looking at magazines and making drawings of the battle scenes from the war that the country had just entered. When Edgar Jr. died, three-year-old Richard tried to stay connected to his brother. "I tried to draw planes and things he had been working on." To help her son work through his grief, Enid found him drawing supplies and plenty of blue paint. His favorite color was blue. "My mother, I think, always encouraged me, because she always bought materials. I think she probably got into it even more after my brother died. I don't know how she pulled that off, but she managed to. . . . In the Copley Square area, [there were] several odd stores. She would go in and buy paints and brushes and things like that."

In addition to furnishing her only surviving son with new art supplies, Enid also salvaged bits of scrap paper and cardboard that were being thrown away by her employers, bringing them home with the laundry that she took in to make ends meet. Occasionally she brought the boy with her to the home of Charles Smith, who owned a Boston furniture store, where she worked as a domestic servant. It was there that Yarde first encountered illustrated art books.

I was fascinated, because [Smith] collected art books. I would go in to help my mother, but there would be these free periods of time, and I would just comb through some of his art books—if I knew what I was looking at—I was curious. . . . I don't remember any place else where I was exposed to that kind of material. It really wasn't until . . . I guess I must have been eight or nine, that I actually started taking classes at the Boston Museum [of Fine Arts] and actually was exposed to paintings.

With his mother's encouragement, Yarde took children's classes at the museum, focusing on drawing and painting, until he aged out when he turned twelve. On Saturday mornings he would walk over to the museum by himself.

Cunard Street was not actually very far from the museum. There was an underground railroad tunnel that basically cut through to save time. I remember going through that and just ending up on Huntington Avenue, right across from the museum. . . . At that point, you could be there as a child, you just had free range in the museum. You couldn't do that today. You'd have to be accompanied by an adult. I would go in and check out . . . I just had certain things that I wanted to look at. I wanted to look at [Paul] Gauguin, and I wanted to look at the [William] Blake watercolors. Those were the two artists that fascinated me.

At the time, the museum's collection of Blake's drawings and prints, including many of his illustrations for John Milton's *Paradise Lost*, were displayed in glass cases on the Fenway side of the building. Their narrative aspect reminded Yarde of the Superman and Captain Marvel comic books that he adored. But there was also "a kind of mystical quality, a religious quality. I think that was what really attracted me, almost a kind of surreal, particularly Blake. He seemed very surreal to me, just mysterious enough to make me want to keep looking at them."

Later, when he was a student at Boston's English High School, Yarde's artistic skills afforded him certain privileges. "Sometimes I would be able to get out of other classes by designing posters for certain things. . . . I would make drawings for a poster for Thanksgiving or Christmas or whatever. I thought that was pretty cool, that I didn't have to be in a regular classroom. . . . Then, my mother always wanted me to make these elaborate posters for the church. It usually involved painting, a lot of painting, you know, an imitation of gothic script."

The Yarde family members were active in the congregation at Union United Methodist Church on Columbus Avenue. While she supported his interest in art, Enid had high hopes that her only surviving son would become a minister. His father just wanted him to be able to earn a living. Not interested in committing his life to the church, during his senior year Yarde applied to college to study engineering but did not receive any offers of admission.

After graduating from high school in 1958, Yarde worked briefly as a stock boy in a factory that made radio parts while also taking night classes. "I took an evening course in advertising and copywriting at Boston University, while I was working [at the factory]. What I remember, the instructor said, you are really pretty lousy and crappy, but you're pretty good at illustration. You've chosen the right area." His instructor encouraged him to apply to the university's art school, and he was accepted. "I was terrified actually. . . . I hadn't taken art in high school. All the students seemed to have come from . . . music and art high schools in New York. . . . They were all pretty practiced, pretty skilled. I just felt like I didn't know anything. I was lucky enough to have Conger Metcalf as my freshman drawing teacher. He really took a huge interest in me. I think by the end of first semester, I was pretty much on par with everybody else. I worked really hard, and he encouraged me."

Conger Metcalf (1914–88) was a transplant from Cedar Rapids, Iowa. Metcalf had studied with the American regionalist painter Grant Wood at the Stone City Art Colony before making his way east to Boston. He had just begun teaching at Boston University (BU) when he met Yarde. Their friendship would continue until Metcalf's death in 1998. "Metcalf would come in early. Class started at 8:30, he would come in at eight o'clock and sit down with me and just go over principles and expose me to certain artists. He was totally into the Renaissance school of drawing. . . . He really liked Leonardo's drawings, Michelangelo, Fragonard, Watteau. . . . Later he said that he felt I was very gifted, and he wanted to try and make something happen for me." Metcalf's support was critical for Yarde. When the young artist couldn't afford the tuition at BU and was contemplating taking a year off to work, Metcalf stepped in on his behalf. "In my first year, there was one scholarship they gave out to a student. They had intended to give it out to someone else. What I learned later was that Conger approached the committee and said, 'If you don't give Richard this scholarship, I'm leaving the school.' That really made all the difference."

As Yarde made his way through the studio curriculum at BU, the courses became more challenging.

By the time I had gotten to my junior year, I was feeling kind of rebellious in some ways. Some part of me was rebelling against the classical approach. I had two drawing instructors in that one year. The one who taught the classical tradition and a sculptor, Hugh Townley, who took a more contemporary approach to drawing. We did all of our drawing for his class outside of class. The classroom was used as a critique session.

That was a ferocious class, I learned a lot from it. He wanted us to basically take over the class and express our opinions. There were two factions in that group. One focusing on figurative work, and the other focusing on abstract. In fact, Brice Marden was in that class. . . . He was abstract, he started early. He did work on figurative work, but when he had the opportunity, he worked abstractly.

While Marden went on to a hugely successful career, most of Yarde's classmates weren't able to make art their sole profession. "There were a lot of people [I thought were good], but not many people make the cut after a few years, it's difficult."

As had been the case in his childhood art classes, Yarde was once again surrounded by white students. "That class that I came in under [at BU] was really the first attempt to integrate the art school. There were five of us, five of us were African American that came in." Fortuitously, Metcalf helped Yarde to connect with members of the Black art community in Boston by helping his most promising student get a job at the Huntington Frame Shop, which was owned by artist and avid golfer Leon Braithewaite:

I was working part-time [at the shop] . . . whatever hours I wanted, I could work. If I wanted to come in there at 12 o'clock at night and work for four hours, I could do that. . . . I was mostly cutting mattes, they nicknamed me "mattes and tones." At that time, frames weren't all prepared in terms of tonalities and stuff. Someone would come in and pick out the tones they wanted, and the framer would create the tone. Whereas today I'm sure it doesn't happen anymore. Even gold leaf, but that was Leon's. . . . That was his handiwork, gold leaf.

By the mid-1960s, Braithewaite had become the preferred framer for William H. Lane, whose celebrated collection of American modernist painting and photography is now held by the Museum of Fine Arts, Boston. During this period Lane was purchasing canvases by Arthur Dove, Stuart Davis, Charles Sheeler, and other modernist American artists. Lane's single limiting criterion was that the painting had to fit in the back of his station wagon. If it didn't fit, he wouldn't buy it. Lane would then drive the piece over to the Huntington Frame Shop to have it framed.

Lane would come in with these works, and he would drive Leon crazy. He wanted exactly the right tone for his frame. Leon would produce a tone, and he'd say, "Oh, it's not quite right." [Leon] would redo it. He couldn't refuse this guy because he was bringing so much business. . . . It was part of my education actually, the shop . . . the mixing tones that was the most helpful, precisely mixing tones. I didn't really get . . . I got a good general sense of mixing color at school, but mixing those beautiful tones was like a real education.

As Yarde completed his studies, the civil rights movement was beginning to explode around him. Many of his friends had become active in demonstrations, which were becoming increasingly violent as protesters clashed with the police. Despite his family's roots in Garvey's Black empowerment movement, Yarde wasn't certain how he fit into the emerging political climate. As graduation approached, a classmate who was preparing to drive cross-country offered Yarde a seat in his car. It was an easy decision.

With his new bachelor of fine arts degree in hand, Yarde headed to California, planning to make a fresh start in the Golden State. While staying with friends in Manhattan Beach, near Los Angeles, he met his future wife. Susan Donovan was outspoken, sensible, and self-assured; she spoke her mind and was always prepared to fight for what she believed was right. She was also an artist who wrote poetry. The two connected over long walks discussing their shared love of art and literature. But not only was Susan white, she was married to someone else at the time, so Yarde decided that there was no future in the relationship, and he hit the road, riding his bicycle up the coast to the San Francisco Bay Area. He had been accepted to a graduate program at the University of California, Berkeley, but could not find a way to raise the out-of-state tuition. He returned to his family's home in Boston to regroup and, after over five hundred miles in the saddle touring California, swore he would never ride a bike again.

Before Yarde's departure from Manhattan Beach, he had lent Susan a few books by Herman Hesse, *Siddhartha* and *The Glass Bead Game*, which she tried to return to him about a year later. Despite his departure she was not ready to let him disappear from her life. "She had come back [East] to live with her grandma. She called me to return the books and said, 'You don't remember me.' I said, 'Oh, yes I do, clearly.' We met on one cold February afternoon at Boston Museum [of Fine Arts]. The day after Malcolm X was killed [on February 20, 1965]." Soon they were living together in an apartment across the Charles River in Cambridge.

Unlike most of Boston, the People's Republic of Cambridge, as it was affectionately called, was a diverse and largely tolerant community. Living together as an interracial couple there was pretty easy. "Cambridge was . . . when we first moved, was kind of an ideal community, because both Black and white folks got along there. We should have stayed there. We should have stayed in that area, because [it] was uncomfortable for everybody [when we left]." But Yarde was restless, and it was hard to get settled in Cambridge. "I think there's personal life and work, right? I think I've separated things out, and I was using my memory for the work, for imagery for the work. I had trouble being in the present. I was recording everything from the past. When we first moved to Cambridge, I tried to drive Susan's friends away. I had my own prejudices about music and everything else. I would go over to Roxbury, go over to meet my parents, and sometimes that wasn't very easy, moving in and out of Roxbury on public transportation."

It was also difficult for the couple to go places together. At the time, interracial marriage was legal in Massachusetts and several other northern and western states. But it was not until *Loving v. Virginia* was ruled on by the Supreme Court in 1967 that it became legal throughout the United States. Even if their relationship was legal, it was not seen as socially acceptable in most places in the country. As an interracial couple, going places together in the highly segregated neighborhoods in Boston could be dangerous.

> Susan and I were just first going out together, we had gone to China-town to have dinner, and then some, I'm assuming these guys were from Southie, they were screaming "N****r lover" and on, and on. Of course, I jumped out of the car, like an idiot, and it turned out that there were three or four of them, as opposed to a single me, and I was going to take them on. But she'd gotten out, unbeknownst to me, she was behind me with a tire iron in her arms ready to defend stupid Richard. Later, Susan said to me, "You know your Ford is a few thousand-pound automobile. Why don't you just pin them to a wall?"

In 1966 their first son was born. "I named him after Marcus Garvey, she named him after Marcus Aurelius. . . . She read his books and thought he was a noble person. . . . She said he was a great king and brought peace in the kingdom." A second son, Owen, followed three years later.

To supplement the intermittent sales of his art and to support his family, Yarde taught painting at Wellesley College, where he was one of three or four Black faculty members, and at BU. It was also a strategy to have a separate studio space to paint in, a luxury that his working-class background and young family did not permit. Until he became a tenured faculty member at the University of Massachusetts Amherst, in the 1980s, he rarely had a committed studio space to call his own and would move his materials in and out of the art buildings in which he taught his classes.

Periodically, he was forced to work at home. It was in part these frequent space restrictions that led him to foreground his work in watercolor. "We went through some changes in terms of our living [space] and everything else where my studio was a kitchen table, basically. That was the only space I had to work on. I didn't have a real space to work on. So, the idea of trying to make oils on the kitchen table, that was not [workable] at all. So, I could always just roll out some paper and work on the table [with watercolor] and roll it back up. But that probably was a big influence too." During the mid-1970s, watercolors moved from serving as studies for Yarde's oil paintings to being the main mode in which he was working.

With his family growing, Yarde began a series of paintings that pictured Black children sitting on the stoops of the decaying brownstones that characterized many of Boston's neighborhoods that had been built in the nineteenth century. "*The Stoops* series of paintings . . . were just trying to have some recall of my experiences growing up in the South End and Roxbury." The works came from a place of nostalgia and mourning for a world that was being bulldozed by aggressive urban redevelopment that was displacing middle- and working-class Black communities across the country. "Life was disappearing. They tore down the buildings and got rid of everything. It was just being pushed off the map. And so, my notion was I wanted some kind of documentation that that was a life that existed at some point. It had been totally removed. I think that was really at the heart of it." But without adequate studio space, it was challenging to work at the monumental scale that Yarde felt the series required, and he struggled to produce the work. "I had done small watercolor studies and large paintings. I remember I was working in an apartment in Cambridge, a small apartment. And I remember the first painting was done in two halves because I couldn't. . . . It was taller than the ceiling to paint. So, I worked on the bottom half and the top half separately and put them together. . . . So, it was about eight feet. The height of the painting was about eight feet. Not a smart thing to do. I felt I needed to work on that scale for some reason."

Working in watercolor had long been a part of Yarde's practice. As a student at BU, he had always begun his paintings with a watercolor study, rather than a graphite or charcoal drawing.

At the school they broke things down into three parts. It started out with a drawing and then some kind of color study. I don't think anybody was working with watercolor except me. But some kind of color study. And that was all a rehearsal for the painting. . . . I think by the time I got to these paintings, I wasn't sketching on canvas, I was just starting with a swatch of paint and just letting it spread out. Many of these paintings [of the 1960s and 1970s], they were made in sections. I didn't have a [set] sense of scale, so I would add pieces on as I went. . . . I didn't make drawings for the watercolors either. I think one thing I liked about the watercolors is they started somewhere and then filled out. I felt more comfortable with that than making a drawing beforehand.

The Stoops drew attention, and soon Yarde began to have exhibitions of his work at Boston galleries, including ones on tony Newbury Street. In 1969–70 art historian Edmund Barry Gaither began to organize a landmark exhibition featuring the work of young Black artists. *Afro-American Artists: Boston and New York* was a collaboration between the Museum of the National Center of Afro-American Artists, the School of the Museum of Fine Arts, and the Museum of Fine Arts, Boston. "I think under [painter] Dana Chandler's pushing . . . [the exhibition] was planned for the museum school, and they somehow managed to get it into the museum. That was the first show I think the museum had done that involved African American artists. Susan said she called Barry and told him he had to get me in the show." White art critic Hilton Kramer gave the exhibition a generally positive review in the *New York Times*, identifying it as "the largest survey of American Black artists ever mounted. Consisting of 158 works—painting, sculpture; drawing, graphics, and other visual media—by 70 artists."[3]

The following year, Yarde's work was scheduled to appear in an even more prestigious exhibition: *Contemporary Black Artists in America* at the Whitney Museum of American Art. The exhibition was initiated by the museum in collaboration with the Black Emergency Cultural Coalition, who later called for a boycott when the museum did not meet the originally agreed-on criteria. The museum moved the show out of its originally scheduled slot during the main season and failed to involve "Black art experts and consultants and/or institutions . . . in the preparation and presentation of all art activities presented by white institutions and involving the Black artist and the Black community" coalition members. Led by painter Benny Andrews, several artists called for artists to pull their work and for the public to boycott the exhibition.[4] Yarde joined Andrews, painter Sam Gilliam, photographer Roy de Carava, sculptor Richard Hunt, and others who either declined invitations to be included in the exhibition or pulled their work from the show as the opening approached. In retrospect, this choice to side with racial solidarity and a righteous demand for systemic change began to feel like a missed opportunity. As many scholars have noted, the mainstream art world has historically integrated its museum walls and gallery spaces at a near-glacial speed, with most American museums still far from reaching any sense of racial or cultural equity in the composition of their permanent collections or in their special exhibition schedules. "There were a lot of protests going on at the time, and so I refused [to show my work at the Whitney]. I don't if that made sense, looking back on it. It doesn't seem to make a lot of sense." Perhaps Yarde should have taken the opportunity to show at the Whitney? As the years passed and comparable opportunities failed to materialize, he often wondered if he had made the right choice.

But this was a moment when the Black Power movement was ascendant, and racial solidarity was increasingly important within the mostly fragmented Black arts community of Boston. "There were these moments when people came together or [would] be brought together by an institution. I remember at the Institute of Contemporary Art there was a [director], Joe Hyde, who brought people together. He tried to bring the work out into the community. They had rented an old electrical building or something and brought teams together from across the community to show. And I remember that very distinctly because that was unusual. That was across color lines. Yeah, that was a very unusual approach, I think, in general." Like its neighborhoods, the Boston art community was very segregated.

Around that time, Yarde began to feel a pull across the river and toward the Black community in Boston.

> I tried to move into Roxbury, which was a disaster. Not something I should have done. I would go to work and Susan would be abused on the phone, and if she did go out on the street, she was abused. We lost a child in that neighborhood. That was a pretty stupid move. . . . That was Black Power period. People were really pissed and angry, [there was a lot of] interracial conflict. . . . I decided I needed to save my homeboys in the hood. That's when we left Cambridge. That certainly didn't work. Not at all. I just put us all into real jeopardy.

At the same time the Black Power movement was ascendant, the rise of the women's liberation movement further complicated the Yardes' marriage.

> I thought it was difficult, but basically what I remember saying [to] Susan, I said, "If you could get through Black Power with me, I can get through feminism with you." Those were two really stressful periods for both of us . . . she was part of an article in *Newsweek.* . . . But yeah, we were both

very split. I was going to Roxbury, and we had these theater performances. Amiri Baraka would put on these plays. I remember his speeches on Malcolm X, and we didn't agree on anything there at the time. But somehow got through it. Yeah. We were very split from those movements.

During the United States' bicentennial in 1976, Yarde was awarded a residency at the Studio Museum in Harlem. "Hilton Kramer reviewed that show, and he didn't like my oil painting at all, but he did like the watercolor. He talked about what he thought was a much more natural response to design, and color, and surface and so on. . . . And that did have an influence on me, I think." Kramer praised the sensitive and exuberant use of color that seemed to flow from Yarde's brush onto the paper, with a freeness that the oil paintings did not match. "The watercolors—not only the *Rally* series [about Malcolm X], but, even more, the studies for the big pictures and the more intimate pictures based on old photographs and firsthand experience—are a distinct success," Kramer declared in his review. "Clarity, precision, and a certain sweetness of feeling are the rule in the watercolors. This more intimate and meticulous medium, which does not permit any second thoughts, allows Mr. Yarde the expression of a lyrical, sometimes nostalgic evocation of experience that is sometimes very moving."[5]

Soon after the Studio Museum show, the Museum of Fine Art's first curator of contemporary art, Kenworth Moffett, began to show an interest in Yarde's work. The two men had first met when they were both teaching at Wellesley.

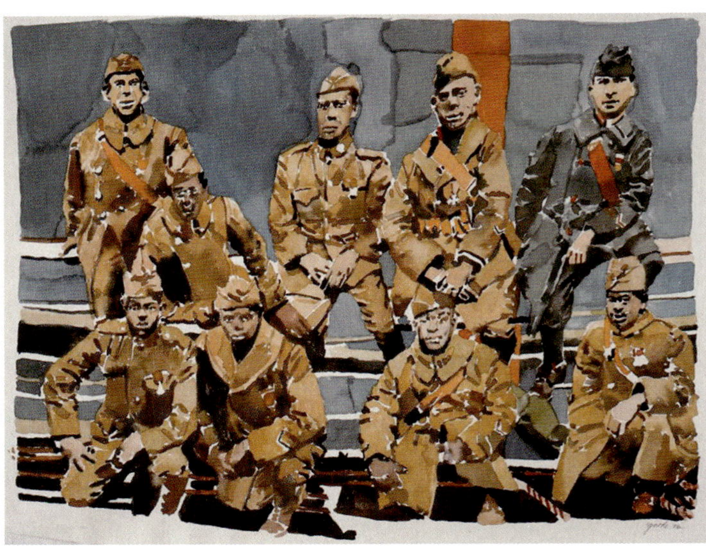

10.2 Richard Yarde, *The Return*, 1976. Museum of Fine Arts, Boston. © Estate of Richard Yarde

Several years after the show *Afro-American Artists: Boston and New York*, Moffett convinced the museum to acquire a watercolor by Yarde that focused on African American history. *The Return* (1976) was based on an archival photograph of a group of Black soldiers from the World War I–era, the 369th Infantry Regiment, popularly known as the Harlem Hellfighters. *The Return* (figure 10.2) was the first of five works that would enter the museum's collection during Yarde's lifetime. As an undergraduate at Columbia, Moffett had been a student of Meyer Schapiro, who mentored him closely and recommended that he do his graduate study at Harvard, where he fell under the sway of modernist critic Clement Greenberg.[6] Moffett saw himself as an aesthete with a connoisseur's eye for quality, with modernist tastes, acquiring work by Jackson Pollock, Morris Louis, and Robert Motherwell for the museum.[7] Yarde's overarching interest in exploring color and shape, as well as his attention to the materiality of his work through the indexical traces of movement that watercolor emphasized, appealed to Moffett, who had little tolerance for the representational materialism that the Warhol effect of pop art was then ushering into the art world.[8]

By this point Yarde was deep into a series of works based on archival photographs. He was drawn primarily to historical figures who exemplified certain aspects of Black masculinity, like the boxer Jack Johnson (figure 10.3). "I think I was an angry young man. I saw [Johnson] as a badass. I certainly related to him. Somebody who did not follow the rules. I certainly wasn't as bad as he was, but he did not follow the rules at all. He married a white woman, and he did everything he wasn't supposed to do." Despite being drawn to Johnson's badassery, Yarde chose to depict the athlete surrounded by flowers. "The Jack Johnson series, there was a lot of flower imagery. He had posed out in the backyard with the flowers around him. And a painting was about the flowers."

Yarde was also exploring the political figures whose legacies had shaped his childhood, focusing on Marcus Garvey and the sociologist W. E. B. Du Bois. "I did this series on African American history, starting with making watercolor studies from photographs of Marcus Garvey. Started branching out a little bit, Jack Johnson and so on. And the Niagara Movement [cofounded by Du Bois]. . . . I was grabbing photographs and making watercolor interpretations. . . . I'd started making drawings based on the Savoy [Ballroom in Harlem] and just started to do some serious research on it."

The project *The Savoy*, which was begun during a one-year teaching appointment at Mount Holyoke College, would be Yarde's first large installation comprising works that were structured around a central theme, in this case the Black dancers who had enlivened the legendary Savoy Ballroom

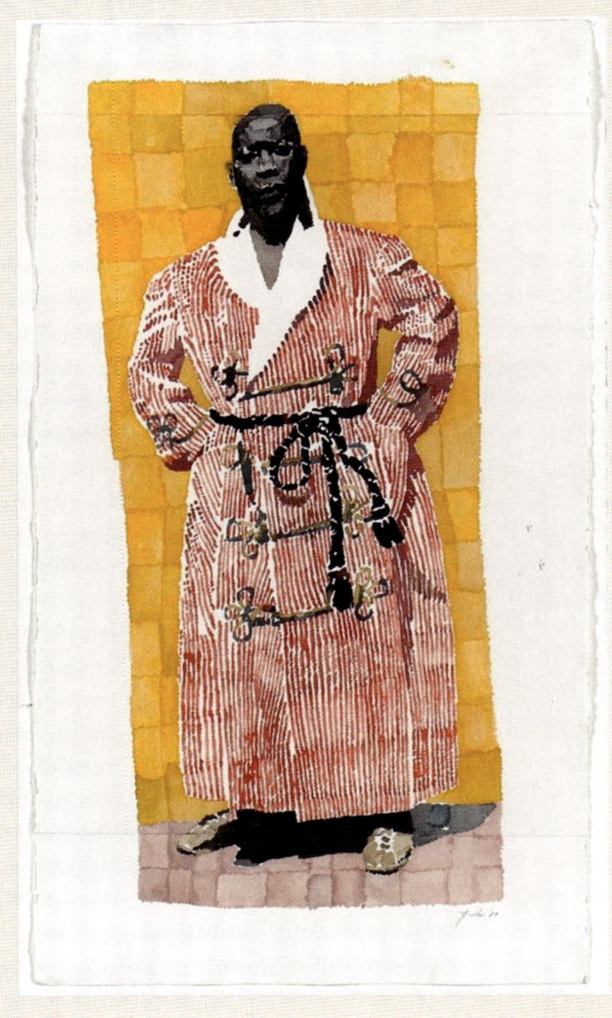

10.3 Richard Yarde, *Jack Johnson*, 1987.
Museum of Fine Arts, Boston. © Estate of Richard Yarde

in Harlem during the Lindy Hop craze of the 1930s. Yarde was drawn to the Savoy (see figure 10.4) as vehicle through which he could explore Black joy.

> Just this idea of dance. Again, I was still thinking in terms of African American culture, but I was starting to think of imagery that was a little more joyous and celebratory. Everybody at the time was working on what I thought was pretty depressing, back when people were doing [art about] lynchings and all kinds of stuff. That's part of life, but that's not the whole picture. . . . [The library at Mount Holyoke] had all kinds of things, and I'd run into people who might have danced there, collected materials, *Life* magazine articles. Material just started flowing. I made watercolor studies, and I decided I wanted to try and do an installation. Mount Holyoke was willing to help with that.

The college assisted with his research and provided a venue for the installation.

> Trying to construct the ballroom, to figure out somewhat what that space was like, because there were fragments. In the photography there were fragments. I figured out that the person who designed the stage of the ballroom . . . had been influenced by Egyptian architecture. Some of the columns, and the tile work . . . the columns were interpreted as lamps, and the tile work was interpreted as carpeting and so on. From the time I was a child, I was interested in Egyptian art. So, I was able to pick up on that pretty quickly . . . the designer [for Savoy Ballroom] had to be influenced by Egyptian art. The carpeting . . . the molding, . . . the bandstand and the lamps, all had been taken from the Temple of Karnak.

The Savoy installation of 1982–83 comprised dozens of just-under-life-size dancing figures that Yarde had rendered in watercolor and attached to cutout supports. They were arranged in an architectural space that evoked the experience of a ballroom and sought to reimagine the sense of freedom and ecstatic release that Lindy Hoppers had felt while swinging their partners though the air to the syncopated rhythm of jazz swing bands. The exhibition originated at Mount Holyoke and then traveled to the San Diego Museum of Art and the Baltimore Art Museum, and wrapped up its tour at the Studio Museum in Harlem. After the exhibition closed, the subject matter offered by the Savoy dancers remained compelling, and Yarde would return to it from time to time and make new watercolor drawings.

In 1988, under the auspices of the Art-in-Architecture Program, the General Services Administration commissioned an indoor mural for the Joseph P. Addabbo Federal Building in Jamaica, New York. But when the commission

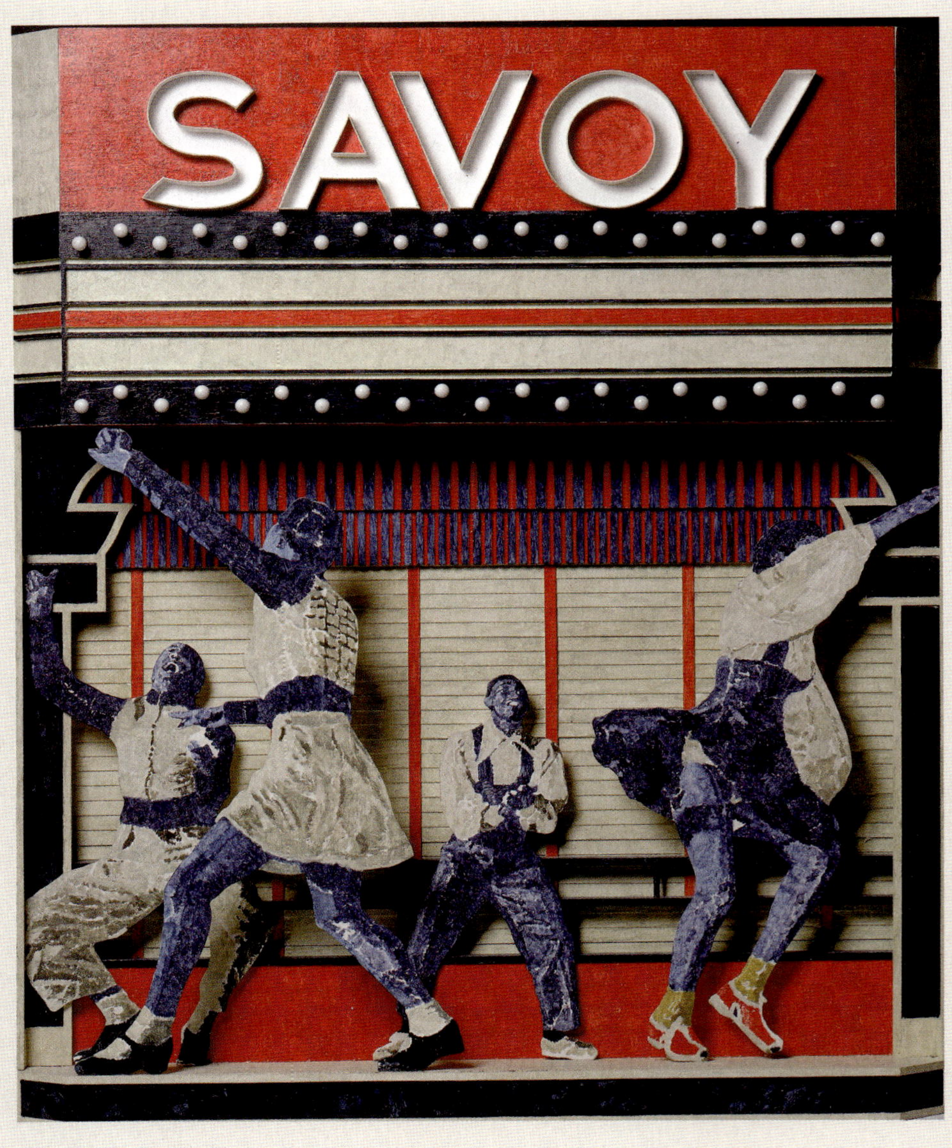

10.4 Richard Yarde, *Savoy*, 1988. Smithsonian American Art Museum, Washington, DC. © Estate of Richard Yarde

was completed, Yarde became disturbed by the Savoy's omnipresence in his practice and the way that it seemed to be impeding his path forward.

> I felt that I didn't want to get stuck in one frame of mind with the work. And just repeat that over and over and over again. I kept looking for new images, but it still seemed to be pretty limited, I think. . . . A collector had asked me to do a large piece, and I worked on it all summer, and then he decided he didn't want to pay the price that was set for it. I was very bummed about it, because I thought, "I'm going back to do something I'm not so sure I want to be doing. I'm not going to even be paid for it."

In the burst of anger that followed the failed commission, Yarde destroyed all the Savoy material remaining in his studio. "I basically tore [up everything] and threw it away. But then I found myself saying, 'Why did I do that?' At least keep the archives, keep a record of everything." Although regret followed the destruction of the material, Yarde did not regret his decision to move on from the topic.

Just a few years later, around 1990, his kidneys began to fail.

> I went on dialysis for about three and a half, four years. And in that period, I think, I stopped working for about a year and a half to two years because I was just overwhelmed physically. And then I distinctly remember starting, what I felt like was starting from scratch. I thought, "Well, I'm going to start again." And what did I do when I first started painting? I started to work with finger paint when I was a child. So, I just went back to pushing paint around with both hands. Not really making images, just getting the feel of the paint. And then I would dry my hands off on a separate piece of paper, and handprints, they just seemed to come forward in a way. I thought I wanted to do something with them.

Not only had the stress of Yarde's illness caused him to take a break from teaching and his regular studio practice, but he had also begun to see a therapist to help him cope with the prospect of death as he waited to be matched for a kidney transplant. The therapist encouraged him to engage with his subconscious. Every morning he would wake up and try to recall his dreams from the night before.

> [I was] trying to get the memory of my dreams coming through more strongly. And it just seemed like the interior of my thoughts just got stronger as I . . . this was the first time I made images [where I did not] have a sense of what the image meant beforehand. I would just put things down,

and then it would occur to me what it might mean later on. . . . At the same time, the Western model for healing wasn't working for me very well. So, this is when I started to [explore other paths to healing].

As Yarde struggled to survive the kidney failure that years of medication for hypertension had created, he began to seek hope in alternative healing communities, and as he began to work on *Mojo Hand*, all this changed. While waiting for an organ transplant, he found solace in the "laying on of hands" that is central to many holistic approaches to healing.[9] He investigated Central and West African beliefs about the magical worlds that control health and illnesses, taking both a visual and intellectual interest in the traditions that were disseminated across the New World through slavery. Yarde moved from venerating and inscribing the past to probing and interpreting the supernatural. By attending to the messages that his unconscious was sending him, by painting this new dreamworld that was born of pain and corporeal doubt, he was able to dedicate concerted attention to his own spirituality and the religious practices of the African diaspora. Through an interrogation of the syncretic Black folk medicine and spiritual culture that still permeates the Caribbean and the Americas, the core of *Mojo Hand* emerged as a visual exploration of universal issues of mortality and transcendence.[10]

Although the popular meaning of the word *mojo* has been affected by its use in popular culture, its traditional meaning has to do with the ability of a specially made charm to do magic, to have mystical powers that will aid its owner. *Webster's Dictionary* defines *mojo* as "[prob. of African origin; akin to Gullah *moco* witchcraft, magic, Fulani *moco'o* medicine man] chiefly South, a voodoo spell or amulet."[11] In practice, mojoes are charm bags made out of variously colored flannel and filled with several different components depending on what they were used for, in Haitian vodou they are called *paket kongo*, or bound medicine packets, and have their roots in the Kongo magic and healing traditions of West Central Africa. These conjure charms are often used to attract the affection of another, as in blues lyrics such as Preston Foster's classic "I Got My Mojo Working." As performed by Muddy Waters and others, the song begins:

> I got my mojo workin' but it just don't work on you
> I got my mojo workin' but it just don't work on you
> I wanna love you so bad, child, but I don't know what to do
> I'm going down to Louisiana, gonna get me a mojo hand Going
>   down to Louisiana, gonna get me a mojo hand. Gonna have all
>   you women under my command.[12]

However, this type of charm only touches on the broader power of mojo charms. In his pathbreaking work *Hoodoo—Conjuration—Witchcraft—Rootwork: Beliefs Accepted by Many Negroes and White Persons These Being Orally Recorded by Blacks and Whites*, folklorist Harry Middleton Hyatt discusses the term *mojo* in the section titled "Hands, Magic Helpers" as an "object or act, which aids a person in obtaining a desire," a desire specific to them alone. Hyatt explains that "Aladdin's lamp was not a hand because anyone could rub it to activate the indwelling spirit," but a hand is "dressed, powered for [the owner] alone." *Mojo* joins *toby, guide, shield, roots*, and *jomo* (a transposition of *mojo*) as a term commonly used for a hand.[13]

Yarde's placement of the twelve hands in *Mojo Hand* was in dialogue with various New World and diasporic African cultural traditions of using images of hands, both upraised and downward pointing, as protective devices. Within African American hoodoo, the upraised Helping Hand, like the popular Catholic hand of power, or *Mano Poderosa*, is often found on candles and curio labels. Downward pointing hands are found in syncretic New World culture as well, for example, the *milagro*, or miracle, charms frequently used in Mexico.[14] Unlike these kinds of iconic curios, the twelve handprints in *Mojo Hand* are not repetitions of a single model; instead, they are individual handprints, each with their own unique lines.

While the palm prints in *Mojo Hand*, made up of the unpainted white space of the paper, are positioned in the manner of Christian benediction and hoodoo prayer, the texture of the small indigo squares of paper mirrors African fabric tonalities. In the way that it visually recalls the rectangular format of West African strip cloth, both that made by the Ewe people of Ghana and Togo and the kente cloth made by the Asante people of Ghana, it references the spiritual source, the site from which all syncretic action issues. Each small square of painted paper, one rubbing up against the next, edges blurring together as they overlap, forms a visual pattern that serves as a repetitious back beat to the forms that populate its surface. And while the elements appear to float on the underlying grid of blue paint, it is really the grid that sutures them together, just as threads of lace knit empty space into evocative designs.

From between the two rows of handprints, the other elements that comprise *Mojo Hand* emerge out of the cloth/paper left unexposed to pigment. The largest element, a found X-ray of the torso of a pregnant woman truncated to show the skeletal makeup of the shoulders and lower pelvis, glows bright white at the center. To the right of the mother's backbone can be seen the stacked vertebrae of the fetus, its ribs nestled along her hip. By placing a skeletal image between the hands, Yarde implies that this woman's body is the focus of their energy, and the skeleton in turn takes on magical import. The skeleton is the part of the body, the single system, that can withstand the ravages of time and that recalls the body's power, its existence, long after the loss of life. In this way, Yarde's inclusion of the X-ray image can be seen as more than a record of a medical procedure; rather, it becomes a reference to the core of the body's temporality.[15] This is the true interior view of life re-creating itself at a structural level. And yet, in the X-ray's creation, in its existence as a record of a medical procedure not normally undergone by healthy pregnant women, lies a warning that there may be something wrong with the mother or the fetus. It is an image of the Madonna and Child, and it is a premonition of the pietà when Mary will once again hold her son after his mortal death. In this way, *Mojo Hand* became Yarde's diasporic African Shroud of Turin resonating with his own memories of the loss of his brother, Edgar Jr. And like the mystical burial cloth that is believed to have recorded the features of the dead Christ as his soul passed through it, *Mojo Hand* is a text of faith, pain, and transcendence.

Beside the ghostly image of the X-rayed torso, where the body's head would be, lies the small diagram of the double helix of DNA. The links between its twisting components are fragmented, broken in spots, overly built up in others. Just as the X-ray hints at danger, so, too, does the mangled DNA. But it also works as a dedicated code, one that describes a unique biological form; it is a blueprint for life. Here, emerging from the blue textural grid of *Mojo Hand*, the double helix (made up of twenty-three elements) marks the existence of life and its infinite variations. It signals the constant mutation inherent in the evolutionary process, the method by which we are all marked as individual, a point that is further emphasized by the two rows of handprints that border the upper and lower edges of the composition.

The rendering of the Twenty-Third Psalm in braille, to the left of the torso, continues this interrogation into the metamorphosis of the body, examining its fragility and its resiliency. By presenting braille, a necessarily three-dimensional entity, on the planar surface of watercolor, the sense of touch is denied. This transposition underscores the need for "helping hands" to take over the job of seeing and reading what the eyes no longer can or have never been able to do. And the psalm, an anagram for the palms that line the top and bottom of *Mojo Hand*, speaks of the safety and guidance that comes from faith.

> The Lord is my Shepherd; I shall not want.
> He maketh me to lie down in green pastures: he leadeth me beside
> the still waters.

He restoreth my soul: he leadeth me in the paths of righteousness for
His name's sake.
Yea, though I walk through the valley of the shadow of death, I will
fear no evil: for thou art with me; thy rod and thy staff, they comfort me.
Thou preparest a table before me in the presence of mine enemies:
thou anointest my head with oil; my cup runneth over.
Surely goodness and mercy shall follow me all the days of my life:
and I will dwell in the House of the lord forever.[16]

The familiar text of this psalm, so often recited by those suffering from illness, acutely aware of the fragility of mortality, serves as a comforting hand
in its invocation of the Shepherd who leads his flock. In this way, the guiding
hand of the Lord, helping those in need, that is found in the Twenty-Third
Psalm is like the belief in the power of a "mojo hand" in New World, African
American religious practices such as hoodoo.

The fabric-like dark blue watercolor background from which the ghostly
forms of *Mojo Hand* emerge not only ties together the hands, bones, and
braille dots but also connects to Yarde's childhood and the indigo blue he
had first gravitated toward in his childhood lessons at the Museum of Fine
Arts. Now that he was facing his own mortality so clearly, the color took on a
broader resonance that reconfirmed his connection to the spiritual influence
of the dreamworld. Yarde recognized that indigo was the medium traditionally used to dye Central African textiles and was the color of fabric used by
hoodoo practitioners for wrapping helping hands that are designed to protect
the well-being of the home.

In 2000 Yarde received a kidney transplant, by which point his work had
changed forever. If *Mojo Hand* had signaled a shift from the historical reportage
found in the work completed prior to his illness, his new projects continued to
revel in a larger diasporic history that fused personal history with cosmic questions, wrestling with magic, mortality, and the fragility of the human condition.
As these works evolved, Yarde began to use double sheets of paper, sutured
together, to form square planes. In *Ring Shout* (2002), the quadrant formed by
doubling the rectangular linear grid of *Mojo Hand* bends to encapsulate a circle
within which the three key elements of mouths, hands, and shoes are marshaled.
Three concentric registers radiate outward from a central grid of blue squares.
The first register contains four open mouths placed at what appear to be the
cardinal locations of north, south, east, and west. The mouths are in turn separated by twelve palm prints, three between each pair of mouths, oriented in a

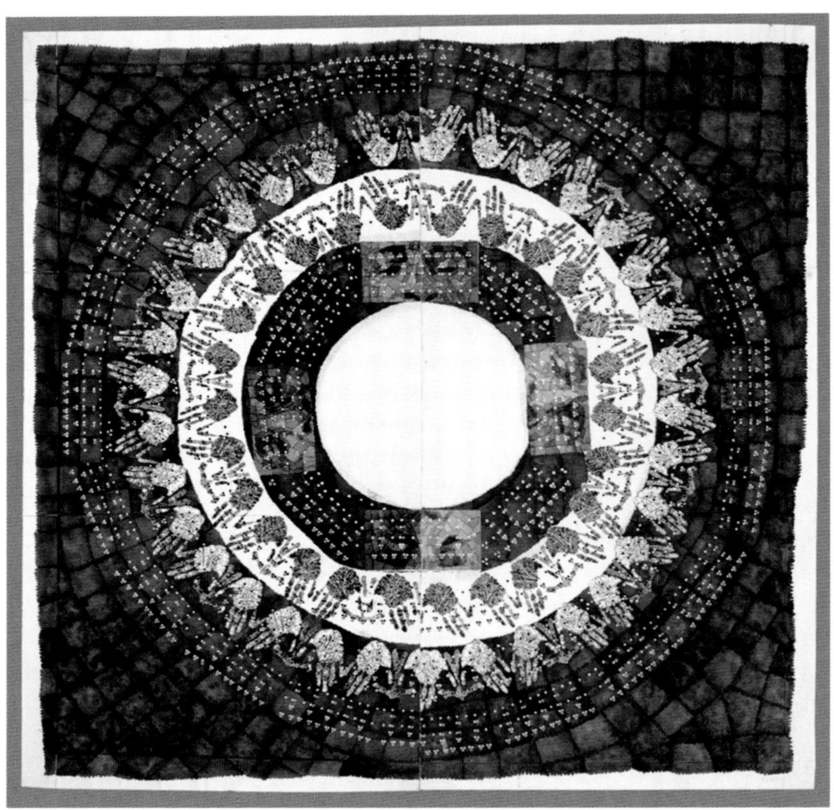

10.5 Richard Yarde, *Pulse*, 2002. United States Department of State, Washington, DC. © Estate of Richard Yarde

counterclockwise direction. The two outer registers comprise identical sets of men's and women's shoes, arranged in pairs, with their toes pointing inward. In a related work, *Pulse*, Yarde inserted images of his own eyes, closed, in the central circle, and handprints in the place of the shoes (figure 10.5).

The title of the series refers to the ceremony of the ring shout, an African American folk ritual with roots in several Central West African traditions, including those of the Bantu, the Igbo and the Akan, the Yoruba, and most significantly the Kongo.[17] The ring shout is characterized by a counterclockwise circumlocution that visually expresses integrated beliefs of cosmic life cycles. Like the hoodoo belief in the power of mojo hands to help their owners, the ring shout is another type of African cultural retention fomented in the southern United States.[18]

During the antebellum period, ring ceremonies held on plantations were often associated with magic and with ancestral life.[19] Historian John Blassingame also cites the ring shout as one of the best examples of the syncretic merging of African and Christian religious practices. Drawing on nineteenth-century sources, Blassingame claims that the shouting, singing, and movement of the ring shout enabled enslaved people to release their despair and to express their desires for freedom.[20] Historian Sterling Stuckey has subsequently argued that the advent of the ring shout in African American culture is best understood in its relation to the Kikongo cosmogram, or Tendwa Nza Kongo.[21]

Representing the "four moments of the sun," the arrangement of a Greek cross surrounded by lines in the Tendwa Nza Kongo embraces the cosmological movement of the sun's rising and setting as a cyclical analogue to the continuing relationship between the living and the dead.[22] It is a reminder of the permeable boundary between this world and the other, the melding of life, death, rebirth, and birth.[23] This African cosmological perspective is reflected in the placement of the hands and mouths in the central register of *Ring Shout*, which also reference the design on the *opon ifa* (divination trays). *Opon ifa* are used by the *babalawo*, the "father of ancient wisdom" who serves as a diviner in the Yoruba belief system of Nigeria and Benin, to help guide his supplicant through a difficult decision by making contact between the human world and the world of the spirits. Stuckey claims that cultural and religious tools like *opon ifa*, the ring shout, and circular imagery in general were an integral part of cultural and religious ceremonies that honored ancestors and asserted people's connection to the land in Africa. This tradition was continued in the close-knit communities of enslaved people in the antebellum South; Stuckey holds that "the use of the circle for religious purposes in slavery was so consistent and profound that one could argue that it was what gave form and meaning to black religion and art."[24]

Yarde's use of shoes references the ring shout's dancelike movement wherein men and women move in separate circles in a sort of shuffling motion, never lifting their feet from the ground, clapping and singing, as described by James Weldon Johnson in his autobiography:

When there was a "ring shout" the weird music and the sound of thudding feet set the silence of the night vibrating and throbbing with a vague terror. Many a time I woke suddenly and lay a long while strangely troubled by these sounds, the like of which my great-grandmother Sarah had heard as a child. The shouters, formed in a ring, men and women alternating, their bodies close together, moved round and round on shuffling feet that never left the floor. With the heel of the right foot they pounded out the fundamental beat of the dance and with their hands clapped out the varying rhythmical accents of the chant; for the music was, in fact, an African chant and the shout an African dance, whole pagan rite transplanted and adapted to Christian worship. Round and round the ring would go. One, two, three, four, five hours, the very monotony of sound and motion inducing an ecstatic frenzy.[25]

And yet in *Ring Shout* the orientation of the shoes does not imply movement; rather, they are shown paired up, attention focused on the central space of the composition, the space of divination. The importance of the cosmogram and the circle to diasporic syncretic religion is witnessed in the use of Cuban *firmas*, *palo mayombe* drawings, flag altars, round sanctuaries, Brazilian *pontos*, and Haitian *véve*.[26] In a similar way to Yarde's use of the ring shout to express community and healing rituals, artist Houston Conwill (1947–2016) created *The New Ring Shout* to commemorate the first graveyard for African Americans in New York City. One of several cosmograms completed by Conwill for public spaces, the piece is embedded in the floor of the General Services Administration building that was built on the site of the graveyard in 1992. Its presence allows visitors to reconnect with an ancestral site that incorporates "memories, histories, and spiritualities that are selectively or forcibly retained, reinvented, or erased."[27]

This desire to connect visually with the spirituality inherent in the divine circularity and spiritual patterns of West Central African healing traditions has been a way for Yarde to address his own personal crisis. His search for transcendence has also been a search for numerological significance in the fundamental structure of the grid, the Twenty-Third Psalm, and the twenty-three fundamental parts to the DNA molecule in *Mojo Hand*. And the doubling of the grid in *Ring Shout*, with its sets of three handprints (a continuation of the three pairs seen in the earlier work) surrounded by neatly mated shoes, continues this investigation into universal questions of structure and spirituality. Through his recent watercolors, Yarde conjured a powerful mixture of history and healing, one that has made dreams real and the real surreal.

Yarde attended an event held by Father Ralph DiOrio, a charismatic priest and faith healer.

I went to his services, and he had something called a laying on of hands there, which I experienced as a partial healing. . . . [After that], I had a couple of dreams that seemed to open up the possibility for the *Mojo Hand* painting. It took me a while to put the images together. I was having a lot of trouble putting the images together. I didn't want to just do an illustration that's parts of the dream that I didn't quite know how things should fit together. [In the dream] I remember the . . . doll's hands, the doll's hands swirling in a dark space. And I tried to be literal with that, and it just didn't work. So, I thought, "Well, I'm going to try my own palms and see what happens there." That seemed to be the [inaudible] pregnant woman. In the dream it was just a woman clothed in a white smock, lying face down. And so I tried to interpret that literally, and that didn't work either. I think I had gotten a lot of X-rays at the time; they were trying to figure out what was going on with me. I just thought, "Let me see what happens if I experiment with the X-rays." There were dots in the dream, which was the first time I started working with braille. Spent some time going to the Perkins School for the Blind in Watertown. I started asking them to translate text into braille. So that's where the 23rd Psalm in braille came from. And just after I put the images together, then I thought of the title. So that was very different for me.

As Yarde began to explore ways of visualizing his dreams, he began to be pulled deeper into the mystical world that Father DiOrio's laying on of hands had opened for him.

Soon, Father DiOrio became a regular presence in Yarde's life as the two men found they had things in common: the priest wanted to be a painter.

It turns out that on his end, he had been painting for many years. . . . His father wanted him to be a painter, and his mother wanted him to be a priest. And he ended up as a priest. My mother wanted me to be a minister. So we were at opposite ends, so to speak. . . . [Father DiOrio] had sent out a prayer asking for help with his painting. And [coincidentally] Susan sent him an invitation to a gallery show I had in New York. And he had his secretary contact me, and I actually got him into UMass, I got him taking courses at UMass. And so we just became friendly. We became very close for a period of time. "You know what?'" he said. "You'd make a terrific priest." I said, "I don't think so. I don't think I could ever go in that direction."

A few months later, Yarde was called with the good news that he had been matched with a kidney from a deceased organ donor. The transplant was successful, but it took its toll on him physically, and the recovery was very slow.

When I had the kidney transplant, I don't think I came back all the way. I was alive, but I think pretty much lacking in spirit. And at night, soon after I had this transplant, around 11:00 or so, the bedroom would fill with this stench. . . . This happened for about a week. Then I called my friend, Father DiOrio, who's the charismatic priest. And [he said] that the spirit of the person whose kidney I was carrying was just in this purgatory, he just couldn't move, in a sense. So, we both prayed for him. And I know it's weird, but I prayed for him one night, and after that, it all stopped. . . . With that kind of operation, it's just a very strange thing that happens. You're carrying around someone else's body part, and will you be able to really connect with it? And what effect does the person have on you?

Despite growing up in the Methodist faith, Yarde had never been particularly religious nor had a deep spiritual feeling about how he moved through the world. His near-death experience with kidney disease, transplantation, and the rush of charismatic energy that he had felt when he met Father DiOrio changed the way he viewed the world and his work. But it didn't completely remove his natural skepticism and his wariness of being drawn in by a charlatan. "I made [Father DiOrio] a painting. His favorite painter was Raphael, and I made him a painting of Christ. It was a Raphael. And he brought it into the church, and he said to me later, 'You realize this person looked at your painting and got a healing. What do you think about that?' And that's when I never went back. I was like, 'Oh no. I'm not being sucked into this.' So, it was part of a number of strange experiences that just happened to me at that time." The healing connection that Yarde made with Father DiOrio did not take away his natural skepticism. Rather, it opened his inner eye to the efforts of his mind, body, and soul to communicate with him through his art.

Beginning with *Mojo Hand*, Yarde explored the fragility of his own body and its relationship to a larger spiritual continuum that reached back through the brutality of enslavement that his ancestors had known on the sugar plantations of Barbados, to the Yoruba, Ibo, and Kongo traditions that their communities had preserved despite the Middle Passage from the Gold Coast of Africa. In the *Ring Shout* series, Yarde visualized the communal healing practices created by African-descended people spread throughout the Atlantic world. And he did so in blue, the color of the oceans though which the diaspora was created and which his parents, Enid and Edgar, had first traveled, both together and alone, to reach the United States. He turned to blue as he confronted his own mortality just as he had first turned to blue when, as a young boy, he sought a reconnection with his beloved deceased brother, Edgar Jr. In the final years of Yarde's life, it was blue paint that filled the most ambitious and expressive watercolors that flowed from his brush.

Part III

BEGINNING AGAIN

The past is a foreign country:
they do things differently there.
—**L. P. HARTLEY**, *The Go-Between* (1953)

If the past is a foreign country where the customs seem strange to those living in the now, is the present a space that is familiar and easily known? Might the present also need to be approached with skepticism and caution so that the disremembered legacies that hover at its edges may be remembered in ways that are reparative rather than exploitative? The reactionary pushback against critical race theory that began to percolate in 2020 is evidence of the willful impulse of some on the political and intellectual right to purposefully disremember the past and disavow its presence within the present. In a moment when the collective consciousness of the present is threatened by individuals and institutions keen on perpetuating a state of radical disremembering, of fake news and purposeful forgetting, of active historical repression, remembering is a scholarly action of increasing critical importance. Now, as we consider the art of the current moment, this work is more socially important and spiritually rewarding than ever.

In my book *Seeing the Unspeakable: The Art of Kara Walker*, I argued for the importance of Kara Walker's transgressive, Black, and female artistic practice as one that repositioned and remembered the past by co-opting an authoritative voice to fashion new visual histories. In this same way, the artist's later work, some of which I discuss in the final section of this book, repositions the dominant historical narrative from a position of mastery by remembering history via a privileging of an alternative set of facts taken from a worldview that is informed by critical race theories of representation. Similarly, in the contemporary practices of remembering employed by Carrie Mae Weems, Sheldon Scott, and Wanda Raimundi-Ortiz, whose work is discussed in two other chapters in this section, inherited visions are also formed and reformed, revealing purposefully or actively disremembered histories.

The book concludes with a critical exploration of the increasing presence of African American and other Black and brown bodies and cultural forms in the contemporary art world. First, I consider how the surge in value and visibility of work by artists of color, in particular African-descended artists, has led to dramatic shifts in the art market and the space of the art museum by centering the ongoing impact of *30 Americans*, the ongoing traveling exhibition of works of art by African American artists from the Rubell Family Collection. Facets of these developments, not all of which appear to be yielding positive impacts, are deeply engaged and further critiqued in the final chapter of this book, which is devoted to a group of highly problematic photographs that were exhibited by photo-based artist Deana Lawson at the Guggenheim Museum during the summer of 2021. This essay ends with a call for more scholarly and intentionally rigorous criticism of contemporary art that foregrounds issues of race in historically white spaces.

The first chapter in this section engages the very recent past of the Hurricane Katrina disaster and considers how it may be remembered by artists working in the present, some in close physical proximity and others at a geographic remove. It begins with an exhibition created and curated in the wake of Katrina by Kara Walker for the Metropolitan Museum of Art in New York City. *After the Deluge* examined the terrifying impact of water, from the biblical deluge (for which Noah built his ark) to the Middle Passage, through which millions of kidnapped and imprisoned human beings were forcibly moved from the African continent to the Americas during the four centuries of the slave trade. In particular, the essay contrasts Walker's display of her own New York–based practice with that of New Orleans–based artists and community members and considers the cyclic nature of disaster for marginalized communities that must regularly weather the impact of racism as well as cataclysm.

The chapter that follows, which centers itself on Carrie Mae Weems's multimedia installation *The Louisiana Project*, also finds its locus in Louisiana and the racialized histories of Mardi Gras. Since the late 1980s, Weems (who is both a photographer and a trained folklore historian) has made an indelible mark on contemporary art by engaging historical images and conjuring disremembered image worlds for contemporary revision. This chapter argues that by stepping into the space of her own work, by photographing herself within it, the artist allows the viewer to see through her the impact of colonization and enslavement that first made it necessary for African-descended people to hide significant aspects of our cultural identities and personal feelings from the eyes of oppressors.

Just as the performative presence of the artist's body has been an integral part of Weems's artistic project, so, too, has it been an essential part of the practices of Wanda Raimundi-Ortiz and Sheldon Scott, whose individual rememberings of the past through contemporary performance art are also examined in this section. The title of this engagement takes its cue from the prose poem "No Man Is an Island," by John Donne, and uses that meditation to consider the ways in which African-descended island-based communities in the South Carolina Sea Islands and in the US territory of Puerto Rico have survived continued colonization and efforts at disempowerment through restorative performances of remembering that recognize the power of cultural traditions and pay homage to ancestral presences.

It still seems a little strange to write about the impact of an exhibition, especially one that is ongoing, instead of the works in that exhibition, but I felt it was important to write about the changes that had in part occurred through the national tour of the landmark exhibition of contemporary African American art *30 Americans*. It had been circulating throughout the United States for over a decade when I served as the guest curator for its stop at the Barnes Foundation in Philadelphia in 2019, and it made a huge impact on my thinking about the power of exhibitions to change the trajectory of art history. As the essay on that exhibition makes clear, the appetite for African American art, from museum audiences and collectors alike, has increased exponentially since the debut of the exhibition in 2008. So, too, has the size of the Rubell Family Collection, from which the show's checklist has been drawn. While the show was still installed at the Barnes, in December 2019, I attended the opening of the new Rubell Museum in Miami, nearly 100,000 square feet of exhibition space showcasing some of the most dynamic and important contemporary art being produced—and acquired—in the country. There was a true resonance between the collecting vision of the Rubells and that of Albert Barnes, as I elucidate in the essay, and seeing this affinity has further clarified for me the many ways that most of our major museums are still failing to collect as expansively and aggressively as they might in areas that will ensure their continued relevance in the coming decades.

In many ways, the final essay in this section has been among the most generative pieces that I have ever written. First published as an opinion piece for Hyperallergic, it is conceived as a combination of review, self-reflection, and a manifesto for contemporary art criticism. Throughout my career I have been keenly aware of the power that a historian of contemporary art or a critic wields when they choose to write about the work of a living artist. We have as much power to lift a career with our words and analysis as to catalyze a negative trajectory if we write something that is less than positive. I took this responsibility seriously as I began to engage the highly problematic work of conceptual photographer Deana Lawson. In my essay I identify numerous instances where the artist, critics, and curators involved needed to be more considerate of the communities and knowledge worlds that their work was both ignoring and involving. It remains my hope that this essay, the others in this section, and the book will be received in the spirit of intellectual openness with which they were all written.

11

REMEMBERING THE REMNANTS

CONTEMPORARY ART
AND HURRICANE KATRINA

Current events often produce historical comparisons, and in an increasingly visual and virtual social culture, the past can seem to inhabit the present in an uncanny way. When the tragedy of Hurricane Katrina became a part of our present in August 2005 and then a part of our past as it is now, it produced many responses, some of them political, others visual and artistic. The various artistic attempts to understand the visual trauma engendered by the flooding and desperation that followed in the wake of Hurricane Katrina, a cataclysm of national and historical importance, mark an important fork in the road toward a postracial America, on the one hand, and a consistently racist America, on the other.

In the wake of the Hurricane Katrina disaster, *After the Deluge* (March 21–August 6, 2006), the artist Kara Walker brought together at the Metropolitan Museum of Art a stunning combination of her own works of art and a number of objects from the museum's collection to create a visual meditation on what the artist termed "the banality of everyday life, water, and its impact (see figure 11.1)." Walker hoped the exhibition would address "the transformative effect and psychological meaning of the sea." In the Met's press release for the show, Walker said, "This show is not simply about the American South or

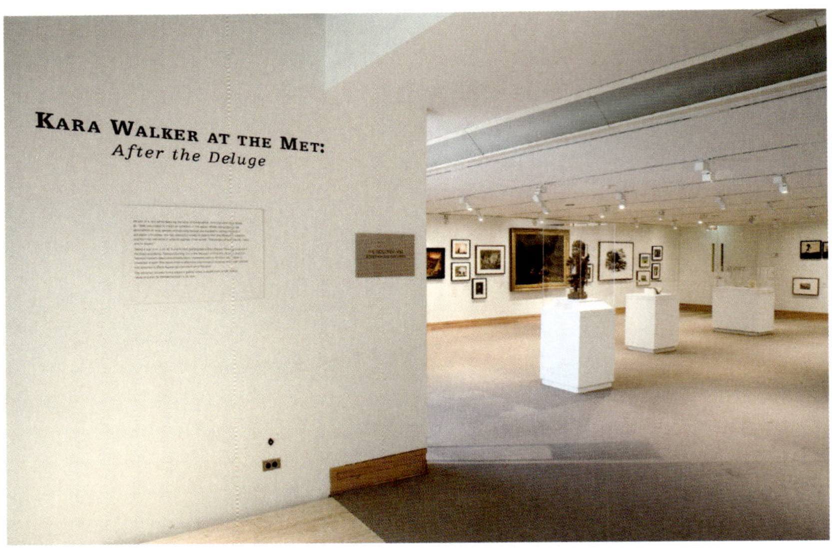

11.1 Installation view, *Kara Walker at the Met: After the Deluge*,
Metropolitan Museum of Art, New York, March 21–July 30, 2006.
© Kara Walker. Courtesy of Sikkema Jenkins & Co. and Sprüth Magers

Hurricane Katrina, although it was inspired by the effect of the chaotic story-telling that erupted in the media during the long, ugly aftermath. I pieced this show together as an attempt to think about visual representations of Black life, in particular, but not exclusively, as it is shaped and transformed by external forces such as the sea, the slave trade, and the failure of retaining walls."[1] Walker wrote on the cover flap of the subsequent book project of the same name that she "created this book because I was tired of seeing news images of (Black) people suffering presented as though it were a fresh new thrilling subject."[2]

In *After the Deluge*, works by Walker, such as *Burn* (1998), *Untitled* (1996), and *Cotton Hoards in Southern Swamp, from the series Harper's Pictorial History of the Civil War (Annotated)* (2005), were installed near a *nkisi nkondi* power figure from the Democratic Republic of the Congo and European and American paintings from the Met's collection, including images of aftermath like Joshua Shaw's *The Deluge towards Its Close* (ca. 1813), which shows the wreckage caused by the biblical deluge that Noah built his ark to avoid (figure 11.2). All of Walker's own works in the exhibition were made prior to Hurricane Katrina. In bringing them together with works from the Met's collections, she worked with the resonance of images, emphasizing

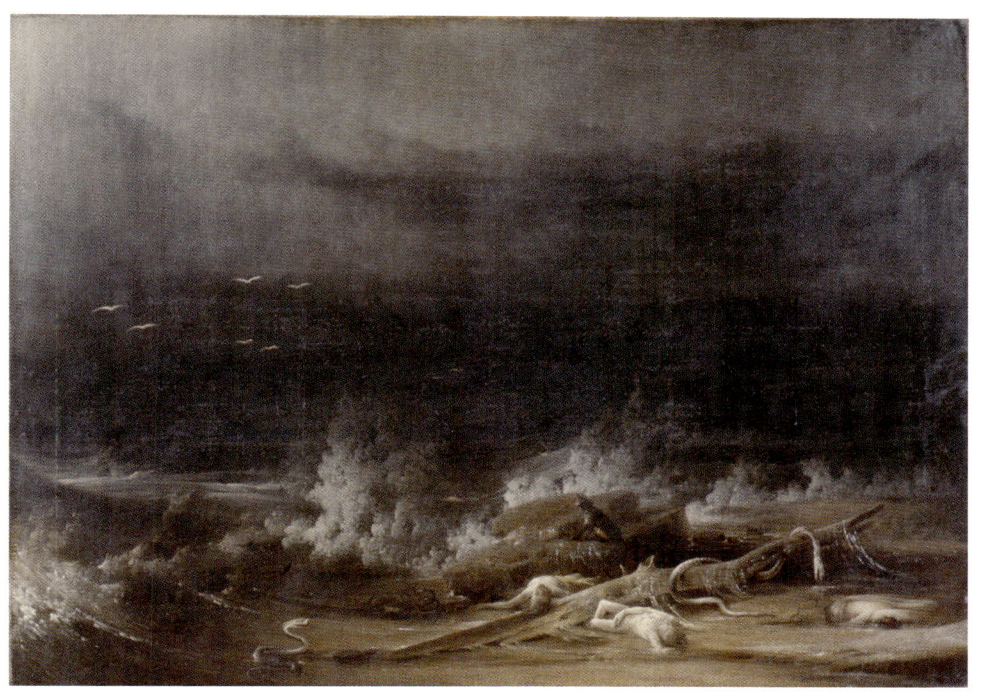

11.2 Joshua Shaw, *The Deluge towards Its Close*, ca. 1813. Metropolitan Museum of Art, New York

that everything we see and create is predicated on what we have already seen and what has already been created. The show was about the shockingly cyclical nature of images; it was also about what has been seen too much, the detrimental power of images, the pornographic nature of pain and suffering, and the things that we refuse to see. For example, Walker included selections from her print series *Harper's Pictorial History of the Civil War (Annotated)*, which highlights the problem of physical invisibility and historical absence. By placing silhouetted figures, whose bodies read as African American, over the pictorial spreads from *Harper's Pictorial History of the Civil War* (1866) Walker's alterations insert a spectral Black presence that effectively derails the narrative structure and historical veracity that the images were originally created to communicate. Walker's remembering of Civil War imagery confronts the viewer with apocryphal narrative. A story that is purposefully anti-Platonic—it is told wrongly—while revealing lost knowledge of the moment. It is an apocryphal story from an "other" time, one that might have been excluded from hegemonic histories of the war, not because it is true or untrue, but because it is undesirable.

In *Cotton Hoards in Southern Swamp* (2005), we see not only the enslaved Black workers and their white overseer quietly poling through a gothic setting of decay and darkness, rotting vegetation, and dripping Spanish moss originally drawn by the unnamed illustrator working in *Harper's Weekly*'s employ but also Walker's contemporary annotation: the silhouetted, colossal black creature rising from the left side of the composition. Festooned with moss, *Cotton Hoards* is all primordial libido—a fantastic cousin of the Swamp Thing or his older sibling, the Creature from the Black Lagoon. All three are gothic by-products of our ambition to control God's creation, evolutionary anomalies grasping for the objects of their desire: an opportunity to procreate amid an environment of unnatural fecundity fed by death.

Rather than depicting "the banality of everyday life," as Walker's introduction promised, most of the images in the exhibition, including *Cotton Hoards in Southern Swamp* and *The Deluge towards Its Close*, were images of death and destruction—of traumatic events and horrific fantasies. Mediatized images of suffering broadcast during and in the aftermath of Hurricane Katrina, and of the devastating flooding that followed, prompted Walker to form her exhibition around the idea of a deluge—a biblical cataclysm—because they resonated so strongly with the many images of suffering that she had been working with in her art for the previous two decades: images of enslavement and torture, dehumanizing images that speak to "man's inhumanity to man" and the ways that people have prioritized their own existence over that of others and then bent those they subordinated to their will.

In assembling these images from the past—both the museum's and her own—Walker attempted not only to confront and control the contemporary images of Katrina's dead or suffering Black people but also to highlight the ways that images of suffering Black folks have long been the stock-in-trade of so much American visual culture. Such images range from nineteenth-century abolitionist imagery advertising the horrors of slavery to contemporary news programs that disproportionately and consistently dehumanize and victimize Black folks—African Americans and Africans alike—routinely shown as impoverished or at the edges of "civilization." Walker's exhibition urged viewers to remember images of a traumatic event in the near present by likening its depiction to innumerable ones that they had seen from the amorphous past, from the space of "postmemory."

Walker's *After the Deluge* attempted to make sense of a devastating event from the still-recent past, a trauma that the artist did not witness personally, and yet one whose imagery was readily available in pictures, newspaper articles and government film, contemporary images that were artistically combined with familiar art historical imagery to create an apocryphal image of a representative episode from that tragedy. As Walker's project points out, homogenizing historical imperatives lead to the repression of dissenting histories, disremembered histories that ultimately lead to the enraged return of the repressed in the form of rememories.

The post-Katrina photographs taken by the Canadian-born photojournalist Robert Polidori appeared both in the *New Yorker* and in a solo exhibition at the Metropolitan Museum of Art that opened a few weeks following the close of *After the Deluge*.[3] Like his earlier images of the atomically ruined Soviet cities of Pripyat and Chernobyl (taken several years after that disaster), Polidori focused his lens on the unpeopled spaces of ruined domesticity, creating a parallel art critic Michael Kimmelman has termed "New Orleans as our modern Pompeii" from the Crescent City's depopulated streets of ruined houses and cars. "A photojournalist's compulsion and problem is always to contrive beauty from misery," writes Kimmelman, "and it is only human to feel uneasy about admiring pictures like these from New Orleans, whose sumptuousness can be disorienting."[4] The artist himself views this highly detailed camerawork as providing a window onto the way that "individuals exteriorize their internal values."[5] In this way, the ruined spaces of New Orleans filled with the material detritus of human occupation evoke what Polidori terms "the materialization of the internal life."[6]

However, Polidori's photographs have been received by some viewers as not only disorientating but also unsympathetic and exploitative as well. For unlike the plaster casts that have been made of gaps in the ash heaps of Pompeii, revealing the shapes of Vesuvius's victims during their last moments, the corpses caught by Polidori's lens have opened the photographer to criticism of unseemly voyeurism and a fetishizing of the pain of others. The Baton Rouge–based photographer and blogger William Greiner, a member of the New Orleans Photo Alliance, immediately criticized Kimmelman's review of Polidori's 2006 show at the Metropolitan Museum of Art by citing the myopia of the New York critic's assessment:

> Nothing is mentioned about the image Mr. Polidori made of a dead man, lying in his own bed and in the privacy of his own home, partially covered by a blanket!
>
> I am a fan, or have been, of Mr. Polidori's work but I think making this image went beyond what is acceptable. I'll put it this way, if that were my brother, father, grand-father or uncle on that bed and I walked in to find this guy with his eight by ten view camera looming over the body, I think

Mr. Polidori would be looking for a good dentist to fit him for dentures right now!

That's what is wrong with this picture![7]

Greiner and other arts bloggers have called on Polidori repeatedly to defend not only the visceral nature of his photographs but also the use to which they have been put beyond the *New Yorker* article for which they were first commissioned.[8] In addition to the Metropolitan Museum of Art exhibition, through which they further became known, and the Steidl book (figure 11.3) in which they were published, Polidori allowed an advertising company in Brazil to utilize one of his Katrina images in an anti-smoking campaign that was anchored by the slogan "Your body is your home. Don't smoke."[9]

Here I would like to give a pointed example of apocryphal history that was reintegrated into the present moment when it became relevant once more though the Katrina disaster: the Seventeenth Street levee break, which flooded the Lower Ninth Ward, leaving hundreds of people dead and thousands homeless. This notorious levee break occurred in what is known as the Industrial Canal, linking Lake Pontchartrain to the Mississippi, and evokes well-worn stories of familial trauma and destruction dating as far back as the Great Mississippi Flood of 1927, when the self-same levees were dynamited on

11.3 Robert Polidori, cover image from *Robert Polidori: After the Flood* (2006)

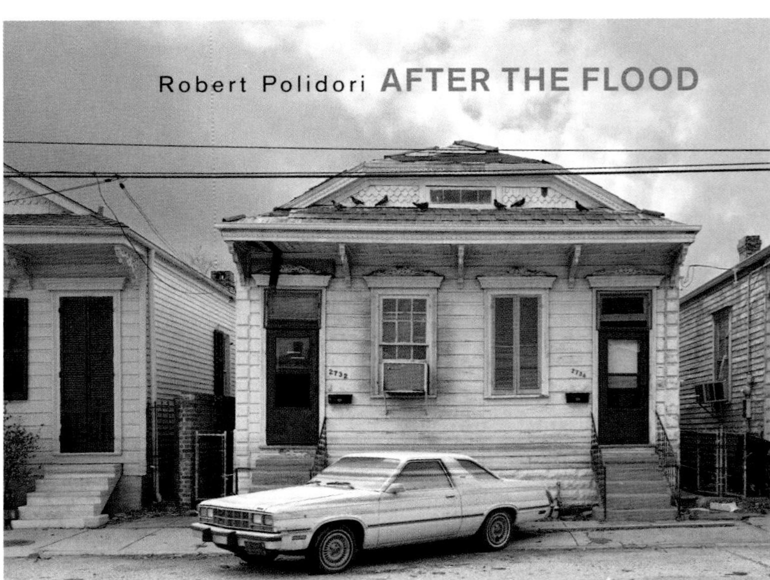

purpose to save wealthier neighborhoods. After Katrina, some residents in the Lower Ninth Ward speculated about the cause of the breach, attributing it to speculators who wanted to clear the neighborhood for future development.[10]

Following the flood of 1927, scores of African American men were wrested from their families and forced at gunpoint to labor on the destroyed levees and on other reconstruction efforts. Numerous examples of organized racial inhumanity during the flooding were recorded. The *New York Times* reported that at one levee, when sandbags ran out, the engineer in charge ordered (and this was an order at gunpoint since all conscripted Black work gangs were run at "concentration camps" manned by armed white guards) "several hundred negroes to lie down on top of the levee and as close together as possible. The black men obeyed, and although the spray frequently dashed over them, they prevented the overflow that might have developed into an ugly crevasse. For an hour and a half this lasted, until the additional sandbags arrived."[11] Such forced labor during and after the flood of 1927 has subsequently been likened to conditional enslavement and belongs to a shameful legacy of American disaster response. Conscripted Black labor was understood in the South at the time as a given mode of Black servitude, a continuation of the tradition of the exploitation of Black people by dominant governmental and commercial structures in the South, and moreover by the American federal government.

It is important to note that the apocryphal histories of 1927 were resurrected in 1965 during the flooding attendant to Hurricane Betsy. Many residents in New Orleans's predominantly Black Saint Bernard Parish believed that their levees had been dynamited—once again—to save more expensive properties upriver in the predominantly white French Quarter. Because the federal government never dispelled these allegations, closure was never achieved. The issue was effectively disremembered. Therefore, when Hurricane Katrina hit, and when the Lower Ninth Ward and Saint Bernard Parish were again flooded, numerous residents believed that the levees had been purposefully breached, thereby reestablishing historically complex race and class divisions and suspicions.

This sentiment continues to resonate loudly in the post-Katrina era in the anger and dissatisfaction that many New Orleanians experienced toward the response of the federal government to their plight. One of the most distressing phenomena has been a sort of contemporary Middle Passage experienced by many poor and Black New Orleanians who were deemed refugees within their own country and who were subsequently spread throughout the land: separated from their families, given no return tickets home, adrift in a new diaspora of dislocation and pain. For many survivors of Hurricane Katrina, the traumatic memories engendered by such a cataclysm are so overpowering, so upsetting, that the cultural circulation of them threatens historical and communal stability rather than reconstructing it.

When the Levees Broke: A Requiem in Four Acts (2006), director Spike Lee's Emmy Award–winning documentary on Hurricane Katrina and its aftermath, like Walker's *After the Deluge*, asks us to see through different eyes and from multiple perspectives to consider potentially competing histories. To do this, Lee combines news clips, still photographs, and original interviews with both well-known locals, such as embattled mayor Ray Nagin and renowned trumpeter Wynton Marsalis, and previously unknown residents. Lee uses many stories and many eyes, including those of Phyllis Montana-Leblanc, who saw their way through a harrowing odyssey of floodwaters and FEMA (Federal Emergency Management Agency) red tape.

By telling her story through Lee's lens, Montana-Leblanc is allowed a place to remember the personal trauma of surviving Hurricane Katrina. For Montana-LeBlanc, Katrina was liberating and life-changing. After appearing in Lee's documentary, she penned a book, *Not Just the Levees Broke*, and moved into acting, with a recurring role in the HBO drama *Treme* (2010–13). In *Treme* Montana-LeBlanc portrayed the hard-edged girlfriend of a struggling musician, struggling to keep her family together amid communal uncertainty and infrequent funds.

Treme, a dramatic series conceived by Eric Overmyer and David Simon, the former writers and producers of the Baltimore-based crime drama *The Wire*, examined the lives of Katrina survivors as they attempted to rebuild their lives in the immediate wake of the storm, starting some three months following the disaster. Like *The Wire*, *Treme* attempted to tell multiple stories that crossed race and class lines, including that of Janette Desautel (Kim Dickens), a restaurateur, and Toni Bernette (Melissa Leo), a lawyer married to a Tulane University English professor, Creighton Bernette (John Goodman). Part of *Treme*'s appeal lay in its interest in moving beyond typical stories of poor Black suffering—that stock-in-trade of disaster and poverty porn that Walker side-eyes—and highlighting instead the lives of white and middle-class New Orleanians, whose experiences were largely absent from the news media's coverage. By writing the white and well-heeled experience back into the post-Katrina narrative, alongside that of the poor, the Black, and the disenfranchised, *Treme* encouraged the inevitable seepage of whiteness back into the stream of discourse around the disaster.

Through documentary and dramatic staging, can we who were not there ever understand the trauma experienced by victims of the storm and its aftermath, or the ways in which the visual and aural horrors of Katrina re-membered the disremembered phantasms rooted in historical rituals of disaster response that were well known to generations of those dwelling on the Mississippi Delta?

If personal trauma is often defined by the secrecy and silence that follow its creation, and if communal silence about trauma is often the result of ex-ternal pressures that are imposed from above by a dominant authority who would prefer to control the discourse surrounding such events, what do we do with the transgressive survivors who refuse to subscribe to such intracultural pacts? What do we do with women like Phyllis Montana-Leblanc, or with the other Katrina survivors who were interviewed by Lee for his film: people who choose to remember the disremembered and in so doing refuse to embrace a hegemonically constructed silence? What do we do with those mouthy out-laws who refute the traditional codes of conduct and opt instead to remember the past by speaking loudly about the scars that are borne by their bodies and minds? What do we do with survivors who refuse to live in the space of silence that results from unequal access to the official discourses of history?

Just as we cannot ignore Montana-LeBlanc, we cannot ignore the experi-ences of the Black people who suffered and died on the levee tops during the Great Mississippi Flood of 1927, thousands of them working at gunpoint in conscripted chain gangs. To wit, a group of thirteen thousand Black people in Greenville, Mississippi, were left for days without food or water atop a levee after having watched whites being loaded onto boats and taken to safety. Weeks later, those who survived the experience found themselves living in squalid refugee camps. Those who could soon fled to the northern cities in search of new homes, work, and educational opportunities for their children, participating in the Great Migration of Black southerners that had begun at the end of the Civil War.

The Tuskegee Institute's president, Robert Russa Moton, commissioned by President Calvin Coolidge's administration to write a report on the condi-tions of the 1927 flood, soon found that his efforts to reveal the extreme racial inequalities in the flood relief were suppressed by President Herbert Hoover, who persuaded him to release the report after the presidential election of the fall of 1928, for fear that he and the Republican Party would lose the race. Moton did so only after he was promised better conditions for Blacks in the South. Once elected, however, Hoover did not keep his end of the bargain. In 1932, when W. E. B. Du Bois was asked why he was not supporting Hoover's reelection, Du Bois explained that Hoover's "refusal to interfere in the case of known injustices to the Negro, as in the unfair distribution of relief after the

Mississippi flood in 1927, and the treatment of Negro workers on the Mississippi levees under government supervision [that] year." For Du Bois, arguably the most powerful African American of the era, it was Hoover's callous treatment of Blacks after the flood that precluded his vote for the Republican candidate, even though it meant breaking his longtime allegiance to the party of Abraham Lincoln.[12]

The tragic irony of the story is that while the Great Mississippi Flood of 1927 may have signaled the beginning of Hoover's presidential career, for George W. Bush, Hurricane Katrina signaled the end. I cannot help but see the Katrina disaster as a part of a larger, inescapable, cyclical history: a cataclysmic flood followed by an epic economic depression. But the greatest (and *not* tragic) irony of this comparison is that unlike Hoover, who was replaced by another elite white (Franklin Delano Roosevelt), Bush was replaced by a bootstrapping African American in the form of Barack Obama.

How can we who were not there remember the desperate circumstances in which much of the poverty-stricken or working-class population in New Orleans found themselves because of the Hurricane Katrina disaster? How can we know their pain when all we have are words and pictures?

Much of the artistic response to Hurricane Katrina by New Orleans–based artists that emerged in its immediate aftermath focused on locating unheroic realities and locating the stories of both victims and survivors. *Floodwall* (2007–11), by New Orleans–based artist Jana Napoli, is an installation of drawers scavenged from the heaps of detritus that lined the city's street in the aftermath of the flood (figure 11.4). It speaks to communal trauma through the lens of destroyed personal belongings. Napoli explained, "Our lives are our neighborhoods, our family, our friends, our neighbors, our workplace, our schools, our communities, our animals, our gardens, our personal property, and even our furniture drawers, the place where we store our secrets, our past lives, our photos, our mementos, our passions and our hopes and dreams."[13]

Floodwall expanded into a multimodal project in which the stories of the drawers themselves were gathered through an online crowdsourcing program to gather oral histories that the original owners associated with the drawers and their contents, and a digital humanities project that mapped the drawers' original locations. The artist then designed several installation configurations for the drawers, and between 2007 and 2011, they traveled throughout the country and then internationally. In 2012, as a part of *Prospect* 2, the second post-Katrina art biennial held in New Orleans, the drawers were exhibited for the last time before being gathered at the edge of the Algiers

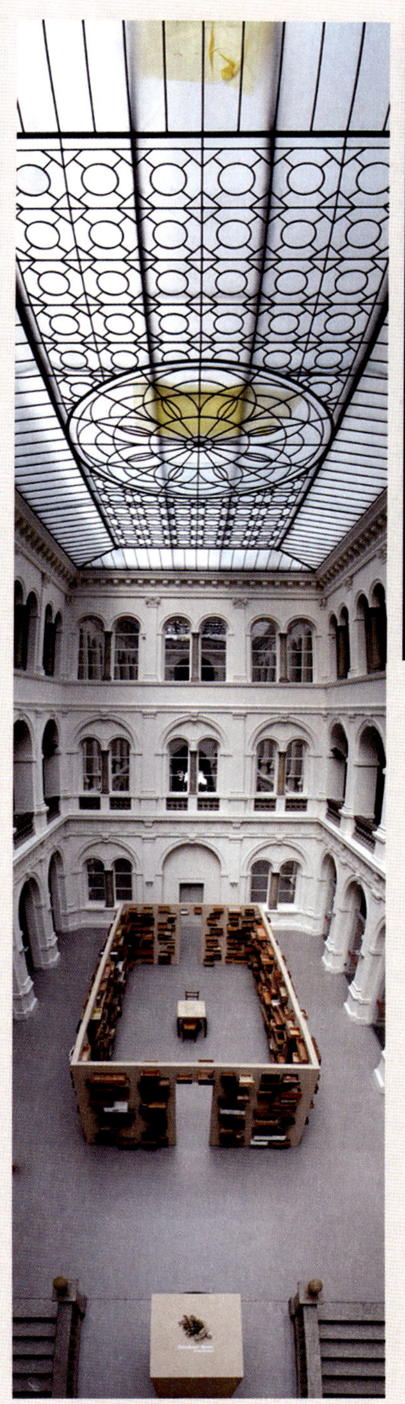

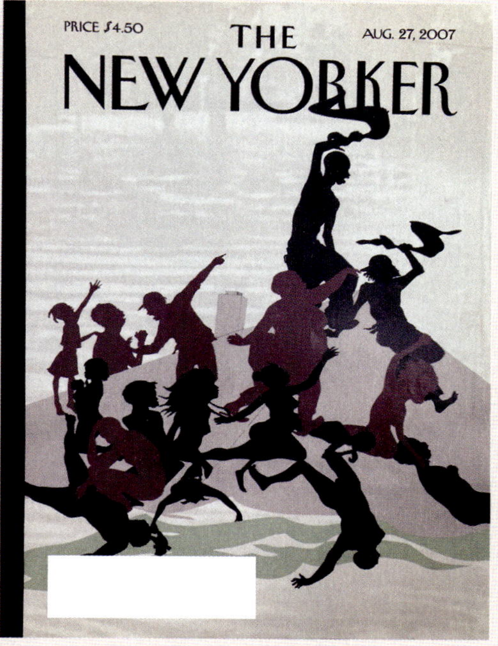

11.4 Photograph of the *Floodwall* exhibition, National Museum, Wrocław, Poland. Photograph by Philip Oeschli

11.5 Kara Walker, *Post Katrina, Adrift*, August 27, 2007, cover for the *New Yorker*

levee to be set ablaze.[14] That same site, near the ferry landing, was one that Walker would also choose to use for the performance of her *Kastawof Kara-van* at *Prospect 4* (February 23–25, 2018).

Napoli's materialization of communal trauma through the ruination of domesticity is emblematic of a significant trend in the Katrina-related visual art that was produced in the immediate aftermath of the disaster. And her decision to torch the drawers that made up *Floodwall* on the banks of the Mississippi River as a part of *Prospect 2* pointed to the role that the river itself has played in the natural and social history of the region.

Unlike Napoli, Kara Walker was not an eyewitness to the recent history with which she was working. Walker's knowledge about the aftermath of Hurricane Katrina came from twenty-four-hour news channels, newspapers, photographic magazines, and the internet. In a sense, Walker looked to past models of history painting, such as Joshua Shaw's *The Deluge towards Its Close* (ca. 1813) and Theodore Gericault's *The Raft of the Medusa* (1818–19), which served as the compositional reference for the August 27, 2007, cover of the *New Yorker* magazine, which commemorated the storm's second anniversary (figure 11.5).

The works of Kara Walker, Jana Napoli, Robert Polidori, and Spike Lee provide multiple points for focalization so that we can remember the nature of both historically remote and more recent traumatic catastrophes. As we consider the enduring landscape and the people who move through it, these multiple points of focalization open onto multiple narratives and visualities. In such a fashion, people are interpolated by the cataclysms of natural and human disasters, which remain eternal and ever changing, enacting relation-ships that are predicated on social structures at once remote and yet wholly familiar. It is so important that we do not underestimate the act of forgetting or refusing to see. We must find ways to remember the past through vision, voice, and a collective disavowal of historical amnesia and communal silence. Otherwise, we have nothing but ruins and no one to blame but ourselves.

12

THE WANDERING GAZE OF CARRIE MAE WEEMS'S *THE LOUISIANA PROJECT*

In 2003 the Newcomb Art Gallery at Tulane University in New Orleans commissioned Carrie Mae Weems (b. 1953) to create a piece in response to the impending bicentennial of the Louisiana Purchase.[1] Comprising over seventy separate photographs and screen prints, a video, and a live performance by the artist at its debut, *The Louisiana Project* examines both the distant past of slaveholding, antebellum Louisiana and its recent present, characterized by economic crisis and racial segregation.[2] *The Louisiana Project* (see figure 12.1) takes as its starting point the ubiquitous New Orleans festival Mardi Gras and the parades and balls associated with the all-white Krewes of Comus, Momus, and Rex—the oldest of the thirty-odd groups who parade through the streets during the annual celebration of Carnival that precedes the Lenten season. *The Louisiana Project* juxtaposes the secrecy that surrounds the Rex ball, an exclusive event attended by members of New Orleans' white upper class, and the not-so-secret sexual liaisons the male scions of these elite families had with African American women from the adjacent community of the *gens du couleur* throughout the nineteenth and twentieth centuries.

In *The Louisiana Project*, Weems continues an artistic practice of reinterpreting the facts of history by placing her own body within the extant detritus

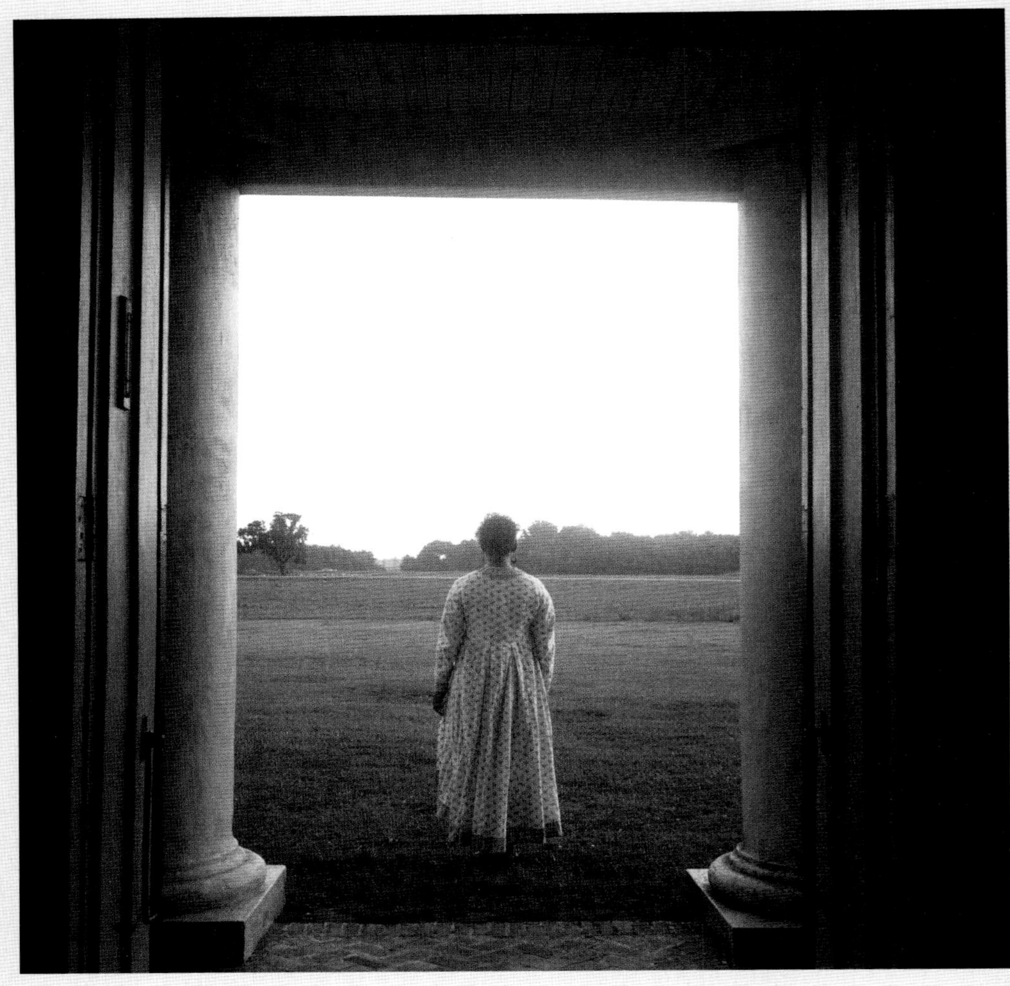

12.1 Carrie Mae Weems, untitled work from *The Louisiana Project*, 2003. © Carrie Mae Weems

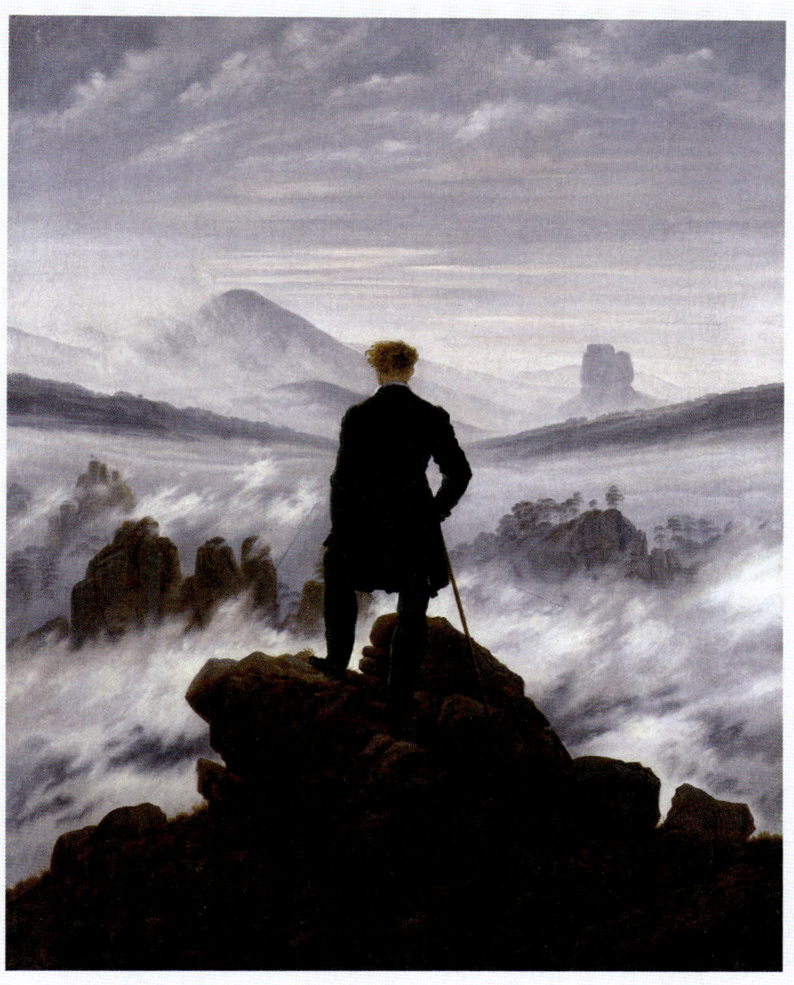

12.2 Caspar David Friedrich, *Wanderer above the Sea of Fog*, ca. 1818. Hamburger Kunsthalle, Hamburg

of its matrix. In many of the photographs that comprise the project, the artist stands with her back to the camera in front of an architectural edifice, amid a rural landscape, or within a domestic interior. She wears period clothing: a plain, long-sleeved dress that falls to the floor, evoking the daily wear of working-class women in the nineteenth century. In other photographs, in which her body faces the camera, she wears masks and men's tuxedos.

Susan Cahan observes in the catalog for the project, "Weems's focus on masking and facades underscores the notion that social hierarchies result from a differential in relations of power, not birthright."[3] The masks, costumes, and choice to turn away from the camera prompt a reconsideration of the physical presence of history. This chapter argues that by turning her back to the viewer, Weems also engages a long history of visual obfuscation associated with the Sublime, a history that may be most powerfully seen in the work of Caspar David Friedrich's (1774–1840) painting *Wanderer above the Sea of Fog* (ca. 1818), which pictures the figure of a man at the top of a craggy peak somewhere in Saxony or Bohemia, looking out over a landscape that is shrouded in mist (figure 12.2). With his back turned to the viewer, not only is his identity concealed but also his expression. Is he delighted with the vista or horrified and aghast? His confident pose, with his left foot planted firmly on the penultimate step of the peak and his right side braced with a walking stick, makes him appear unaffected by the strong wind that briskly blows his blond hair to one side. There is little indication of a vertiginous instability, only a sense of mastery despite the seeming insignificance of the lone walker himself.

Like Friedrich's wanderer, we do not have to *see* through Weems to know what she is seeing. Instead, we can see *through* Weems. Weems prompts us to reconsider our understanding of domestic spaces and architecture as we gaze on a photograph of her sitting on the grass before a Greek revival–style plantation home. "Who lived here?" "Who looked out of these windows?" "Who walked these halls?" "Who died here?" "Whom did they love?" "What fate befell them?" This process of remembering history through Weems's body and gaze indicates that the landscape and the buildings that populate it are always key players in multiple histories. By seeing *through* Weems as she moves through space, time, and place, we are privy to visions both real and ethereal. And in these pictures we see a place that is on the edge of expiration and yet struggles valiantly to hold its own decay at bay.

In his 2002 book *The Landscape of History: How Historians Map the Past*, John Gaddis ruminates on Friedrich's *Wanderer*, using the painting and its sole figure as a metaphor for the way that we as historians can only "represent" the past by portraying it as a near or distant landscape. "We can perceive shapes through the fog and mist, we can speculate as to their significance, and sometimes we can even agree amongst ourselves as to what these are," argues Gaddis. "We pride ourselves on not trying to predict the future, as our colleagues in economics, sociology, and political science attempt to do. We resist letting contemporary concerns influence us—the term 'presentism,' among historians, is no compliment. We advance bravely into the future with our eyes fixed firmly on the past: the image we present to the world is, to put it bluntly, that of a rear end."[4] In *The Louisiana Project*, Weems shows us her backside to emphasize her own privilege as the primary holder of vision.

Here, Weems is the revenant among the exteriors and interiors of Greek revival plantation homes; the disremembered specter standing on a stretch of deserted railroad; a restless spirit traversing aboveground tombs, standing still like Friedrich's figure in the *Wanderer*, poised on the brink, having come to a sublime vista just a bit too late to find it at its peak. She makes us a witness to the landscape around her. Here, Louisiana has become the object of her gaze. A gaze that reads different visions than those seen by others, apocryphal visions. Through her wandering gaze, we encounter a landscape that juxtaposes the slowly evanescing Greek revival architecture of the 1840s with the decrepit expanse of a mid-twentieth-century public housing project (a sort of postbellum slave quarters). In its poignant repetition of condition, it is a space that is oddly predictive; in its mix of past and present, the landscape of *The Louisiana Project* is profoundly prescient in nature.

A key component of the installation is a video that intercuts television footage from 2003 of Rex, the king of Mardi Gras, dancing with his queen at the Rex ball, with a shadow drama of characters dressed in eighteenth-century clothes engaging each other in a silhouetted tableau of domesticity, masquerade, and sexual domination. Mardi Gras marks the annual outing of rituals that are both creative and destructive, defining and mystifying, a world in which things are turned on their head on purpose, a world in which transgression is constantly rewarded so long as it follows tradition. By providing the viewer with an "other" way to see Mardi Gras, and the parades of Rex, Endymion, Orpheus, Zulu, and Bacchus, Weems remembers a new Carnival through the age-old tradition of topsy-turvy. Mikhail Bakhtin describes this tradition as practiced in pre-Enlightenment Europe as a social institution in which the "temporary suspension of all hierarchic distinctions and barriers among men . . . and of the prohibitions of usual life" was the rule.[5] For Bakhtin, *carnivalesque*, the term used to describe the kind of behavior displayed during these periods, is both the description of a historical phenomenon—the activities that took place during the great medieval carnivals of Europe—and the designation for specific literary tendencies as well as a relation to our understanding of the physically grotesque. Bakhtin viewed such raucous festivities as regulated moments in time when the social authority of secular and religious authorities was suspended at least momentarily for the ascendance of licensed transgression. Such communally sanctioned, and essentially participatory, festivals of the grotesque and fantastic allow participants to move beyond a regular membership within a crowd, to become part of a whole. In this way, to participate in Carnival, and in the case of New Orleans to attend the parades of Mardi Gras, is to become a part of a collective, a collective in transgression. Within Carnival, asserts Bakhtin, "all were considered equal. . . . Here, in the town square, a special form of free and familiar contact reigned among people who were usually divided by the barriers of caste, property, profession, and age."[6] Carnival and its progeny, the Mardi Gras of New Orleans, both construct and deconstruct the social rules that govern transgression and trauma.

The visual drama of Weems's video is accompanied by an audio track of the artist's voice slowly reciting a detailed poem of remembrance. The audio and video work combine to conjure up a world of faded majesty remembered beneath a veneer of deceit, an imaginary that evokes Louisiana's complicated and uneasy mythic legacy of race and gender, an imaginary in which Weems has inserted herself as a real and figurative witness to the romantic tales that we tell ourselves about slavery and interracial sexuality in the creole south, tales about the voodoo priestess Marie Laveau and Labelle's "[Creole] Lady Marmalade," tales that veil the legacy of enslavement and the conflicting truths about interracial sexual liaisons in the eighteenth and nineteenth centuries.[7]

Of all the myriad elements of *The Louisiana Project*, it is Weems's solitary Friedrichian wanderer and the physical constancy of the landscape in which she moves—a landscape that is as much a constructed character as the ones that Weems creates and embodies—that holds the pain of the past and the possibility of a future. I argue strongly for the project's prescience, for its ability to help us envision the future through visions of the past, for its oracular gift to see the reflexive nature of the present in relation to history. *The Louisiana Project* transforms Weems's body into a vehicle through which we are made to *see*, and at other times into a body that we are made to see *through*. This task of specular transcendence is accomplished through images that posit the artist's physical presence in the picture plane as a momentary and yet ever-present imprint on time and space, so that representations of many pasts and recent futures can be seen from multiple perspectives. In this way, both her body and the landscape in which she moves are made to hold the past and the pain of our individual and our collective trauma of enslavement as well as the historical blindness that has affected our understanding of the past, present, and possible futures of Louisiana, and especially of New Orleans just two years following the traumatic experience of Hurricane Katrina. Ultimately, the prescient nature of *The Louisiana Project* helps us to remember several traumatic pasts, all of which bear the mark of New World slavery.

To experience *The Louisiana Project*, in which Weems constantly positions herself as a witness to both past and future histories, is to be confronted by one's own position as a viewer and to acknowledge the ever-present power of the gaze and the perpetual struggle by women artists, in their work and in their persons, to control it. Much of Weems's work during the past three decades has been about controlling the gaze, from the *Kitchen Table Series* of 1990, in which we are asked to virtually join the artist and her models at one end of a table as silent witnesses to dramatic domestic events that unfold over a series of photographs, to *The Jefferson Suite* from 2001, where our spectatorial presence is elided and rechanneled as we consider the ramifications of genetic research in relation to race, ethics, and morality as well as the American judicial system.

To control both the narrative and the gaze, Weems enters her own work through a process of self-objectification. In *The Jefferson Suite*, we see the artist in several guises but most strikingly in the role of President Thomas Jefferson's enslaved consort Sally Hemings. In *The Jefferson Suite*, Weems served as her own model, a role that she has frequently inhabited in her work. Alternately dressed as Hemings and undressed as an example of a genetic topos, Weems functioned as the focalizer for a visual tale of sexual attraction, political intrigue, and social deception that led the viewer from the eighteenth century through to the 1998 "revelation" of the Jefferson DNA study that scientifically demonstrated the connections between the "Black" Hemings and the "white" Jefferson families. Weems collapsed time and space in *The Jefferson Suite* and rechanneled the authority of voice into the body of one whose enslavement had imposed a loud silence in history. By juxtaposing this staged photograph with a more "natural" one of our forty-second president, William Jefferson Clinton, and his much younger mistress, White House intern Monica Lewinsky, Weems encourages our gaze to wander across a historical legacy of unequal power relations and sexual attraction that spans over two hundred years of American history. In *The Louisiana Project*, Weems continued the practice of inserting herself into a truly apocryphal version of history. In this way, Weems mobilizes what I call a "wandering gaze."

As an art historical theory of spectatorship, the gaze has its origins in film theory and the work of Laura Mulvey. Mulvey's 1975 essay "Visual Pleasure and Narrative Cinema" introduced the gaze as a theory of gendered spectatorial differences in popular twentieth-century film that help to explain the ways that men and women view the world and each other on-screen. Mulvey asks that we imagine a darkened movie theater in which every member of the audience has their eyes locked on the screen. All vision follows the cone of light that travels from one side of the theater to the other, from the projection booth to the screen. In this scenario Mulvey places an active male viewer seated in the theater and a female image on the screen. It is a kind of perennial geometry through which male vision consumes the female image. In the past thirty-plus years, much has been written to dispute Mulvey's argument that cinematic vision is posited as male and heterosexual. Feminist film scholars from B. Ruby Rich, to Teresa de Lauretis, to Linda Williams have since argued that the relationship of female viewers to the screen image is less patriarchal and more dialectical.[8] They argue that the female viewer retains more agency through a selective filtering process. Williams encourages a questioning of "the orthodoxies of a classical spectatorship without abandoning the fundamental [importance of] the spectators who gaze at [film], glance at it, or avert their eyes from it."[9] Rich pushes back a bit more firmly against the dominance of gaze-based Lacanian psychoanalytic feminist film criticism, charging it with an unblinking ahistoricity that fails to account for "the key determinants of context, audience, or even aesthetic fashion."[10] Similarly, Lauretis argues the importance of "engaging all of the codes of cinema . . . to articulate the conditions and forms of vision for another social subject" as a way to broaden the possibilities for the "production and counterproduction of social vision."[11] The idea that the only person who could be interpellated into the subject of the gaze, the primary person who could be called forth to be the "gazer" if you will, would be a man whose sexualized vision would contain the female object on the screen in an unequal power relation is simply not tenable when you begin to think about the multiplicity of points of vision that are possible in a contemporary, expanded viewing environment. Simply put, there are multiple points of view. Weems's "wandering gaze" allows multiple individuals to occupy the position of power as the holder of the gaze regardless of gender identity, sexual orientation, or race.

With the "wandering gaze" we can allow ourselves the freedom to move into an expanded field of vision. If we begin to conceive of visual art as unbound narrative, we can read images as connecting not only to a past but also to a present, and to a future as well. In this way, we begin to see how a multifold increase in the diversity of vision would inform the interpretation of the moment of viewing in more complicated ways than those provided for by the simple assumption of a uniform, heterogeneous, white world, a world in which the ability of class, ethnicity, and education to separate whites from one another is ignored and sublimated beneath a brittle veneer of pink-skinned sameness.

The "wandering gaze" allows us to step inside the skin of Friedrich's omniscient white viewer, who, above the mists, commands the landscape below him. We are aware of our own significance, standing astride the peaks of history, and our utter insignificance as one of many who have risen to consciousness only to fall. We not only dominate our field of vision but also falter in its sublimity, which proves to diminish our standing. What is offered by an expansion into the "wandering gaze" is an ever more inclusive theory of vision in which myriad spectators, regardless of race, gender identity, or sexual orientation, can be the empowered agents of their own pleasure and (I would argue) their own pain, experiencing vision as an ever-widening field of subjective choice and experience. In this way, multiple identifications are possible.

Increasingly, we are better able to grasp the association of power with various raced and gendered positions in society and to see how a multifold increase in the diversity of vision would inform the interpretation of the moment of viewing in more complicated ways and allow for multiple identifications.

And it is this type of viewing, that of gazing back at the past from the perspective of the present, that *The Louisiana Project* opens for its audience. Weems's photographs push us to recognize that you can see *through* me, and you can see through *me*, regardless of my original position or yours. After all, all forms of knowledge are channeled through our experience as individuals within specific cultural moments; as the artist allows their work to move out into the world, it is constantly reinterpreted through each individual act of viewing.

The photographs of *The Louisiana Project* present multiple visualities rather than being the result of a single visualization. In this expanded visual and temporal field, we begin to see that in *The Louisiana Project*, vision is embodied in the "wandering gaze" as an intervention into the metanarrative, creating several differing histories beyond the present and into the past and into the ever-present, yet ever-changing, landscape. However, such an approach requires that the viewer not be lured into the notion that Weems the narrator is the same person as Weems the model, for these images and those she has created previously in the *Kitchen Table Series* or *The Jefferson Suite* are not unbidden snapshots or autobiographical records but rather are staged images in which the artist has assumed a role that is of her own conception and creation. It is not Carrie Mae Weems the narrator who stands in the doorway of a Greek revival plantation house with her back to the camera. That Weems stands outside the photograph in the role of what Mieke Bal would call the visual "focalizer," initiating and directing vision into the distance.[12] We are view-pointed *by* her, *to* her, and *through* her we see the land beyond the building. She is the intercessor through whom we come to know the landscape of the past in a new and different way.

Through the "wandering gaze" of *The Louisiana Project*, we are able to see the relation of trauma to the visualization of memory, and the act of forgetting or refusing to see, in relation to our irrevocable separation from the Lacanian notion of the real.[13] To view *The Louisiana Project* is to see the (un)dead New Orleans of the past, a world that is no more and yet resists erasure through the reassurance of ritual. *The Louisiana Project* creates a space for the dramatization of individual and collective memory, a space in which personal and communal trauma is shared. Through these multiple points of focalization that Weems's wandering gaze marshals, viewers become open to the multiple narratives that are possible within the spaces of her address. Domestic architecture is no longer home so much as it is place, place in which reanimated bodies move through a landscape and architecture that is eternal and ever changing, enacting relationships that are predicated on social structures at once remote and yet wholly familiar. It is the scene of the crime, and Weems's presence in it is as much accusation as it is reflection. As our wandering gaze is focalized through Weems's, we see New Orleans as a matrix of communities afloat in the wake of an antebellum history of enslavement, a postbellum product of segregation, and in the contemporary moment a city still marked by post-Katrina displacement, creative resurrection, and creeping gentrification. To view and review *The Louisiana Project* is to see the future through visions of the past and, through this oracular gift, to see the ever-reflexive nature of the present in relation to the past.

The act of prescient reconstruction and stitching back together of the past, effected by Weems's wandering gaze, brings into focus terrestrial revenants to cloud our vision like the mists before Friedrich's wanderer. In the absences, in the vacated landscapes that endure both before and beyond, we may reflect on the roles we ourselves have played in the past, in the present, and in the future.

13

TEN YEARS OF
30 AMERICANS

Since its December 2008 premiere at Art Basel Miami Beach art week, *30 Americans* has become the most viewed exhibition of its kind. Curated from the extensive holdings of contemporary art owned by the Rubell family, the exhibition includes works by thirty-one African American artists, who explore contemporary social issues and personal mythologies through various modes of abstraction and diverse representational strategies. All these artists occupy complex subject positions, so to say that they share a common identity as African Americans belies the richness of their varied and often intersectional experiences as men, women, straight, gay, queer, wealthy, working-class, and so forth. Just as there is no single type of work in this exhibition, which includes sculpture, painting, video, and installation, neither is there one kind of "Black" artist in the group.

Along with the diversity of the work included, a major attraction of *30 Americans* has been its rarity. Important exhibitions of challenging, contemporary art that reflects or interrogates the lived realities of being nonwhite, queer, or working-class in our society are rarely shown by mainstream museums. During the past century, as museums in this country filled their galleries and storage vaults with works of art, their mostly white and mostly male leadership has consistently failed to acquire work by minority and women artists. Recent studies have shown that most major museum collections in the United States contain just a small percentage of works by artists who are white women or people of color, or who openly represent LGBTQ+ communities.[1] Regardless of their institutional holdings, most museums that purport to serve general audiences rarely have more than a few works by such artists on view, and if museumgoers are not already familiar with the backgrounds of those artists, that diversity might go unnoticed. Not surprisingly, curious and excited audiences from all backgrounds and walks of life have flocked to see *30 Americans*, and their enthusiasm has translated to record attendance. Well over one million viewers have seen this exceptional exhibition.

After ten years traveling the country, *30 Americans* finally came to Philadelphia and the Barnes Foundation, an institution like the Rubell Family Collection that maintains a private collection amassed by a visionary art lover. Nearly a century ago, in the 1920s, after he had amassed a large collection of avant-garde European art, decorative objects, and sub-Saharan African masks and sculpture, Dr. Albert C. Barnes began supporting the work of self-taught and classically trained African American artists like Horace Pippin and Aaron Douglas. Not only did Dr. Barnes purchase several works by Pippin to hang on the walls of his eponymous foundation, he also encouraged Pippin to take classes at the Barnes. In 1928 he arranged for Douglas and the writer Gwendolyn Bennett to study in the foundation's collection of African art. On a personal level, Dr. Barnes felt that he had unique insights into African American culture, which he wrote about in an essay that was included in the highly influential and generative 1925 anthology *The New Negro*, edited by the rationalist philosopher and aesthete Alain Locke.[2] The tone taken in Dr. Barnes's writings about Black musicality and religiosity is characteristically patronizing—he was a remarkably self-satisfied and imperious individual—and the essay reflects the attitudes of a man of his time who clearly had an appreciation for Black culture but who did not necessarily feel that Blacks (or most whites) were his social or intellectual equals.

Unlike Dr. Barnes, the Rubells have largely been able to avoid being viewed as "patronizing" white patrons of African American art by remaining dedicated to the visions of the artists they collect (rather than trying to impose their own ideas of what Black art should look like or mean on the works in their collection). Overall, the Rubell family's efforts have helped broaden the visibility of the African American artists included in *30 Americans* as well as many who are not in the exhibition or in the Rubell Family Collection. This essay attempts to summarize the extraordinary impact of *30 Americans*. It begins to assess what the exhibition has meant for the Rubell family, for the critics who have written about their experiences seeing it, for the museums that have hosted it, for the visibility of African American art and those who collect it, and for the American public at large. "That's the bigger point you should take away from *30 Americans*. African-American art isn't just about identity, or slavery, or advertising, or any one theme. Just as Latino art isn't, and white art isn't, and German art isn't. It's diverse and spectacular and evolving and hard to contain—and that's the real power of this show."[3]

In 2015, when *30 Americans* arrived at the Arkansas Art Center in Little Rock, it was the museum's first exhibition of contemporary art by African American artists in its fifty-five years of operation. The show was praised as "innovative" by the critic Cyd King, who reviewed it for the *Arkansas Democrat-Gazette*.[4] By that time, over one million visitors had seen *30 Americans*, and many of the artists who had been "emerging" at the time of its organization in 2008, like Shinique Smith and Mickalene Thomas, had staged high-profile solo shows and won further national and international recognition. The following year, when the exhibition arrived in Tacoma, Washington, it was lauded as a "game-changer for art," having given "more regular Americans . . . a much broader concept of contemporary art, one that includes black artists."[5]

Over the years, while celebrated by many critics, *30 Americans* has confounded others who were unable to recognize the curatorial rationale for an exhibition devoted to contemporary art made by artists of African descent working in the United States. "It's not the brainchild of a museum or of professional curators, but of Mera and Don Rubell, two high-visibility collectors who buy what they like and show it however they damn well please," wrote art critic Jeffry Cudlin in 2011 when the exhibition opened at the Corcoran Gallery of Art in Washington, DC. Cudlin opined that the label text and didactics that accompanied the Corcoran's presentation fell short. He was left questioning "why and how these artists came to make these works; how the works function in the art world at large; or why, aside from the color of their skin, any of these artists belong in a room together."[6] Other critics, such as visual studies scholar Tiffany Barber, whose research and writing have been almost exclusively dedicated to African American art and culture, asserted that a curatorial rationale could be found in the way that "many of the artists in *30 Americans* use figuration, narrative, and other aesthetic strategies oft associated with explorations of identity to interrogate the very nature of representation."[7] Similarly, in his review of the Corcoran show, *Washington Post* art critic Philip Kennicott wrote:

You sense from most of the artists that they are keenly aware of the paradox, that they know full well how much the art world participates in the same efforts to categorize, reduce, brand and market racial identity to the world at large. In the end, the work that matters, that survives the complicated game of making an exhibition about race when everyone acknowledges that there is no agreement about what race means, or should mean, is the work that resists to the very end, that refuses to participate, that bears some final trace of something elementally human, whatever that means.[8]

Lauren Meir, a writer for the London-based art market website MutualArt, felt the exhibition was organized around the ways that each artist "contends with the concept of Black identity in the United States, touching on issues reflected in popular culture, the media, and the fight for civil rights."[9] And after questioning the viability of race as an organizing rubric for an exhibition of contemporary art, Miami-based curator Claire Breukel noted that after "moving through the exhibition, it [became] apparent that *30 Americans* is investigating cause-and-effect channels of influence between the younger and the more established generations."[10]

Other reviewers, particularly those whose journalistic practice had investigated racial polarization, discrimination, and dissonance, were profoundly moved by the exhibition. The *Cincinnati Enquirer*'s Mark Curnutte wrote, "In this exhibit, I saw faces and heard voices of black people I'd met since undertaking a life-changing project in 1993 here at *The Enquirer*. The series titled 'A Polite Silence' unfolded that November in six parts from five months of reporting and 350 interviews, a learning process that helped me fully recognize and accept my white privilege."[11] Curnutte was deeply touched by *30 Americans* and recognized in it his experience of his racially divided hometown:

I walked through *30 Americans*, stopping several times: Nick Cave's *Soundsuit, 2008* is a mannequin wrapped in fabric, fiberglass and metal. It's the black man protecting himself against violence and racial stereotypes. I've written about him, many times over. Hank Willis Thomas' *Branded Head*, a profile photograph of a black man with a Nike logo etched above the ear, is in the section of the exhibit titled "The Economy, Class, and Commodification." NFL players are well aware of the high-risk/high-reward nature of their work. Both on and off the record, a few players told me they wanted to play long enough to make as much money as possible—including endorsements—and retire with minimal damage to their bodies and minds.[12]

The exhibition also moved Curnutte to emphasize the rarity with which many white Americans actively engage issues of racial disparity or difference or choose to confront the legacies of slavery that all Americans have inherited but bear in disproportionate ways.

Many white Americans don't want to know the ugly details of slavery and post-reconstruction racial violence. The truth is uncomfortable, and, besides, we weren't the ones holding the nooses. Yet, African-Americans cannot nor should not forget what their race—their ancestors—suffered, and the many ways large and small that racism continues today. White America needs to engage, to meet African-Americans on a single path toward better race relations. *30 Americans* is an opportunity to start your own journey. [The] Cincinnati Art Museum is a safe place, less confrontational to some [white] people than the National Underground Railroad Freedom Center, which they view as a "black museum."

The notion that there are "white" and "Black" cultural spaces, and that confronting the history of slavery and continued reality of racial inequality in our society and cultural institutions is a task only for "Black museums," is troubling yet unsurprising. Because many mainstream museums have failed to collect or exhibit contemporary works by racially diverse artists, they can appear as spaces reserved for the delectation of white viewers. By choosing not to regularly display works that visualize (or otherwise make apparent through auditory, haptic, or other sensory means) the histories and lived realities of individual people of color and minority communities, such museums repeatedly reify and venerate the specific artistic traditions that dominant, overwhelmingly white communities have valued historically. As a result, the disturbing realities of racial inequality and social discord and the enduring segregation still present in American cities like Cincinnati, Little Rock, and nearly every other metropolitan area visited by *30 Americans* remain largely unaddressed by a significant number of art institutions. Racially conscious critics, such as the *Cincinnati Enquirer's* Mark Curnutte, immediately recognized the major contribution that *30 Americans* made to disrupting long-standing practices of curatorial omission and exclusion.

Many African American collectors and philanthropists have been key in shifting the tide (I discuss just a handful of them later in this essay), yet the role that high-profile white collectors like the Rubells have played in helping dominant cultural institutions to recognize the egregious gaps in their permanent collections and exhibition schedules cannot be understated. Most of the works by African American artists in the Museum of Fine Arts (MFA),

Boston, for example, were acquired in a special purchase from the collector John P. Axelrod, who spent much of the 1990s and early 2000s building a representative collection of historical and contemporary works. Through Axelrod's vision and generosity, the MFA resolved the absence of any work by critically important contemporary African American artists like Kerry James Marshall.[13] But this example highlights how long-term, comprehensive change in most mainstream US museums remains tied almost exclusively to the efforts of wealthy white collectors. As the primary donors to museums, wealthy white art patrons often serve as trustees and advisers, and their voices are the ones most easily heard and most often respected by museum directors, who have the final say in what is exhibited and collected. "It's the museum's first significant show of African-American art in five years, and the challenge is to curate it for audiences of all races in a way that goes beyond tokenism to understanding."[14]

At each venue, *30 Americans* has been rethought and reinstalled in accordance with the spatial limitations of the hosting institution and the professional tastes of the curatorial team. An exhibition that could include as many as two hundred different works of art has in many venues featured as few as fifty. At the Chrysler Museum in Norfolk, Virginia, the organizing curators interspersed works from the museum's own permanent collection among those on the original checklist.[15] Similarly, the curators at the Cincinnati Art Museum dispersed the show throughout the museum's galleries, interweaving it through the permanent collection to draw visitors through the space as a whole and to highlight the museum's own holdings of works by Lorna Simpson, Glenn Ligon, and Nick Cave.[16]

By the time that *30 Americans* arrived in Detroit in 2015, the rarity of exhibitions of contemporary art by Black artists at the Detroit Institute of Arts (DIA) had become a major issue for the local art community. Detroit's population is 80 percent Black, and even though General Motors had endowed a center for African American art at the museum nearly two decades earlier, DIA had been remarkably hesitant to embrace the needs of its largest racial and ethnic demographic. "The museum has failed to capitalize on what it has [locally]," George N'Namdi, founder of the N'Namdi Center for Contemporary Art in Detroit and a prominent dealer of African American art, told the *Detroit Free Press*. "This was one of the major collecting spots in the country for African-American art. The museum should be a leader in this area for the population that's here, and because it could really distinguish itself in this area."[17] Thankfully, the arrival of *30 Americans* at DIA lent support to the long-standing efforts of Valerie Mercer, curator of the General Motors Center, to expand the institution's collection of art by Black artists.

Attendance for the exhibition was 16 percent higher than the museum's original target, and African American visitors made up 41 percent of the total.[18] These numbers went a long way to convincing the museum's leadership that a greater commitment to African American art would diversify the museum's audience and help DIA establish itself as a visibly progressive force in the Motor City. In 2016 the museum launched a formal initiative, spurred by a $125 million grant from the Ford Foundation, to redress the absences in its collection by purchasing works of art by African American artists. "Museums today are about more than just art on the walls," Ford Foundation president Darren Walker told the *Free Press*. "The best museums today take seriously the responsibility to build communities. Museums should educate and empower the citizenry, and nothing is more empowering for African Americans than seeing great art by African Americans on the walls of a museum like the DIA."[19]

Other venues for the exhibition have also seen their collecting and exhibiting programs positively impacted by the "*30 Americans* effect." Linda Johnson Dougherty, the chief curator and curator of contemporary art at the North Carolina Museum of Art, has said the exhibition had a "huge impact" on their acquisitions and resulted in works by Mickalene Thomas, Kehinde Wiley, Hank Willis Thomas, Purvis Young, and others entering the collection. She also credits *30 Americans* for their upcoming solo exhibition of Leonardo Drew.[20] Similarly, the Joslyn Museum moved to purchase works by Thomas, Wiley, Kara Walker, and Rashid Johnson within months of the show's opening there in the winter of 2019.[21]

If museums have sat up and taken notice since *30 Americans* came on the scene, then the secondary art market and the collecting world have been standing at attention when it comes to many of the artists included in the show. In the years immediately preceding the organization of *30 Americans*, the secondary art market had already begun to recognize the investment value of works by Jean-Michel Basquiat, for example, when one of his paintings fetched a record-setting $14.6 million at a 2007 auction. A decade later, auction prices for Basquiat paintings had risen dramatically. In May 2017 *Untitled* (1982) garnered an astronomical sum of $110.5 million.[22] In 2014 one of Glenn Ligon's white text paintings sold for $3.9 million, while a piece by David Hammons garnered $3.5 million. In March 2018 Mark Bradford set a record auction price for a work by a living African American artist when his piece *Helter Skelter I* (2007) sold for nearly $12 million. That record was soon broken: Kerry James Marshall's epic painting *Past Times* (1997) sold for $21.1 million.

Past Times was purchased by rapper and hip-hop producer Sean "Diddy" Combs, who joined a growing group of Black music industry titans who have focused increasingly on collecting contemporary African American art as a cultural statement and a financial investment. Producer Kasseem "Swizz Beatz" Dean and his wife, the pianist and vocalist Alicia Keys, have collected over four hundred pieces—many by *30 Americans* artists such as Mickalene Thomas, Nina Chanel Abney, and Kehinde Wiley—putting the couple at the forefront of this movement.[23] And while Swizz Beatz has become well known for his interest in collecting and promoting Black art, Beyoncé Knowles Carter and her husband, Shawn "Jay-Z" Carter, have been the most publicly visible and broadly influential members of the hip-hop aristocracy to make themselves a part of the African American contemporary art scene.

In addition to collecting art, the Carters have shared numerous photographs of themselves with works of art, and they allude to art history on their social media accounts and in their creative production. Their 2014 Halloween costumes—where Beyoncé dressed as Frida Kahlo and Jay-Z went as Jean-Michel Basquiat—created a significant buzz, as did an image of Beyoncé mimicking a Kerry James Marshall painting on exhibition at David Zwirner Gallery in London. A music video in which Beyoncé danced around her living room with a David Hammons "basketball painting" in the background revealed a small glimpse of how the couple lives with their art collection.[24] And in 2013, when Jay-Z shot a performance art–inspired video for his song "Picasso Baby" on location at Pace Gallery in New York, he invited a number of contemporary artists of African descent, including Fred Wilson and Jacolby Satterwhite, to participate. In 2018, working together under their married name, the Carters arranged to shoot the video for "Apeshit"—an infectious ode to fame, good taste, and success—in the Louvre Museum in Paris. Over the course of a remarkably brisk six minutes, the gloriously decked-out couple poses amid the Hellenistic Nike of Samothrace (190 BCE) and the Venus de Milo (101 BCE), while groups of beautifully diverse Black dancers execute routines in front of familiar works of art, including Leonardo da Vinci's *Mona Lisa* (1503), Théodore Gericault's *The Raft of the Medusa* (1818–19), and Marie-Guillemine Benoist's *Portrait of a Black Woman* (1800). Interwoven into these shots are cutaways to young Black models whose intricate poses echo the works around them in highly contemporary *tableau vivant*. One senses the influence of Kehinde Wiley's painting practice in this final gesture of co-optation and signification. The unparalleled popularity of the "Apeshit" video (it was viewed over 150 million times in its first twelve months of release) led to a 25 percent increase in attendance at the Louvre from 2017 to 2018.[25] In response, the Louvre began offering a ninety-minute tour that included all the works of art featured in the video.[26] Like the art they collect, the Carters have proven themselves to be enormously powerful influencers.

In addition to changes in the art market and the collecting habits of hip-hop royalty, the influence of *30 Americans* can be seen in the visually prominent, yet thoroughly fictional collection of art owned by the music mogul Lucious Lyon on the Fox television show *Empire*. The serial melodrama, which debuted in 2015 and entered its sixth and final season in 2019, focuses on a highly successful and ridiculously stylish family of African American musicians, producers, and entrepreneurs. Remarkably, contemporary African American art is as much a part of the show's vibe as the musical interludes and fashionable clothing that distinguish its characters' lives from other primetime fare. The artworks shown in the background of scenes present viewers with a who's who from the checklist of *30 Americans*. And while immediately recognizable works by Mickalene Thomas, Kehinde Wiley, Jean-Michel Basquiat, Barkley L. Hendricks, and Kara Walker have been featured on *Empire*, works by artists not in *30 Americans*, such as Jamea Richmond-Edwards and Michael Savoie, have gained considerable exposure by being in their company. By spotlighting real-life works of art—present on set in the form of high-quality facsimiles—*Empire* has helped to make contemporary art by African American artists increasingly visible in American popular culture.

In a wide-ranging essay published in 2016, *New York* magazine art critic Jerry Saltz placed *30 Americans* squarely within the legacy of the 1993 Whitney Biennial, which many considered to be the most influential and polarizing exhibition of fin de siècle contemporary art. In titling his piece "The Reviled Museum Show That Forever Changed Art," Saltz indicated the extreme vitriol that disaffected establishment critics levied at what they derisively dubbed the "diversity biennial" because of its inclusion of historically underrepresented artists and its presentation of works that tackled themes of racial, sexual, and social discord—artistic positions that had mostly been absent from previous biennials.[27] "For the first time, biography, history, the plight of the marginalized, institutional politics, context, sociologies, anthropologies, and privilege [were all being] recognized as 'forms,' 'genres,' and 'materials' in art. Possibly the core materials," argued Saltz. "That shift put the artistic self front and center, making it perhaps the primary carrier of artistic content since the 1990s."[28] To support this argument, Saltz pointed to the enduring role that white collectors such as the Rubells have played in helping to attract a mainstream white audience to African American art. "'You're out of your mind to be white collectors doing [*30 Americans*,] a show by black artists.' People were saying, 'You're walking into a beehive here,'" Mera Rubell told Saltz in an interview for the article. "'You're going to be accused and embarrassed' and, honestly, there was a moment where we wondered as a family, are we willing to take the risk?"[29] Much of the Rubells' trepidation centered around issues of their own racial position in relation to the works of art from their collection that they hoped to share with the public. "Every single white person said, 'Don't do it. You will embarrass yourself, you will destroy the reputation of the collection, and this is a weird thing—white collectors doing a black show.'"[30]

When the Rubells spoke privately with Rashid Johnson and the other artists they wanted to include in *30 Americans*, both parties were reassured about the show's premise. On the whole, the artists were honored to be in the company of their peers and those like Basquiat and Robert Colescott, who had been strong influences on their artistic practices.[31] While some were initially hesitant about being included in a "Black art show," the prospect of being a part of *30 Americans*, where their work would be placed in direct dialogue with that of their contemporaries (rather than as a part of a historically open-ended survey), was a very attractive idea.

The Rubell family's commitment to supporting the artists by buying directly from them and their designated representatives, rather than purchasing works from the secondary art market, has endeared them to the artists whose work they collect. This practice of direct and unconditional support has fostered an uncommon degree of loyalty and sense of reciprocity. "Artists would say, 'I don't want to be ghettoized, I'd rather hang with Richard Prince than be in a show with 'black artists' because what do I have in common with black artists as such?'" Mera Rubell told Saltz. "But we met with Rashid Johnson . . . and we said you're one of the younger artists we're curating into the show and we want to know how you feel about it. Do you feel it makes sense to do a black show? And he says, 'Why not? You own the work.' I don't know if he even knew Glenn Ligon or Mickalene Thomas was in the show then, but he said it would be such an honor to be in the same show as [David] Hammons."[32] In a 2014 interview, Johnson "recalled that [the Rubells] engaged in soul-searching sessions with several artists to ensure they were behind the project's premise."[33]

The Rubells' decision to seek the approval of the artists whom they hoped to include in *30 Americans* ultimately made a great difference. "The artists know that we believe in the work," Mera Rubell asserted.[34] The Rubells' unwavering belief in the power and personal authenticity of each artist's vision, regardless of (and because of) the artist's identity, ultimately propelled their curatorial vision for *30 Americans*.

Given the small number of exhibitions of contemporary art by African American artists shown at major art museums in the United States, it is unsurprising that *30 Americans* has had such an impact. But the power and quality of the work collected by the Rubells has accounted for the tremendous response and the continued flow of visitors into each respective venue. If not for the efforts of the Rubell family, "how else would we be able to have a conversation about American history in front of a monumental bale of cotton, as in Leonardo Drew's *Number 25*, or a circle of Klansman hoods surrounding a noose, as in Gary Simmons' *Duck, Duck, Noose?*" wrote Laura Hutson in her 2013 review for *Nashville Scene* when *30 Americans* came to the Frist Center for the Visual Arts. "How else could we see Glenn Ligon's massive text paintings, Nick Cave's sound suits, and Kerry James Marshall's beautiful comic canvases, and be able to bring our children through the galleries to discuss all the ways contemporary art is perfectly suited to discuss complex issues like race, and to see that influence spill over onto the work of our poets and writers, informing the conversation we have about identity in America for years to come? This is an unforgettable exhibit, and its importance should not be underestimated."[35]

H IS FOR HAPPENS TO BE BLACK

Obama, it is said, is a presidential candidate that "happens to be black." This is despite the fact that he is biracial and chose to call himself an African American. I happens to be black too, though I don't know how it happened. Because I never felt I was in a position to choose my racial identity, it never occurred to me that blackness was something that could happen to you, like being mugged, or winning the lottery. I thought one was just black and that was that.[36]

Though planning and preparation for the launch of *30 Americans* began long before the November 2008 election, Barack Obama's subsequent victory and his impending inauguration as the first African American president of the United States helped catalyze interest in the show when it opened at the Rubell Family Collection in Miami in December 2008. In the months leading up to the election, the increasing momentum of the Obama campaign—and the previously unimaginable possibility of an America in which the son of a Black Kenyan and a white Kansan could ascend to the highest elected office—not only buoyed the Rubells but also inspired those who wrote for the

30 Americans catalog. Furthermore, the Obama era and *30 Americans* "effect" would have a lasting impact on American art, visual culture, and identity.

The nation's excitement at the idea of an African American president permeates the essays completed in the spring of 2008 for the first edition of the *30 Americans* catalog. In her essay "The African Sublime," cultural critic Michele Wallace compared the shifting terrain of African American art and culture during the late twentieth century with that of the politics of the nation at large: "Barack Obama has been nominated as the Democratic candidate for office of President of the United States by unanimous acclamation, something that has never happened to an African-American in the history of the United States. (Indeed, by the time this essay is published he may be president.)"[37] By adding the last sentence parenthetically, Wallace seems to hedge her bets, not wanting to be predictive or to jinx the course of history in any way.

The prospect of Obama's presidency and what it might mean for racial representation and African American cultural change is most palpable in Glenn Ligon's alphabetically bulleted essay. In it, Ligon uses the mixed-race Obama as a trope for thinking about racial identification. By questioning the ways that skin color and parentage seem to be used arbitrarily in this country to decide who gets to choose their racial identity, the artist emphasizes that a fixed reality exists for dark-skinned folks that isn't as fluid as that experienced by Black-identified individuals who may choose to claim "mixedness" by having a white parent. The issue of racial liminality in relation to Obama's candidacy was also taken up by art historian Robert Hobbs, whose essay for the catalog explores the future president's status as a "cultural mulatto," someone who is not bound to a single racial or social status, who is at ease in both Black and white worlds and unhindered by class barriers.[38]

Once in office, the Obama family very quickly demonstrated a sincere and profound interest in promoting and living with African American art that would become an important part of their enduring legacy. Almost immediately after assuming the role of First Family in January 2009, the family borrowed an oil stick text piece by Glenn Ligon, titled *Black Like Me #2*, from the Smithsonian's Hirshhorn Museum. Here, Ligon has stenciled across the surface of the canvas a quotation from the 1961 memoir *Black Like Me* by white journalist John Howard Griffin, who transformed himself into a Black man so that he could write about his experiences and help support African American civil rights in the era leading up to the Voting Rights Act of 1965.[39] *"All traces of the Griffin I had been were wiped from existence." "All traces of the Griffin I had been were wiped from existence." "All traces of the Griffin I had been were wiped from existence."* Stenciled repeatedly, until the once clear message has itself slipped away into a sticky smudge of black illegibility, meaning becomes obscure, riffing on an enduring modernist mode to destabilize a present sense of selfhood and social knowledge.

"It's in the private quarters of the White House," Ligon told the *Guardian* newspaper in 2013 when he was asked about the placement of *Black Like Me #2*.

> So I can't see it. But I met Obama once, backstage at the Apollo in Harlem. I was with my friend and a woman said, "I wonder if you have a moment to meet the president?" And, you know, we had dinner reservations—but OK. So we go downstairs and there's Obama with the chief of staff, who says, "Mr. President, this is Glenn Ligon. *Black Like Me #2* is in your personal quarters." And Obama looks at me and goes, "Oh, yeah, we have a set of prints too! But they had to move them out, because of the light. I really miss them." I thought, "Oh wait, this is real! They live with art, they take their children to look at art, they're not scared of artists. This is not some bullshit. This is not on his talking points." I was super impressed.[40]

As the president's attachment to *Black Like Me #2* demonstrates, the Obamas were deeply interested in contemporary art and artists. It should come as no surprise, then, that when *30 Americans* arrived at the Corcoran Gallery in 2011, the Obamas went to see the exhibition. Several weeks into the engagement, Michelle Obama called the museum's offices to see if it was an appropriate exhibition for her young daughters to view. She was probably told that there was nudity, that some of the work was sexual in nature, and that other works contained violent imagery. Accordingly, she visited the exhibition first by herself before returning the next day with her daughters. The Obamas must have been especially struck by the Kehinde Wiley paintings that dominated the installation. The family's interest in promoting contemporary African American art, and in Wiley's uniquely vivid style of anachronistic portraiture, would soon help to visually define the legacy of the Obama presidency.

In the winter of 2016–17, as he prepared to leave office, President Obama began consulting with the staff of the Smithsonian's National Portrait Gallery regarding the commissioning of the official presidential portrait and portrait of the First Lady destined to be installed in the ongoing *America's Presidents* and *First Ladies* exhibitions. A year later, on February 12, 2018, when the portraits of the now former president and his wife, by Kehinde Wiley and Amy Sherald respectively, were revealed, they created a national sensation. The distinctive portraits quickly became the most viewed images in the history of the National Portrait Gallery, logging over 2.3 million visitors in their first year.

When Amy Sherald presented her portrait of Michelle Obama to the nation that February, she was an unfamiliar face to most in the art world. Already an accomplished conceptual portraitist, her work had only recently emerged onto the national stage when she won the 2016 Outwin Boochever Portrait Competition, the National Portrait Gallery's triennial juried exhibition of American portraiture. In contrast, the work of Kehinde Wiley was some of the most celebrated and widely exhibited by a living African American artist. By the time Wiley began his portrait of Obama, his work had been featured in over two dozen solo exhibitions around the world, from New York to London to Beijing, making it some of the world's most recognizable contemporary portraiture.

Wiley's portrait shows Obama sitting on an ornate chair surrounded by lush foliage that includes white jasmine flowers native to his birthplace in Hawaii and to Indonesia, where he spent his childhood; purple African lilies, representing his Kenyan heritage; multicolor chrysanthemums, symbolizing his life in Chicago; and rosebuds for love and courage.[41] In person, the portrait has an almost mesmerizing effect on viewers. Some have detected hidden meanings or seen coded script embedded in the green leaves that curl about Obama's body as he perches on his modest throne, leaning toward the picture plane and almost into the space of the viewer. Secret language or no, there is nothing else even remotely like it in the *America's Presidents* exhibition. While most of the presidential portraits assert the power embodied in their subject through the direct and penetrating gaze of the subject, none of these looks seems to go as fiercely deep as that of Wiley's Obama.

Amy Sherald's portrait of Michelle Obama has proven just as powerful to an often-overlooked group of American viewers: African American and other girls of color. In Sherald's composition, the First Lady sits on a low platform facing the viewer wearing an evening gown from Milly, designed by Michelle Smith. "It has an abstract pattern that reminded me of the Dutch artist Piet Mondrian's geometric paintings," Sherald explained at the portrait's unveiling. "But Milly's design also resembles the inspired quilt masterpieces made by the women of Gee's Bend, a small remote black community in Alabama, where they compose quilts in geometries that transform clothes and fabric remnants into masterpieces."[42] A painterly statement about sartorial history and women's arts, the patterns of quilts made by female ancestors are spread out below Mrs. Obama's bare and legendarily well-toned arms.

The profound and very particular importance of Sherald's portrait was witnessed just two weeks after its unveiling, when DC resident Jessica Curry took her two-year-old daughter, Parker, to see the painting. Parker was stunned by the image of a beautiful Black woman, whom she described to her mother as a "queen." A photograph of that moment taken by another museum visitor quickly went viral. "This is what America is all about," tweeted an Atlanta man. "This young girl can now dream about being someone like Michelle Obama."[43] When Sherald posted the image to her Instagram account, she wrote:

> When I look at this picture I think back to my first field trip in elementary school to a museum. I had only seen paintings in encyclopedias up to that point in my life.... There was a painting of a black man standing in front of a house. I don't remember a lot about my childhood, but I do have a few emotional memories etched into my mind forever and seeing that painting of a man that looked like he could be my father stopped me dead in my tracks. This was my first time seeing real paintings that weren't in a book and also weren't painted in another century. I didn't realize that none of them had me in them until I saw that painting.... I knew I wanted to be an artist already, but seeing that painting made me realize that I could. What dreams may come? #representationmatters.[44]

A week later, Michelle Obama posted to Instagram some photos and a video of her and Parker dancing in a room of the Kalorama mansion that the Obamas moved to in January 2017. She wrote, "Parker, I'm so glad I had the chance to meet you today (and for the dance party)! Keep on dreaming big for yourself... and maybe one day I'll proudly look up at a portrait of you." Over 1.5 million people liked the images, but only a few noticed the print by Kerry James Marshall and the fire-hose piece by Theaster Gates in the background. The works are evidence of the continuous commitment that the Obamas have made to contemporary art and to Black Chicago-based artists like Marshall and Gates in particular. The following Halloween, now three-year-old Parker Curry chose to go as Sherald's vision of Michelle Obama, as did an untold number of other young girls of color.

Sherald's painting has become a remarkably powerful image that represents not just the culmination of Michelle Obama's process of "becoming" (as the former First Lady titled her best-selling memoir) but also a key icon impacting the positive identity formation of young girls of color, giving them a way to begin to visualize themselves as beautiful, powerful women with leadership potential. And while the Halloween photos of girls dressed and posed as in Sherald's painting are tremendously moving, another little girl's choice to go as "Amy Sherald, American artist" is equally inspiring.

"I bet many people come, and many school tours come, and just like when I was a kid—I'm tearing up now," *30 Americans* artist and Baltimore native Shinique Smith related in 2011 while the exhibition was on view at the Corcoran. "I just realized that when young people come to the museum to see the show, there will be kids like me . . . seeing Lorna Simpson and Carrie Mae Weems, and thinking 'I could be in this museum . . .' I think that's an amazing thing."[45]

Works of art can incite change and inspire us, not just to view or acquire them but also to envision ourselves as the creators of our own culture. The picture of a little Black girl who imagines herself not as a queen, or as the accomplished wife of a former president, but as a famous artist fills one with hope for the future. A future in which the people who pursue roles of cultural leadership in the United States, and who are also recognized for doing so, it will be as rich and diverse as the nation itself. It is a future that the very remarkable exhibition *30 Americans* has helped many to envision as perhaps being possible.

14

"NO MAN IS AN ISLAND"

THE DIASPORIC PERFORMANCES
OF WANDA RAIMUNDI-ORTIZ
AND SHELDON SCOTT

> No man is an island entire of itself; every man
> is a piece of the continent, a part of the main;
> if a clod be washed away by the sea, Europe
> is the less, as well as if a promontory were, as
> well as any manner of thy friends or of thine
> own were; any man's death diminishes me,
> because I am involved in mankind.
> And therefore never send to know for whom
> the bell tolls; it tolls for thee.
> —**John Donne, "No Man Is an Island" (1624)**

John Donne wrote *Meditation XVII* in 1624, just five years after the first enslaved Africans were sold at Jamestown. Great Britain had just declared war on Spain, seeking to gain control over Puerto Rico and the other islands strategically located between the two American continents. The major European imperial powers battled over territory once controlled by Native peoples for the next century, until the former British colonies that became the United States asserted their hegemony over the remaining Spanish colonies and, in so doing, became an empire. Throughout this period the danger of human disconnection that Donne laments was a horrific reality for the millions of kidnapped Africans who survived the transatlantic slave trade's Middle Passage.

When Africans arrived in the Americas, colonial slavery was already decimating Indigenous populations, including the Guale people of the Sea Islands off the coast of what is now Georgia and South Carolina, and the Arawak peoples throughout the Caribbean islands. These disparate groups survived by merging into new communities of color, which in turn created hybrid cultural forms that evolved over generations as their descendants endured unrelenting forced labor. Today the persistence of colonialist attitudes and exploitative economic practices tests the cultural tenacity of the Gullah Geechee Black folks of the Sea Islands, descendants of Guale and West Africans, and the Afro-Taíno-Latinx communities living on Puerto Rico or residing stateside.[1]

In their reparative performance art practices, Wanda Raimundi-Ortiz and Sheldon Scott materialize and animate the diasporic consciousnesses that are foundational to the cultural texture of communities of color in the American South.[2] The New York–born Raimundi-Ortiz maintains strong connections to her Afro-Latinx family in Mayagüez and Bayamon, Puerto Rico. Scott was born and raised in a Gullah Geechee family on Pawley's Island, off the coast of South Carolina, and spends part of each year in Washington, DC. Both emphasize embodied presence to honor the dignity of their communities in the present and to reconnect to their ancestors. They draw on the visual and gestural vocabularies of Black performance art while incorporating site-specificity and contextual references to ground their work in a history of trauma and healing. Through their performances Raimundi-Ortiz and Scott seek to reestablish interpersonal connections, making unique interventions into cyclical histories of violent separation, to remind their audiences that "no man is an island."

Scott and Raimundi-Ortiz were both commissioned by the National Portrait Gallery to make performances as a part of Identify, an ongoing performance art series intended to represent the people who are absent from most of the works in the museum's collection due to histories of repression and exclusion. Scott's *Precious in Da Wadah* (2016) activated the spaces of the museum's Kogod Courtyard and Great Hall to create a moving portrait of the kidnapped Africans who brought their agricultural ingenuity from their homelands to the Sea Island rice plantations. Scott enlisted dozens of collaborators to symbolically enact the planting of rice shoots in the courtyard's fountains before having himself bound to a rice mortar. The following year, for her *Pietà* performance, Raimundi-Ortiz cradled thirty-three men and women of color in her arms for three minutes and thirty-three seconds each—a duration referring to Jesus's age of thirty-three at the time of his death. The tender gesture was meant to soothe the overwhelming fear of loss that people of color carry with them due to the vulnerability of their children to state violence.

Late in the summer of 2019, Scott and Raimundi-Ortiz both created new works in the South that recognized the epigenetic pain of their respective Gullah Geechee and Puerto Rican island communities. In their works these artists amplify John Donne's entreaty, honoring the ways that island-bound, African-descended communities have retained their spiritual and corporeal integrity, so as not to be swept out to sea like a clod of earth with no meaning, no matter, no elegy to lament their passing.

On a hot August day, from sunup to sundown, over a duration of twelve hours, twenty minutes, and fifty-seven seconds, a single video camera recorded Scott as he knelt in an overgrown rice field near his family home on Pawley's Island. Wearing a black suit, white shirt, and black tie, Scott labored continuously before the camera's lens, hulling grains of Carolina Gold rice by hand. As the sun slowly crossed the sky, he sought shelter in the shadows of the moss-shrouded trees, communing with grasshoppers, white egrets, and a swarm of fire ants crawling at his feet. Each return of his hand to the bag of fragrant heirloom rice at his side—rice that was originally grown in the Senegambia region from which his ancestors were forcibly taken—intensified Scott's corporeal and empathic connection to the soil beneath. This performance, *Portrait, Number 1 Man (Day Clean ta Sun Down)*, conjured enslaved men of Scott's family who labored on the old Brookgreen Plantation (figure 14.1). To be a "number 1 man" in the parlance of slavery was to be designated the most valued object on a list of human property.

Over the course of that August day, the artist worked to limit the movements of his body to either kneeling or standing while hulling the rice. Despite the extreme heat of the South Carolina summer, Scott wore the black suit that has become essential to his performance practice. Within the African American community, black business suits have long signaled the masculine respectability that is so often denied to Black men in their daily lives. It is for this reason that civil rights activists in the late 1950s and early 1960s like Martin Luther King Jr. and Malcom X always wore suits; it is also why Pope.L chose to wear them in his Crawls, to exaggerate the abjection of his prone movement along the dirty city streets. Scott was also barefoot, so that when he stood, he could feel the damp earth between his naked toes. The artist has explained that his choice to go barefoot in his performances is intended to

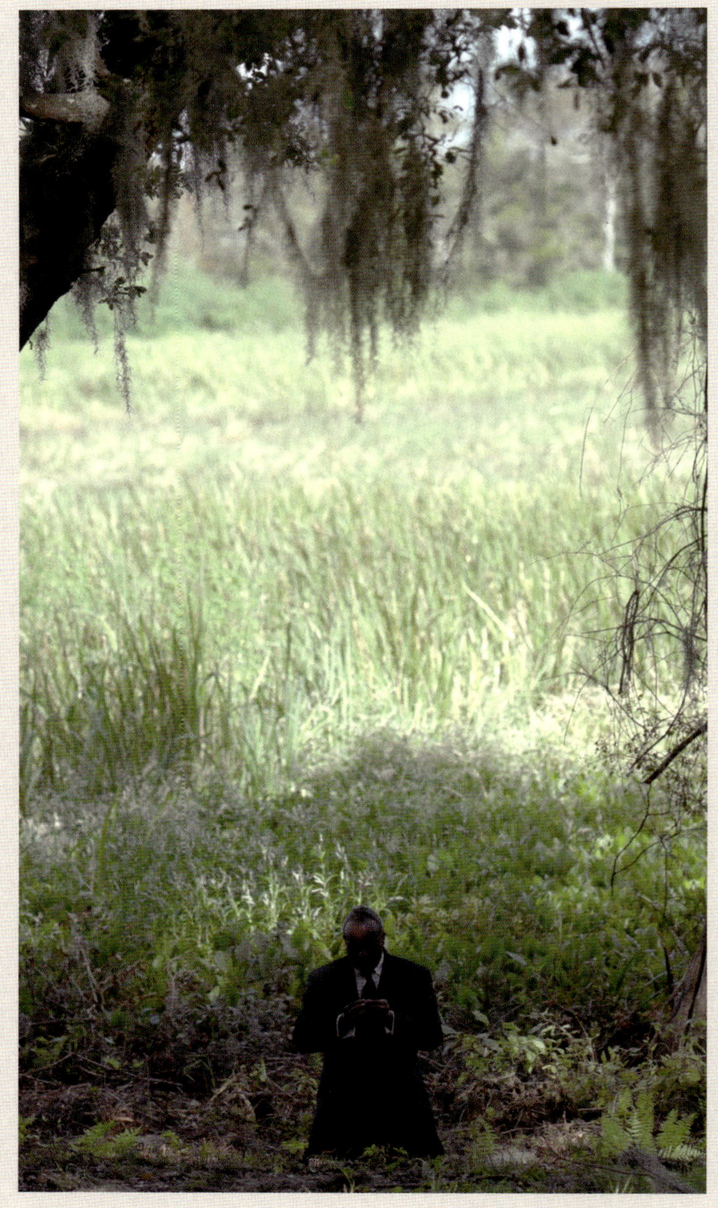

14.1 Sheldon Scott, *Portrait, Number 1 Man (Day Clean ta Sun Down)*, 2019. Video still, index of performance events, run time 12:20:00. Cinematography: Jon-Sesrie Goff; composition: Tamarkali. © Sheldon Scott, courtesy of CONNERSMITH

refute the myth that people can rise from poverty by "pulling themselves up by their bootstraps." "But what if you have no shoes?" asks Scott. Then what do you use to ascend the social and economic hierarchy, to climb "up from slavery" like Booker T. Washington?

Most enslaved people were never provided with shoes to protect their feet. Some African-descended communities saw the vital contact between skin and earth as essential for communion between the living and the dead. Scott told me that he felt his feet absorb the sweat, pain, and suffering from spectral presences who had once walked on African soil before they were put to work on Pawley's Island. This energy, he said, occasionally made his breathing difficult, as did the presence of the ancient trees that surrounded him, living witnesses to the pain of previous generations.

In its act of "bearing the weight," Scott's work recalls the endurance art of Sherman Fleming, such as the performance *Something Akin to Living* (1979), in which the artist stood in a doorway and adjusted his body to support an increasing number of wooden slats that were placed there by audience members until he finally relinquished his position. But Scott's connection to site takes this gesture out of the realm of metaphor and gives it concrete historical meaning. Scott labored in a space of brutal beauty and past agony, amid the presence of his Gullah Geechee ancestors, still unsettled and roaming what was once a vast carceral agricultural complex covering most of Pawley's Island. In moments of whiteout, he felt the spirits of the enslaved men and women who had performed the highly specialized work that his own ceremonial work was now honoring. Work that was physically and mentally numbing. Work that was done six days a week, from sunup to sundown—a rhythm invoked by the performance's duration. Work that is mirrored in the continuing struggle of working-class descendants of enslaved people to retain homesteads in the face of encroaching golf courses and resorts built for and occupied by the new ruling class.

A month later and 450 miles farther south, the sound of metal debris being dragged across pavement announced the presence of Raimundi-Ortiz in Orlando's downtown arts district. She was resplendent in a long, ruffled dress—an unruly wearable assemblage of bright blue construction tarps, orange plastic temporary fencing, and other bits of detritus (figure 14.2). These materials had been scavenged with her own hands from the thousands of emergency home repairs that followed Hurricane Maria's destructive path across the island of Puerto Rico in 2017. A red, white, and blue Puerto Rican flag fluttered atop Raimundi-Ortiz's back, and her long skirt spread out in a swirl around her ankles. At the center of her chaotic costume, she resembled the eye of the hurricane itself as she serenely strode up to the front door of a local performing arts center and into the central salon.

Once inside, Raimundi-Ortiz greeted a band of musicians by walking a circle before them and a crowd of onlookers. By lifting the hem of her skirt, she initiated the bomba, a dance form that for centuries has been central to Black self-expression in Puerto Rico. In bomba, musicians, singers, and dancers all interact with one another in exchanges derived from West African dance and drumming traditions. The drums are accompanied by maracas and *cúa*, the Taíno Arawak musical instruments endemic to the island. For centuries, a gathering for bomba was one of the few creative outlets that allowed the island's enslaved to resist the social death engendered by their relentless labor on the sugar plantations that have long characterized much of the Global South. When contemporary African-descended Puerto Ricans like Raimundi-Ortiz dance bomba, they use their movement to both honor and embody the spirits of their ancestors.

To perform bomba is to champion the anthem of the displaced. To sing its verses is to remember ancient histories. To enter the circle made by the musicians and the crowd is to be transported back to the space of the *batey*, the plaza found at the center of the living areas for the enslaved on colo-

14.2 Wanda Raimundi-Ortiz, *Exodus|Pilgrimage*, 2019. Documentation of live performance. Courtesy of the artist

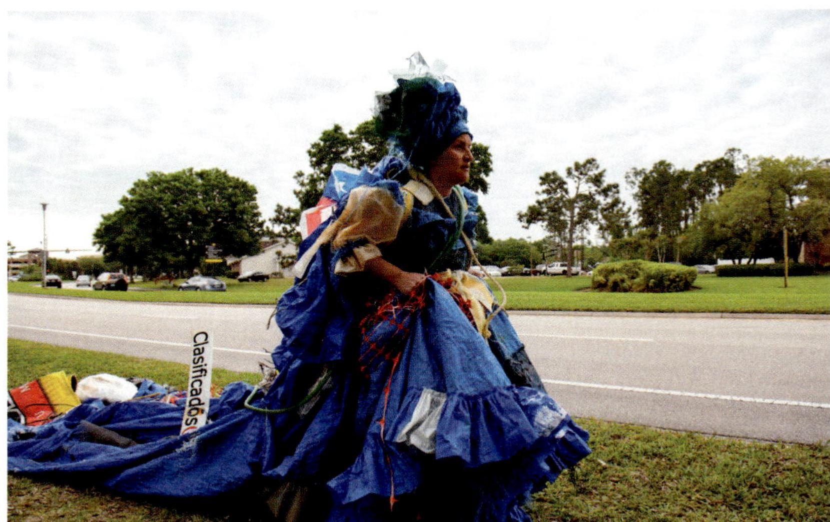

nial sugar plantations. Bomba reminded the African-descended people on plantations of their true origins. Today it does the same for contemporary Puerto Ricans living in Florida and throughout the South. "Just because you live here," Raimundi-Ortiz told me, "does not mean you are from here." Like Shaun Leonardo's performance *El Conquistador vs. The Invisible Man* (2005–7), in which the Afro-Dominican artist mobilized a popular wrestling format to explore the challenges of being seen as both Black and Latino by a dominant culture that fails to comprehend much about either, Raimundi-Ortiz's work serves as a reminder that the histories of the Global South are rooted in complex individual identities.

Raimundi-Ortiz's performance in downtown Orlando, *Exodus|Pilgrimage*, was a refusal to allow the horrific destruction of Hurricane Maria in 2017, and the displacement that it caused for so many Puerto Ricans, to go unseen by those living stateside. The bipartite title evokes both the biblical departure of the enslaved Hebrews from Egypt and the journeys made by believers to holy shrines. For each Floridian who lost power for a week after the hurricane, there were hundreds of Puerto Ricans who lived without electricity for nine months or more. After desperately needed relief failed to materialize from the federal government, the immense hardship that came with Hurricane Maria forced thousands of Puerto Ricans to leave the island. *Exodus|Pilgrimage* draws on Puerto Rico's deeply imbricated histories of Taíno Arawak genocide, African enslavement, labor exploitation by the sugar industry over centuries, and the continuing colonial status of the island as a neglected territory of the United States. As Raimundi-Ortiz proceeded through the streets of Orlando, she was dragging more than just the trauma of Hurricane Maria, woven as it was into the debris that trailed behind her. She was pulling the weight of the island's contemporary experience of oppression and the exodus of those who had fled its unchecked destruction into the field of vision of those who had long been shielded from that reality by virtue of their economic and geographic positions, comfortably middle class, residing stateside.

This use of elaborate costumes and markers of Latinx femininity conjures Coco Fusco's *Better Yet When Dead* (1997), in which the artist cast herself as dead predecessors like Frida Kahlo and Ana Mendieta, whose fame came in part through the visibility of their suffering. Fusco turned the gallery into a site of elaborate funerary services, invoking the West African spiritual beliefs that spread throughout the Caribbean and Latin America during enslavement under the guise of the permitted veneration of Catholic saints. Santeria, Espiritismo, Candomblé, the cult of María Lionza, and other diasporic practices that have their roots in West African religions remain essential to the integrity of many Latinx communities both in and outside of the United States. They have evolved over centuries of attempted suppression and demonization. In the spiritual practices of Ifa, which originated with the Yoruba people of Nigeria and spread throughout the Americas with the growth of the African diaspora, blue and white, the colors of Raimundi-Ortiz's bomba dress, are associated with the worship of the orisha, or deity, Yemaya. While the Yoruba people believe that Yemaya makes her home in the rivers, in the context of the Americas she is associated with the ocean and white flowers. In Afro-Brazilian Candomblé, she is worshipped in the aspect of Our Lady of Navigators. On New Year's Eve, believers bring offerings of white flowers and candles to Brazil's beaches in hope of good luck for the coming year. In Cuba she is one with the Virgin of Regla, who makes her terrestrial appearance as a Black woman in a blue gown holding a white child, a trenchant reminder of the forced maternity endured by enslaved women who were also made to nurse the children of their oppressors.

If Yemaya's benevolent dominion over the rivers, oceans, and seas is believed to have protected the Africans who endured the Middle Passage, this power was thrown into doubt when Hurricane Maria ravaged Puerto Rico. "Right now, I have a problem with Yemaya," Raimundi-Ortiz told me after I remarked on this connection, expressing her frustration that the orisha had not protected her spiritual children in their time of need. Even so, the artist's embodiment of Yemaya in *Exodus|Pilgrimage*, like her embodiment of the Virgin Mary in *Pietà*, reveals her continued investment in the promise and possibility of divine intervention that these holy figures represent to the faithful.

Raimundi-Ortiz and Scott reveal the enduring presence of Afro-diasporic culture and spirituality within the contemporary consciousness of the American South, both stateside and throughout Latin America. When Raimundi-Ortiz embodies Yemaya to dance bomba, and when Scott dons a black suit to peel grains of rice, each artist evokes a tender retrieval of the millions of lives that have been wrested from natal lands or taken from their families through state violence and neocolonial exploitation. The artists and their works offer respect to the spirits of the dispossessed and the deceased, both ancient and immediate, by confronting the painful truths of our reality. The presence of the past within the present is honored by these reparative performances, as are the legacies of resilience that characterize all African-descended communities and, indeed, all mankind.

15

WHAT DEANA LAWSON WANTS

The text that the Guggenheim Museum had placed on the web page for *Centropy*, Deana Lawson's Hugo Boss Prize exhibition, was indeed intriguing. It promised a body of conceptual photography in which "the everyday is transfigured into the uncanny and the magnificent" by drawing on "the legacies of historical portraiture, documentary photography, and the family album, but [it] transcends these traditions, constructing scenes that merge lived experience with imagined narratives.... The aesthetics and intergenerational connectivity of the Black diaspora guide Lawson's choice of subject matter. Each of her works takes its place in an overarching project, cohering into what she terms 'an ever-expanding mythological extended family.'"[1]

But what did *centropy* mean? A Google search revealed only links to Lawson's show and a stray entry in the online Urban Dictionary. Was this a bespoke term for the new visual order that Lawson had miraculously achieved? How was this fantastical language, and the highly orchestrated images that Lawson made by placing models that she had specifically sought out or strangers that she had approached in public places and then paid to pose in locations of the artist's choosing, changing the ways that Black people are

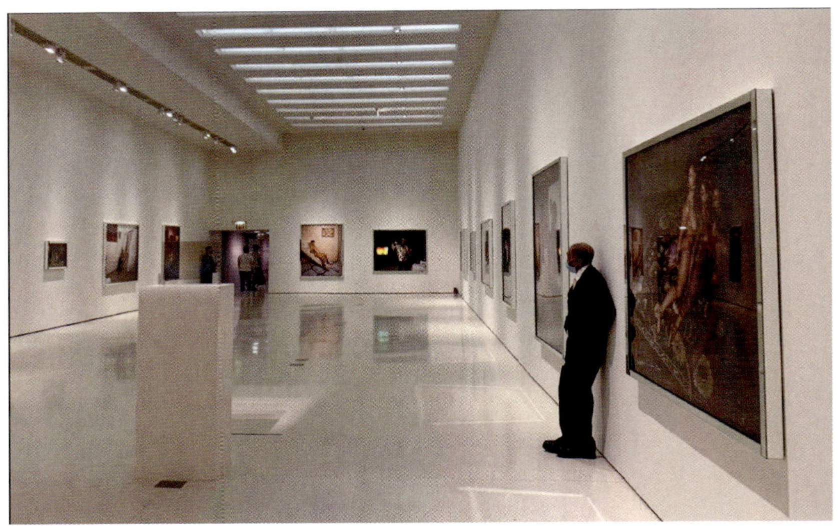

15.1 Installation view of Deana Lawson's exhibition *Centropy*,
Guggenheim Museum New York, May 7–October 11, 2021.
Photo by Lakshmi Amin for Hyperallergic

being seen in the space of the gallery or museum? Was Lawson really picturing Black people in a transcendent and "magnificent" new way, I wondered.

Over the past three or four years, I had become familiar with Lawson's work but had yet to see it in person. Since an appreciation for and curiosity about the aesthetic expressions of Black life in the United States and throughout the African diaspora is a key motivator for my own work, I wanted to see *Centropy* for myself.[2]

Compelled by the spirit of "intergenerational connectivity," I thought it would be helpful to encounter the show with my good friend and former student Brittany, a Brooklyn-born and -based television writer who specializes in hip-hop and youth culture and is just young enough to be my daughter.

A few weeks later, we spent an afternoon in *Centropy*, talking through the work surrounded by the large crystals, holograms, lenticular images, and other shiny objects that Lawson had included in her installation. Brittany began by confessing to me that while she had always loved Lawson's work when she scrolled past it on her phone, now that she was encountering the same images almost life-size, framed within wide bands of mirrored glass, the work was having a different effect. Yet it was still gratifying to see familiar spaces of Black life finally being presented in the space of one of the world's most important museums. She pointed to *Barrington and Father* (2021) and related how the mirrored wall behind the two male figures resembled one from the 1970s in the living room of the Clinton Hill apartment that she had inherited from the grandmother who had raised her. I agreed with her; there was a highly satisfying nostalgia quotient that felt familiar to me. I can vividly recall my own five-year-old thighs sticking painfully to the plastic slipcovers that protected the Louis XV sofas in my Nana Shaw's tiny, subsidized apartment in Blackity-Black Roxbury, Massachusetts. But as we moved through the exhibition, we became increasingly concerned by the ways that Black people were being presented in other examples of Lawson's work.

"That lady there, who looks like she might be sleeping," Brittany said, indicating *Deleon? Unknown* (2020), a piece that appeared to be a blown-up snapshot of a pregnant woman lying on a bed with a scribble of ballpoint ink across its surface. "Look at her hair. No Black woman that I know would ever let anyone take her picture with her hair sticking up like that. It's so clear she has no idea what's going on. What about consent?"

I wondered whether some of Lawson's images were other people's personal snapshots that had been appropriated without the subjects' or makers' knowledge. But I couldn't be sure, since adding digital effects to provide a faux-historical patina is one tool in Lawson's complex of methods.

And what about the subjects who either were not looking back at the camera or seemed unaware of its presence? Their numbers felt significant since the searing gazes of Lawson's subjects are often referenced as the method by which her images subvert or challenge the violence that photography has historically imposed on Black people. "Their stares place our focus not on their naked bodies or on the acts in which they may be engaged, but on their faces," explains Steven Nelson in an important essay on the artist from 2018. "Lawson's figures, aware of being seen, watch us watch them—and in doing so, our very right to look at them is called into question."[3]

Lawson's *Axis* (2018), which depicts three naked women doing the splits on a shabby rug in a dingy room surrounded by painted wood paneling, is one such image where the viewer's gaze is not defiantly returned, where our right to look is indulged rather than challenged. Taken from above, this portrait of three pierced, tattooed, and cosmetically altered female bodies, posed chest-to-back against one another in an ombre arrangement that cast their melanin from light to dark, speaks of unglamorous sex work and insurmountable poverty. I would like to agree with Tina Campt's assertion in *A Black Gaze: Artists Changing How We See* that "we must work to confront our resistance to seeing flawed but beautiful bodies of Black women [in

Lawson's work] who refuse to be shamed as they display themselves publicly with dignity and purpose," but I was not seeing much that was dignified in *Axis*.[4] These women who could be my sisters had been directed to line up with their genitals brushing against a dirty rug in what appeared to be a dank basement room, arranged before the photographer and her assistants, the hot lights bearing down on them as the eye of the large-format camera captured their vulnerability. Only one of the women looks at the camera, and she seems barely able to meet its gaze. These women do not appear to be "doing their own thing," and they do not exude a kind of specifically Black claim to individuality that is described by the celebrated filmmaker Arthur Jafa in Lawson's twenty-minute film *Centropy* (produced by the Guggenheim with support from Lawson's galleries, Sikkema Jenkins in New York, and David Kordansky Gallery in Los Angeles) that was posted on the Guggenheim website.[5] What I saw in *Axis* was a group of working-class Black women once more being asked to make the difficult choice to swap access to their bodies for some coin. And while it is not my place to judge what any woman chooses as survivance, I know many women who have posed, stripped, or tricked to pay the bills, and I am compelled to question the logic of how sex work is presented in Lawson's images.

In *Axis* and other pieces in *Centropy*, I could not find any of the earned intimacy that pointed to the artist's own personal experience or long-term communal investment in most of what she was depicting. I think of this in contrast to Nan Goldin's 1985 *The Ballad of Sexual Dependency*, the brutal autobiographic ode to sex, drugs, and urban rave culture of the early 1980s. Instead, it makes me concerned that Lawson is adopting the artistic models presented by white male sado-Marxist provocateurs like the Spanish-born Santiago Sierra, whose performance works have included paying people to engage in outrageously abject activities in the middle of a public gallery to highlight the debasing processes of capitalism.

In a world where Black women and femmes have been continually exploited in real life, in popular and visual culture, and in fine art, I am not sure that there is a true willing consent in Lawson's prurient nudes, which is why I did not reproduce her photos with this essay. The glossy lighting and shiny skin that structure many of these images, such as *Nicole* (2016), *Soweto Queen* (2017), or *Eternity* (2018), are about selling. Whether they are posed standing with their behinds to the camera or reclining on a piece of furniture, their formal grammar is resoundingly commercial. And while the settings in which they appear may at first be novel to some viewers in the art world, one can quite easily find remarkably similar greased-up naked bodies photographed in low-rent interiors in a spread from a *Black Tail* porno magazine, or on the monumentally enlarged cover of a *King* magazine that the white male American artist Kelley Walker has covered with jism-like smears of toothpaste. Lawson's modus operandi seemed to be following troublesome, pornotropic strategies of artistic mastery.

Is it just a difference in scale that transforms Lawson's gallery-hung nudes into fine art rather than blowups of cheap paper trim that may be held in one hand? Is it a matter of price point that makes them fine art—thousands of dollars for an image by Lawson versus $75 for a vintage copy of *Black Tail* on eBay? After all, what does it really change if commodified pornographic images of Black women are being made by a Black woman?

Lawson's images, and the ways that she has discussed her process, seem to be actively reproducing the kind of big-dick energy power dynamics of white male artists who also claim mastery over their subject matter. "Someone said that I'm ruthless when it comes to what I want," reveals Lawson. "Maybe that's part of it: I have an image in mind that I have to make. It burns so deeply that I have to make it, and I don't care what people are going to think."[6] Unfortunately, this kind of totalizing control isn't good for anyone except Deana Lawson and the people who are making bank off it while blinding most of the art world to the consequences of this problematic artistic strategy.

A photograph Lawson made while traveling in Brazil, titled *An Ode to Yemaya* (2019), tipped me off to the artist's misunderstanding of the communities that she encountered in other parts of the African diaspora. It depicts an older woman in a blue-and-white patterned dress holding a little girl wearing a beaded ceremonial mask that hides her face. While the style of the child's headdress and costume links her to the Yoruba-derived spiritual practice of Brazilian Candomblé, the golden color of the beads and the yellow of the satin bodice on the handmade dress she wears are not the colors that are traditionally associated with the orisha Yemaya, the protector of all who endured the Middle Passage from Africa to create the diaspora in which we Black folks now live. The costume and beads should have been blue and white if the child was being presented as Yemaya. Instead, the gold beads and yellow satin that the girl wears evoke the presence of Yemaya's sister deity, the orisha Oshun, who is associated not only with sensual love and fertility but also with jealousy and spitefulness. If the child was the focus of the piece, Lawson wasn't photographing Yemaya. And if the old woman in her blue-and-white dress was the Yemaya of Lawson's title, then the compositional structure belied an ignorance of the representational strategies of Candomblé, failing to connect viewers with key referents.

The headdress worn by the child in Lawson's image is there to protect the face of the god from those who should not look on it. In Yoruba culture on the African continent, this kind of beaded headdress is also worn by the *oba*, or king, to protect his face from the gaze of those who are not worthy to look on him. In an article from the *New York Times Magazine*, "When the Camera Was a Weapon of Imperialism. (And When It Still Is.)," critic Teju Cole writes eloquently about how British colonial powers used photography to control and visually subjugate the Ejebu people of Lagos, to forcefully pull back the beads from the face of the *oba*. "The dominant power decided that everything had to be seen and cataloged, a task for which photography was perfectly suited. . . . When we speak of 'shooting' with a camera, we are acknowledging the kinship of photography and violence."[7]

In this exhibition Lawson is formulating deceptive myths of diasporic culture, ones that large segments of her audience may be ill equipped to recognize. She is also attempting to assert her brand of visual mastery over a community whose syncretic religious practices are complicated and should be afforded respect by outsiders. As a controlling director, Lawson has adopted a specific kind of power mode that historically operated exclusively within dominant white male artistic culture. "When I don't get what I want, it's abject failure. There's moments where I felt I had this opportunity to make a really amazing photograph that I let slide, which still haunt me to this day," Lawson said in a 2018 conversation with the celebrated filmmaker and artist Arthur Jafa before describing her feelings over having failed to take a picture of a woman that she saw in a historically maroon community in Jamaica. "But I should have photographed her. I took a picture of her from a distance, but I actually should have taken that moment to pose her against a tree and take a real picture of her, and she would have let me—I know she would have."[8] It matters little, I would argue, whether a Black woman or a white man is overseeing "the shoot" on a photo safari in the Global South, when violent appropriation is occurring.

When I speak about Lawson's work with other Black colleagues who also teach and write about contemporary African American art and culture, we tend to commiserate about the precarity that we feel, as comfortably upper-middle-class and middle-aged intellectuals voicing any discomfort with a young Black artist's work (as I have just done). We worry that doing so might brand us as out of touch with the kind of lives that other Black folks live, the aesthetics they embrace. This fear to speak out is pervasive even though most of us are strivers who have roots and living relatives in what used to be called the ghetto. We all still carry a bit of this precarity, this ghetto striving, with us despite laying claim to being among the few Black folks who have perse-vered in unwelcoming academic environments for long enough to walk away with PhDs in art history. We come from households and communities that strongly resemble those shown in Lawson's images. And we haven't forgotten what it means to be a part of those worlds. None of us wants to be cast as the second coming of Betye Saar trashing the next Kara Walker—particularly me. But photographs and silhouettes are not the same; the space of imagination works differently in the realm of photography.

In the spring of 2021, art historian Kobena Mercer gave a brilliant caution-ary talk at the annual James A. Porter Colloquium, cosponsored by Howard University and the National Gallery of Art, about the speed with which Black images by African-born and African American artists were entering the market, moving into collections as financial investments that doubled as symbols of wokeness but were not publicly visible long enough to be engaged critically by art historians.[9] Mercer openly questioned whether the plethora of easily consumable images of Blackness and Black people on the market is a good thing.

Sadly, engaging Lawson's work at a critical level has not been an easy thing for scholars to do without encountering significant pushback from the artist and the forces that support her practice. Steven Nelson, the distinguished scholar of African and African American art who is now the dean of the Center for the Advanced Study in the Visual Arts at the National Gallery of Art, ran afoul of the Lawson promotional machine in 2018 when he was commissioned by *Aperture* to provide a historical context for the artist's work. When Nelson chose to center his analysis around a group of works by the artist that had been published in *Time* magazine, Lawson and her represen-tation, Rhona Hoffman Gallery, denied Nelson the right to reproduce any of her images, thus causing *Aperture*, and later *Frieze*, to decline publication. When Nelson's essay (cited earlier in this chapter) finally ran on Hyperal-lergic, it was without images and accompanied by a coda describing efforts by the artist, her representatives, and the establishment art press to bury his engagement with her work.

Since Nelson's experience, the art press has seemed more concerned with echoing the rhetoric that the museum and gallery complex was coauthoring to promote the artist's work and drive high-priced sales. While I am im-pressed by Lawson's ability to influence the conversations that are being had around her work, I am also concerned that some of this control is coming at the expense of both the Black people who are outside of her circle of influence and those whom she tries to bring within her orbit.

It was a rainy Thursday, and the Guggenheim's atrium was closed to visitors for reinstallation, so *Centropy* was mostly empty, except for Brittany and me, a stray gallery attendant who wandered in and out, and a handful of other visitors, mostly white people. After about an hour, we left the museum, stopping at Le Bilboquet for two glasses of rosé (accompanied by something strange called "cajun chicken" that was served with walk-in freezer pommes frites for $38 a plate). As the only Black people in the restaurant besides one young busboy in training, we received unabashed stares from our fellow diners throughout our meal. We then continued downtown to the Armory Show.

In the Javits Center, there were more Black people on the walls than in the halls. We were about halfway through the maze of booths when a tiny old white man in a ratty double-breasted cream-colored suit ran up to Brittany, breathlessly proclaimed her beauty, shoved a business card in her hand, and offered to take her to lunch to "help" her. "And your friend can come, too!" he exclaimed. We were still muttering about that encounter when a well-dressed Black man mistook me for a good friend and colleague, thinking that I was a different tall, light-skinned African American art historian with freckles and shoulder-length hair. He apologized when I told him that he was mistaken but that I knew exactly who he thought I was. While my anti-COVID mask had undoubtedly contributed to his error, it wasn't the first time that, while moving through the art world, I have been confused with this person, or been asked if I was her sister or (quite unbelievably) her daughter. I immediately texted my friend about it, and she wrote back, "You must be looking fabulous! ☺" Not compared to the young woman with me, I thought.

Brittany and I were each erroneously interpolated in a matter of minutes—she was taken for a brown sugar baby who might welcome the "help" of a horny old white guy rather than being recognized as the hugely accomplished, Ivy-League-degree-holding television writer that she is, and I was confused within the interchangeable sign that is bougie Black lady art historian (after all, how many of them can there be?). Neither of us seemed to be all that far removed from Lawson's subjects when it came to how the art world both saw and failed to see us. And this was a problem that the images in *Centropy* were reifying rather than transforming.

I suspect that most of the people who walked through *Centropy* while Brittany and I were there had little or no experience with Candomblé, nor was it likely that the white viewers had personal experience being on the receiving end of the kind of abject objectification that Black people, and especially Black women and femmes, experience on a daily basis, regardless of how we look, how old we are, or where we find ourselves.

Many of Lawson's pictures continue a tradition of degradation and exploitation that may not be easily recognized as problematic by those who are distanced from it by virtue of their class position or racial identity. What might Lawson's representations of oiled-up and provocatively posed Black people and exotically displayed diasporic religious practices mean to them? Shouldn't these meanings be part of the conversation about her work?

A Black woman behind the camera changes little for anyone other than the photographer if she thinks she is entitled to make whatever images she chooses. Real damage may be done if Lawson's viewers come away thinking that they are viewing documentary images of real Black people, in their own spaces, doing "their own thing," rather than playacting the fantasies of an artist auteur. And real damage may be done if an artist is using her own Blackness as a tool of false solidarity to entice working-class Black subjects into a visual order that perpetuates the exploitation of their bodies and cultural forms. After all, visual colonialism is not enacted only via a white gaze. As an elder recently said to me, "Black snakes bite, too."

What do we all have to sacrifice for Deana Lawson to get what she wants?

Notes

Introduction

1. A note on terms: Throughout this essay I use the terms *Black* and *African American* to refer to peoples of African descent born or living in the United States. You will also see the terms *black* (without capitalization) and *African-American* (with a hyphen) used by other writers. While I have preserved the original style of these terms for citational accuracy, my preference is for the capitalized *Black*, which implies a broadly, but not monolithically, shared ethnic identity, like *Jewish*; and for *African American*, which emphasizes the temporal and continental bridging that the bodies of people of African descent represent in contemporary American life—and, grammatically, I do not feel that the hyphen is necessary.

2. Hartman, "Venus in Two Acts," 12.

3. Mitchell, "Narrative, Memory, and Slavery," 200.

4. For a discussion of the ongoing nature of the colonial project, see Quijano, "Coloniality of Power."

5. Walker, "Kara Walker Interview," 168–69.

6. Foucault and Deleuze, "Intellectuals and Power," 209.

7. The full course description reads:

ARTHIST 261: Black Aliveness (AFRICAAM 261, AMSTUD 261A). Based on Kevin Quashie's 2021 book 'Black Aliveness, or A Poetics of Being,' this seminar will explore moments of possibility, love, and being in works of literature and art. With Quashie as our guide, we will look closely at poems, stories, photographs, and paintings by, among others, Lucille Clifton, Audrey Lorde, Gwendolyn Brooks, Toni Morrison, Toi Derricotte, Gordon Parks, and Henry

Ossawa Tanner. Featuring intense discussion and emphasis on developing powers of black aliveness in one's own writing.

Description of ARTHIST 261 from Stanford University's ExploreCourses, accessed July 24, 2023, https://explorecourses.stanford.edu/search?view =catalog&filter-coursestatus-Active=on&page=0&catalog=&q=ARTHIST+261%3 A+Black+Aliveness&collapse=.

8. See Driskell, *Two Centuries*.

Chapter 1. Facing Phillis Wheatley

This chapter combines, in much-expanded form, portions of my article "'Moses Williams, Cutter of Profiles': Silhouettes and African American Identity in the Early Republic," *Proceedings of the American Philosophical Society* 149, no. 1 (March 2005): 22–39, with ideas developed in "'Interesting Characters by the Lines of Their Faces': Moses Williams's Profile Portrait Silhouettes of Native Americans," in *Black Out: Silhouettes Then and Now*, ed. Asma Naeem (Washington, DC: National Portrait Gallery, 2018), 60–73. Exhibition catalog.

1. Many variations on the frontispiece have been reproduced in the nineteenth, twentieth, and twenty-first centuries. In addition to its publication in the beginning of *Poems on Various Subjects, Religious and Moral*, the original engraving of the frontispiece adorned the cover of Bickerstaff's *Boston Almanack for 1782*. After Isaac Bickerstaff's various adaptations, the portrait was reproduced repeatedly throughout the nineteenth century. The version that accompanied the 1834 edition of the poems, which included Margaretta Odell's anonymous memoir of Wheatley, was relatively faithful to the original, but the book resting on the table was greatly reduced in size. An unlocated and undescribed portrait of Wheatley, possibly the original painting from which the frontispiece was taken, would be displayed at the Columbianum exhibition in the Pennsylvania state house between May and July 1795 to celebrate the establishment of the new republic's first academy of art (see Bellion, "Illusion and Allusion"). In 1856 a hand-drawn version of the image, which eliminated the book and chair and changed the colonial pewter inkstand into a more contemporary glass bottle, was included in E. and G. Duykinck's *Cyclopedia of American Literature*, and Benson J. Lossing's volume *Our Country, or, Brief Memoirs of Eminent Americans*, from 1859, featured a variation that changed the shape of the table at which Wheatley sits from oval to rectangle and smoothed her wooly hair into gentle waves. However, neither of these later versions faithfully reproduced the upward gaze that so powerfully animates the sitter in the original: an expression of intelligence that establishes Wheatley as a divinely inspired, reflective individual rather than as an enslaved person. See Robinson, *Phillis Wheatley and Her Writings*?

2. Wheatley, *Poems on Various Subjects*.

3. Gates, *Figures in Black*, 25.

4. Gilroy, *Black Atlantic*, 153.

5. Erkkila, "Revolutionary Women," 202.

6. Since the original publication of this essay in 2006, further research and writing on the frontispiece of Wheatley has been conducted by Megan Walsh; see Walsh, *Portrait and the Book*.

7. Porter, *Modern Negro Art*, 8–9.

8. In 2013 Eric Slauter added a great deal more to our understanding of Moorhead's life; see Slauter, "Looking for Scipio Moorhead."

9. We are told by Wheatley's modern biographer, William H. Robinson, that S.M. was identified as Scipio Moorhead "from a penciled note in a 1773 volume of Phillis's *Poems* housed at the American Antiquarian Society." Robinson, *Phillis Wheatley and Her Writings*, 274.

10. See Bearden and Henderson, *History of African American Artists*, x; S. Lewis, *African American Art and Artists*, 11–12; and Pohl, *Framing America*, 126.

11. Patton, *African-American Art*, 44.

12. In her discussion of portraiture in a colonial context, Beth Fowkes Tobin argues, "Whoever pays for them, portraits imply an empowered subject. . . . Even though the identity of the figures in a portrait are often lost over time, they are still somebodies who for various ideological and material reasons have achieved the status of subject." Tobin, *Picturing Imperial Power*, 17.

13. The schooner *Phillis*, under the command of Captain Peter Quinn, arrived in Boston on July 11, 1761, with a cargo of kidnapped Africans to be sold into slavery. An advertisement was placed in the *Boston Gazette* and the *Boston Country Journal* for July 29 that read, "To be Sold: A Parcel of likely Negroes, imported from Africa, cheap for cash, or short credit; enquire of John Avery, at his House next Door to the White-Horse, or at a Store adjoining to said Avery's Distillery House, at the South End, near the South Market; Also, if any Persons have any Negro Men, strong and hearty, tho' not of the best moral character which are proper Subjects for Transportation, may have an Exchange for small Negroes" See Robinson, *Phillis Wheatley and Her Writings*, 3–5.

14. Odell, "Memoir," 1. Odell was the great-grandniece of Susanna Wheatley. A facsimile is included in Robinson, *Phillis Wheatley and Her Writings*, 430–50.

15. Odell, "Memoir," 2.

16. The February 29, March 14, and April 18, 1772, issues of the *Boston Censor* carried a subscription advertisement for Wheatley's poems. "Much supported by Loyalist Governor Hutchinson and his equally Loyalist brother-in-law, Lieutenant-Governor Andrew Oliver, the *Boston Censor* was pointedly ignored by Patriot Bostonians, and the paper ceased publication after only seven months of unheeded existence," explains Wheatley biographer William H. Robinson. "Not enough Boston subscribers—printers usually required 300—could or would agree that the poems of the proposals were written by a Negro." Robinson, *Phillis Wheatley and Her Writings*, 27–28.

17. The following text, which the Wheatleys hoped would serve to verify Phillis's authorship of her poems and to establish a case for her intellectual abilities, accompanied the book in the form of a printed card that was inserted by the publisher, Archibald Bell:

> TO THE PUBLIC: As it has been repeatedly suggested to the publisher, by persons who have seen the manuscript, that numbers would be ready to suspect they were not really the writings of PHILLIS, he has procured the following attestation, from the most respectable characters in Boston, that none might have the least ground for disputing their Original.
>
> We whose Names are under-written, do assure the World, that the Poems specified in the following page were (as we verily believe) written by PHILLIS, a young Negro Girl, who was, but a few years since, brought, an uncultivated Barbarian, from Africa, and has ever since been, and now is, under the disadvantage of serving as a Slave in a family in this town. She has been examined by some of the best judges, and is thought qualified to write them.

Among the eighteen signatures were those of His Excellency Thomas Hutchinson, Governor; The Hon. Andrew Oliver, Lieutenant Governor; Hon. James Bowdoin; John Hancock, Esq.; Rev. Samuel Mather; and Rev. John Moorhead. Literary historian Henry Louis Gates writes extensively on this "examination" in his book, *The Trials of Phillis Wheatley: America's First Black Poet and Her Encounters with the Founding Fathers.*

18. Papers of Selina Hastings, Countess of Huntingdon, Churchill College, Cambridge, England, reprinted in Jackson, "Letters of Phillis Wheatley," 212.

19. Captain Robert Calef, who commanded the schooner *London*, which was owned by John Wheatley and had transported the poems across the Atlantic to Bell, reporting to Susanna Wheatley. Quoted in Robinson, *Phillis Wheatley and Her Writings*, 31.

20. Lovell, "Eighteenth-Century American Family Portraits."

21. See Edwards, *History of the British Colonies*, frontispiece.

22. I refer here to Jürgen Habermas's *Structural Transformation of the Public Sphere.*

23. Gilroy, *Against Race*, 116–20.

24. Gates, *Signifying Monkey*, 159.

25. Wheatley departed for England on May 8, 1773, and arrived in London on June 17, 1773, where she stayed until the middle of August.

26. For more on ekphrasis, see Hollander, *Gazer's Spirit.*

27. Wheatley, *Poems on Various Subjects*, 114.

28. See Rebora et al. *John Singleton Copley in America.* Copley would become the leading portrait painter in Boston between the 1750s and 1774. When he and his Loyalist in-laws were forced to depart for England, his first exposure to art and to portraiture came through his stepfather, Peter Pelham, who was an engraver and one of the chief producers of colonial mezzotints in New England

during the 1720s and 1730s. Pelham's prints enjoyed wide distribution throughout Boston, and his son, Copley's half-brother Henry Pelham, seen as a youth in Copley's 1765 painting *Boy with a Squirrel*, also became a printmaker and continued the rich tradition in Boston of making mezzotint portraits and scenes.

29. In the past, many art historians interpreted American portraitists' borrowing from prints as evidence that colonial painters lacked access to formal training. Trevor Fairbrother claims that Copley "manipulated these sources to suit his pictorial needs" rather than simply being derivative (Fairbrother, "John Singleton Copley's Use," 122). Margaretta Lovell argues that Copley's use of prints is a sign of his sophistication as opposed to his technical limitations. Lovell, "Mrs. Sargent," 22–23.

30. Porter, *Modern Negro Art*, 8.

31. Strong et al., *British Portrait*, 200.

32. It is true that Wheatley's writings, and the portrait frontispiece that accompanied them, have long been important to the work of African American writers and activists because of the way they denied her status as a "slave" and as someone else's property. In her diary entry from July 28, 1854, African American abolitionist Charlotte Forten Grimké recorded that she had just read the Wheatley's poems and that "she was a wonderfully gifted woman and many of her poems are very beautiful." Grimké also noted that Wheatley's "character and genius provide a striking proof of the falseness of the assertion made by some that hers is an inferior race." Grimké, *Journals of Charlotte Forten Grimké*, 92. Half a century later, African American education activist Lucy Craft Laney would also cite Wheatley as one of the few early "isolated cases of men and women of high moral character and great intellectual worth . . . whose work and lives should have taught, or at least suggested to their instructors, the capabilities and possibilities of their dusky slave pupils." Laney, "Burden of the Educated," 297.

Chapter 2. Profiling Moses Williams

1. James Rush was the son of the pioneering American medical doctor Benjamin Rush. The younger Rush studied medicine at the University of Pennsylvania and the University of Edinburgh, where he developed an interest in psychology. Toward the end of his life, Rush published *Outline of an Analysis of the Human Intellect*, which argued that character was formed by vocation. See Kurtz, "James Rush." Since the original publication of my work on Moses Williams in the *Proceedings of the American Philosophical Society* (Shaw, "'Moses Williams'"), the Library Company of Philadelphia has added Moses Williams to the contributor section of the object's file.

2. For detailed information on Peale and his family, there is a large body of scholarship, including museum exhibition catalogs; see Miller, *Peale Family*.

3. Sacco, "Spectacular Masculinities," 50–52, 60.

4. The physiognotrace was a machine created in the late 1790s by an English inventor, John Isaac Hawkins. They were expensive to make, and only a few

of them were used in the United States between 1802 and 1840. However, the operators of these devices, including Charles Fevret de Saint-Mémin, produced a huge number of images. The Peale family of Philadelphia owned several. The one that was operated by Moses Williams under their auspices at the museum they maintained in the Longroom of Independence Hall was used for tracing as many as eight thousand profiles in one year. See Elam, *Peale Family*, 110.

5. This shift from an individual image to an infinitely reproducible generalization raises many issues about the silhouette's nature as sign. These issues are addressed in Benjamin's germinal essay "The Work of Art in the Age of Mechanical Reproduction."

6. Brigham, *Public Culture*, 70.

7. Charles Willson Peale to John Isaac Hawkins, December 17, 1805, December 22, 1805, and December 25, 1805, in C. Peale, *Selected Papers*, 2:916.

8. Rembrandt Peale, "The Physiognotrace," 308.

9. Charles Willson Peale to Raphaelle Peale, July 18, 1803, in C. Peale, *Selected Papers*, 2:542.

10. Charles Willson Peale to Rembrandt Peale, September 11, 18, 1808, in C. Peale, *Selected Papers*, 2:1138.

11. Other Peale children expressed whatever anxiety and anger they had regarding their father through different means. Raphaelle rejected the portraiture practice that his father would have had him do in favor of constructing highly personalized still life paintings. And Titian Ramsay Peale II, the youngest son, made a curious and imaginative drawing of his father's severed head on the last page of a sketchbook (*Decapitation*, ca. 1822, Sketchbook 15c, 29r, American Philosophical Society, Philadelphia). This image, which Kenneth Haltman claims to be an oedipal projection in which the adult child fantasizes about his father's gruesome death, is eerily like a silhouette in its profile orientation and dark cast shadow. See Haltman, "Titian Ramsay Peale's Specimen Portraiture," 191. Sacco gives great attention to the role that Williams played in the museum, functioning both as a concessionaire and as a racialized display. Sacco, "Spectacular Masculinities," 71–72.

12. Charles Willson Peale, Diary 17, Cape May, New Jersey, May 30 to June 12, 1799, in C. Peale, *Selected Papers*, 2:241.

13. 1820 US Census, Philadelphia Lower Delaware Ward, Philadelphia, Pennsylvania, NARA roll M33_108, p. 252, image 273, Ancestry.com (images reproduced by FamilySearch).

14. 1810 US Census, Philadelphia North Mulberry Ward, Philadelphia, Pennsylvania, roll 55, p. 350, image 00127, Family History Library microfilm 0193681, Ancestry.com (images reproduced by FamilySearch).

15. Sacco, "Racial Theory, Museum Practice," 28.

16. Sacco, "Racial Theory, Museum Practice," 28.

17. R. Stein, "Charles Willson Peale's Expressive Design." This piece is an exhaustive study of Peale's process of creating an emblematic painting with spe-

cifically American sources. It offers a detailed look at the methodology behind the creations of the painting and the museum that is represented within its imaginary space.

18. Ewers, "'Chiefs from the Missouri and Mississippi,'" 10–11.

19. Foster, *Jeffersonian America*, 21, quoted in Miles, *Saint-Mémin*, 144–45.

20. "From Thomas Jefferson to Osage Nation, 31 December 1806," Founders Online, National Archives, accessed August 18, 2023, https://founders.archives .gov/documents/Jefferson/99-01-02-4778.

21. There is a thirteenth silhouette present in the collection that is now housed in the Anthropological Archives of the Smithsonian, but since it is of a very adult-looking Titian Ramsay Peale (1799–1885), it seems unlikely that it was one of the originals taken on that day, when he would have been less than seven years old. See "Silhouettes of Members of a 1805–6 Delegation to Washington and Others, February 1806," Manuscript 7129, National Anthropological Archives, Smithsonian Institution, https://sova.si.edu/record/NAA.MS7129?s=0&n=10&t =C&q=%E2%80%9CSilhouettes+of+Members+of+a+1805%E2%80%936+Delegati on+to+Washington+and+Others%2C+&i=0.

22. Charles Willson Peale to Thomas Jefferson, February 8, 1806, manuscript/ mixed material, Papers of Thomas Jefferson, Library of Congress, retrieved from Founders Online, National Archives, https://founders.archives.gov/documents /Jefferson/99-01-02-3205.

23. Rafter, Posick, and Rocque, "Phrenology."

24. Nash and Soderlund, *Freedom by Degrees*, 108.

25. Stevens, "Collectors and Museums," 481.

26. Adrienne Kaeppler noted that the painting "obviously did not depict a Hawaiian." Kaeppler, "Rembrandt Peale's Ethnographic Still Life," 235. Sacco has deduced that because Williams was the correct age at the time of the painting and was already exoticized within the museum, he was the most likely candidate. Sacco, "Spectacular Masculinities," 110–12.

27. Nash, *Forging Freedom*, ch. 2.

28. Brigham, *Public Culture*, 71.

29. James Rush was fascinated with the development of character and its linkage to mental conditioning through work. Rush's interest in the psycho-logical ramifications of vocation may have driven his interest in collection Williams's portrait. While the silhouettes that Rush bequeathed to the Library Company included ones of notable Philadelphians and national figures, includ-ing the philanthropist Rebecca Gratz and the ex-patriate painter Benjamin West, they also included hundreds of unidentified sitters, some in duplicate. James Rush's silhouette collection may be found at the Library Company of Philadel-phia, https://digital.librarycompany.org/islandora/object/digitool%3A109074 #page/1/mode/1up.

30. Gates, *Signifying Monkey*, xxiii.

31. Frank Colliger, "Peale's Philadelphia Museum, & c.," Recollections of the Past, *Philadelphia Daily News*, undated clipping in Charles A. Poulson's Scrapbook of Philadelphia History, 8:18–24, collection of the Library Company of Philadelphia.

32. Sacco, "Spectacular Masculinities," 51.

Chapter 3. The Freedom to Marry for All

This chapter was first published under the same title in Kirk Savage, ed., *The Civil War in Art and Memory* (Washington, DC: National Gallery of Art and Yale University Press, 2016), 5–14.

1. Loving v. Virginia, 388 U.S. 1 (1967).

2. Mildred Loving, "Loving for All: Prepared for Delivery on June 12, 2007, the 40th Anniversary of the *Loving vs. Virginia* Announcement," http://www.scribd .com/doc/3897600/mildred-lovingstatement.

3. Franke, "Becoming a Citizen," 252.

4. Currently on long-term loan to the Philadelphia Museum of Art, the portraits of the Montiers descended through their family and are in the collection of Mr. and Mrs. William Pickens III. They were the center of an exhibition, *The Montiers of Philadelphia*, on view at the museum in 2009–11 and curated by Mark D. Mitchell. See the exhibition website, https://www.philamuseum.org /calendar/exhibition/the-montiers-of-philadelphia.

5. See Davies, "Class, Culture, and Color," 95.

6. Pitts, "'Richard Morrey, Gent.'"

7. William Pickens III, phone conversation with the author, April 10, 2014.

8. "Deed of Bargain and Sale," January 6, 1746, Philadelphia County Deed Book G-7:539–543, Philadelphia City Archives.

9. Their ages are estimated from the 1850 census records: 1850 US Census, Philadelphia New Market Ward, Philadelphia, Pennsylvania, NARA, roll M432_817, p. 417A, image 427, Ancestry.com (images reproduced by FamilySearch).

10. Census records; see chap. 2, note 9.

11. Black, *Civil War in Pennsylvania*.

12. Census returns for 1861, roll C-1106–1107, Library and Archives Canada, Ottawa, Ontario. Agnes Street no longer exists. It is now a part of Dundas Street, which runs for several miles through the heart of Toronto. The section of Dundas that was once Agnes is near the intersection with University Avenue, near the Art Gallery of Ontario.

13. Letter from Toronto, *Weekly Anglo-African*, March 17, 1860, p. 1, col. 2, Negro Newspapers for the American Council of Learned Studies, Library of Congress, Washington, DC.

14. In the 1865 issue of *Mitchell's Toronto Directory*, Hiram Montier is listed as a boot maker and shoemaker, while his twenty-three-year-old son Adrien is inscribed as a tobacco worker. See *Mitchell's Toronto Directory, for 1864–65*, 118.

15. Registrations of Marriages, Ontario, 1869–1928, microfilm, MS932, reels 1–833, 850–880, Archives of Ontario, Toronto.

16. City Directory, Baltimore, Maryland, 1868, p. 641, U.S. City Directories, 1821–1989, Ancestry.com; and 1870 US Census, Philadelphia Ward 8, District 22 (2nd Enum.), Philadelphia, Pennsylvania, NARA roll M593_1421, p. 295A, image 593, Family History Library microfilm 552920, Ancestry.com (images reproduced by FamilySearch).

17. Adrien Montier and Emma Chase were married at the Church of the Epiphany in Philadelphia on January 30, 1871. Historic Pennsylvania Church and Town Records, reel 230, HSP. The US census for 1880 lists Montier as a widower living with his children and several of his wife's relatives in Philadelphia. 1880 US Census, Philadelphia, roll 1170, p. 173B, enumeration district 127, image 0530, Family History Library microfilm 1255170, Ancestry.com (images reproduced by FamilySearch).

18. Philadelphia Ward 36, 1900, Family History Library microfilm 1241477, NARA roll 1477, p. 5B, enumeration district 0916, Ancestry.com (images reproduced by FamilySearch).

19. 1850 US Census, Boston Ward 2, Suffolk, Massachusetts, NARA roll M432_334, p. 162B, image 330, Ancestry.com (images reproduced by FamilySearch).

20. See chap. 2, note 19.

21. Birth records for Margaret Copeland, Massachusetts, 1840–1915, Massachusetts Town and Vital Records, 1620–1988, Ancestry.com.

22. The 1860 census lists Samuel Copeland's personal wealth at $3,500 and the value of his home at 237 Chestnut Street in Chelsea, North Boston, at $9,500. The entry also includes a twenty-three-year-old white, Irish-born servant, Mary Conway, in the Copeland household. See 1860 US Census, Chelsea, Suffolk, Massachusetts, NARA roll M653_526, p. 798, image 170, Family History Library microfilm 803526, Ancestry.com (images reproduced by FamilySearch). In 1870 the census taker noted a drop in the value of Copeland's property, down to $4,000, and his net worth was recorded as $2,500. A widower, with five minor children living with him, he was employing a thirty-four-year-old white, English-born servant named Margaret Rodman as his housekeeper.

23. In addition to the three daughters painted by Prior, the Copelands would go on to have four more children between 1855 and 1860: Sophia, James, Jennie, and Edward. See the 1870 US Census, Chelsea, Suffolk, Massachusetts, NARA roll M593_650, p. 80A, image 166, Family History Library microfilm 552149, Ancestry.com (images reproduced by FamilySearch).

24. *Three Sisters of the Copeland Family*, 1854, Museum of Fine Arts, Boston (48.467); for provenance records, see Museum of Fine Arts, Boston, "*Three Sisters of the Copeland Family*," http://www.mfa.org/collections/object/three-sisters-of-the-copeland-family-33213.

25. Augusta Savage (1892–1962), *Bust of Dr. William Pickens Sr.*, 1932–33, plaster, approximately 16 inches high, Studio Museum in Harlem, Gift of Mr. William Pickens III, New York (02.12.2).

26. Obergefell v. Hodges, 576 U.S. 644 (2015).

27. Craven, "Seventeenth-Century New England Mercantile Image," 4.

Chapter 4. Landscapes of Labor

This chapter was originally published with the same title in Barbara McCaskill and Caroline Gebhard, eds., *Post-bellum, Pre-Harlem: African American Literature and Culture, 1877–1919* (New York: New York University Press, 2006). Epigraph source: Jennings, "Introduction," 22.

1. The best source of biographical information on Robert Scott Duncanson is Joseph D. Ketner's *The Emergence of the African American Artist*. Ketner's exhaustive archival research established an extensive biographical history for Duncanson as well as reproducing many of the artist's paintings for the first time. Recent work on Mary Edmonia Lewis has been done by Kirstin Pai Buick; see Buick, *Child of the Fire*.

2. According to the record of his marriage to Christiana Babcock on June 10, 1857, Bannister was born in St. Andrews, New Brunswick. See Massachusetts, U.S., Town and Vital Records, 1620–1988, Babcock.

3. Conversation with Corrine Jennings, January 26, 2002. Significant work on Bannister has been done by, and under the auspices of, collector and independent art historian Corrine Jennings. Through Jennings's New York City gallery, Kenkeleba House, two retrospectives of Bannister's work were mounted in the 1990s. The catalogs for these two shows are the primary sources for information on the artist. Please see the fine essay by Juanita Holland, "Reaching behind the Veil"; and Holland, *Edward M. Bannister*, for more complete biographical information.

4. Dr. DeGrasse gave Bannister his first nonportrait commission in 1854 for *The Ship Outward Bound*. King, *Edward M. Bannister, 1828–1901*, 5. More information on the DeGrasse family and their role in African American life in nineteenth-century Boston can be found in the DeGrasse-Howard Papers at the Massachusetts Historical Society: "DeGrasse-Howard Papers," Collection Guides, accessed January 10, 2023, https://www.masshist.org/collection-guides/view /fa0153.

5. Patrick Reason, who was probably based in Philadelphia, is better known for his print *Am I Not a Man and a Brother?*, which is based on the late eighteenth-century Josiah Wedgwood plaque that first showed a shackled and kneeling man pleading for freedom, than for his paintings. Almost as little is known about the life of William Matthew Prior, who is often called a "plain painter" or a "limner," terms that refer to the flat linearity of his images. His extant work is significant for the fact that many of the portraits he did are of Black sitters, including one of the abolitionist and Underground Railroad conductor William Whipper (1848), which would

seem to indicate his own antislavery sentiments quite clearly. His works date mostly from the 1840s and 1850s and were done in Massachusetts and New York.

6. Katie Mullis Kresser argues that the white Brahmin community of Boston sought to wrest the memory of Shaw's sacrifice from what they deemed to be the inappropriate hands of Black artists like Bannister and Lewis by systematically marginalizing and discounting Black participation in various memorial efforts. She states that Shaw, as a favorite scion of Boston's prosperous Brahmin community, was greatly mourned when he fell at Fort Wagner in the campaign to take Charleston, South Carolina, in 1863. Over the next fifty years, his memory would be increasingly revered in artwork until his martyrdom reached a Christ-like level in the *Shaw Memorial* (1893) on Boston Common, by the white sculptor Augustus Saint-Gaudens, which shows him on horseback as though he were entering Jerusalem. Kresser, "Power and Glory."

7. Up until the Civil War, Duncanson found support for his artistic career from abolitionist patrons. But this generous, politically motivated help came with certain thematic strings attached. At least once, as evidenced by his 1853 painting *Uncle Tom and Little Eva* (Detroit Institute of Arts), Duncanson uncharacteristically opted to render popular subject matter. In the composition, Eva and Tom, two characters from Harriet Beecher Stowe's 1852 serialized antislavery novel *Uncle Tom's Cabin*, are shown discussing the heavenly reward that awaits her purity and his loyalty. This work of sentimental fiction was extremely appealing to many abolitionists, and it is likely that the painting was commissioned since nothing else like it appears in Duncanson's oeuvre.

8. Holland, *Edward M. Bannister*, 27.

9. Holland, *Edward M. Bannister*, 4.

10. According to Jay Coughtry's *The Notorious Triangle: Rhode Island and the African Slave Trade, 1700–1807*, between 1709 and 1807, nearly a thousand voyages to Africa were made by vessels that were registered in the Narragansett Bay region. The slave ships would travel first to the Gold Coast of Africa, where they would collect kidnapped Africans in exchange for rum and brandy. Then they would proceed south to the West Indies, where they would offload most of their human captives and take on a cargo of molasses before returning home to Rhode Island, where the remaining Africans would be sold and the molasses made into rum. Through this type of triangular trade, over 100,000 Africans, nearly one-fifth of the total number of people who were kidnapped and forcibly brought to North America during the period, found themselves on vessels owned by Rhode Islanders.

11. This idea of a racialized landscape in which African American religious culture can be read into the natural surroundings is put forth first by art historian David Lubin in his essay on Robert Scott Duncanson. See Lubin, *Picturing a Nation*, 107–57.

12. Kirsten Pai Buick's essay "The Ideal Works of Edmonia Lewis: Invoking and Inverting Autobiography" argues that the artist used both white racial features

and biblical subject matter to approach difficult racial topics and to push for the inclusion of Black females into the cultural space of womanhood.

13. See Childs, "Tanner in Oriental Africa."

14. Judith Wilson's essay "Lifting the 'Veil': Henry O. Tanner's *The Banjo Lesson* and *The Thankful Poor*" makes a strong argument for Tanner's desire to make Black folk into ideal American peasants.

15. George Whitaker, "Edward Mitchell Bannister," undated typescript, pp. 4–5, Edward Mitchell Bannister Papers, Archives of American Art, Smithsonian Institution, Washington, DC, quoted in Holland, *Edward M. Bannister*, 29–34.

16. See Locke, "Legacy of the Ancestral Arts."

Part II. Modern Blackness

1. In August 2023, the Metropolitan Museum of Art announced plans for an exhibition focused on the Harlem Renaissance, to open in 2024.

2. Basualdo, *Barbara Chase-Riboud*.

Chapter 5. "This Gifted Sculptress of the Race"

1. Although there is no mention of Mary Magdalene's hair in the New Testament, and although there are only few references to her in the Gospels and other apocryphal texts, the sixth-century writings of Pope Gregory I, who in Homily 33 identified the Magdalene as a repentant prostitute, are most often cited as the source for the association of her hair, which Gregory describes as a tool once used by Magdalene to enhance her beauty that now dries her tears.

2. Nelson, "White Marble, Black Bodies."

3. "A Story in Clay," Men of the Month, *Crisis* 12, no. 6 (October 1916): 278.

4. My use of the term *intersectional* is an adaptation of the analytical framework first posited by legal theorist Kimberlé Crenshaw in 1989. In Crenshaw's original usage, intersectionality is the way in which an individual's various public and personal identities (social, political) can coincide to generate different spaces of privilege and/or discrimination given the different systems of power that are associated with those with those identity positions. See Crenshaw, "Demarginalizing the Intersection."

The term New Negro was commonly used beginning in the early 1910s to describe African Americans who were more culturally, socially, and economically ambitious than their ancestors. There were two main ideas about what characterized the New Negro. The first version came from the middle-class Black intelligentsia, which saw the New Negro as a figure that would lead the descendants of formally enslaved people into a homogeneous, bourgeois American propriety. This was the New Negro that was promoted in the pages of the *Crisis* (the NAACP's magazine) and *Opportunity* (published by the National Urban League). The second version may be found in philosopher Alain Locke's 1925 essay "The New Negro," which used the figure to encourage creative Black folk to move toward individuality of expression rather than toward artificial forms of prescribed racial normalcy. The idea of the "Talented Tenth" came from a 1903 essay of the same name by W. E. B. Du Bois, which began with the declaration, "The Negro race, like all races, is going to be saved by its exceptional men. The problem of education, then, among Negroes must first deal with the Talented Tenth; it is the problem of developing the Best of this race that they may guide the Mass away from the contamination and death of the Worst, in their own and other races." Du Bois, "Talented Tenth," 33.

5. Pennsylvania Academy of the Fine Arts (PAFA), "Register of Students, 1894–1895," PAFA Archives, Philadelphia.

6. Pennell, *Adventures of an Illustrator*, 54.

7. Quoted in Belle Case La Follette and Caroline L. Hunt, "Woman of the Hour: May Howard Jackson," *La Follette's Magazine* 4 (June 22, 1912): 10. The only mention of Floarda Howard's wife that I have been able to locate is found in the listing for Floarda Howard Jr., in Stowe, *Stowe's Clerical Directory*, 138.

8. William Still lived at 244 South Twelfth Street from the 1840s until his death in 1902. During the antebellum period his home was used as a stop on the Underground Railroad, helping over a hundred people to successfully free themselves from enslavement.

9. The Institute for Colored Youth was located at 915 Bainbridge, four blocks away from the Howard residence. In 1902 the school moved to a donated estate on the rural Delaware and Chester County line, becoming what is today Cheyney University.

10. The enumerator recorded that all four members of the Howard family could read and write. Floarda Jr.'s secondary education was taken at Philadelphia's famed Central High School, the integrated alma mater of Alain Locke, Albert Barnes, and many other Philadelphia-raised luminaries. Further, *Stowe's Clerical Directory* lists Floarda Howard Jr., who later became an Episcopal priest, as having attended Central High School and the University of Pennsylvania for his doctor of divinity. See Stowe, *Stowe's Clerical Directory*, 138.

11. The same birthplace of Maryland and birth date of July 1848 is given for the two Floarda Howards. See 1900 US Census, Atlantic City Ward 3, Atlantic, New Jersey, roll T623_953, p. 1B, enumeration district 13; and 1900 US Census, Philadelphia Ward 2, Philadelphia, Pennsylvania, roll T623_1452, p. 9B, enumeration district 53, Ancestry.com.

12. Jacob Lawrence, oral history interview, October 26, 1968, Archives of American Art, Smithsonian Institution, http://www.aaa.si.edu/collections /interviews/oral-history-interview-jacob-lawrence-11490.

13. Her brother, Floarda Howard Jr., became an Episcopal priest, and both of her sisters were married to ministers who were prominent in the New York Black Episcopal Church. Elizabeth, known as Bessie, married James Wesley Loguen, a descendant of Jermaine Wesley Loguen, who became a bishop in the African Methodist Episcopal Zion Church after escaping from enslavement. The formerly

enslaved elder Loguen had authored an autobiography, *The Rev. J. W. Loguen, as a Slave and as a Freeman, a Narrative of Real Life*.

14. *The Colored American*, April 19, 1902, 12 (image 13), https://chroniclingamerica.loc.gov/lccn/sn83027091/1902-04-19/ed-1/seq-13/.

15. Evan J. Albright, "Blazing the Trail: A Slice of History," *Amherst Magazine*, Winter 2007, https://www.amherst.edu/aboutamherst/magazine/issues/2007_winter/blazing/slice.

16. Jackson went on to become the school's vice principal after sexism caused Anna Julia Cooper to be dismissed in 1906, the same year that the school was renamed in honor of Paul Laurence Dunbar.

17. La Follette and Hunt, "Woman of the Hour."

18. W. E. B. Du Bois to May Howard Jackson, May 2, 1907, W. E. B. Du Bois Papers, MS 312, Special Collections and University Archives, University of Massachusetts Amherst Libraries.

19. "Music and Art," *Crisis* 4, no. 4 (August 1912): 169.

20. La Follette and Hunt, "Woman of the Hour."

21. Dunbar, *Lyrics of the Hearthside*, 40.

22. The bust appears at the center of the photo montage that accompanies the Men of the Month feature. The other four men who are profiled in the article are all represented by formal studio portrait photographs. *Crisis* 15, no. 1 (November 1917): 23.

23. "Annual Art Exhibit of Washington Art Club," *Washington Bee*, June 12, 1915, [1], Readex: America's Historical Newspapers.

24. "Note of Arts," *Washington Bee*, March 10, 1917, 8, Readex: America's Historical Newspapers.

25. "Poet Dunbar," *Washington Bee*, March 27, 1920, 1, Readex: America's Historical Newspapers.

26. "Dunbar in Bronze," *Negro Star*, July 2, 1920; and "Bust of Paul Dunbar," *Washington Bee*, July 3, 1920, 2, Readex: America's Historical Newspapers.

27. Locke, quoted in Reynolds and Wright, *Against the Odds*, 23.

28. LeFalle-Collins, *Sargent Johnson*, 36.

29. Buick, "Ideal Works of Edmonia Lewis."

30. In her 1966 article "The Cult of True Womanhood: 1820–1860," historian Barbara Welter describes the "cult of domesticity" and sexual stereotyping that was created around the lives of American women to establish the "proper role" of women as limited to the domestic sphere of husband and family.

31. Cover of *Crisis* 17, no. 6 (April 1919).

32. "Crisis Advertisers," *Crisis* 17, no. 6 (April 1919): 299.

33. I am not aware of extensive scholarship in this area; however, my own research has not revealed much evidence for the widespread collection of original sculpture within even the most elite Black households of the period, except perhaps those that had the excess income that enabled them to commission painted family portraits.

34. May Howard Jackson, Harmon Foundation exhibition application, September 7, 1928, Harmon Foundation Records, Library of Congress, Washington DC. I wish to thank collector Derrick Lackey, whom I met in March 2015 while he was conducting research at the Archives of American Art, for alerting me to the valuable materials on May Howard Jackson in the Harmon Foundation Records at the Library of Congress that are cited herein.

35. May Howard Jackson to Dr. George Haynes, November 26, 1928, box 19, Harmon Foundation Records.

36. May Howard Jackson to Dr. George Haynes, January 15, 1929, box 19, Harmon Foundation Records.

37. "Harmon Foundation Winners Announced," *Omaha World Herald*, January 3, 1929, NewsBank/American Antiquarian Society; see also "Five Women Represented in Current Exhibition of Negro Art, One Wins Harmon Foundation Award for Portrait Bust," *New York Sun*, January 18, 1929, 34. For her submissions, see May Howard Jackson, Harmon Foundation exhibition application.

38. May Howard Jackson to Alain Locke, January 14, 1929, Alain Locke Papers, box 164–39, Moorland-Spingarn Research Center, Howard University, Washington, DC, quoted in Farrington, *Creating Their Own Image*, 74.

39. 1910 US Census, Precinct 8, Washington, District of Columbia, roll T624_153, p. 3A, enumeration district 0144, image 151, Family History Library microfilm 1374166, Ancestry.com (images reproduced by FamilySearch).

40. For more on Madame Walker's parties, see Hagedorn, *Savage Peace*, 37. For information on Georgia Douglass Johnson's "Halfway House" parties, see D. Lewis, *W. E. B. Du Bois*, 184–85. In 1938, when Du Bois was beginning work on the encyclopedic project he called the Africana, he received a letter from Johnson expressing her interest in writing an entry on Howard Jackson and "certain others." Georgia Johnson to W. E. B. Du Bois, November 10, 1938, W. E. B. Du Bois Papers, MS 312, Special Collections and University Archives, University of Massachusetts Amherst Libraries.

41. 1930 US Census, Washington, Washington, District of Columbia, roll 297, p. 22B, enumeration district 202, image 798.0, Family History Library microfilm 2340032, Ancestry.com (images reproduced by FamilySearch).

42. These included a house at 318 South Alfred Street, another structure next door at 320 South Alfred Street, and two other houses (one with an undeveloped lot) ten blocks directly north at 812 Madison Street. Washington Post Bureau, "News of Alexandria," *Washington Post*, September 11, 1919; and "Washington Post Bureau, News of Alexandria," *Washington Post*, October 4, 1919, 3, both from ProQuest Historical Newspapers.

43. Howard Jackson's regular stays at her summer home were noted by the Black press. "Out of Town Society News," *New York Amsterdam News*, August 25, 1927, 5.

44. 1930 US Census, Washington, Washington, District of Columbia.

45. While the Jacksons never had children of their own, they are often discussed in relation to the biography of the sculptor Sargent Johnson (1889–1967), Sherman Jackson's nephew. This familial connection was never acknowledged publicly during May Howard Jackson's life. This was probably deliberate, considering Howard Jackson's service as a judge for several of the Harmon Foundation art exhibitions in which Johnson exhibited. Their familial connection could have been viewed as a conflict of interest, something the two ambitious artists surely wished to avoid. In the foundational biographical work done on Johnson by Evangeline J. Montgomery, who interviewed Johnson in the 1960s before his death in 1967, early contact between Howard Jackson and Johnson following the death of his parents, when he was thought to have temporarily stayed with the Jacksons, is cited as one of his early inspirations to become a sculptor. Unfortunately, the date of the Jacksons' marriage and census records do not support this story.

46. On April 12, 1919, she attended a reception at the Brooklyn Academy of Music. "Academy of Music Reception" (April 19, 1919). *Chicago Defender* (Big Weekend Edition) (1905–1966), 5, ProQuest Historical Newspapers.

47. See "Mrs. May Jackson, Noted Artist, Dies," *New York Amsterdam News*, July 15, 1931, 19.

48. W. E. B. Du Bois, "Postscript: May Howard Jackson," *Crisis* 40, no. 10 (October 1931): 351.

Chapter 6. Singing Saints

1. "The Chronicle's Offer: Signed Prints in Limited Editions," *San Francisco Chronicle*, March 18, 1940.

2. "Today's Contemporary Graphic," *San Francisco Chronicle*, March 17, 1940.

3. The *Chronicle*'s failure to connect Johnson's print with the Gertrude Stein–Virgil Thomson opera may have been due to the limited information provided by the artist. Or perhaps its writers and editors were simply unaware of the opera—a possibility that would point to the provincialism of San Francisco's most prominent morning daily newspaper.

4. Thomson and Stein, *Four Saints*, 1. "Its principal characters are Saint Teresa of Avila, Saint Ignatius Loyola, and their respective confidants, Saint Settlement and Saint Chavez—both of these last without historical prototypes." The opera also included several other saints, both real and made up, and a compère and a "commère" who comment on the progress of the opera to one another and the audience. It included a representation of a religious procession and several ballets.

5. Thomson and Stein, *Four Saints*, 2–3.

6. Thomson and Stein, *Four Saints*, 1.

7. On the first public performance, see "To Produce Opera at Harlem Church," *New York Amsterdam News*, January 24, 1934, 3, ProQuest Historical Newspapers Online.

8. For many years *Four Saints in Three Acts* held the record for the longest-running opera to appear on Broadway. It had a long afterlife and a significant impact on its audiences and its participants. In December 1934 the *New York Amsterdam News* reported that original cast member Edward Matthews was performing selections from the opera along with songs by Johannes Brahms and Franz Schubert at New York's Town Hall, with Virgil Thomson accompanying him on the piano; for reviews of Edward Matthews's performances, see Olin B. Downes, "Matthews Heard in a Song Recital," *New York Times*, December 3, 1934; and Frances Moss Mann, "Music News," *New York Amsterdam News*, December 8, 1934. Matthews's presence was also noted in Chicago, where he was performing as part of the cast of *Run Little Chillun*; see "Going Backstage with the Scribe," *Chicago Defender*, national edition, November 24, 1934. *Four Saints* was broadcast as a concert oratorio in 1942 and 1947 and was revived on the stage in 1952 (starring Leontyne Price), in 1973, and again in 1981, in honor of Thomson's eighty-fifth birthday.

9. Thomson would later compose *The Mother of Us All* (1942) about the life of Susan B. Anthony, again with a libretto by Stein.

10. In the 1920s the *New York Amsterdam News* reached upward of 100,000 subscribers, with seven or eight times that number of total readers.

11. Both the *Chicago Defender* and the *Pittsburgh Courier* were available in the Bay Area. They were "sold at certain newsstands, usually in Black neighborhoods. . . . One would also find them in barbershops, restaurants and other small Black-owned enterprises." Thomas C. Fleming, "Oakland: Where the Trains Stopped," *Free Press*, June 10, 1998, http://www.freepress.org/fleming/flemng38.html.

12. George W. Streator, "4 Saints in 3 Acts," *Crisis* 41, no. 4 (April 1934): 104. Streator's comments hint at the problems engendered by continuing notions of inherent African American musicality that Thomson and Stein's opera recapitulates with its unworried voices. It is important to consider the sense of African American simplicity that Thomson's reputed comments evoke, for they offer a window into a particularly uncomplicated view of race relations in the Jim Crow era.

13. "Miss Stein Uses Saints as Scenery; They 'Exist and Converse, but Don't Do Anything,' She Says in Explaining Her Opera," *New York Times*, November 17, 1934, 13.

14. Edward Alden Jewell, "New Display of Art Made by Negroes: Exhibition at New School Has Fewer Entries, but Shows Interesting Subjects," *New York Times*, May 1, 1934.

15. Stein's visit received no fewer than eight different mentions in the *San Francisco Chronicle* between March 26 and April 12, 1935. See "Gertrude Stein," *Women's City Club Magazine*, March 1935, 8, http://www.archive.org/stream /nationalleaguefo81936wome#page/n3/mode/2up. Johnson knew the Women's City Club, which was affiliated with the National League for Women's Service and had even donated "an illustrated poem" to a benefit for the legal defense of the Scottsboro Boys held there in March 1934. According to the Associated Press, a benefit auction was hosted by the actor James Cagney at the Women's City Club

in San Francisco: "Sargent Johnson, famous Berkley Sculptor . . . contributed an insight into a poet's workshop by offering three versions of a poem, showing the original and two corrected copies." "Manuscript Auction Nets \$1,300 for Scottsboro Defense Fund," *Philadelphia Tribune*, March 15, 1934. The auction was also reported without mention of Johnson in the *Daily Worker* on March 3, 1934. The event was apparently not sponsored by the club as there is no mention of it in the club's monthly magazine, where all sponsored events, including Stein's visit, were listed.

16. "Miss Stein Uses Saints as Scenery," *New York Times*, November 17, 1934.

17. Linda Simon, "Gertrude Stein," in *The Shalvi/Hyman Encyclopedia of Jewish Women*, Jewish Women's Archive, last updated June 23, 2021, http://jwa.org /encyclopedia/article/stein-gertrude.

18. Saint Ignatius Church was severely damaged in the 1906 earthquake, and its reconstruction at Parker Avenue and Fulton Street was not completed until 1914.

19. Watts, "'Can Women Have Wishes,'" 53.

20. Watson, *Prepare for Saints*, 44.

21. Watson, *Prepare for Saints*, 44.

22. Watson, *Prepare for Saints*, 44.

23. Watson, *Prepare for Saints*, 44.

24. "Miss Stein Uses Saints as Scenery," *New York Times*, November 17, 1934.

25. Stein's embrace of Catholicism for creative purposes did not erase her Jewish identity, however. In an 1896 essay, "The Modern Jew Who Has Given Up the Faith of His Fathers Can Reasonably and Consistently Believe in Isolation," that Stein wrote as an undergraduate at Radcliffe College, she asserts that Jews should publicly assimilate into the dominant culture in which they live while maintaining their religious identities on a private level; she saw writing as an "asemantic medium for sketching mobile identities." Stein and Feinstein, " Modern Jew," 416; these attitudes would be sorely tested when World War II came. During the German occupation of France, Stein had to hide both her American and Jewish identity from the collaborationist Vichy government.

26. Watts, "'Can Women Have Wishes,'" 59–60.

27. Mitrano, *Gertrude Stein*, 113.

28. Marranca, "St. Gertrude," 107.

29. Marranca, "St. Gertrude," 108–11.

30. Watson, *Prepare for Saints*, 44–45.

31. Regarding Stein's attitude, see Marranca, "St. Gertrude."

32. "It was then that she had to take her turn in the delivering of babies and it was at that time that she noticed the negroes and the places that she afterwards used in the second of the *Three Lives* stories, Melanctha Herbert, the story that was the beginning of her revolutionary work." Gertrude Stein, *Autobiography of Alice B. Toklas*, 44.

33. "Here Are Artists and Their Work: Artist Sargent Johnson's 'Singing Saints,'" *San Francisco Chronicle*, March 17, 1940, 8.

34. Thomson and Stein, *Four Saints in Three Acts*, 1–2.

35. Bourdieu's idea of cultural capital was first introduced in the essay "Cultural Reproduction and Social Reproduction," coauthored with Jean-Claude Passeron.

36. Jefferson, *Notes on the State of Virginia*, 275n31.

37. In *The Clansman*, Northerner Elsie Stoneman plays the banjo in the hospital where wounded Confederate colonel Ben Cameron is recovering. "The banjo had come to Washington with the negroes following the wake of the army. She had laid aside her guitar and learned to play all the stirring camp-songs of the South." Dixon, *Clansman*, 9–10. Later in the book, its appearance helps to set the scene for Marion's and her mother's suicides following the girl's rape by Black soldiers. "As they sat in brooding anguish, floating up from the river valley came the music of a banjo in a negro cabin, mingled with vulgar shout and song and dance." Dixon, *Clansman*, 306.

38. See, for example, Johannes Vermeer, *Woman Playing a Guitar*, 1672, Kenwood, London; Jean-Baptiste Greuze, *Bird-Catcher Plays the Guitar*, n.d., Muzeum Nardowe, Warsaw; and Nicolas Poussin, *Bacchanal with the Guitar Player (The Great Bacchanal)*, ca. 1627–28, Musée du Louvre, Paris.

39. See, for example, Pierre-Auguste Renoir, *Woman with a Guitar*, 1918, Philadelphia Museum of Art; Edgar Degas, *Degas's Father Listening to Lorenzo Pagans Playing the Guitar*, ca. 1869–72, Museum of Fine Arts, Boston; and Édouard Manet, *Still-Life, Guitar and Sombrero*, 1862, Musée Calvert, Avignon.

40. See, for example, any of the works in the 2011 exhibition *Picasso: Guitars 1912–14*, at the Museum of Modern Art, New York; Joan Miró, *Tumbler with Guitar*, n.d., Museo Thyssen-Bornemisza, Madrid; and Juan Gris, *Guitar and Glasses*, 1914, Museum of Modern Art, New York.

41. See Montgomery, *Sargent Johnson*, 10 (for discussion of Johnson's early music training), 23 (for mention of his adult interest in the guitar).

42. None of the contemporary coverage of the opera mentioned the prominent role that the saint and his guitar had in the third part of the first act. Perhaps Johnson did, in fact, see the New York production, or perhaps photographs of the performers onstage or in costume somehow made their way within his orbit.

Chapter 7. Norman Lewis's *Dan Mask*

This chapter was first published as "Norman Lewis's *Dan Mask* and the Challenge of the African 'Thing' in the 1903s," in "*Norman Lewis (1909–1979): Art and Legacy*," *International Review of African American Art* 26, no. 1 (2015): 6–9.

1. R. Fine, "Sense of Place," quoted in Hills, *Painting Harlem Modern*, 317n36.

2. Museum of Modern Art, press release announcing *African Negro Art* exhibition, released March 16 or 17, 1935, https://www.moma.org/momaorg/shared/pdfs/docs/press_archives/233/releases/MOMA_1934-35_0048_1935-03-09_11-3-9-35.pdf.

3. Virginia-Lee Webb discusses the importance of photographic documentation by Charles Sheeler, who photographed the brochure for de Zayas's exhibi-

tion *African Negro Sculpture* at his Modern Gallery in 1918 as well as for Walker Evans's 1935 portfolios for the MoMA show. See Webb, "Art as Information."

4. Webb, introduction to *Perfect Documents*, 13.

5. Walker Evans, *Mask, Ivory Coast*, 1935, Victoria and Albert Museum, http://collections.vam.ac.uk/item/O1100205/mask-ivory-coast-photograph-walker-evans/.

6. In the meticulously researched and argued *Painting Harlem Modern: The Art of Jacob Lawrence*, Patricia Hills outlines the impact that the 1935 MoMA exhibition had on Harlem-based African American artists, including Lawrence, who saw the exhibition with the historian Charles Seifert (23). See also Locke, "Legacy of the Ancestral Arts"; Locke, *Negro Art*; and Langston Hughes, "The Negro Artist and the Racial Mountain," *Nation*, June 23, 1926.

7. Shaw, "Creating a New Negro Art."

8. Locke, "Legacy of the Ancestral Arts."

9. Brooks, "On Creating a Usable Past."

10. B. Brown, "Thing Theory," 4.

11. Césaire, "Between Colonizer and Colonized," 20–25.

12. Norman Lewis, *Every Atom Glows: Electrons in Luminous Vibration*, 1951, Museum of Fine Arts, Boston, https://collections.mfa.org/objects/555109/every-atom-glows-electrons-in-luminous-vibration?ctx=27321f12-1e8d-4d9c-9fe0-f08b0771360f&idx=0; and Norman Lewis, *Evening Rendezvous*, 1962, Smithsonian American Art Museum, https://americanart.si.edu/artwork/evening-rendezvous-33910.

13. Defrantz, *Dancing Many Drums*, 146.

Chapter 8. "Bolshevized by Conditions"

This chapter was published as "African American Artists and Mexican Muralism," in *Vida Americana: Mexican Muralists Remake American Art, 1925–1945,* , edited by Barbara Haskell, 220–25 (New York: Whitney Museum of American Art; New Haven, CT: Yale University Press, 2020).

1. For more on the Talladega College murals, see Mayer, Ater, and Woodruff, *Rising Up*.

2. Orozco, *Autobiografía*, 65, quoted in Tibol, "Foreword," 11.

3. T. R. Poston, "Murals and Marx: Aaron Douglas Moves to the Left with PWA Decoration," *New York Amsterdam News*, November 24, 1934, 9.

4. Douglas, quoted in Poston, "Murals and Marx."

5. Poston, "Murals and Marx."

6. Prigoff and Dunitz, *Walls of Heritage*, 17–18.

7. Dickerman et al., *Jacob Lawrence*.

8. See Schreiber, "Dislocations of Cold War Cultures," 283.

9. For more on Catlett and her politics, see Washington, *Other Blacklist*, 268–69.

10. Plessy v. Ferguson, 163 U.S. 537 (1896).

11. The Kanders-Safariland-Whitney connection was first reported by Hyperallergic on November 27, 2018. See Jasmine Weber, "A Whitney Museum Vice Chairman Owns a Manufacturer Supplying Tear Gas at the Border," Hyperallergic, November 27, 2018, https://hyperallergic.com/472964/a-whitney-museum -vice-chairman-owns-a-manufacturer-supplying-tear-gas-at-the-border/. Three days later, a letter signed by more than a hundred Whitney staff members was delivered to the museum's leadership voicing outrage and demanding the museum respond to the Hyperallergic report. See Hrag Vartanian, Zachary Small, and Jasmine Weber, "Whitney Museum Staffers Demand Answers after Vice Chair's Relationship to Tear Gas Manufacturer Is Revealed," Hyperallergic, November 30, 2018, https://hyperallergic.com/473702/whitney-tear-gas-manufacturer-is-revealed. The first public protest was organized by Decolonize This Place and staged at the museum on December 9. See Ilana Novick and Hakim Bishara, "Activists Protest at Whitney Museum Demanding Vice Chairman and Owner of Tear Gas Manufacturer 'Must Go,'" Hyperallergic, December 9, 2018, https://hyperallergic.com /475198/activists-protest-at-whitney-museum-demanding-vice-chairman-and -owner-of-tear-gas-manufacturer-must-go/. The following month, Decolonize This Place organized a town hall meeting at Cooper Union in New York to strategize further protest action against the Whitney. See Alex Greenberger, "'Whitney Museum, Shame on You': Decolonize This Place Holds Town Hall on Warren B. Kanders Controversy," *ARTnews*, January 26, 2019, http://www.artnews.com/2019 /01/26/whitney-museum-decolonize-this-place-town-hall-warren-b-kanders/. Kanders remained on the museum's board until July 24, 2019.

12. Safariland promised to stop selling tear gas in 2020. See Robin Pogrebin, "Warren Kanders Says He Is Getting Out of the Tear Gas Business," *New York Times*, June 9, 2020, https://www.nytimes.com/2020/06/09/arts/design/tear-gas -warren-kanders.html. A search of Safariland's online store confirms that they continue to sell a dizzying array of holsters for gun and handcuffs, tactical gear, body armor, and other equipment for military and police officers.

Chapter 9. Malcom X Rising

This chapter was previously published as "Barbara Chase-Riboud's Phenomenological Art," in *Barbara Chase-Riboud: The Malcolm X Steles*, edited by Carlos Basualdo, 21–31 (Philadelphia: Philadelphia Museum of Art in association with Yale University Press, 2013).

1. Chase-Riboud, "On Her Own Terms," 747.

2. Chase-Riboud, "On Her Own Terms," 747–48.

3. This and the following quote are from Barbara Chase-Riboud in the film *Five*, produced by Milton Meltzer and Alvin Yudkoff.

4. Chase-Riboud, in Meltzer and Yudkoff, *Five*.

5. E. Fine, "Mainstream, Blackstream," 374–75.

6. E. Fine, "Mainstream, Blackstream," 375.

7. Chase-Riboud, quoted in Thomas A. Johnson, "Paris: Negroes' Way Station: 'The Action' Is at Home in U.S., Many Feel," *New York Times*, March 19, 1969, ProQuest Historical Newspapers Online.

8. Hilton Kramer, "Black Experience and Modernist Art: Romare Bearden Uses Photos in Collages; Malcolm X Is Subject of Barbara Riboud," *New York Times*, February 14, 1970, ProQuest Historical Newspapers Online.

9. Henri Ghent, letter to the editor, "Art Mailbag," *New York Times*, April 19, 1970, ProQuest Historical Newspapers Online.

10. Tom Carhart, "Insulting Vietnam Vets," *New York Times*, October 24, 1981, ProQuest Historical Newspapers Online.

11. Roberta Smith, "Barbara Chase-Riboud," *New York Times*, July 23, 1999, ProQuest Historical Newspapers Online.

12. According to the plans, Chase-Riboud's Middle Passage Monument, a yet-unrealized memorial commemorating those who died on the perilous sea voyage between Africa and the New World, would be far more ambitious in scale than *Africa Rising*.

13. Miranda and Spencer, "Omnipresent Negation."

14. Miranda and Spencer, "Omnipresent Negation," 923.

Chapter 10. Richard Yarde's Mojo Blues

1. Over the course of two months in the spring of 2011, I spoke with Richard Yarde at least four times. The biographical sketch that follows draws on those conversations, using the artist's own words and my own historical research to provide context. It aims to provide a sketch of Yarde's life story and seeks to lend insight into the works that he made from the late 1960s through the early 2000s. It begins in childhood; moves through Yarde's time as an art student at Boston University, his early teaching experiences, and the challenges of exhibiting his work in the highly segregated art world of the 1970s and 1980s; and ends with the remarkable spiritual journey that he undertook during a long battle with kidney disease. When Yarde and I spoke, his transplanted kidney was rapidly failing, and he knew that his time was limited. Some of our conversations would end with the arrival of the doctor. It seemed providential when, in the winter of 2020, I was asked to contribute a piece of writing to a catalog that the Baltimore Museum of Art was planning to accompany an exhibition of Yarde's work. At their request, I chose to revisit my conversations with the artist to remember his life story by merging it with earlier writing that I had done on his work for the Institute of Contemporary Art, Boston. See Shaw, "Mojo Hand."

2. A topical discussion of Yarde's working practice and an overview of his career can be found in Alona Horn, "Showing Vital Signs: The Watercolors of Richard Yarde," *American Visions*, February–March 1998.

3. Hilton Kramer, "Black Artists' Show on View in Boston," *New York Times*, May 22, 1970, 34.

4. Grace Glueck, "15 of 75 Black Artists Leave as Whitney Exhibition Opens," *New York Times*, April 6, 1971, 50.

5. Hilton Kramer, "Art: Portraits by Richard Yarde Evoke Black Heroes," *New York Times*, March 6, 1976, 13.

6. Kenworth Moffett, "Kenworth Moffett and the MFA," Berkshire Fine Arts, February 25, 2015, https://www.berkshirefinearts.com/02-25-2015_kenworth -moffett-and-the-mfa.htm.

7. Moffett, "Kenworth Moffett and the MFA." See also Kenworth Moffett (1934–2016), June 27, 2016, at 9:13am, https://www.artforum.com/news/kenworth -moffett-1934-2016-61363.

8. Moffett, "Moffett and the MFA."

9. For an alternate discussion of Yarde's spiritual journey during his dialysis, see Jeffries, "Going Under."

10. I use the term *syncretic* (and *syncretism*) as an adjective describing "the developmental process of historical growth within a religion by accretion and coalescence of different and often orig. conflicting forms of belief and practice through the interaction with or supersession of other religions." *Webster's Third International Dictionary*, Unabridged (Online Version, 1999–2000 Bell & Howell Information and Learning Company), s.v. "syncretism."

11. *Webster's Third International Dictionary*, Unabridged (Online Version, 1999–2000 Bell & Howell Information and Learning Company), s.v. "mojo."

12. This song has been recorded by numerous artists and innumerable variations on its lyrics exist. See "Got_My_Mojo_Working," *Wikipedia*, accessed August 22, 2023, https://en.wikipedia.org/wiki/Got_My_Mojo_Working.

13. Hyatt, *Hoodoo—Conjuration—Witchcraft—Rootwork*, 1:519.

14. For a more complete discussion of hands, hoodoo, and mojo, see Catherine Yronwode's online book, *Hoodoo in Theory and Practice: An Introduction to African-American Rootwork*, and her Lucky W Amulet Archive (https://www.luckymojo .com/luckyw.html). In *Mules and Men*, Zora Neale Hurston's record of the hoodoo practices and beliefs that thrived in the 1930s, root doctor Luke Turner describes his grandmother, the renowned hoodoo priestess Marie Laveau, beginning a curse by placing her hands flat on the table. Hurston, *Mules and Men*, 196–97.

15. For several Native American cultures, including the Inuit peoples of the Arctic Circle and those living farther south along what is today the northwest coast of British Columbia and Washington State, the skeleton is also a traditional shamanic image. For these people the skeleton signifies that part of the shaman's body that would survive the impact of the elements long after they died. In this way the bones were the core of the shaman's power, emblematic of the second sight with which a magical community healer was ritually endowed.

16. Psalm 23:1–6 (King James Version).

17. Historian Michael Gomez discusses the origins of the African American ring shout in this region of sub-Saharan Africa. Gomez, *Exchanging Our Country Marks*, 118, 135, 149.

18. Gomez, *Exchanging Our Country Marks*, 250.

19. In a traditional story of how a group of enslaved Igbo people flew back to Africa from Ebo Landing, a location on St. Simons Island off the Georgia coast, the captives' flight was preceded by a ring dance that grew faster and faster until they took flight. See Gomez, *Exchanging Our Country Marks*, 118.

20. Blassingame, *Slave Community*, 134–35.

21. Stuckey, *Slave Culture*. For another discussion of the Kongo cosmogram and its impact on diasporic African visual culture, see the work of art historian Robert Farris Thompson, in particular *Flash of the Spirit: African and Afro-American Art and Philosophy* and *The Four Moments of the Sun: Kongo Art in Two Worlds*.

22. In addition to their impact on various ring ceremonies in West Central Africa and the southern United States, Kongo cosmograms have been found at archaeological sites in material recently unearthed from cabins where enslaved people lived, including the "curer's cabin" at the Levi Jordan Plantation in Brazoria, Texas. See K. Brown, "Material Culture and Community Structure."

23. Stuckey, *Slave Culture*, 8–99.

24. Stuckey, *Slave Culture*, 11.

25. Johnson, *Along This Way*, 22, quoted in Hail, "African Religious Retentions," 108.

26. For more on these see Thompson, *Face of the Gods*.

27. Frohne, "Commemorating the African Burial Ground."

Chapter 11. Remembering the Remnants

1. "Kara Walker Exhibition at Metropolitan—Inspired by Hurricane Katrina—Explores Theme of 'After the Deluge' through Works by Artists through the Ages," Metropolitan Museum of Art, press release, March 20, 2006, https://www.metmuseum.org/press/exhibitions/2006/kara-walker-exhibition-at-metropolitan—inspired-by-hurricane-katrina—explores-theme-of-after-the-deluge-through-works-by-artists-through-the-ages.

2. Walker, *After the Deluge*.

3. *New Orleans after the Flood: Photographs by Robert Polidori*, exhibition at the Metropolitan Museum of Art, September 19–December 10, 2006, https://www.metmuseum.org/exhibitions/listings/2006/robert-polidori.

4. Michael Kimmelman, "Art Review: What's Wrong with This Picture?," *New York Times*, September 22, 2006.

5. Robert Polidori, "*New Orleans after the Flood: Photographs by Robert Polidori*," Metropolitan Museum of Art (podcast), August 29, 2006, http://www.metmuseum.org/audio/exhibitions/mmaExhibPodcast.08292006.mp3 (no longer available).

6. Polidori, *"New Orleans"* (podcast).

7. William Greiner, "What's Wrong with This Picture?," *William Greiner: Making Stuff about My Life* (blog), September 22, 2006, http://fotoarttoo.blogspot.com/2006/09/whats-wrong-with-this-picture.html.

8. Doug McCash, "Robert Polidori Defends His Post-K Decisions," July 20, 2007, http://blog.nola.com/dougmaccash/2007/07/robert_polidori_defends_his_po.html (no longer available).

9. Polidori, *Robert Polidari*.

10. Brinkley, *Great Deluge*, 621.

11. Quoted in Barry, *Rising Tide*, 131.

12. W. E. B. Du Bois to Dr. Henry Hugh Proctor, pastor of the First Congregational Church in Atlanta, September 28, 1932, in *Correspondence of W. E. B. Du Bois*, 1:463.

13. Jana Napoli, *Floodwall*, accessed July 29, 2023, http://www.floodwall.org/index.php.

14. The bonfire for *Floodwall: Cremation* was lit on December 3, 2011, on the Algiers levee near the ferry landing in New Orleans. Jana Napoli, "Exhibitions," *Floodwall: A Tribute to New Orleans in the Aftermath of Katrina*, accessed July 29, 2023, http://www.floodwall.org/exhibitions.html.

Chapter 12. The Wandering Gaze of Carrie Mae Weems's *The Louisiana Project*

1. I was asked to speak about Weems's *The Louisiana Project* in 2006, when it was installed at the Selby Gallery at the Ringling School of Art and Design in Sarasota, Florida. The exhibition space was small, and the many components of Weems's photographic and video installation were overwhelming. At the time, I managed to assemble a reasonably coherent lecture for the gallery's visitors, but I did not feel comfortable publishing it until almost twelve years later. I had to ruminate on it for a long time before I was willing to share it in print. I had to allow myself to remember.

2. Weems, Cahan, and Metzger, *Louisiana Project*.

3. Cahan, "Carrie Mae Weems Reflecting Louisiana," 8.

4. Gaddis, *Landscape of History*, 2–3.

5. Bakhtin, *Rabelais and His World*, 15.

6. Bakhtin, *Rabelais and His World*, 10.

7. For more on the woman known as Marie Laveau, see Ward, *Voodoo Queen*. The song "Lady Marmalade," about a creole prostitute, was written by Bob Crewe and Kenny Nolan in 1974 for the group Eleventh Hour. It was later popularized by the group Labelle, featuring Patti Labelle.

8. See Rich, *Chick Flicks*; Lauretis, *Figures of Resistance*; and Williams, *Viewing Positions*.

9. Williams, *Viewing Positions*, 4.

10. Rich, *Chick Flicks*, 292.

11. Lauretis, *Figures of Resistance*, 34.

12. Bronzwaer, "Mieke Bal's Concept of Focalization."

13. For Jacques Lacan, our relationship to a natural state, a state of the real, is lost once we enter the practice of language. For more, see Eyers, *Lacan*.

Chapter 13. Ten Years of *30 Americans*

1. Topaz et al., "Diversity of Artists."

2. Barnes, "Negro Art in America," in Locke, *New Negro*.

3. Rosemary Ponnekanti, "*30 Americans* Wows with Size, but Leaves You Wondering about Subtleties," *News Tribune*, October 4, 2016, updated October 9, 2016, https://www.thenewstribune.com/entertainment/arts-culture/article105792431 .html.

4. Cyd King, "Innovative Exhibit Explores Black Contemporary Art," *Arkansas Democrat-Gazette*, May 24, 2015, https://www.arkansasonline.com/news/2015 /may/24/miami-couple-interweave-art-collecting-/.

5. Ponnekanti, "*30 Americans* Wows with Size."

6. Jeffry Cudlin, "*30 Americans* Has Little to Say about Its 31 Artists," *Washington City Paper*, October 7, 2011, https://www.washingtoncitypaper.com/arts /museums-galleries/article/13041483/30-americans-has-little-to-say-about-its-31 -artists.

7. Tiffany Barber, "Now Dig This! Art and Black Los Angeles 1960–1980 and *30 Americans*," CAA *Reviews*, October 2, 2012, http://www.caareviews.org/reviews /1880#.W_7MTxNKiuU.

8. Philip Kennicott, "*30 Americans*: A Challenging Study of Identity," *Washington Post*, September 30, 2011, https://www.washingtonpost.com/lifestyle/style /30-americans-a-challenging-study-of-identity/2011/09/28/gIQAHTnaAL_story .html.

9. Lauren Meir, "The Evolution of Change: African American Art," Mutual-Art, September 21, 2011, https://www.mutualart.com/Article/The-Evolution-of -Change—African-America/8A81D2A9CD275C2B.

10. Claire Breukel, "*30 Americans*," ARTPULSE, November 2008, http:// artpulsemagazine.com/30-americans.

11. Mark Curnutte, "My Journey across the Color Line," *Cincinnati Enquirer*, June 25, 2016, updated June 26, 2016, https://www.cincinnati.com/story/opinion /contributors/2016/06/25/my-journey-across-color-line/86194788/.

12. Curnutte, "My Journey."

13. As an honorary lifetime adviser at the MFA Boston, John Axelrod has also sponsored a series of lectures on African American art and, with his partner, Darwin Cordoba, a series on Latin American art at the museum. For an idea of the scope and importance of the Axelrod collection within the holdings of the MFA, see Sims, *Common Wealth*.

14. Rosemary Ponnekanti, "*30 Americans* Confronts Issues of Race at Tacoma Art Museum," *News Tribune*, September 21, 2016, updated September 25, 2016, https://www.thenewstribune.com/entertainment/arts-culture/article105792431.html.

15. "*30 Americans* Surveys African-American Artists over Three Decades," *ARTFIXdaily*, March 1, 2012, http://www.artfixdaily.com/artwire/release/3811–30-americans-surveys-african-american-artists-over-three-decades.

16. Maria Seda-Reeder, "Exhibit Navigates Life via Black Artists' Eyes," WCPO 9 News, March 18, 2016, https://www.wcpo.com/news/insider/30-americans-at-cincinnati-art-museum-explores-life-through-black-artists-eyes.

17. Mark Stryker, "DIA Launches Multimillion-Dollar Effort to Acquire African-American Art," *Detroit Free Press*, July 20, 2016, updated November 18, 2016, https://www.freep.com/story/entertainment/arts/2016/07/20/dia-african-american-art-david-hammons/87291024/.

18. Carey Dunne, "Detroit Institute of Arts Launches Initiative to Deepen Collection of African American Art," Hyperallergic, July 28, 2016, https://hyperallergic.com/314143/detroit-institute-of-arts-launches-initiative-to-deepen-collection-of-african-american-art/.

19. Stryker, "DIA Launches Multimillion-Dollar Effort." A similar grant from the National Endowment for the Arts was used by the MFA Boston to increase its holdings of art by historically underrepresented artists. Today those funds and others raised by the museum are part of its Heritage Fund, which encourages various departments to pursue the purchase of works made by more racially and ethnically diverse artists from the United States.

20. Juan Roselione-Valadez, director of the Rubell Family Collection, email correspondence with the author, August 7, 2019.

21. Juan Roselione-Valadez, director of the Rubell Family Collection, and Karin Campbell, Phil Willson Curator of Contemporary Art, Joslyn Art Museum, email correspondence, June 21, 2019.

22. Basquiat's *Untitled* (1982) was purchased by Japanese entrepreneur Yusaku Maezawa at Sotheby's evening auction for $110.5 million. Mark Bradford's *Helter Skelter I* (2007) sold for £8,671,500, about $10.4 million (nearly $12 million including fees), at Phillips London on March 8, 2018.

23. M. H. Miller, "How Swizz Beatz Bridged the Worlds of Hip-Hop and Contemporary Art," *New York Times Style Magazine*, February 13, 2019, https://www.nytimes.com/2019/02/13/t-magazine/swizz-beatz-art.html.

24. "Who Does Beyonce Collect? See the Queen Bey's Fierce Art Collection," Artspace, February 23, 2018, https://www.artspace.com/magazine/interviews_features/how_i_collect/who-does-beyonce-collect-see-the-queen-beys-fierce-art-collection-55260.

25. Kristin Corry, "Beyoncé and Jay-Z Helped the Louvre Break Attendance Records: The Louvre Believes the Carters Got 10 Million People to Go 'APESHIT' at the Museum This Year," *Vice*, January 4, 2019, https://www.vice.com/en_us/article/mbyy73/beyonce-jay-z-the-louvre-record-breaking-attendance.

26. As a part of its "Visitor Trails" series, the Louvre offers "Jay-Z and Beyoncé at the Louvre." Francesca Street, "The Louvre Launches Beyonce and Jay-Z Tour," cnn, updated July 11, 2018, https://www.cnn.com/travel/article/louvre-beyonce -jay-z-tour/index.html.

27. Jerry Saltz, "How Identity Politics Conquered the Art World: An Oral History," by Jerry Saltz and Rachel Corbett, Vulture, April 2016, https://www.vulture .com/2016/04/identity-politics-that-forever-changed-art.html.

28. Quoted in Saltz, "Reviled Museum Show."

29. Quoted in Saltz, "Reviled Museum Show."

30. Quoted in Saltz, "Reviled Museum Show."

31. Quoted in King, "Innovative Exhibit Explores."

32. Saltz, "Reviled Museum Show."

33. Diane Solway, "Family Affair," *w Magazine*, December 1, 2014, https://www .wmagazine.com/story/rubell-family-art-collection.

34. Quoted in Robin Pogrebin and Brett Sokol, "Art Basel Miami Beach: A Focus on Female Artists," *New York Times*, November 26, 2015, https://www. nytimes.com/2015/11/27/arts/design/art-basel-miami-beach-a-focus-on-female -artists.html.

35. Laura Hutson, "The Frist Exhibit *30 Americans* Provides an Essential Survey of Contemporary African-American Art: A New Sensation," *Nashville Scene*, November 21, 2013, https://www.nashvillescene.com/arts-culture/article/13051502 /the-frist-exhibit-30-americans-provides-an-essential-survey-of-contemporary -africanamerican-art.

36. Glenn Ligon, "Untitled," in Valadez, *30 Americans*, 84.

37. Michele Wallace, "African Sublime," in Valadez, *30 Americans*, 122.

38. Robert Hobbs, "Looking B(l)ack: Reflections of White Racism," in Valadez, *30 Americans*, 163.

39. Bruce Watson, "*Black Like Me*, 50 Years Later: John Howard Griffin Gave Readers an Unflinching View of the Jim Crow South. How Has His Book Held Up?," *Smithsonian Magazine*, October 2011, https://www.smithsonianmag.com /arts-culture/black-like-me-50-years-later-74543463/.

40. Jason Farago, "He's Barack Obama's Favourite Artist. But Is Britain Ready for Glenn Ligon?," *Guardian*, April 2, 2015, https://www.theguardian .com/artanddesign/2015/apr/02/glenn-ligon-artist-obama-favourite-encounters -collisions-interview.

41. Kim Sajet, "In Obama's Official Portrait the Flowers Are Cultivated from the Past," *Smithsonian Magazine*, February 20, 2018, https://www.smithsonianmag .com/smithsonian-institution/obamas-official-portrait-flowers-cultivated-from -past-180968200/#oOml2uLK741Po5sD.99.

42. Amy Sherald, public remarks at the National Portrait Gallery, February 12, 2018.

43. Michael S. Rosenwald, "'A Moment of Awe': Photo of Little Girl Captivated by Michelle Obama Portrait Goes Viral," *Washington Post*, March 4, 2018, https://

www.washingtonpost.com/local/a-moment-of-awe-photo-of-little-girl-staring
-at-michelle-obama-portrait-goes-viral/2018/03/04/4e5a4548-1ff2-11e8-94da
-ebf9d112159c_story.html.

44. Amy Sherald, Instagram, March 2, 2018.

45. Emily Friedman, "*30 Americans* and the Impact of African-American Art,"
WAMU Radio, September 30, 2011, https://wamu.org/story/11/09/30/30_americans
_the_impact_of_african_american_art/.

Chapter 14. "No Man Is an Island"

This chapter was previously published as "No Man Is an Island" in *Art in
America/ArtNEWS*, November 2021.

1. For more on the Gullah Geechee communities of the Sea Islands, see Holladay and Roberts, *Gullah Geechee Heritage.* For more on Afro-Caribbean identity
in Puerto Rico and stateside, see Reid-Merritt and Rodriguez, *Race and Identity.*

2. Thanks to Sheldon Scott for speaking with me at length about his practice
from his family's home on Pawley's Island on June 19, 2020, and thanks to Wanda
Raimundi-Ortiz, who did the same from her backyard in Orlando on June 23, 2020.

Chapter 15. What Deana Lawson Wants

Parts of this essay first appeared as "The Many Problems with Deana Lawson's
Photographs," Hyperallergic, September 23, 2021, https://hyperallergic.com
/679220/the-many-problems-with-deana-lawsons-photographs/.

1. The Hugo Boss Prize 2020: Deana Lawson, *Centropy*, Solomon R. Guggenheim Museum, May 7–October 11, 2021, https://www.guggenheim.org/exhibition
/the-hugo-boss-prize-2020-deana-lawson.

2. An abbreviated version of this essay first appeared on Hyperallergic. It was
commissioned by senior editor Seph Rodney after I left an assortment of stink-
eye emojis in response to a series of images by the photographer Deana Lawson
that he posted to Instagram. He followed up, asking me what my emojis meant,
and I replied that Lawson's work made me feel dirty, sort of like watching videos
of the sexual predator R Kelly peeing on young girls. Rodney said that he felt this
was a response that might resonate with the site's readers, and he encouraged me
to go to the show and write an opinion piece in response. I did. But as part of my
writing process over the course of a long weekend, I circulated essay drafts to several close colleagues for feedback. Although I do not credit them by name, many
of the most powerful parts of this essay were suggested or encouraged by these
colleagues. Since the essay's publication, I have received nothing but positive
feedback although I suspect that there are a fair number of people who dislike or
disagree with what I say. But that is the beauty of writing a deeply informed and
highly researched opinion piece: it can be exactly what you think it should be
based on the facts that you are able to gather and deploy.

3. Steven Nelson, "Issues of Intimacy, Distance, and Disavowal in Writing about Deana Lawson's Work," Hyperallergic, June 4, 2018, https://hyperallergic .com/444883/issues-of-intimacy-distance-and-disavowal-in-writing-about-deana -lawsons-work/.

4. Campt, *Black Gaze*, 40.

5. Deana Lawson, dir., *Centropy*, 2021, 23 minutes, https://www.imdb.com/title /tt15482706/.

6. Deana Lawson and Arthur Jafa, "A Match Made in Heaven: Deana Lawson and Arthur Jafa on Destiny, Intuition, and Influence," *Garage Magazine*, September 4, 2018, https://garage.vice.com/en_us/article/paww9m/deana-lawson-arthur -jafa-interview.

7. Teju Cole, "When the Camera Was a Weapon of Imperialism. (And When It Still Is)," *New York Times Magazine*, February 6, 2019, https://www.nytimes.com /2019/02/06/magazine/when-the-camera-was-a-weapon-of-imperialism-and -when-it-still-is.html.

8. Lawson and Jafa, "Match Made in Heaven."

9. Mercer, "Flowback."

Bibliography

Bakhtin, Mikhail. *Rabelais and His World*. Translated by Hélène Iswolsky. Bloomington: Indiana University Press, 1984.

Bal, Mieke. "Dispersing the Gaze: Focalization." In *Looking In: The Art of Viewing*, 41–61. London: Routledge, 2001

Barnes, Alfred C. "Negro Art in America." In *The New Negro*, edited by Alain Locke, 19–25. New York: Albert and Charles Boni, 1925.

Barry, John M. *Rising Tide: The Great Mississippi Flood of 1927 and How It Changed America*. New York: Simon and Schuster, 1998.

Basualdo, Carlos, ed. *Barbara Chase-Riboud: The Malcolm X Steles*. Philadelphia: Philadelphia Museum of Art in association with Yale University Press, 2013. Exhibition catalog.

Bearden, Romare, and Harry Henderson. *A History of African American Artists: From 1792 to the Present*. New York: Pantheon Books, 1993.

Bellion, Wendy. "Illusion and Allusion: Charles Willson Peale's 'Staircase Group' at the Columbianum Exhibition." *American Art* 2003 17, no. 2 (2003): 19–39.

Benjamin, Walter. "The Work of Art in the Age of Mechanical Reproduction." In *Illuminations*, 217–52. New York: Schocken Books, 1968.

Black, Samuel W., ed. *The Civil War in Pennsylvania: The African American Experience*. Philadelphia: Pennsylvania Heritage Foundation, 2013.

Blassingame, John. *The Slave Community: Plantation Life in the Antebellum South*. New York: Oxford University Press, 1979.

Bourdieu, Pierre, and Jean-Claude Passeron. "Cultural Reproduction and Social Reproduction." In *Knowledge, Education and Cultural Change: Papers in the*

Sociology of Education, Explorations in Society, edited by Richard K. Brown, 71–112. New York: Harper and Row, 1973.

Brigham, David. *Public Culture in the Early Republic: Peale's Museum and Its Audience*. Washington, DC: Smithsonian Institution Press, 1994.

Brinkley, Douglas. *The Great Deluge: Hurricane Katrina, New Orleans, and the Mississippi Gulf Coast*. New York: William Morrow, 2006.

Bronzwaer, W. "Mieke Bal's Concept of Focalization: A Critical Note." *Poetics Today* 2, no. 2 (1981): 193–201. http://www.jstor.org/stable/1772197.

Brooks, Van Wyck. "On Creating a Usable Past." *The Dial* 64, no. 7 (April 11, 1918): 337–41.

Brown, Bill. "Thing Theory." *Critical Inquiry* 28, no. 1 (Autumn 2001): 1–22.

Brown, Kenneth L. "Material Culture and Community Structure: The Slave and Tenant Community at Levi Jordan's Plantation, 1848–1892." In *Working toward Freedom: Slave Society and Domestic Economy in the American South*, edited by Larry E. Hudson Jr., 95–118. Rochester, NY: University of Rochester Press, 1995.

Buick, Kirsten Pai. *Child of the Fire: Mary Edmonia Lewis and the Problem of Art History's Black and Indian Subject*. Durham, NC: Duke University Press, 2010.

Buick, Kirsten Pai. "Confessions of an Unintended Reader: African American Art, American Art, and the Crucible of Naming." In *The Routledge Companion to African American Art History*, edited by Eddie Chambers, 82–91. London: Routledge, 2019.

Buick, Kirsten Pai. "The Ideal Works of Edmonia Lewis: Invoking and Inverting Autobiography." *American Art* 9, no. 2 (Summer 1995): 4–19.

Cahan, Susan. "Carrie Mae Weems Reflecting Louisiana." In *The Louisiana Project*, edited by Carrie M. Weems, Susan Cahan, and Pamela R. Metzger, 7–16. New Orleans: Newcomb Art Gallery, Tulane University, 2004. Exhibition catalog.

Campt, Tina. *A Black Gaze: Artists Changing How We See*. Cambridge, MA: MIT Press, 2021.

Césaire, Aimé. "Between Colonizer and Colonized." 1955. In *Discourse on Colonialism*, translated by Joan Pinkham, 9–61. New York: Monthly Review Press, 1972.

Chase-Riboud, Barbara. *Hottentot Venus: A Novel*. New York: Doubleday, 2003.

Chase-Riboud, Barbara. *I Always Knew: A Memoir*. Princeton, NJ: Princeton University Press, 2022.

Chase-Riboud, Barbara. "On Her Own Terms: An Interview with Barbara Chase-Riboud." Interview by Suzette A. Spencer. *Callaloo* 32, no. 3 (Summer 2009): 736–57.

Chase-Riboud, Barbara. *Sally Hemings*. New York: Ballantine Books, 1979.

Childs, Adrienne L. "Tanner in Oriental Africa." In *Henry Ossawa Tanner: Modern Spirit*, edited by Anna O. Marley, 98–108. Philadelphia: Pennsylvania Academy of the Fine Arts; Berkeley: University of California Press, 2012. Exhibition catalog.

Coughtry, Jay. *The Notorious Triangle: Rhode Island and the African Slave Trade, 1700–1807*. Philadelphia: Temple University Press, 1981.

Craven, Wayne. "The Seventeenth-Century New England Mercantile Image: Social Content and Style in the Freake Portraits." In *Reading American Art*, edited by Marianne Doezema and Elizabeth Milroy, 1–11. New Haven, CT: Yale University Press, 1998.

Crenshaw, Kimberlé. "Demarginalizing the Intersection of Race and Sex: A Black Feminist Critique of Antidiscrimination Doctrine, Feminist Theory and Antiracist Politics." *University of Chicago Legal Forum* 1989, no. 1: 139–67. https://archive.org/details/DemarginalizingTheIntersectionOfRaceAndSex ABlackFeminis/mode/1up?view=theater.

Davies, John. "Class, Culture, and Color: Black Saint-Dominguan Refugees and African-American Communities in the Early Republic." PhD diss., University of Delaware, 2008.

Defrantz, Thomas F. *Dancing Many Drums: Excavations in African American Dance*. Madison: University of Wisconsin Press, 2001.

Dickerman, Leah, and Elsa Smithgall. *Jacob Lawrence: The Migration Series*. With contributions by Jacob Lawrence, Elizabeth Alexander, Rita Dove, Nikky Finney, Terrance Hayes, Tyehimba Jess, Yusef Komunyakaa, et al. New York: Museum of Modern Art; Washington, DC: Phillips Collection, 2015.

Dixon, Thomas. *The Clansman: An Historical Romance of the Ku Klux Klan*. New York: Doubleday, 1905.

Donne, John. "No Man Is an Island." In *Devotions upon Emergent Occasions*, edited by John Sparrow, 98. Ann Arbor: University of Michigan Press, 1959.

Driskell, David. *Two Centuries of Black American Art*. Los Angeles: Los Angeles County Museum of Art, 1976. Exhibition catalog.

Du Bois, W. E. B. *The Correspondence of W. E. B. Du Bois*. Vol. 1, *Selections, 1877–1934*. Edited by Herbert Aptheker. Amherst: University of Massachusetts Press, 1973.

Dunbar, Paul Lawrence. *Lyrics of the Hearthside*. New York: Dodd, Mead, 1899.

Duykinck, E., and G. Duykinck. *Cyclopedia of American Literature*. New York: Charles Scribner, 1855.

Edwards, Bryan. *History of the British Colonies in the West Indies*. Vol. 2. London: John Stockdale, 1801.

Elam, Charles H. *The Peale Family: Three Generations of* American *Artists*. Detroit: Detroit Institute of Arts and Wayne State University Press, 1967.

English, Darby. *To Describe a Life: Notes from the Intersection of Art and Race Terror*. New Haven, CT: Yale University Press, 2019.

Equiano, Olaudah. *The Interesting Narrative of the Life of Olaudah Equiano, or Gustavus Vassa, the African*. London: T. Wilkins, 1789.

Erkkila, Betsy. "Revolutionary Women." *Tulsa Studies in Women's Literature* 6, no. 2 (Autumn 1987): 189–223.

Ewers, John C. "'Chiefs from the Missouri and Mississippi' and Peale's Silhouettes of 1806." *Smithsonian Journal of History* 1 (Spring 1966): 10–11.

Eyers, Tom. *Lacan and the Concept of the Real.* Basingstoke, UK: Palgrave Macmillan, 2012.

Fairbrother, Trevor J. "John Singleton Copley's Use of British Mezzotints for His American Portraits: A Reappraisal Prompted by New Discoveries." *Arts Magazine* 55, no. 7 (March 1981): 121–30.

Farrington, Lisa E. *Creating Their Own Image: The History of African-American Women Artists.* Oxford: Oxford University Press, 2005.

Fine, Elsa Honig. "Mainstream, Blackstream and the Black Art Movement." *Art Journal* 30, no. 4 (Summer 1971): 374–75.

Fine, Ruth. "A Sense of Place—Norman Lewis in Harlem: 'An Inquiry into the Laws of Nature.'" Lecture at the National Gallery of Art, Washington, DC, January 15, 2006. http://www.nga.gov/content/ngaweb/audio-video/audio /sense-of-place-fine.html.

Foster, Augustus John. *Jeffersonian America: Notes on the United States of America, Collected in the Years 1856–7 and 11–12.* Edited by Richard Beale Davis. Westport, CT: Greenwood, 1980.

Foucault, Michel, and Gilles Deleuze. "Intellectuals and Power." In *Language, Counter-Memory, Practice: Selected Essays and Interviews*, edited by D. F. Bouchard. 205–17. Ithaca, NY: Cornell University Press, 1977.

Franke, Katherine M. "Becoming a Citizen: Reconstruction Era Regulation of African American Marriages." *Yale Journal of Law and the Humanities* 11, no. 2 (Winter 1999): 251–309. http://digitalcommons.law.yale.edu/yjlh/vol11/iss2/2.

Frohne, Andrea. "Commemorating the African Burial Ground in New York City: Spirituality of Space in Contemporary Art Works." *Ijele: Art eJournal of the African World* 1, no. 1 (2000). https://www.africaknowledgeproject.org /index.php/ijele/article/view/1292.

Gaddis, John Lewis. *The Landscape of History: How Historians Map the Past.* Oxford: Oxford University Press, 2002.

Gates, Henry Louis, Jr. *Figures in Black: Words, Signs, and the "Racial" Self.* New York: Oxford University Press, 1987.

Gates, Henry Louis, Jr. *The Signifying Monkey: A Theory of African American Literary Criticism.* New York: Oxford University Press, 1989.

Gates, Henry Louis, Jr. *The Trials of Phillis Wheatley: America's First Black Poet and Her Encounters with the Founding Fathers.* New York: Basic Civitas Books, 2003.

Gilroy, Paul. *Against Race: Imagining Political Culture beyond the Color Line.* Cambridge: Belknap Press of Harvard University Press, 2000.

Gilroy, Paul. *The Black Atlantic: Modernity and Double Consciousness.* Cambridge, MA: Harvard University Press, 1993.

Gomez, Michael. *Exchanging Our Country Marks: The Transformation of African Identities in the Colonial and Antebellum South.* Chapel Hill: University of North Carolina Press, 1998.

Griffin, John Howard. *Black Like Me.* Boston: Houghton Mifflin, 1961.

Grimké, Charlotte Forten. *The Journals of Charlotte Forten Grimké.* Edited by Brenda Stevenson. New York: Oxford University Press, 1988.

Guernsey, Alfred H., and Henry M. Alden. *Harper's Pictorial History of the Civil War.* Chicago: Star Publishing, 1894.

Guernsey, Alfred H., and Henry M. Alden. *Harper's Pictorial History of the Great Rebellion.* Chicago: McDonnell Bros., 1866–68.

Habermas, Jürgen. *Structural Transformation of the Public Sphere.* 1962. Translated by Thomas Burger. Cambridge, MA: MIT Press, 1989.

Hagedorn, Ann. *Savage Peace: Hope and Fear in America, 1919.* New York: Simon and Schuster, 2008.

Hall, Robert L. "African Religious Retentions in Florida." In *Africanisms in American Culture,* edited by Joseph E. Holloway, 224–48. Bloomington: Indiana University Press, 1990.

Haltman, Kenneth. "Titian Ramsay Peale's Specimen Portraiture; or Natural History as Family History." In *The Peale Family: Creation of a Legacy, 1770–1870,* edited by Lillian B. Miller, 186–201. New York: National Portrait Gallery with Abbeville Press, 1996. Exhibition catalog.

Harmon Foundation. *Exhibit of Fine Arts; Productions of American Negro Artists. Under Auspices of the Harmon Foundation and the Commission on the Church and Race Relations, Federal Council of Churches.* New York: Harmon Foundation, 1928.

Hartley, L. R. *The Go-Between.* New York: New York Review of Books, 1953.

Hartman, Saidiya. "Venus in Two Acts." *Small Axe* 12, no. 2 (26) (2008): 1–14. https://muse.jhu.edu/article/241115.

Hills, Patricia. *Painting Harlem Modern: The Art of Jacob Lawrence.* Berkeley: University of California Press, 2009.

Hobbs, Robert. "Looking B(l)ack: Reflections of White Racism." In *30 Americans,* 4th ed., edited by Juan Valadez, 156–73. Miami: Rubell Museum, 2017. Exhibition catalog.

Holladay, Patrick J., and Amy Lotson Roberts. *Gullah Geechee Heritage in the Golden Isles.* Mount Pleasant, SC: Arcadia, 2019.

Holland, Juanita Marie. "Reaching behind the Veil: African American Artist Edward Mitchell Bannister." In *Edward Mitchell Bannister, 1828–1901,* 17–60. New York: Kenkeleba House and Whitney Museum of Art at Champion, 1992. Distributed by Harry N. Abrams, New York. Exhibition catalog.

Hollander, John. *The Gazer's Spirit: Speaking to Silent Works of Art.* Chicago: University of Chicago Press, 1995.

Hudson, Larry E., Jr., ed. *Working toward Freedom: Slave Society and Domestic Economy in the American South.* Rochester, NY: University of Rochester Press, 1995.

Hurston, Zora Neale. *Mules and Men.* Philadelphia: Lippincott, 1935.

Hyatt, Harry Middleton. *Hoodoo—Conjuration—Witchcraft—Rootwork: Beliefs Accepted by Many Negroes and White Persons, These Being Orally Recorded by Blacks and Whites*. Hannibal, MO: Western Publishing, 1970.

Jackson, Sara Dunlap. "Documents: Letters of Phillis Wheatley and Susanna Wheatley." *Journal of Negro History* 57, no. 2 (April 1972): 211–15.

James Pott & Co. Letter to W. E. B. Du Bois, January 12, 1903. W. E. B. Du Bois Papers (MS 312). Special Collections and University Archives, University of Massachusetts Amherst Libraries.

Jefferson, Thomas. *Notes on the State of Virginia*. 1785. Electronic Text Center, University of Virginia Library. https://docsouth.unc.edu/southlit/jefferson /jefferson.html.

Jeffries, Tamara. "Going Under: Artists on the Healing Power of Art Making." *International Review of African American Art* 16, no. 4 (2000): 2–15.

Jennings, Corinne. Introduction to *Edward Mitchell Bannister, 1828–1901*, by Juanita Marie Holland, 9–14.

Johnson, James Weldon. *Along This Way: The Autobiography of James Weldon Johnson*. New York: Da Capo, 1973. First published 1933.

Kaeppler, Adrienne. "Rembrandt Peale's Hawaiian Ethnographic Still Life." *Hawaiian Journal of History* 27 (1993): 227–38.

Ketner, Joseph D. *The Emergence of the African American Artist*. Columbia: University of Missouri Press, 1993.

King, Roger. *Edward M. Bannister, 1828–1901: A Centennial Retrospective*. Newport, RI: Roger King Gallery of Fine Art, 2001. Exhibition catalog.

Kresser, Katie Mullis. "Power and Glory: Brahmin Identity and the Shaw Memorial." *American Art* 20, no. 3 (Fall 2006): 32–57.

Kurtz, Stephen G. "James Rush, Pioneer in American Psychology, 1786–1869." *Bulletin of the History of Medicine* 28, no. 1 (1954): 50–59. http://www.jstor .org/stable/44446412.

Laney, Lucy Craft. "The Burden of the Educated Colored Woman." In *Black Women in Nineteenth-Century American Life: Their Words, Their Thoughts, Their Feelings*, edited by Bert James Loewenberg and Ruth Bogin, 297–301. University Park: Pennsylvania State University Press, 1976. Originally published as *Report of the Hampton Negro Conference* no. 3 (July 1899): 37–42.

Lauretis, Teresa de. *Figures of Resistance: Essays in Feminist Theory*. Edited by Patricia White. Urbana: University of Illinois Press, 2007.

Lee, Jarena. *The Life and Religious Experience of Mrs. Jarena Lee*. Philadelphia: published for the author, 1849. First published 1836.

Lee, Spike, dir. *When the Levees Broke: A Requiem in Four Acts*. Four-part documentary film. Aired August 21–24, 2006, on HBO.

LeFalle-Collins, Lizzetta. *Sargent Johnson: African American Modernist*. San Francisco: San Francisco Museum of Modern Art, 1998. Exhibition catalog.

Lewis, David Levering. *W. E. B. Du Bois: The Fight for Equality and the American Century, 1919–1963*. New York: Henry Holt, 2000.

Lewis, Samella. *African American Art and Artists*. 3rd ed. Berkeley: University of California Press, 2003.

Ligon, Glenn. "Untitled." In *30 Americans*, 4th ed., edited by Juan Valadez, 83–97. Miami: Rubell Museum, 2017. Exhibition catalog.

Locke, Alain. "The Legacy of the Ancestral Arts." In *The New Negro*, edited by Alain Locke, 254–71.

Locke, Alain. *Negro Art: Past and Present*. Washington, DC: Associates in Negro Folk Education, 1936.

Locke, Alain. "The New Negro." In *The New Negro*, edited by Alain Locke, 3–18.

Locke, Alain, ed. *The New Negro: An Interpretation*. New York: Albert and Charles Boni, 1925.

Loguen, Rev. J. W. *The Rev. J. W. Loguen, as a Slave and as a Freeman, a Narrative of Real Life*. Syracuse, NY: J. G. K. Truair, 1859.

Lossing, Benson J. *Our Countrymen, or, Brief Memoirs of Eminent Americans*. New York: Ensign, Bridgman and Fanning, 1855.

Lovell, Margaretta M. "Mrs. Sargent, Mr. Copley, and the Empirical Eye." *Winterthur Portfolio* 33, no. 1 (Spring 1998): 1–39.

Lovell, Margaretta M. "Reading Eighteenth-Century American Family Portraits: Social Images and Self-Images." *Winterthur Portfolio* 22, no. 4 (Winter 1987): 243–64.

Lubin, David. *Picturing a Nation: Art and Social Change in Nineteenth-Century America*. New Haven, CT: Yale University Press, 1994.

Marranca, Bonnie. "St. Gertrude." *Performing Arts Journal* 16, no. 1 (January 1994): 107–12.

Mayer, Stephanie, Renée Ater, and Hale Woodruff. *Rising Up: Hale Woodruff's Murals at Talladega College*. Atlanta, GA: High Museum of Art, 2012. Exhibition catalog.

Meltzer, Milton, and Alvin Yudkoff, producers. *Five*. 16 mm film. 29:44. Norwalk, CT: Silvermine Films, 1971. http://youtu.be/9mVZXFoZDp8.

Mercer, Kobena. "Flowback—How Africa Is Redefining Today's Diaspora." Lecture at Defining Diaspora: 21st-Century Developments in Art of the African Diaspora, 31st Annual James A. Porter Colloquium, Howard University and the Center for Advanced Study in the Visual Arts, National Gallery of Art, Washington, DC, April 16, 2021. https://www.nga.gov/research/casva/meetings/porter-colloquium.html.

Miles, Ellen. *Saint-Mémin and the Neoclassical Profile Portrait in America*. Washington, DC: National Portrait Gallery, Smithsonian Institution, 1994.

Miller, Lillian B., ed. *The Peale Family: Creation of a Legacy, 1770–1870*. New York: Abbeville, 1997. Exhibition catalog.

Miranda, Carlos A., and Suzette A. Spencer. "Omnipresent Negation: *Hottentot Venus* and *Africa Rising*." *Callaloo* 32, no. 3 (Summer 2009): 910–33.

Mitchell's Toronto Directory for 1864–5. Toronto: W. C. Chewett, 1864. https:// digitalarchive.tpl.ca/objects/237318/mitchells-toronto-directory-for-18645.

Mitchell, W. J. T. "Narrative, Memory, and Slavery." In *Picture Theory: Essays on Verbal and Visual Representation*, 183–207. Chicago: University of Chicago Press, 1994.

Mitrano, G. F. *Gertrude Stein: Woman without Qualities*. Aldershot, UK: Ashgate, 2005.

Montana-Leblanc, Phyllis. *Not Just the Levees Broke*. New York: Simon and Schuster, 2008.

Montgomery, Evangeline J. *Sargent Johnson: Retrospective*. Oakland, CA: Oakland Museum, 1971.

Morgan, Jessica, ed., *Pulse: Art, Healing, and Transformation*. Göttingen, Germany: Steidl; Boston: Institute of Contemporary Art, 2003. Exhibition catalog.

Morrison, Toni. *Beloved*. New York: Alfred A. Knopf, 1987.

Mulvey, Laura. "Visual Pleasure and Narrative Cinema." *Screen* 16, no. 3 (Autumn 1975): 6–18.

Nash, Gary B. *Forging Freedom: The Formation of Philadelphia's Black Community, 1720–1840*. Cambridge, MA: Harvard University Press, 1988.

Nash, Gary B., and Jean R. Soderlund. *Freedom by Degrees: Emancipation in Pennsylvania and Its Aftermath*. New York: Oxford University Press, 1991.

Nelson, Charmaine. "White Marble, Black Bodies and the Fear of the Invisible Negro: Signifying Blackness in Mid-Nineteenth-Century Neoclassical Sculpture." In *Representing the Black Female Body in Western Art*, 139–57. London: Routledge, 2010.

Odell, Margaretta Matilda. "Memoir." In *Memoir and Poems of Phillis Wheatley: A Native African and a Slave*, 9–29. Boston: George W. Light, 1834. https:// docsouth.unc.edu/neh/wheatley/wheatley.html.

Orozco, José Clemente. *Autobiografía*. Mexico City: Ediciones Occidente, 1945.

Patton, Sharon. *African-American Art*. Oxford: Oxford University Press, 1998.

Peale, Charles Willson. *The Selected Papers of Charles Willson Peale and His Family*. Vol. 1, *The Artist as Museum Keeper*, edited by Lillian B. Miller. New Haven, CT: Yale University Press, published for National Portrait Gallery, Smithsonian Institution, 1983.

Peale, Rembrandt. "The Physiognotrace." *Crayon* 4 (1857): 307–8.

Pedrosa, Adriano, and Tomás Toledo, eds. *Afro-Atlantic Histories*. With text by Ayrson Heráclito, Deborah Willis, Hélio Menezes, Kanitra Fletcher, Lilia Moritz Schwarcz, and Vivian Crockett. New York: DelMonico Books; São Paulo: Museu de Arte de São Paulo, 2021. Exhibition catalog.

Pennell, Joseph. *The Adventures of an Illustrator: Mostly in Following His Authors in America and Europe*. Boston: Little, Brown, 1925.

Pitts, Reginald H. "'Richard Morrey, Gent.,' of Cheltenham Township and His 'Negro Woman Mooney.'" *Bulletin of the Historical Society of Montgomery County* 30, no. 4 (Spring 1999): 261–99.

Pliny, the Elder. *Pliny: Natural History in Ten Volumes*. Translated by H. Rackham, W. H. S. Jones, and D. E. Eichholz. New York: Harvard University Press, 1938–63. http://attalus.org/info/pliny_hn.html.

Pohl, Frances K. *Framing America: A Social History of American Art*. London: Thames and Hudson, 2002.

Polidori, Robert. *Robert Polidori: After the Flood*. Göttingen, Germany: Steidl, 2006.

Porter, James A. *Modern Negro Art*. 1943. Washington, DC: Howard University Press, 1992.

Prigoff, James, and Robin J. Dunitz. *Walls of Heritage, Walls of Pride: African American Murals*. San Francisco: Pomegranate, 2000.

Quashie, Kevin. *Black Aliveness, or A Poetics of Being*. Durham, NC: Duke University Press, 2021.

Quijano, Aníbal. "Coloniality of Power, Eurocentrism, and Latin America." Translated by Michael Ennis. *Nepantla: Views from South* 1, no. 3 (2000): 533–80. https://muse.jhu.edu/article/23906.

Rafter, Nicole, Chad Posick, and Michael Rocque. "Phrenology: The Abnormal Brain." In *The Criminal Brain: Understanding Biological Theories of Crime*, 2nd ed., 44–69. New York: New York University Press, 2016. https://www.jstor.org/stable/j.ctt1bj4qgv.10.

Rebora, Carrie, Paul Staiti, Erica E. Hirshler, Theodore E. Stebbins Jr., and Carol Troyen. *John Singleton Copley in America*. New York: Metropolitan Museum of Art, 1995.

Reid-Merritt, Patricia, and Michael S. Rodriguez. *Race and Identity in Hispanic America: The White, the Black, and the Brown*. Santa Barbara, CA: ABC-CLIO, 2020.

Reynolds, Gary A., and Beryl J. Wright. *Against the Odds: African American Artists and the Harmon Foundation*. Newark, NJ: Newark Museum, 1989.

Rich, B. Ruby. *Chick Flicks: Theories and Memories of the Feminist Film Movement*. Durham, NC: Duke University Press, 1998.

Robinson, William H. *Phillis Wheatley and Her Writings*. New York: Garland, 1984.

Rush, James. *Brief Outline of an Analysis of the Human Intellect*. Philadelphia: J. B. Lippincott, 1865.

Sacco, Ellen [Ellen Sacco-Fernandez]. "Racial Theory, Museum Practice: The Colored World of Charles Willson Peale." *Museum Anthropology* 20, no. 2 (September 1996): 25–32.

Sacco, Ellen [Ellen Sacco-Fernandez]. "Spectacular Masculinities: The Museums of Peale, Baker and Bowen in the Early Republic." PhD diss., University of California, Los Angeles, 1998.

Schreiber, Rebecca M. "Dislocations of Cold War Cultures: Exile, Transnationalism, and the Politics of Form." In *Imagining Our Americas: Toward a Transnational Frame*, edited by Sandhya Shukla and Heidi Tinsman, 282–312. Durham, NC: Duke University Press, 2007.

Sharpe, Christina. *In the Wake: On Blackness and Being*. Durham, NC: Duke University Press, 2016.

Shaw, Gwendolyn DuBois. "Creating a New Negro Art in America." *Transition*, no. 108 (2012): 75–87.

Shaw, Gwendolyn DuBois. "'Interesting Characters by the Lines of Their Faces': Moses Williams's Profile Portrait Silhouettes of Native Americans." In *Black Out: Silhouettes Then and Now*, edited by Asma Naeem, 60–73. Princeton, NJ: Princeton University Press, 2018. Exhibition catalog.

Shaw, Gwendolyn DuBois. "Mojo Hand: History, Healing and Hoodoo in the Watercolors of Richard Yarde." In *Pulse: Art, Healing and Transformation*, edited by Jessica Morgan, 63–72. Göttingen, Germany: Steidl; Boston: Institute of Contemporary Art, 2003.

Shaw, Gwendolyn DuBois. "'Moses Williams, Cutter of Profiles': Silhouettes and African American Identity in the Early Republic." *Proceedings of the American Philosophical Society* 149, no. 1 (March 2005): 22–39.

Shaw, Gwendolyn DuBois. *Portraits of a People: Picturing African Americans in the Nineteenth Century*. Seattle: University of Washington Press, 2006.

Shaw, Gwendolyn DuBois. *Seeing the Unspeakable: The Art of Kara Walker*. Durham, NC: Duke University Press, 2004.

Shaw, Gwendolyn DuBois. "The Wandering Gaze of Carrie Mae Weems's *The Louisiana Project*." *Panorama: Journal of the Association of Historians of American Art* 4, no. 1 (Spring 2018). http://journalpanorama.org/the-wandering-gaze.

Sims, Lowery Stokes. *Common Wealth*. Boston: Museum of Fine Arts, 2015.

Slauter, Eric. "Looking for Scipio Moorhead: An 'African Painter' in Revolutionary North America." In *Slave Portraiture in the Atlantic World*, edited by Agnes Lugo-Ortiz and Angela Rosenthal, 89–118. Cambridge: Cambridge University Press, 2013.

Sollors, Werner. *Ethnic Modernism*. Cambridge, MA: Harvard University Press, 2008.

Stein, Gertrude. *The Autobiography of Alice B. Toklas*. Toronto: Ryerson University and Pressbooks.com, 2019. First published 1933.

Stein, Gertrude, and Amy Feinstein. "The Modern Jew Who Has Given Up the Faith of His Fathers Can Reasonably and Consistently Believe in Isolation." 1896. PMLA 116, no. 2 (March 2001): 416–28.

Stein, Gertrude. *Three Lives*, New York: Grafton, 1909.

Stein, Roger B. "Charles Willson Peale's Expressive Design: The Artist in His Museum." *Prospects: The Annual of American Cultural Studies* 6 (October 1981): 139–85.

Stevens, Scott Manning. "Collectors and Museums: From Cabinets of Curiosities to Indigenous Cultural Centers." In *The Oxford Handbook of American Indian History*, edited by Frederick E. Hoxie, 475–96. New York: Oxford University Press, 2016.

Stowe, Harriet Beecher. *Uncle Tom's Cabin; or, Life among the Lowly*. Boston: John P. Jewett, 1852.

Stowe, Rev. Andrew, ed. *Stowe's Clerical Directory of the American Church, 1920–21*. Minneapolis: A. D. Stowe, 1920.

Strong, Roy, Brian Allen, Richard Charlton-Jones, Kenneth McConkey, Christopher Newell, Martin Postle, Frances Spalding, and John Wilson. *The British Portrait, 1660–1960*. Woodbridge, UK: Antique Collectors Club, 1991.

Stuckey, Sterling. *Slave Culture: Nationalist Theory and the Foundations of Black America*. New York: Oxford University Press, 1987.

Thompson, Robert Farris. *Face of the Gods: Art and Altars of Africa and the African Americas*. New York: Museum for African Art; Munich: Prestel, 1993.

Thompson, Robert Farris. *Flash of the Spirit: African and Afro-American Art and Philosophy*. New York: Random House, 1983.

Thompson, Robert Farris. *The Four Moments of the Sun: Kongo Art in Two Worlds*. Washington, DC: National Gallery of Art, 1981.

Thomson, Virgil, and Gertrude Stein. *Four Saints in Three Acts, an Opera by Gertrude Stein and Virgil Thomson, Scenario by Maurice Grosser*. Edited by Wiley Hitchcock and Charles Fussell. Middleton, WI: A-R Edition, 1949.

Tibol, Raquel. "Foreword: In the Land of Aesthetic Fraternity." In *In the Spirit of Resistance: African American Modernists and the Mexican Muralist School*, by Lizzetta LeFalle-Collins and Shifra M. Goldman, 9–13. New York: American Federation for the Arts, 1996.

Tobin, Beth Fowkes. *Picturing Imperial Power: Colonial Subjects in Eighteenth-Century British Painting*. Durham, NC: Duke University Press, 1999.

Topaz, Chad, Bernhard Klingenberg, Daniel Turek, Brianna Heggeseth, Pamela Harris, Julie C. Blackwood, C. O. Chavoya, Steven Nelson, and Kevin M. Murphy. "Diversity of Artists in Major U.S. Museums." *SocArXiv*, January 4, 2019. https://osf.io/preprints/socarxiv/nhdmk/.

Valadez, Juan, ed. *30 Americans*. 4th ed. Miami: Rubell Museum, 2017. Exhibition catalog.

Walker, Kara Elizabeth. *Kara Walker: After the Deluge*. New York: Rizzoli, 2007.

Walker, Kara Elizabeth. "Kara Walker Interview with Silke Boerma." In *Kara Walker: Kunstverein Hannover*, edited by Stephan Berg, 165–73. Hanover, Germany: Modo Verlag, 2002.

Wallace, Michele. "The African Sublime." In *30 Americans*, edited by Juan Valadez, 120–27.

Walsh, Megan. *The Portrait and the Book: Illustration and Literary Culture in Early America*. Iowa City: University of Iowa Press, 2017.

Ward, Martha. *Voodoo Queen: The Spirited Lives of Marie Laveau*. Jackson: University Press of Mississippi, 2004.

Washington, Mary Helen. *The Other Blacklist: The African American Literary and Cultural Left of the 1950s*. New York: Columbia University Press, 2014.

Watson, Steven. *Prepare for Saints: Gertrude Stein, Virgil Thomson, and the Mainstreaming of American Modernism*. Berkeley: University of California Press, 2000.

Watts, Linda. "'Can Women Have Wishes': Gender and Spiritual Narrative in Gertrude Stein's 'Lend a Hand or Four Religions.'" *Journal of Feminist Studies in Religion* 10, no. 2 (Fall 1994): 49–72.

Webb, Virginia-Lee. "Art as Information: The African Portfolios of Charles Sheeler and Walker Evans." *African Arts* 24, no. 1 (January 1991): 56–63, 103–4.

Webb, Virginia-Lee, ed. Introduction to *Perfect Documents: Walker Evans and African Art, 1935*, 13–15. New York: Metropolitan Museum of Art and Harry N. Abrams, 2000.

Weems, Carrie M., Susan Cahan, and Pamela R. Metzger. *The Louisiana Project*. New Orleans: Newcomb Art Gallery, Tulane University, 2004. Exhibition catalog.

Welter, Barbara. "The Cult of True Womanhood: 1820–1860." *American Quarterly* 18, no. 2, pt. 1 (Summer 1966): 151–74.

Wheatley, Phillis. *Poems on Various Subjects, Religious and Moral, by Phillis Wheatley, Negro Servant to Mr. John Wheatley, of Boston, in New England*. London: A. Bell, Bookseller, Aldgate; Boston: Messers Cox and Berry, King Street, 1773.

Wilderson, Frank, III. *Afro-pessimism*. New York: Liveright, 2020.

Williams, Linda. *Viewing Positions: Ways of Seeing Film*. New Brunswick, NJ: Rutgers University Press, 1995.

Wilson, Judith. "Lifting the 'Veil': Henry O. Tanner's *The Banjo Lesson* and *The Thankful Poor*." In *Critical Issues in American Art*, edited by Mary Ann Calo, 199–220. New York: Routledge, 1998.

Yronwode, Catherine. "Hoodoo in Theory and Practice: An Introduction to African-American Rootwork." Lucky Mojo, accessed July 26, 2023. https://www.luckymojo.com/hoodoo.html.

Index

Bartolozzi, Francesco: *Portrait of Ignatius Sancho* (engraving, after Thomas Gainsborough), 30, *32*

Basquiat, Jean-Michel, 12, 219–22; *Untitled*, 219

Bearden, Romare, 23, 133, 153–54

Bell, Archibald, 26, 39, 250n17

Bell, John: *The Octoroon*, 93

Bender, Frank: *Unearthed*, 157

Benjamin, Walter, 45

Bennett, Gwendolyn, 214

Benoist, Marie-Guillemine: *Portrait of a Black Woman*, 220

Berlo, Janet, 11

Beyoncé. *See* Carter, Beyoncé Knowles

Bible, 5–6

Bickerstaff, Isaac, 248n1

Black art: accessibility of, 2, 14; Black collectors of, 219–21; in Civil War era, 76; critical reception of, 83; exhibitions of, 170, 213–25, 227–28; the Obamas and, 224–27; origins of, 41; politicized approaches to, 88; in popular culture, 221; present-day interest in, 188, 189, 215, 243; representation of Blackness in, 2, 79–83, 101, 213–28, 237–45; significance of, 13–14; transatlantic contexts for, 24, 41; white collectors of, 217–18, 221–22. *See also* Black artists; Harlem Renaissance

Black artists: and African art, 131, 134, 266n6; biographical approaches to, 89, 146; and Black identity, 216; expectations and opportunities for, 152, 170–71, 216; identities of, 213; Mexican muralism's influence on, 10, 87–88, 135–43; political and social views of, 88, 133, 135–42; present-day interest in, 1–2, 85, 188, 219–20; racism's impact on, 82, 86, 94–95, 99, 116, 171; women, 86, 94, 96. *See also* Black art

Black Arts Movement, 152

Black Emergency Cultural Coalition, 170

Black identity: in American art, 13, 67, 81–82, 121; American egalitarianism and, 17; Black artists and, 213, 216; Black families and, 17; *Kara Walker at the Met:*

After the Deluge and, 192; Lawson's work and, 237–45; racism's impact on, 108–10; self-constructions of, 14, 17; significance of Wheatley's poetry and portrait for conceptions of, 21, 24, 27–28, 30, 35, 248n1, 251n32; slavery in relation to, 15, 57–58; Stein and, 120, 124; stereotypes of, 13, 120, 216; Williams and, 16–17, 60

Black Lives Matter, 8

Black Out: Silhouettes Then and Now (catalog), 16

Black portraiture, origins of, 16, 20–21, 23–24

Black Power movement, 8, 153, 171

Black Tail (magazine), 241

Black women: as artists, 86, 94, 96; Black representations of, 101, 104–5; demeaning images of, 27–28, 35, 41, 91, 93, 239–41, 244–45; sexualized representations of, 27–28, 91, 93; significance of Wheatley's frontispiece portrait for the representation of, 24, 27–28, 30, 35, 37, 39, 41

Blake, William, 164; *Flagellation of a Female Samboe Slave* (engraved after a drawing by John Gabriel Stedman), 27–28, *29*

Blassingame, John, 183

bomba, 234–35

Bonaparte, Napoleon, 51

Bonvicini Brothers Foundry, 147, 153

Boston, Joseph, 98

Boston, Massachusetts: African Americans and race relations in, 67, 70, 76–78, 168–69, 171, 257n6; cultural sphere in, 25–26, 35, 37, 250n28; Wheatley in, 20, 23, 25–26

Boston Censor (newspaper), 25

Boston News Letter (newspaper), 25

Boston University (BU), 165–66, 169–70

Botticelli, Sandro: *St. Augustine*, 34, *36*

Bourdieu, Pierre, 121

Bradford, Mark: *Helter Skelter I*, 219

Braithewaite, Leon, 166–67

Breukel, Claire, 216

Brigham, David: *Public Culture in the Early Republic*, 44

Newcomb Art Gallery, Tulane University, New Orleans, 203

New Deal, 133, 137

New Negro movement: and African art, 134; concepts and principles of, 131, 258n4; Douglas and, 137; and the Harlem Renaissance, 83, 85, 131; Howard Jackson and, 93–94, 99, 108; Johnson and, 10, 86; Locke and, 83, 131, 137, 214; and Mexican muralism, 135; and modernism, 133

New Orleans, Louisiana, 10, 188–89, 195–203, 208–9, 212. *See also* Hurricane Katrina

New Orleans Cotton Centennial Exposition, 83

New Orleans Photo Alliance, 195

Newport Museum (Rhode Island), 81

New School for Social Research (New York), 117, 136

New York (magazine), 221

New York Amsterdam News (newspaper), 116, 137–38, 263n10

New Yorker (magazine), 195–96, *201, 202*

New York Times (newspaper), 117–19, 153–54, 156, 170, 197

New York Times Magazine, 242

Niagara Movement, 173

Nike of Samothrace, 220

N'Namdi, George, 218

N'Namdi Center for Contemporary Art, Detroit, 218

North Carolina Museum of Art (Raleigh), 219

Nugent, Richard Bruce, 109

Obama, Barack, 200, 223–26

Obama, Michelle, 225–27

Odell, Margaretta Matilda, 25, 248n1, 249n14

135th Street Library, Harlem, 137, 139

Opportunity (magazine), 258n4

Orozco, José Clemente, 138, 139; *The Epic of American Civilization*, 135; *Table of Universal Brotherhood*, 136

Overmyer, Eric, 198

Pace Gallery, New York, 220

PAFA. *See* Pennsylvania Academy of the Fine Arts

paper silhouettes. *See* silhouettes

passing (intentional or unintentional), 60, 66, 86, 99

patriarchy, 53–54

Patton, Sharon: *African-American Art*, 23–24

Pawley's Island, South Carolina, 230–33

Peale, Angelica Kauffman, 47–48

Peale, Charles Willson, 16, 44–50, 53–54, 56, 58–59, 61, 252n11; *The Artist in His Museum*, 48, *49,* 50

Peale, Raphaelle, 42, 44, 47–48, 56, 61, 252n11

Peale, Rembrandt, 47–48; *Man in a Feathered Helmet,* 54, *55,* 56

Peale, Titian Ramsay, II, 252n11

Peale, Titian Ramsay, 47

Pelham, Henry, 251n28

Pelham, Peter, 250n28

Penn, William, 63

Pennsylvania Academy of the Fine Arts (PAFA), 86, 87, 93–95, *96, 97,* 110

phenomenological experience of art, 146, 148–52, 154–56, 159–60

Philadelphia, Pennsylvania: African Americans in, 48, 65, 94–95, 98–99

Philadelphia Centennial Exposition, 82

Philadelphia Museum of Art, 71

Philadelphia Public Schools, 94

Phillips Collection, Washington, DC, 139

Phillis (schooner), 249n13

photography, 16, 45–46, 66

phrenology, 53–54

physiognotrace, 45–47, *46,* 50, 56, 60, 252n4

Picasso, Pablo, 124

Pickens, William, III, 71

Pickens, William, Sr., 71

Pickens family, 71

Pike, Elijah, 70

Pine, Robert Edge, 39

Pippin, Horace, 214

Pittsburgh Courier (newspaper), 116, 263n11

Plessy v. Ferguson (1896), 142